INTRODUCTION TO MASS COMMUNICATIONS

INTRODUCTION TO MASS COMMUNICATIONS

SIXTH EDITION

WARREN K. AGEE
University of Georgia

PHILLIP H. AULT
South Bend *Tribune*

EDWIN EMERY
University of Minnesota

HARPER & ROW, PUBLISHERS
New York, Hagerstown, San Francisco, London

Sponsoring Editor: *Alan Spiegel*
Project Editor: *Karla B. Philip*
Designer: *Gayle Jaeger*
Production Manager: *Marion A. Palen*
Compositor: *Ruttle, Shaw & Wetherill, Inc.*
Printer and Binder: *The Murray Printing Company*
Art Studio: *Eric G. Hieber Associates, Inc.*

INTRODUCTION TO MASS COMMUNICATIONS, Sixth Edition

Copyright © 1979 by Harper & Row, Publishers, Inc.

Library of Congress Cataloging in Publication Data
Agee, Warren Kendall.
    Introduction to mass communications.
Bibliography: p.
    Includes index.
    1. Mass media.   I. Ault, Phillip H., Date____
joint author.   II. Emery, Edwin, joint author.
III. Title.
P90.A35   1979   301.16'1   78-19851
ISBN 0-06-040172-9

P90
A35
1979

pg 139

CONTENTS

5-22-80 Speech comm.

5
Growth of Radio, Television, and Film   80

III

CRITICISMS AND CHALLENGES   103

6
Crisis of Credibility   105

7
The Media and Social Issues   139

8
Economic Problems of the Media   178

IV

THE MASS COMMUNICATIONS INDUSTRIES AND PROFESSIONS

195

9
Newspapers

197

10
Magazines

238

11
Book Publishing

252

12
Radio and Recordings

265

FOREWORD

The sixth edition of this book, like the earlier ones, is designed to give readers a full description of the mass communications industries, to introduce them to all the areas of professional work in journalism and mass communications, and to illuminate for them the importance of the communicator in modern society. It thus seeks to give all readers a comprehensive picture of the mass media upon which we depend so heavily as citizens. For those who are considering careers in mass communications, it offers detailed analyses of the communications agencies that seek their talents. The sixth edition has been updated throughout.

Part I, "The Role of Mass Communications," is an introductory essay that describes briefly and simply the communication process and the role of the mass media in developing the political, social, and economic fabrics of a modern democratic society. In it, and throughout the book, the authors' aim is to answer in a positive yet realistic way the question: Is mass communications a desirable profession, important to society?

The development of the mass media is related in Part II, "The Historical Perspective." One chapter describes the basic theories of the press developed during the past five centuries and reviews the unending battle to win and preserve the rights to print, to criticize, and to report the news. Another offers a comprehensive synthesis of the history of the print media in terms of journalistic trends and the contributions of the men and women who helped to shape the American newspaper and magazine. Included are sections dealing with the New Journalism and the black press. A third chapter traces in detail the relatively brief histories of radio, television, and film, focusing on the news and opinion roles of these essentially entertainment media.

During the past decade a greatly increased awareness of the role of the mass media in influencing decisions and shaping our very life-styles has dawned upon most Americans. The media have been the focal point of much controversy. Consequently, the authors have found it necessary to revise the book more frequently than in previous years and also greatly to expand and update Part III, "Criticisms and Challenges." An entirely new arrangement of Part III was provided in the fifth edition.

Chapter 6, "Crisis of Credibility," describes the credibility duel between the media and government, and between the media and the public, that reached its zenith during President Nixon's second term in office.

The civil riots and the political and student demonstrations, which set the stage for this dramatic confrontation, are discussed, as well as the Pentagon Papers case, "The Selling of the Pentagon" dispute, and other developments, including the classification of public documents, the issuance of a growing number of subpoenas and "gag" orders by the courts, and the employment of journalists by the CIA.

Chapter 7, "The Media and Social Issues," reviews such controversial subjects as violence; obscenity; sex and good taste; the media and the individual, including the problems of free press and fair trial, libel and slander, privacy, and copyright; access to the media, including minority pressures, the fairness doctrine, and the powerful consumer movement, with its demands for countercommercials; other criticisms of advertising; and the media's continuing efforts to improve their performance.

Chapter 8, "Economic Problems of the Media," discusses such important subjects as the growth of monopolies; group ownership of the media, including the rise of cross-media conglomerates; economic pressures brought to bear on the media by minority groups and others, including license renewal threats; audience responses and preferences; and the effects of inflation and new technological developments on media ownerships. Much new material may be found in these chapters and in those that follow.

The major section of the book is Part IV, "The Mass Communications Industries and Professions." Twelve chapters—including a recently added chapter dealing with radio and recordings—describe how the mass media and related agencies are organized, their current sizes and roles, and opportunities and qualifications for those contemplating professional careers in them. The authors' aim in each chapter is to present a unified picture of a major area of communications work and to note the interrelationships among the media and among their various functions.

The descriptive materials and figures contained in these chapters have been brought up to date. The chapters introduce the reader to the various media and professional areas: the changing newspaper, in which stress is placed on the technological revolution in production and editing, and efforts to learn why fewer Americans were reading newspapers than in the past; the magazine, including general and specialized periodicals, industrial editing, and freelance writing; book publishing; radio and recordings; television, including cable television, videocassette and videodisc TV, and public broadcasting; the film, including entertainment, documentary, industrial, and educational films, and film criticism; photographic communication; press associations; advertising, including the media, agency, and company department fields; public relations; and the growing fields of mass communications research and education.

A nationally known public relations practitioner, J. Carroll Bateman of the Insurance Information Institute, New York, has revised the chapter on public relations, which he wrote for the fifth edition.

A selected, annotated bibliography is offered readers who wish to explore further some of the many facets of mass communications.

Also available is a revised instructor's manual, which contains study questions and projects, lesson plans, and examination questions. The manual incorporates a number of successful approaches to the study provided by instructors who have taught the introductory course during the last fifteen years or longer and whose adoption of the book has made it the most widely used textbook in its field.

The book throughout represents a pooling of the professional media experience and scholarly interest of its authors, who wish to thank the more than 100 journalism and communications professors whose suggestions and criticisms, elicited by questionnaire, have helped shape these six editions. We also wish to thank especially a number of other persons for their aid and interest in the project. R. Smith Schuneman of the University of Minnesota wrote the chapter on photographic communication in consultation with the authors. Barbara McKenzie of the University of Georgia wrote the chapter on the film, with later updating provided by Gayla Jamison of the same institution. Joining Jack B. Haskins of the University of Tennessee in assisting with the chapter on mass communications research were Emery L. Sasser of the University of South Florida and Leo Jeffres of Cleveland State University. Leslie G. Moeller of the State University of Iowa reviewed the manuscript for the first edition and made many valuable suggestions and criticisms; Joseph A. Del Porto of Bowling Green State University read galley proofs and made helpful comments. John T. McNelly of the University of Wisconsin and Hugh E. Curtis of Drake University supplied criticisms in preparation for the second edition.

Among professionals in the mass media with whom the authors have consulted (including their titles at the time) were James A. Byron, general manager and news director, WBAP and KXAS-TV, Fort Worth; Jack Douglas, general manager of WSBT and WSBT-TV, South Bend, Indiana; Andrew Stewart, president, Denhard & Stewart, Inc., advertising agency, New York; David F. Barbour, copy chief, Batten, Barton, Durstine & Osborn, Inc., Pittsburgh office; Chandler Grannis, editor-at-large, *Publishers' Weekly;* Earl J. Johnson, vice president, United Press International; William C. Payette, president, United Feature Syndicate, Inc., New York; K. P. Wood, vice president, American Telephone & Telegraph Company; and William Oman, vice president, Dodd, Mead & Company, Inc.

Professors of journalism or communications who proved helpful in contributing to or reviewing chapters of the book during the past two decades were Milton Gross, University of Missouri; Max Wales and Warren C. Price, University of Oregon; R. C. Norris, Texas Christian University; Baskett Mosse, Northwestern University; Scott M. Cutlip, University of Georgia; William Mindak, Tulane University; Sam Kuczun, University of Colorado; Harold W. Wilson; and Roy E. Carter, Jr., University of Minnesota; John R. Wilhelm, Ohio University; Michael C. Emery, California State University, Northridge; Emma Auer, Florida State University; Mel Adams and Lee F. Young, University of Kansas; James E. Dykes, Troy State University; and James L. Aldridge, William S. Baxter, A. Edward Foote, Worth McDougald, Ronald Lane, Frazier Moore, Charles Martin, and J. Thomas Russell, University of Georgia.

The authors wish to thank all these persons, as well as others who have expressed their interest in the book since it first helped establish the introductory mass communications course in American universities almost twenty years ago. Thanks also are extended to the International Communication Agency (formerly USIA), which has placed successive editions of the book in its reading libraries throughout the world and for which translations have been published in Korean, French, Spanish, and Portuguese, joining the editions published in India, Taiwan, and the Philippines. We hope that the many changes incorporated in this sixth edition will meet with the approval of all who read it.

Warren K. Agee
Phillip H. Ault
Edwin Emery

PART I

THE ROLE OF MASS COMMUNICATIONS

CHAPTER 1
COMMUNICATION AND THE MASS MEDIA

THE IMPACT OF MASS COMMUNICATIONS

Mass communication—the delivery of news, ideas, and entertainment to thousands or millions of people simultaneously—is a force with incalculable impact on today's world. In an era when messages and pictures are bounced off a satellite 20,000 miles out in space and back into our homes within seconds, those persons who work in and direct the media influence their fellow humans far more significantly than ever before. The new styles of living that mark the difference between today's generation and earlier ones have been fostered by the instant communications that penetrate into every remote spot on earth.

As mass communications has increased its grip on our minds, communication among individuals has diminished. Yet an anomaly exists. The success of every mass communication effort, whether visual, written, or spoken, rests upon the skill of the communicator to stimulate the recipient's thinking, to stir emotions, to persuade him or her to action. Mass communication is the one-to-one impact of one human intelligence upon another, carried on a thousandfold simultaneously among individuals who have no direct personal contact.

Political, social, and economic aspects of contemporary life are molded by our ability to communicate swiftly and voluminously. Riots, wars, and the fall of governments follow in the wake of news reports at a pace inconceivable at earlier points in history. Information is available through television and radio, newspapers, magazines, books, films, and recordings.

The challenge is clear: Mass communicators must be among our best-educated, most responsible citizens. And every person must learn how to read, listen, and watch—critically and intelligently—so as to order his life most efficiently and satisfyingly.

Those who choose to report, interpret, and perform in the mass media can expect meaningful, often exciting, lives. As mass communicators, they will help shape our destiny.

Mass communicators, for example:

Report the achievements, and the transgressions, of men and women in public office.

Interpret the aspirations of all peoples, including minorities, for a better way of life.

Design a newspaper, magazine, book, film, or broadcast program so as to make people read, watch, and listen . . . and think and act.

Speed a press association report to millions within a matter of minutes.

Turn a public spotlight upon the activities of antisocial groups and individuals.

Persuade a community, state, or the nation to improve its educational programs, control air and water pollution, and build more efficient and safe transportation systems.

Advertise products and services aimed at improving our standard of living and keeping our economy sound.

Entertain with movies, accounts of sports events, comics, stories of fact and fiction, and dramatic and musical programs of every sort.

In short, mass communications provides the very fabric with which our lives are ordered. Were mass communications suddenly to cease, our civilization would collapse. That is why this book was written: To promote a better understanding of our world of mass communications, and to inspire the brightest young men and women to seek socially useful and rewarding careers in a field whose importance is second to none.

WHAT COMMUNICATION MEANS

Mankind has another fundamental need beyond the physical requirements of food and shelter: the need to communicate with our fellow human beings. This urge for communication is a primal one and, in our contemporary civilization, a necessity for survival.

Simply defined, *communication* is the act of transmitting information, ideas, and attitudes from one person to another.

Upon this foundation society has built intricate, many-faceted machinery for delivering its messages. The unfolding achievements of science are making this communication machinery more and more fantastic in its ability to conquer the physical barriers of our world. Our minds and our electronic devices are reaching into areas not considered even remotely possible by our grandparents.

Astronauts hurtling through space send back radio and color television reports of what they experience. Cameras mounted on space vehicles give us closeup televised photographs of the moon and the planet Mars and of men walking on the moon itself. Television programs are transmitted from one side of the world to another by bouncing their signals off a satellite in orbit. Each year brings additional wonders in the craft of communicating our messages. With computers and instantaneous transmission systems, we are bending time and space to our will.

Yet all this costly structure is a meaningless toy unless its users have something significant to say. The study of communication thus involves two aspects—a broad comprehension of the mechanical means and the underlying theories of communication and, more important, an understanding of how we use these tools in our daily round of informing, influencing, inspiring, convincing, frightening, and entertaining one another.

Each of us communicates with another individual by directing a message to one or more of his senses—sight, sound, touch, taste, or smell. This is known as *interpersonal communication,* in contrast with *intrapersonal communication,* in which a person "talks to himself." Both forms are subjects of much research study. When we smile, we communicate a desire for friendliness; the tone in which we say "good morning" can indicate feelings all the way from surliness to warm pleasure; and the words we choose in speaking or writing convey a message we want to "put across" to the other person. The more effectively we select and deliver those words, the better our communication.

Contemporary society is far too complex to function only through direct communication between one individual and another. Our important messages, to be effective, must reach many people at one time. A consumer who is angry at high meat prices may talk to a half-dozen neighbors about organizing a boycott, but if the editor of the local newspaper publishes a letter from the consumer, the idea is communicated to hundreds of others in a fraction of the time it would take to visit them individually. The politician running for the Senate spends much time visiting factories and meetings, shaking hands with the citizens in the hope of winning their votes. The candidate knows, however, that only a small percentage of the voters can be reached this way, so time is bought on television and radio to deliver the message to thousands of voters simultaneously. This is *mass communication*—the process of delivering information, ideas, and attitudes to a sizable and diversified audience through use of media developed for that purpose.

The art of mass communication is much more difficult than that of face-to-face discussion. The communicator who is addressing thousands of different personalities at the same time cannot adjust an appeal to meet their individual reactions. An approach that convinces part of the audience may alienate another group. The successful mass communicator is one who finds the right method of expression to establish empathy with the largest possible number of individuals in the audience. In some instances, such as network television shows, the audience for a message numbers in the millions. In the case of weekly newspapers, it may be only a few thousand. The need to catch and hold the individual's attention remains the same.

The politician reaches many more individuals with a single television speech than through handshaking tours, but that person's use of mass communication may be a failure if the same feeling of sincerity and ability that is conveyed through a handshake and smile cannot be projected over the air.

Thus the mass communicator's task breaks down into two parts, knowing *what* to communicate and *how* to deliver the message to make the deepest possible penetration into the minds of the audience. A message of poor content, poorly told to millions of people, may have less total effective impact than a well-presented message placed before a small audience.

Every day each of us receives thousands of impressions. Many of these pass unnoticed or are quickly forgotten. The effectiveness of the impression is influenced in part by the individual's circumstances. A news story from Washington about plans by Congress to increase unemployment benefits raises hopes in the mind of the person who fears being laid off a job; the same dispatch may disturb the struggling small businessman or woman who sees in it the possibility of higher taxes. The communicator's message has had differing effects upon these two members of the audience; it may have none at all upon another reader who is somehow distracted while scanning the newspaper or listening to a newscast.

Obviously, the mass communicator cannot know the mental outlook and physical circumstances of everyone to whom the message goes. There are many principles and techniques that can be used, however, to ensure that the message has an effective impact upon the greatest possible number of individuals in the largest possible audience. Some of these are learned by mastering the basic techniques of journalistic communication (writing, editing, newscasting, graphic presentation); others are learned by studying the mass communication process and by examining the character of the mass media.

THE COMMUNICATION PROCESS

Researchers call our attention to four aspects of the communication process: the *communicator,* the *message,* the *channel,* and the *audience.* (In research language, the communicator is also known as the *encoder;* the message—whether words, pictures, or signs—becomes *symbols;* the channel, in the case of mass communication, is one of the mass *media;*

the person in the audience is known as the *decoder.*) A properly trained person understands the social importance of the communicator's role and also knows what to transmit as the message. The communicator understands the characteristics of the channels (media) to be used and studies the varying interest and understanding levels of groups of people who make up the total audience. The message is molded to the requirements of each channel used and to the capabilities of the audiences being sought. The communicator knows about the limitations and problems communication researchers have studied.

FIGURE 1.1   The communication process: Communicator (C) places a message in selected channel to reach audience (A) but is subject to "noise" interferences.

One of these is *channel noise,* a term used to describe anything that interferes with the fidelity of the physical transmission of the message (such as static on radio or type too small to be read easily); but broadly speaking, channel noise may be conceived of as including all distractions between source and audience. The professional communicator helps overcome its effects by attention-getting devices and by careful use of the principle of *redundancy* (repetition of the main idea of the message to make sure it gets through even if part of the message is lost).

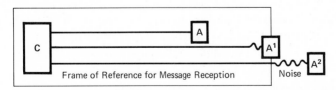

FIGURE 1.2   Communicator and audience member A have the same frame of reference; A^1 is only partially receptive; A^2 is unable to understand.

A second kind of interference, called *semantic noise,* occurs when a message is misunderstood even though it is received exactly as it was transmitted. The communicator, for example, might use words too diffi-

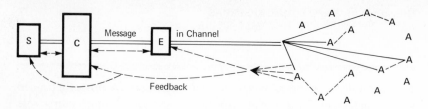

FIGURE 1.3 Mass communication for a given message at one moment in time is illustrated here: Source (S) has the message reported by communicator (C) in channel controlled by editor (E); some audience members (A) receive the message directly, others indirectly, but some are inattentive; feedback interactions may occur along the communication route.

cult for an audience member to understand or names unknown to him or her (material outside that person's *frame of reference*). Or the words used may have one meaning for the communicator and another for the listener or reader (the common or dictionary meaning is called *denotative,* the emotional or evaluative meaning is called *connotative*—a word like "socialist" has widely differing connotations). Semantic noise can be reduced if the communicator will take pains to define terms and adjust vocabulary to the interests and needs of the audience. Sometimes, difficult or strange words are understood because the reader grasps the *context* in which they appear, but it is also possible for a poorly defined word to be misunderstood this way. And if the material presented is too complex, the reader either will be forced to *regress* and restudy the message or, more likely, will turn to some other more rewarding and pleasant material.

Even if all these hurdles are surmounted, the communicator still has other problems in message reception. The receiver interprets the message in terms of a frame of reference, we have said. Each person has a *stored experience,* consisting in part of individual, ego-related beliefs and values and in part of the beliefs and values of the groups to which he or she belongs (family, job, social, and other groups). A message that challenges these beliefs and values may be rejected, distorted, or misinterpreted. Conversely, one whose beliefs on a given subject are under pressure may go out of the way to seek messages bolstering his or her viewpoint. In cases where beliefs are firmly fixed, the communicator finds it is often more effective to try to redirect existing attitudes slightly than to meet them head on. Another audience problem is called *dissonance.* This occurs when an action is taken that is inconsistent with what a person knows or has previously believed, or the action is taken after two or more attractive alternatives are considered. The person is uncomfortable until he or she achieves some dissonance-reduction by seeking out messages that help adjust beliefs to action (a familiar example is the person who, having bought one make of car from among several attractive ones, continues to read advertisements for the car purchased; if makes have been switched, even more reassurance is required).

The communicator is aided by what are called *feedback effects.* These are reactions that take place along the communication process and that are transmitted backward: by the communicator (reporter) to the original news source; by another media worker (editor) to the reporter; by members of the audience to the editor, the reporter, or the news source; and by different persons in the audience to each other. Obviously there is much more discernible feedback in person-to-person communication than in mass media communication, and thus a better opportunity to deliver a convincing message face to face. But the communicator who has knowledge of feedback reactions in mass communication and who solicits them may enhance acceptance of the messages.

Nonverbal communication is an important aspect of the communication process. Popularly known as "silent language" or, in some of its aspects, "body language," nonverbal communication may involve such attributes as facial expression, eye movement, posture, dress, cosmetics, voice qualities, laughing, and yawning. For example, a TV newscaster may, consciously or unconsciously, alter the meaning of the spoken message through a lifted eyebrow or a shrug of the shoulders. A weak voice may convey uncertainty or an arms-folded stance defiance. A politician's rolled-up sleeves and tie-less shirt may produce votes from laborers. Such examples are endless.

All this is summed up in Professor Harold D. Lasswell's question: "Who, says what, in which channel, to whom, with what effect?" Chapter 19 on mass communications research examines the different types of studies carried on by the mass media and by individual scholars to aid in more effective communication. The first steps for the would-be communicator, however, are to gain an understanding of the role of the communicator in our contemporary society and to examine the mass media through which audiences are reached. To take the communicator through these steps is the purpose of this book.

WHAT ARE THE MASS MEDIA?

A message can be communicated to a mass audience by many means: hardly an American lives through a day without feeling the impact of at least one of the mass media. The oldest media are those of the printed word and picture, which carry their message through the sense of sight: the weekly and daily newspapers, magazines, books, pamphlets, direct mail circulars, and billboards. Radio is the mass communications medium aimed at the sense of sound, whereas television and motion pictures appeal both to the visual and auditory senses.

The reader turns to a newspaper for news and opinion, entertainment, and the advertising it publishes. In the weekly the focus is upon the reader's own community; in the daily, upon the nation and the world as well. Magazines provide background information, entertainment, opinion, and advertising; books offer a deeper and more detailed examination of subjects, as well as entertainment; pamphlets, direct mail pieces, and billboards bring the views of commercial and civic organizations. Films may inform and persuade as well as entertain. Television and radio offer entertainment, news and opinion, and advertising messages and can bring direct coverage of public events into the listener's home.

Important agencies of communication are adjuncts of the mass media. These are (1) the press associations, which collect and distribute news and pictures to the newspapers, television and radio stations, and news magazines; (2) the syndicates, which offer background news and pictures, commentary, and entertainment features to newspapers, television and radio, and magazines; (3) the advertising agencies, which serve their business clients on the one hand and the mass media on the other; (4) the advertising departments of companies and institutions, which serve in merchandising roles, and the public relations departments, which serve in information roles; (5) the public relations counseling firms and publicity organizations, which offer information in behalf of their clients, and (6) research individuals and groups, who help gauge the impact of the message and guide mass communicators to more effective paths.

Who are the communicators who work for and with these mass media? The list is extensive. They include the reporters, writers, editors, photographers, cinematographers, announcers, and commentators for newspapers, magazines, television and radio, press associations, and syndicates; book and publication editors and creative personnel in the graphic arts industry; advertising personnel of all types; public relations practitioners and information writers; business management personnel for the mass media; radio-television script and continuity writers; film producers and writers; trade and business publication writers and editors; industrial publication editors; technical writers in such fields as science, agriculture, and home economics; specialists in mass communications research; and teachers of journalism and mass communication. Actors and actresses in television and motion pictures also are communicators in a special sense, for they add emotional impact to the written script.

WHAT IS JOURNALISM?

A somewhat narrower definition is traditionally applied to the use of the mass media in order to identify the role of the journalist. In journalism there is an element of timeliness not usually present in the more leisurely types of writing, such as the writing of books. Journalism is a report of things as they appear at the moment of writing, not a definitive study of a situation. Historically, the journalist has been identified by society as carrying out two main functions: reporting the news and offering inter- pretation and opinion based on news. A journalist may write an account that is entertaining as well as newsworthy; but a person who writes for sheer entertainment only, such as some television scriptwriters, is not a journalist.

Periodical journalism is the oldest and most widely identified area. Periodicals are printed at regular and stated intervals. To be considered newspapers, periodicals must appear at least weekly in recognized news- paper format and have general public interest and appeal. Commonly identified as "journalists" are the reporters, writers, editors, and column- ists who work for newspapers, press associations and syndicates, news magazines, and other magazines devoted largely to public affairs. The print media they serve have been known collectively as "the press," although many newspaper men and women reserve that term for their medium.

News reporting and commentaries delivered by television and radio are equally a form of journalism, as are public affairs documentaries, direct broadcasts of news events, and filmed and videotaped documenta- ries. The reporters, writers, editors, and photographers in the television- radio-film area point out that the general descriptive term "the press" applies to them as well as to the print media people when they are deal- ing with news and opinion. But they tend more often to identify them- selves with the name of their medium than with the collective word "journalist." So do others in the list of communicators given above— photographers, book editors, advertising specialists, industrial editors, and so on.

The ephemeral nature of journalistic writing does not mean that it is poor and careless writing, as is sometimes assumed. Quite the contrary is true in many cases. Journalistic writing is a contemporary report of the changing scene, intended to inform readers of what is happening around them. The impact of journalism can and often does influence the course of events being reported, because it brings public opinion into focus and sometimes creates it. Thus the newspaper and broadcast reports of a street or campus demonstration can touch off strong reaction among the citizenry and force a shift in local, state, or national policy.

Journalists deal in immediacy; they enjoy the stimulation of being close to events and the knowledge that their efforts can help shape the future. They are *communicating* the developments of the day to an audience whose lives are affected by the events they discuss. The sum total of articles printed in the continuing issues of a periodical constitutes a big slice of history as it is being made. Many of the facts reported in any issue soon are outdated by later developments; yet they are true at the moment of writing.

Television and radio journalists communicate news of contemporary events by means of electronic devices rather than with paper and ink. Although this makes the transitory nature of airwave journalism even more pronounced than that of the written word, it is not necessarily less effective and may often be more so. Events with strong elements of sound or sight, such as a forest fire, a football game, or a political convention, are especially well communicated by television and radio.

Dramatic evidence of how electronic and newspaper reporting can dominate the life of the world during a great crisis is found in the reporting of the assassination of President John F. Kennedy and Senator Robert F. Kennedy and the astronauts' journey to the moon and "handshake" in space. Television, radio, newspapers, and magazines provided a massive portrayal of events and held the world tightly in the grip of intense emotion.

ALL MEDIA ARE INTERRELATED

Trying to separate the various mass media into tight compartments is a futile task, and pointless, too. They are closely interrelated, both in functions and in personnel. Employees shift from one medium to another with comparative ease. Certain details of technique are different and must be learned by newcomers, no matter how much experience they may have in other fields, but the principles of mass communication among humans are remarkably similar in all media.

The newspaper reporter who happens to have a good voice may become a radio commentator. He or she must learn to write copy in a more narrative style to please the ear rather than the eye, but the precepts of objectivity, fair play, and persistent digging for facts learned on the newspaper beat still apply. Press associations supply the same daily budget of world and national news to radio and television stations as to newspapers, although the reports are prepared in slightly different form to meet the technical requirements of the various media. The broadcaster, desiring to see a viewpoint preserved in more durable form, may write a magazine article or a book. An author whose novel becomes a best seller may soon be in a Hollywood studio writing screen plays at an exceptionally large salary.

A hard line of demarcation between motion pictures and television was maintained by the film industry during television's early years immediately after World War II. The filmmakers feared the commercial competition of TV. Inevitably this separation broke down because the two media are linked so closely in appeal and techniques. Hollywood studios that once put clauses in their stars' contracts forbidding them to appear on television now film dozens of TV shows on their sound stages and outdoor sets. Numerous prominent motion picture actors "break in" on television, then move into films. Scripts first shown to the public as TV shows have been successfully expanded into feature-length motion pictures. Newspaper publishers also own almost one-fourth of our television stations and almost one-tenth of our radio stations.

The mass media have a common need for men and women with creative minds who can use words and pictures effectively to transmit information and ideas. This is true whether the communication is intended to enlarge the recipient's knowledge, entertain, or convince the person through advertising that a commercial product or service should be purchased.

Advertising is an essential part of the major media and constitutes an additional service to persons seeking that type of information. In newspapers and magazines, stories and advertisements appear side by side and are absorbed by the reader's mind almost simultaneously. On radio and television, presentation of the commercial has been developed into an intricate art, and is often closely integrated with the entertainment portion of the program, which the advertiser also controls. At times, unfortunately, more ingenuity and effort go into the commercial than into the program itself. Large national advertisers conduct sales campaigns for their products in the press and on the air at the same time, spending huge sums to make certain that their messages reach a mass audience as frequently as possible. They are employing the proved technique of repetition. Without advertising revenue, newspapers and magazines could not be sold at their present prices and radio and TV programs could not be provided without charge.

Advertising also has an important function in attracting an audience for the various media. The film studios, theaters, and television producers are heavy advertisers in newspapers and magazines, and newspapers take commercial time on radio and television to publicize their features in an effort to build circulation. Public relations men and women provide a steady stream of stories, photographs, and motion picture film for use by the mass media.

Thus it is evident that the mass media are heavily dependent upon each other. They turn to common sources for talent, for news, for ideas, and even for ownership. In the early days of radio, newspapers feared that the competition of this swift news-dispensing medium would ruin them; when television came along, newspapers, magazines, and motion pictures all were frightened of it at first. Gradually they learned that there is room and a need for all and that no medium need ruin another. The older media had to develop fresh techniques to meet the newcomer's challenge, and they improved themselves in doing so.

In the United States the mass media are commercial ventures, without government subsidy, and survive only if they make money. This is in the best tradition of the free enterprise system. They compete with each other for the audience's time and the advertiser's dollar. Yet all realize that basically they are serving the same purpose—to provide a transmission belt for the free flow of ideas.

CHAPTER 2
THE SOCIAL IMPORTANCE OF COMMUNICATORS

THE COMMUNICATOR'S TASK

Recording history as it happens is an exciting assignment. In this day of almost instantaneous mass communications, members of the mass media are doing even more than recording history; they are helping to shape it. The responsibility is stimulating. From its practitioners, mass communications work demands broad knowledge, sound judgment, quick decisions, and the realization that the words they write or speak may influence the lives of many millions of people.

This sense of influence and responsibility extends to others in mass communications work than those dealing with breaking news. Their opportunities to reach wide audiences and to affect attitudes may be as great. Perhaps all this sounds overwhelming, and in some ways it is. But an intelligent, college-educated man or woman who approaches the job with a proper sense of ethical responsibility and adequate knowledge of the basic techniques will find the work satisfying, mentally and financially, and at times truly exciting.

There is the excitement of creative accomplishment: writing a series of stories exploring the successes and failures of a ghetto youth club project; helping to entertain a nation with a television program and having millions adopt a line like "sock it to me" as their own; writing a story for *Esquire* interpreting the personality of a noted musician; helping to solve a marketing problem for a great industry through an advertising campaign; coming up with the magic of a slogan like "We try harder"; or shooting a photo series that catches the hopes and feelings of the participants in an Upward Bound program.

There is the additional sense of participation felt by those handling the flow of the day's news. Their reporting and commenting take many forms: it may be a television reporter's on-the-scene description of a forest fire as massive flames illuminate the sky, a newspaper writer's word-for-word account as the jury delivers the verdict in a murder trial, a radio reporter's summary of the world's main news developments packed tightly into a five-minute period, or an editorial writer's analysis of the forces shaping a foreign policy decision by the president of the United States. Just as important, it may be a conference by the little-publicized persons behind the news, the editors. They must decide which stories in the day's flow of events deserve the most prominent place in print or on the air. Or it may be a political news writer patiently checking the advance text of a prominent political leader's speech against its actual delivery to see whether an unscheduled piece of major news has been inserted. That is exactly the way President Lyndon Johnson unexpectedly informed the world that he would not run for reelection in 1968 at the height of the Vietnam conflict.

Mass communications work is not always exciting. To pretend that it is would be misleading and unrealistic. As in any business, there are hours of routine, often repetitive work. A solid, disciplined routine and a well-defined set of operating principles underlie everything. What makes news work so intriguing, however, is that exciting events may break loose at the most unexpected moment. Then, in an instant, the reporter's or editor's training, experience, and judgment are called into action. The instantaneous quality of radio and television has added even greater challenges for all those seeking to provide fair and objective presentation of news.

Throughout the mass media of communication, the challenge of social responsibility is felt by those at work. Frequently their judgment is tested under pressure in matters of taste, social restraint, and fairness, with few absolute rules to guide them. The jobs they perform make possible the general diffusion of knowledge about life in today's world and, more than that, influence many aspects of our social, political, and economic patterns. By the way they select and present information, they help in sometimes small, sometimes unintentional, ways to shape our society.

Our mass media illuminate the social fabric of the nation. They are essential to the continued development of the economic fabric in a modern industrial state. And they continue to fulfill their historic role in protecting and improving the political fabric of a democracy. Among the many opportunities enjoyed by the communicator, none is more important than the opportunity to help shape public opinion.

COMMUNICATION, PUBLIC OPINION, AND DEMOCRACY

Public opinion is the engine that keeps the wheels of democracy turning. Although we elect public officials to conduct our government's business and give them power to make decisions controlling our lives, we do not let them exercise arbitrary power as leaders do in a dictatorship. They are restrained by the influence of public opinion, the very instrument that put them into office. This public opinion is expressed primarily through the news media. If the official strays too far from the desires of the mass of the public, counterforces go to work. The most potent and obvious of these is the threat of defeat at the next election, a fact always near the surface of a professional officeholder's mind. More subtle forms of pressure also may be applied by adverse public opinion, such as moves to restrict the power of, damage the prestige of, or discredit the official in public.

Mass media that do not deal in the urgency of spot news—books, most magazines, and films, and a large portion of radio and television programs—also are vital in the formation of public opinion. They examine important contemporary issues in a reflective manner that is possible because their writers and editors have more time to consider the ramifications of events. Social attitudes and political viewpoints can be examined with telling impact through fictional narrative as well as by factual reporting.

Sometimes an excessive amount of time is required to correct a flagrant misuse of governmental authority, but ultimately it is almost always accomplished. In the long run, a democracy gets the kind of government that the majority of its people desires. To be successful, a political leader must convince the voters that he or she represents the viewpoint of the majority, or that his or her policies are wise and should be endorsed by the voters.

How is public opinion brought to bear in political affairs, above and beyond the impact of events themselves? This is a complicated process insofar as arrival at a decision on an issue or an election contest is concerned. The average person is likely to be affected more strongly by social pressures, group associations, and the attitudes of "opinion leaders" than by direct use of the mass media. Since the social group and the opinion leader also reflect information and opinions gained from the mass media, there is a close interrelationship among the three—the mass media, opinion leaders, and the social group—in the decision-making process.

But whatever other forces come into action, it is clear that the mass media of communication have a key role in the building of the political fabric of a democracy. They are the widely available channels through which political leaders express their views and seek to rally public backing for their policies. The president of the United States makes a statement in a press conference, and within minutes the news is sped around the world by the press associations and broadcasters. President Franklin D. Roosevelt found his famous "fireside chats" on radio during the 1930s to be an effective tool in winning support for his economic reforms and later in alerting the American people to the dangers of fascist aggression. Development of television gave later presidents even greater access to the American mind. President John F. Kennedy used live televised news conferences with exceptionally good effect because of his easy delivery and quick wit. On the other hand, President Lyndon Johnson failed to develop an empathy with millions of Americans in his television appearances. His personality was not conveyed well by the cameras, and he appeared cold, calculating, and less than candid. This intangible weakness on television contributed to charges of a "credibility gap" that undermined his power in the later years of his term.

The media also work in the reverse direction to bring the officials news of what the people think and desire. Newspapers publish stories reporting the viewpoints of political opponents and the actions taken in public meetings concerning government policy; on their editorial pages they express their own reactions to developments and make suggestions; frequently newspapers publish the interpretative comments of well-known columnists. In the columns of letters to the editor the readers express their views.

Television and radio help to publicize this interplay of opinion through news reports similar to those appearing in the newspapers, interviews, and panel discussions. An especially effective television technique is found in programs such as "Meet the Press," in which a public official submits to intensive and sometimes belligerent questioning by a group of journalists.

Weekly news magazines have become a significant factor in the two-way transmission of political policy and reaction. With more leisurely deadlines than the daily newspapers have, these periodicals provide background for the news developments and seek to put them into context. Magazines of opinion examine the news critically and express their views on its meaning, much as newspaper editorials do; scholarly periodicals published at intervals of a month or longer delve more deeply into specialized aspects of the contemporary scene.

Books, particularly the heavy-selling paperbacks, convey facts and opinion about public candidates and officeholders. In many respects the paperback, often heavily subsidized and promoted by political factions, has replaced the political tract, such as Thomas Paine's *Common Sense* (1776), which was widely circulated in an effort to influence public opinion.

Public opinion polls, reported widely in the print and broadcast media, have become important elements in the shaping of public opinion as well as the measuring of it by public officials, political candidates, journalists, and the public. Hundreds of survey organizations now probe public sentiment on all important issues and seek to predict the outcomes of elections. Political candidates measure public concerns and attitudes, then shape their campaigns and their statements to the media in light of the findings. On election night they end up with poll point-spreads like football teams.

Even though in the last three presidential elections the final Gallup and Harris polls have been accurate within their stated margins of error, many persons have grave doubts about the polling procedure. How can samples of 1500 or 1600 adults accurately reflect the opinions of 145 million adult Americans? Yet that is all that are needed, providing skilled polling scientists select the proper random sample. And with modern probability methods of sampling (in which each individual in a given population has a known cause of falling into the sample), it is possible to measure just how good the sample is. That is, through probability theory and statistics, it is possible to estimate the chances that the sample is valid or erroneous.

Other possibilities for error in polling include poor wording of questions, thus introducing bias and influenced responses; inadequate interviewing, particularly if the questioning of respondents is done by telephone; and errors in tabulation and analysis. Screening questions are vital in polls attempting to predict how persons will vote: questions dealing with issues, interest in the election, previous voting record, and general attitudes toward the candidates.

Allowing the pollsters their stated 3 to 4 percent margin of error, methodology has become sufficiently sophisticated that most reputable polls have an excellent record in general elections. Gallup, for one, has been off an average of only 1.2 percentage points in national elections since 1952. If the candidates finish only 1 or 2 percent apart, the task of the pollsters is indeed difficult.

Yet it is this precision in election forecasting that gives credibility to the poll findings on attitudes and issues, in which public opinion is tested on such topics as gun control, food stamps, federal aid to education, abortion, and busing. Everyone, from public official to newspaper editor, can ponder the results. The growing use of the polling technique to probe in issue-oriented fashion has helped the media press government for responsive action.

The news media also have the vital role of "watchdog" over the government, searching out instances of malfunctioning and corruption. Without the searching eyes and probing questions of reporters, the public would have far less control over the affairs of city, state, and national governments than it does. Many significant congressional investigations have been started as the result of revelations in the press. President Richard M. Nixon was forced to resign, in part because reporters Bob Woodward and Carl Bernstein uncovered evidence of his unethical and illegal conduct.

Once a bad situation is exposed, public opinion can quickly be brought to bear for reform; but without alert reporters to disclose the misbehavior, the situation might remain uncorrected indefinitely. Generally, the news media have been less zealous in observing the misdeeds of business enterprises, even when these have affected the general public welfare, than they have been in watching over the government.

Plainly, then, in a democracy the press is the "marketplace" of political thought. The policies and aims of government are made known through the channels of the press and are examined exhaustively by opposition political figures, and by commentators, editors, and the public at large. Stories from the newspapers and newscasts are used as the basis for discussions in classroom and clubs. A high government official, wanting to test public reaction to a policy idea, often sends up a "trial balloon" in the form of a guarded newspaper interview suggesting the possible advantages of such a step, or has a friendly columnist discuss the advisability of the move. Other editors and commentators pick up the proposal and examine it in print or on the air. Soon millions of Americans are aware of the tentative plan and are expressing either favorable or negative opinions. The official and staff members keep close watch on this reaction. If the plan encounters heavy opposition, perhaps stirred up by an antagonistic pressure group, the official quietly abandons it; but if it receives popular support, he or she takes positive steps to put it into operation, either by legislation or executive order. It is in such ways that public opinion shapes government policy in a democracy. Note the contrast in a dictatorship, where the ruling clique issues decrees arbitrarily and enforces them regardless of the public's feelings.

COMMUNICATIONS AND THE ECONOMIC FABRIC

Without an extensive and swift system of mass communications, the economic life of a major industrial country cannot function properly.

When we think how large the continental United States is—more than 3000 miles in width and covering many kinds of terrain, population, and living conditions—the degree of economic cohesion is remarkably high. People in the deserts of Arizona drive the same kinds of automobiles, wear the same makes of shoes, and eat the same brands of breakfast food as their fellow Americans in chilly New England. They are able to do so because of two major factors in contemporary American life—

good transportation for moving the goods from the factory and a highly developed system of advertising and marketing.

Students of mass communications should be very conscious of the role and influence of advertising. It informs readers and listeners about the products the manufacturer and merchant offer for sale; it influences them by stimulating their desire for those commodities; and, if it is successful, it convinces them that they should purchase the goods as soon as possible or as soon as they are needed.

Ever since this country was founded, Americans have lived in an expanding economy, except for a few temporary periods of depression. As the population grew and pushed westward, it automatically created a need for goods and services. But if Americans had not learned to want the products of factories, population growth would not have been sufficient to keep the nation's industrial plants growing and its economy expanding. Americans' desire for new products and their demonstrated willingness to purchase them encourage producers to develop attractive new commodities. With few exceptions, companies that spend money to advertise their goods become larger and more profitable than their competitors which do not. This lesson has been driven home so firmly that modern business practice leads most successful companies to expend fixed percentages of their income on advertising. The advertising budget has become as essential in a company's financial operations as money designated for salaries, factory operating expenses, and distribution of the products.

It is no exaggerated claim for advertising to state that it has played a major role in the steady rise of the American standard of living, which has now risen to the highest point of any country in history. The existence of a free enterprise economy such as ours without advertising is inconceivable.

From the consumer's standpoint, the rival advertising of competing companies increases the range of choice and actually saves time and money. From reading or viewing the advertising for new automobiles, the consumer learns what new features each line of cars offers and sees photographs in color of the body designs. If personal inclinations and social group influences have given that person a casual, indefinite idea of trading in an old car for a new one this year, the advertising brings action. He or she visits the showrooms, and probably comes home with a purchase contract.

On a smaller scale, the dollars-and-cents importance of advertising in everyday living is evident if we watch a person read the grocery ads in a newspaper. A weekend shopping list is built from these announcements. One market offers a special price on soap, another nearby market lists a bargain on pork roast. He or she decides to shop first at the market offering the pork roast, but may also visit the store featuring a special price on soap. Without advertising, the customer might have found these bargains by a prolonged search among the shelves, if time were available. Or the person might have missed them and paid full price at still another market. By checking the advertisements, the consumer can shop more rapidly and effectively, and with an actual saving of money.

How does the food store benefit if it spends money on advertising to attract a shopper who buys goods at special low prices, thus reducing the shop's profit margin on those items? The answer to that question contains the secret of price advertising. The consumer saves money on the advertised items, but having been attracted to the store by them, is beguiled by point-of-purchase displays of additional items and buys these, too. The advertisement creates foot traffic in the market, and it is an axiom of merchandising that the more traffic that goes through a store, the more goods are sold. These additional purchases beyond actual realized needs help build our expanding economy.

Advertising in the United States is divided into two broad categories, national and local. National advertising is used by manufacturers to inform a nationwide audience, or perhaps a large regional one, about the advantages of their products. Sometimes a company devotes its advertising space to creating an image of itself in the public mind, emphasizing its reliability, friendliness, or public service, rather than concentrating upon a direct selling message for its products. This is institutional advertising, whose results cannot be measured directly upon a sales chart. Large corporations also use institutional advertising to influence public opinion on matters of national economic policy that are important to them. National advertisers use television, magazines, newspapers, and radio for the bulk of their advertising. Placement of the advertising campaigns is done through large advertising agencies, many of which have their head offices along Madison Avenue in New York City; these agencies earn their money principally by receiving a percentage of the price charged by the media for their space and time.

Local advertising is placed by merchants in their community newspapers and on local television and radio stations. It is directed to a well-defined, easily comprehended audience. Rarely does local advertising appear in magazines, because few periodicals have sufficient circulation concentrated in a single community. Chain-store merchandisers also use direct mail to distribute hundreds of thousands of advertising pieces called "mailers" at bulk rates. Sometimes these multiple-page advertisements are published simultaneously in newspapers. Whereas the main function of national advertising is to present products to a huge audience and to stimulate buying interest in them, local advertising is largely concerned with direct sales, making the cash register ring. Emphasis upon price is much greater in local advertising copy, because an attractive price is often the stimulus that converts the potential customer from intention to action.

The automobile manufacturer introduces new models in the autumn with an elaborate national network television program featuring famous entertainment personalities and glamorous shots of the automobiles surrounded by attractive men and women. That is the national approach. A few days later, the community auto dealer purchases time on a home-town television station. The dealer appears on the screen, fondly patting the fender of a new model, and tells each viewer, "You can have this beautiful car for only $500 down. Come in and see it tonight; we are open until 9 P.M." That is the local follow-up.

A department store may take a half-page advertisement in a local newspaper just to publicize a bargain price for nylon hose. It knows that the expenditure will be profitable if the advertisement is attractive enough to draw a throng of women into the store. The item chosen is a low-cost one, regarded by most women as a necessity, and with a frequent replacement need. Thus, if it is sufficiently attractive, thousands of readers almost automatically are potential customers for such a sale.

At the end of the day the department manager can tell exactly how many pairs of hose have been sold and compare this with a normal day's total. Thus the pulling power of the advertisement can be measured. However, the item may have been priced so low that, with the cost of the advertising added, the store may have lost money on the sale. The venture would still be regarded as highly successful if a large percentage of the sale shoppers bought additional unadvertised merchandise while they were in the store.

The mass media, then, play key roles in the business life of the country, at both the national and local levels of production and sales, by providing channels for advertising messages. They also help in other ways to shape the economic fabric of the country. They bring people, from industrial leaders to laborers, the necessary information upon which their business and personal decisions are based. They help the public to crystallize its attitudes on matters of national economic policy. They serve as sounding boards of public opinion for business, labor, agriculture, and other segments of society. Deprived of rapid and effective mass communications, a country whose sections and people have become as closely interdependent as ours would quickly tumble into economic and social chaos.

THE MASS MEDIA AS SOCIAL INSTRUMENTS

So far we have looked briefly at the mass communicator's role as a transmitter of political opinions in a democracy and in promoting the country's economic growth. Equally vital is the reporting of swiftly changing American social customs and opinions.

The upheaval that struck many aspects of American life during the past two decades was abundantly reported and analyzed in the media. Indeed, television, radio, newspapers, magazines, and books were responsible for publicizing such phenomena as the miniskirt, leading to its adoption even by women whose desire to be fashionable was stronger than the warnings they saw in the mirror. The outburst of college protests and violence could be traced from campus to campus by televised and printed news stories. Within a few hours, methods used by protesters in one part of the country were adopted on other campuses thousands of miles away. The techniques of racial protest could be traced from city to city in much the same manner.

Even the increase in public use of language previously considered indecent and the growing interest in displays of public nudity have been reflected in the news media. Notably, however, newspapers are far more cautious in their use of increasingly uninhibited visual and spoken material than magazines, books, motion pictures, and the stage.

Virtually no aspect of our habits, desires, and relationships escapes examination in our public media. As the years have passed, discussion has become increasingly frank; for better or worse, the evasions have all but disappeared. Some portions of the mass media have forced this trend; others have followed reluctantly.

Our curiosity about each other as individuals is intense. We want to know how the other person lives. We chuckle at the ludicrous situations in which fellow humans involve themselves, and we read with sympathy of their tragedies. No matter how sternly they may deny it, all people have a little of the back-fence gossip in their souls. They like to peek into the lives of others, whether for mere satisfaction of curiosity or for the higher purposes of social research. As we absorb our daily quota of stories, abundantly provided by the media, we are, without fully realizing it, receiving a multicolored picture of the contemporary social scene.

The news media are the recorders of day-by-day history on a broader scale than ever before. Historians who try to reconstruct life in the centuries before there were newspapers would give much to have similar material available about those days.

Always in news coverage there is the underlying pressure of the necessity for speed. Few mass media workers enjoy the luxury of time for philosophical reflection. Theirs is a "now" business. Decisions must be made quickly, often when all the facts are not yet available. The deadline is ever-present—most urgently for press association, daily newspaper, and television reporters and editors, but to a lesser degree for others, too. Mass communications work is for men and women who can think rapidly, act decisively, and report the world with clarity and compassion.

PART II

THE HISTORICAL PERSPECTIVE

CHAPTER 3
THEORIES AND REALITIES OF PRESS FREEDOM

SOCIETY'S CRUCIAL FREEDOMS

The history of journalism and of the development of the mass media begins with the story of man's long struggle for personal liberty and political freedom, upon which the freedom to write and speak depends. Without that freedom, the magic of print and electronic technologies is of no value to free minds. One basic tenet of Anglo-American society has been freedom to print without prior restraint. How fragile such concepts are became apparent in 1971 when, for the first time in the history of the American republic, a president sought to impose prior restraint upon his country's newspapers. He succeeded for fifteen days. And although then overruled, he clouded the future of press freedom. The roots of the Pentagon Papers case are found in the historic duel between the people's press and the people's governors.

Five centuries ago the printing press began to revolutionize man's ability to communicate information and ideas. But almost from the moment Johann Gutenberg introduced movable type to the Western world around 1440 in Germany, barriers were erected against its use to influence public opinion through the free flow of news and opinion. In the English-speaking world printers and writers struggled until 1700 to win the mere right to print. They fought for another century to protect that liberty and to win a second basic right: the right to criticize. Addition of a third right—the right to report—came equally slowly and with less success. Today's journalist knows that there remains a constant challenge to the freedoms to print, to criticize, and to report and that therefore the people's right to know is in constant danger. This is true in the democratic Western world, where freedom of the press is a recognized tenet, as well as in the larger portion of the world where it is denied. And it is true of the twentieth-century additions to the printing press: film, radio, and television.

Freedom of the press is intertwined with other basic freedoms. These are freedom of speech, freedom of assembly, and freedom of petition. Upon these freedoms rest freedom of religious expression, freedom of political thought and action, and freedom of intellectual growth and communication of information and ideas. A society possessing and using these freedoms will advance and change as it exercises democratic processes. Very naturally, then, these freedoms will come under attack from those opposed to any change that might diminish their own power or position in society—today as in past eras. The press, occupying a key role in the battle for these basic freedoms, is a particular target. To the closed mind, the press always has been a dangerous weapon to be kept as far as possible under the control of adherents of the status quo; to the inquiring mind, it has been a means of arousing interest and emotion among the public in order to effect change.

The social and political environments of the past five centuries have produced two basic theories of the press. The older we call the *authoritarian theory*. The controlled society of the Renaissance era, into which the printing press was introduced, functioned from the top down; a small and presumably wise ruling class decided what all of society should know and believe. This authoritarian concept of the relationship between man and the state could brook no challenge from those who thought the rulers were reflecting error, not truth. Publishing therefore existed under a license from those in power to selected printers who supported the rulers and the existing social and political structure. The authoritarian press theory still exists today in those parts of the world where similar controlled societies are dominated by small ruling classes. A variant of this theory, called the *Soviet Communist theory* of the press by the authors of *Four Theories of the Press* (Fred S. Siebert, Theodore Peterson, and Wilbur Schramm; University of Illinois Press, 1956), arose with the twentieth-century dictatorship. Whether fascist or communist, it exalts the state at the expense of individuals and its government-owned and party-directed press is dedicated to furthering the dictatorship and its social system.

As the Western world advanced through the Renaissance and Reformation into the democratic modern era, the second basic theory of the press developed. This we call the *libertarian theory*. Its roots extend back into the seventeenth century, but it did not become dominant in the English-speaking world until the nineteenth century. In libertarian theory, the press is not an instrument of government or a spokesman for an elite ruling class. The mass of people are presumed able themselves to discern between truth and falsehood, and having been exposed to a press operating as a free marketplace of ideas and information, will themselves help determine public policy. It is essential that minorities as well as majorities, the weak as well as the strong, have free access to public expression in the press of a libertarian society.

In the battle against authoritarianism, the printer gradually became an ally of thinkers and writers who struggled for religious, political, and intellectual freedom and of the rising commercially based middle class that demanded economic freedom and political power in its contest with feudalism. Slowly the journalist developed dual functions: the opinion function and the news function. His media were the printed broadside and the pamphlet before he developed regularly issued newspapers in an established format. These appeared on the European continent before 1600, in England after 1622, and in the American colonies after 1704. In the eighteenth century they were joined by the early magazines. By our standards early newspapers were poorly printed, haphazard in content, and limited in circulation. But their influence can be measured by the amount of effort expended by those in authority to erect barriers against them and the stimuli to thought and action they contained. The traditions of freedom their printers and editors won by breaking down the barriers in the seventeenth and eighteenth centuries are the heritage of the modern newspapers and magazines developed in the nineteenth and twentieth centuries and of the film and electronic media of our times.

It was John Milton in his *Areopagitica* of 1644 who argued against repression of freedom of expression by advocating reliance upon truth: "Let her and Falsehood grapple: who ever knew Truth put to the worse in a free and open encounter?" Those who are afraid of truth will of course seek to prevent its entrance into a free marketplace of thought, but those who believe in the public liberty should realize that its existence depends upon liberty of the press. Thomas Jefferson put it well in a letter to his friend, Carrington, in 1787:

I am persuaded that the good sense of the people will always be found to be the best army. They may be led astray for a moment, but will soon correct themselves. The people are the only censors of their governors; and even their errors will tend to keep these to the true principles of their institution. To punish these errors too severely would be to suppress the only safeguard of the public liberty. The way to prevent these irregular interpositions of the people, is to give them full information of their affairs through the channel of the public papers, and to contrive that those papers should penetrate the whole mass of the people. The basis of our government being the opinion of the people, the very first object should be to keep that right; and were it left to me to decide whether we should have a government without newspapers, or newspapers without a government, I should not hesitate a moment to prefer the latter.

Jefferson qualified his final statement, however, by adding: "But I should mean that every man should receive those papers, and be capable of reading them." Jefferson used the word "reading" because the problem of literacy still was a major one in his day; he also meant "understanding" in the sense of intellectual literacy. In these words of Milton and Jefferson are found the libertarian arguments for freedom of printing and other forms of communication, for freedom to criticize, and for freedom to report. They also argue for public support of the kind of mass media that carry out their responsibilities to provide the free flow of news and opinion and to speak for the people as "censors of their governors." The ability of journalists to discharge their responsibilities to society is conditioned, as Jefferson warned, by the level of public education and understanding; there is a public responsibility implied in this philosophic statement of the role of press liberty in supporting all of society's crucial freedoms.

There is also a public responsibility, and a journalistic one, to maintain the libertarian theory that everyone can be freely heard in the press, through a variant concept called the *social responsibility theory* of the press. Today it is no longer economically feasible for anyone so minded to start printing or airing his views. Concentration of much of the mass media in the hands of a relatively few owners imposes an obligation on them to be socially responsible, to see that all sides of social and political issues are fairly and fully presented so that the public may decide. The social responsibility theory contends that should the mass media fail in this respect, it may be necessary for some other agency of the public to enforce the marketplace of ideas concept.

THE RIGHT TO PRINT

William Caxton set up the first press in England in 1476. It was more than two centuries later, in 1694, before the freedom to print without prior restraint became a recognized liberty of the English people and their printer-journalists.

Prior restraint means licensing or censorship before a printer has a chance to roll his press. Unauthorized printing in itself becomes a crime. Under our modern concept anyone is free to have his or her say, although subject to punishment if what is printed offends society (obscenity, sedition) or harms another individual (libel). Authoritarian government does not care to grant this much freedom; it wishes to control communication from the start and to select the communicators.

Caxton printed the first books in the English language and otherwise aided in bringing the culture of the Continent to England. He enjoyed royal support and needed subsidizing by the ruling class, since his market was so limited by illiteracy. He and his successors improved the quality and volume of printing during the next half-century, which saw the rise of the Tudor dynasty. Henry VIII, in his efforts to grasp absolute power, issued a proclamation in 1534 requiring printers to have royal permission before setting up their shops. This was a licensing measure, imposing prior restraint. Except for short periods, the theory of prior restraint remained in effect in England until 1694.

Henry VIII took other measures to control the press, including banning foreign books, issuing lists of forbidden books, and punishing ballad printers who offended Henry and his powerful Privy Council. But neither he nor Queen Elizabeth I was able to frighten all the printers and writers into compliance. After 1557 the Stationers Company, an organization of the licensed publishers and dealers, was given power to regulate printing and to search out bootleg jobs that had not been registered with it. Severe penalties for unauthorized printing were imposed in 1566 and 1586, in the latter year by the authority of the infamous Court of the Star Chamber. But despite arrests and smashing of presses of unlucky printers, some defiance always remained.

The struggle between the rising commercial class and the crown, which broke out into revolution in 1640 and brought the establishment of the Commonwealth in 1649 by Oliver Cromwell, gave printers some temporary freedom. James I and succeeding Stuart kings found that Puritan opposition was increasingly difficult to contain, and the journalists were more alert to their opportunities. Public interest in the Thirty Years' War on the Continent and in other political and economic affairs inevitably brought increased publication. Nathaniel Butter, Thomas Archer, and Nicholas Bourne produced the first regularly issued news book in 1621, on a weekly basis. Containing translated news from European news sheets, it was called a coranto. Diurnals, or reports of domestic events, appeared first as handwritten newsletters and later, after the Long Parliament raised the crown's ban on printing in 1641, in print.

But freedom was short-lived. By 1644 Milton was protesting against new licensing laws. After the execution of Charles I in 1649, Cromwell and his Puritan regime permitted only a few administration publications, censored by none other than Milton. The return of the Stuarts under Charles II in 1660 merely brought a switch in the licenser and censor to the royal party and more strict repression of unauthorized printing. Noteworthy, however, was the founding of the court newspaper, the London *Gazette,* in 1665. It remains today the oldest English newspaper.

The decline of the Stuarts, preceding the Revolution of 1688 that brought William and Mary to the throne, restored freedom to printers.

Parliament allowed the licensing act to lapse in 1679. It was revived temporarily but finally died in 1694. Though severe seditious libel laws remained, and taxes on print paper and advertising were to be instituted beginning in 1712, the theory of prior restraint was dead. Newspapers by the score appeared in London, among them the first daily, the *Daily Courant,* in 1702. The early eighteenth century saw a flowering of newspapers and popular "essay" papers, edited by such figures as Daniel Defoe, Richard Steele and Joseph Addison, and Samuel Johnson.

Licensing and the theory of prior restraint did not die immediately in the American colonies. The Puritans imported the first press to New England in 1638 to print materials for their schools and Harvard College. Commercial presses followed, and some news broadsides and pamphlets appeared. In 1690 a refugee editor from London, Benjamin Harris, issued the first number of a Boston newspaper, *Publick Occurrences,* but his frank reporting nettled the colonial governor and council, which promptly ruled him out for not having a license. When the postmaster, John Campbell, brought out the first regular weekly paper, the Boston *News-Letter,* in 1704, he voluntarily trotted to the authorities for advance censorship and put "Published by Authority" at the top of his columns. It was not until 1721, when James Franklin began publishing his famed *New-England Courant,* that a colonial editor printed in defiance of authority.

Freedom to print became an accepted principle in America; nine colonies had already provided such constitutional protection by 1787, when the Constitutional Convention met in Philadelphia. Many felt it was a state matter, but when the Bill of Rights was added to the Constitution, the First Amendment included freedom of the press among the basic liberties which Congress could not violate. Under British common law and American judicial interpretation, prior restraint violates press freedom. Suppression of publications in anticipation of wrongful printing, or licensing measures to control those who would publish, cannot be authorized by Congress. In 1931 the Supreme Court for the first time applied the press guarantees of the First Amendment to the states, through the due process clause of the Fourteenth Amendment. The ruling came on an appeal against suppression of a Minneapolis news sheet under the Minnesota "gag law" of 1925 permitting suppression of malicious and scandalous publications. The court held the Minnesota law unconstitutional because it permitted prior restraint and said that those damaged by the newspaper had proper recourse through libel action.

There was a flaw in the courts' protection of the press, however. Was the prohibition of prior restraint absolute? When the New York *Times* in 1971 began publication of a summary of the secret Pentagon Papers laying bare U.S. decisions to escalate the Vietnam war, the government won a temporary restraining order prohibiting more stories. Shaken, the newspaper attorneys retreated, arguing only that the government had failed to show a danger to national security. The Supreme Court agreed, 6 to 3, but legal scholars warned that the ban on prior restraint could not be considered absolute. Part III will examine reasons for this setback.

The Post Office, with its power to exclude publications from the mails under certain conditions, has given publishers many censorship troubles. Matters came to a head in 1946 after it sought to withdraw use of the second-class mailing rate from *Esquire* magazine on the grounds that the rate was a privilege intended only for those making a "special contribution to the public welfare." *Esquire,* faced with an additional half-million dollars a year in postal bills, appealed to the Supreme Court, which ruled in its favor. The court commented, "But to withdraw the second-class rate from this publication today because its content seemed to one official not good for the public would sanction withdrawal of the second-class rate tomorrow from another periodical whose social or economic views seemed harmful to another official." The decision put the Post Office back to judging specific issues on the basis of obscenity or inclusion of illegal news of lotteries.

The motion picture industry instituted its own regulatory code in 1922, as a form of self-censorship, through the Motion Picture Association of America. Even before that date, state and city censorship boards were exercising precensorship functions by viewing and clipping films in advance of movie showings, or banning them, a practice that still continues despite court challenges. Extralegal pressures have been brought by such unofficial groups as the former Legion of Decency. The same informal pressures have affected book publication and book purchases by public libraries and school systems. In addition, book publishers run the risk of having specific volumes barred from the mails as obscene. (Supreme Court decisions on obscenity are reviewed in Chapter 7.)

Radio and television, like the printed media, are not subject to precensorship. But more charges of "censorship" are raised in their cases, with the objection being to self-censorship or control of content in anticipation of adverse reaction. The broadcast media are more sensitive on this score because their managers realize that violations of what is considered to be "good taste" might cause difficulties for an individual station with the Federal Communications Commission under broadcasting licensing provisions (see Chapter 7).

If history has proved licensing to be a dangerous practice inimical to press freedom, why did the American public agree to licensing of radio and television stations? The answer is that by common consent we have recognized that broadcast channels are in the public domain. Congress in 1912 first legislated that the Department of Commerce should issue licenses to private broadcasters and assign them wavelengths so that they would not interfere with government wavelengths. During World War I all wireless operations were put under government control, but by 1919 private broadcasters were again experimenting. Numbers of stations increased rapidly and chaos developed on the airwaves. The radio industry, the National Association of Broadcasters, the American Newspaper Publishers Association, and other groups petitioned the government for relief.

This came from Congress through the Radio Act of 1927, which established a five-man commission to regulate all forms of radio communication. The government retained control of all channels, granting three-year licenses to broadcasters "in the public interest, convenience, or necessity" to provide "fair, efficient, and equitable service" throughout the country. Federal authority was broadened in 1934, with establishment of the seven-man Federal Communications Commission to exercise jurisdiction over all telecommunications. The responsibility of the license holder to operate his station in the public interest was more clearly spelled out. The commission was given the power to refuse renewal of a license in cases of flagrant disregard of broadcasting responsibility, but the FCC rarely has used this power. The law forbids any attempt at censorship by the commission; no station can be directed to put a particular program on or off the air. But the FCC undeniably is able to exercise indirect pressure upon license holders, who are understandably wary of its ultimate powers. FCC insistence upon stations' building some record for broadcasting in the public interest has led to attention to news and public affairs programs; on the other hand, the licensing problem has led to broadcasters dragging their feet in airing controversial issues.

American radio and television are as free as American newspapers and magazines to provide whatever news their news editors see fit. Radio and television have also widely broadcast the opinion programs of individual commentators. But they have been reluctant until recently to broadcast opinion as that of the station itself. The FCC in 1941 issued a ruling that "the broadcaster cannot be advocate"; then in 1949 the commission decided that stations could "editorialize with fairness" and urged them to do so. Many broadcasters felt they did not have the trained staffs to do effective editorializing or did not wish to identify the station management as an advocate in controversial situations, but twenty-five years later more than half the stations were broadcasting editorial opinions.

THE RIGHT TO CRITICIZE

Winning the liberty to print without prior restraint did not free the press from the heavy hand of government. In eighteenth-century England, and in the American colonies, the laws of seditious libel ran counter to the philosophical theory that the press should act as "censor of the government." To the authoritarian mind, the mere act of criticism of officials was in itself a crime, and "the greater the truth, the greater the libel" was an established tenet. This meant that publishing a story about a corrupt official was all the more seditious if the official indeed was corrupt.

The journalist's problem was to establish the principle of truth as a defense against charges of sedition or criminal libel. Mere fact of publication then would not be sufficient to determine guilt, and the accused printer or editor would be able to present his case in open court, preferably before a jury. Once the principle of truth as a defense could be won, governments would be less likely to press sedition charges, and laws defining what constitutes sedition could be revised.

The landmark case in what is now the United States was that of John Peter Zenger, who was tried in New York colony in 1735 for seditious libel. Zenger was an immigrant printer who lent the columns of his weekly paper, the *Journal,* to the cause of a political faction opposed to the royal governor. Some of the leading citizens of the colony were aligned with Zenger in the struggle against the governor, whom they accused of various arbitrary actions in the *Journal's* columns. Zenger was jailed and brought to trial in a hostile court. At this juncture a remarkable eighty-year-old lawyer from Philadelphia, Andrew Hamilton, entered the case as Zenger's attorney.

The crown prosecutor reviewed the laws of seditious libel and argued that since Zenger had admitted publishing the newspaper issues in question, the trial was as good as over. His aged opponent skillfully tilted with the presiding justice and the prosecutor and insisted that truth should be permitted to be offered as a defense, with the jury to decide upon the truth of Zenger's publications. These arguments were denied by the court, but Hamilton ignored the ruling and delivered a stirring oration to the jury. He ended with a plea for the jury to take matters into its own hands: "The question before the court . . . is not just the cause of the poor printer. . . . No! It may in its consequence affect every freeman . . . on the main of America. It is the best cause; it is the cause of Liberty . . . the liberty both of exposing and opposing arbitrary power . . . by speaking and writing Truth."

Zenger was acquitted, and the court did not challenge the jury's verdict, even though it ignored existing law. A similar court victory on the issue of admission of truth as evidence was not won in England itself until the 1770s. The threat of trials for seditious libel remained until the end of the century, although in the colonies no further court trials of editors were held. Some editors were harassed by governors and their privy councils, but in general the colonial press was free to criticize the English authorities and to promote the cause of American independence (the reverse was not true, however, and Tory editors were suppressed by colonial radicals). By the early 1770s such papers as the Boston *Gazette* were openly seditious in their attacks upon constituted authority, but they continued to appear and to fan the fires of revolution.

Once the revolution was won, there was sharp cleavage along political and economic lines in the new nation. The newspapers continued to take pronounced partisan stands. The two political factions, the Federalists headed by Alexander Hamilton and the Republicans headed by Thomas Jefferson, split on many domestic issues and particularly over the country's emotional reaction to the French Revolution. Most of the weeklies and the few dailies that had started after 1783 were published in seaboard towns for the commercial classes and tended to be Federalist in sympathy. Hamilton sponsored some party organs in addition: John Fenno's *Gazette of the United States,* Noah Webster's *American Minerva,* and William Coleman's New York *Evening Post.* Topping the Federalist editors in partisan criticism was William Cobbett with his *Porcupine's Gazette.*

Jefferson countered with Philip Freneau's *National Gazette* and also had other Republican supporters, including William Duane and Benjamin Franklin Bache at the *Aurora.* The impulsive Bache, grandson of Benjamin Franklin, more than matched Cobbett in vituperative criticism. When it appeared that war with France was imminent in 1798, the Federalists decided to crack down on their tormentors.

The Alien and Sedition Acts they passed in 1798 were aimed at deportation of undesirable aliens and at curbing criticism of the government. Undesirable aliens in Federalist eyes were those who supported Vice-President Jefferson; some were deported and others were harassed. The Sedition Act by its terms restricted prosecutions to those who "write, utter, or publish . . . false, scandalous and malicious writing" against the federal government, its officials and legislators, or its laws (including the Sedition Act itself). It provided for admission of truth as a defense. In theory, only false criticism was to be punished; but in practice, Federalist politicians and judges set out to punish anti-Federalist editors. One, for example, was jailed and fined for printing a letter to the editor which accused President John Adams of "ridiculous pomp, foolish adulation, and selfish avarice."

Vice-President Jefferson, fearful for his own safety, retired to Monticello, where he and his supporters drafted the Virginia and Kentucky Resolutions, advocating the theory of nullification by the states of unconstitutional acts of the Congress. But the issue did not need to be joined; Federalist excesses in administering the Alien and Sedition Acts contributed to a popular revulsion and to Jefferson's election as president in 1800. The dangerous Alien and Sedition Acts expired the same year. Jefferson insisted that his administration permit partisan journalism, "to demonstrate the falsehood of the pretext that freedom of the press is incompatible with orderly government." He urged that individuals protect themselves against journalistic excesses by filing civil suits for libel. The calm course Jefferson took was vindicated when his party retained control of the government for a generation. Party newspapers, with one-sided news and fiercely partisan opinion, continued to flourish, but after the great crisis of 1798 no federal administration attempted to repress criticism. Soon after 1800 the libertarian theory of the press had eclipsed the authoritarian theory by common consent.

During wartime, national safety requirements and emotional feelings bring some restriction of criticism. The Civil War saw suppression of a few newspapers in the North, but considering the violence of many editors' criticisms, retaliation by Lincoln and his generals was almost negligible. During World War I, the Espionage Act of 1917 widened the authority of the Post Office to bar periodicals from the mails, and the Sedition Act of 1918 made it a crime to write or publish "any disloyal, profane, scurrilous or abusive language" about the federal government. The ax fell heavily upon German-language newspapers, in many cases unfairly. It also fell upon Socialist magazines and newspapers, because they opposed the war, and upon pacifist publications. Max Eastman's brilliant magazine, *The Masses,* was barred from the mails, as were two leading Socialist dailies, the New York *Call* and the Milwaukee *Leader.* Socialist party leader Eugene Debs went to prison for criticizing America's allies as "out for plunder." Clearly the theory of liberty to criticize was disregarded in these violations of minority opinion rights. During

World War II only a few pro-Nazi and Fascist publications were banned —and they had few friends to plead their cause.

The right to criticize needs constant protection, as was demonstrated when Louisiana political boss Huey Long attempted to punish newspaper opponents through taxation. Long and his political machine imposed a special tax on the advertising income of larger Louisiana dailies, virtually all of which were opposed to him. The Supreme Court held the punitive tax unconstitutional in 1936. In the early 1950s courageous newspapers and magazines that spoke out against Senator Joseph McCarthy of Wisconsin and what became known as McCarthyism were harassed and denounced. But neither McCarthy nor his followers could bring about actual legislation restricting criticism, much as they might have liked to do so.

Contempt-of-court citations bring about another kind of clash over the right to criticize. A series of Supreme Court decisions in the 1940s widened the freedom of newspapers to comment upon pending court cases and actions of judges. This was done by applying the "clear and present danger" theory to a judge's contention that administration of justice was being impeded by newspaper comment. But judges have great power in contempt-of-court matters, and editors remain wary of criticizing their acts without pressing need to do so.

THE RIGHT TO REPORT

The right to report is not nearly as much a right safeguarded by law and legal precedent as the right to print and the right to criticize. Rather, it is based on a philosophical argument. What would be gained through the right to print and to criticize if no news were forthcoming? What good would a free press be for the reader if editors and reporters had no way to find out what government was doing? Denial of the right of access to news is a denial of the people's right to know, the journalist maintains.

Yet, no person can be compelled to talk to a reporter; no government official need grant an interview or hold a press conference; courts and legislatures admit the press through historical tradition and have the power to eject the press (unless specific statutes have been passed requiring open legislative sessions). There is another side to the coin: No newspaper can be compelled to print any material it does not wish to use, including paid advertising.

While the laws of seditious libel were in vogue, no right to report was recognized. The mere reporting of a government official's action, or of a debate in Parliament, was likely to be construed as seditious (unfavorable) by some person in authority. William Bradford in Pennsylvania,

James Franklin in Massachusetts, and other colonial editors were haled before authorities for reporting a disputed action of government. In England, reporting of the proceedings of Parliament was banned until 1771, when the satirical writings of Dr. Samuel Johnson and the open defiance of newspaper publisher John Wilkes crumpled the opposition.

The House of Representatives of the American Congress opened its doors to reporters in 1789, two days after it was organized as a legislative body. The Senate, however, excluded reporters until 1795. Congress came to depend upon journalists, particularly the editors of the Jeffersonian party organ, the *National Intelligencer,* to publish a record of debates and proceedings. Not until 1834 did the government publish its own records.

Today there is little likelihood that Washington correspondents will be denied access to the congressional press galleries, except when the legislators are meeting in emergency executive session (a rare event). But reporters are admitted to sessions of legislative committees only with the consent of the committee chairman and members. Some 40 percent of congressional committee sessions are closed to the press. The situation in state capitals is similar. Television and radio reporters and photographers have won access to legislative sessions only by persistent effort, and their ability to use all their equipment is often circumscribed.

Reporters similarly are admitted to court sessions only by the agreement of the presiding judge. They may be excluded, with other members of the public, if the court deems it necessary. Juvenile courts, for example, operate without reportorial coverage in most cases. Ordinarily reporters are free to attend court sessions, since public trials are the rule, but they have no automatic right of attendance. Photographers and TV-radio reporters have had only spotty success in covering trials with cameras and microphones, due to restrictions applied to them by Section 35 of the Canons of Judicial Ethics of the American Bar Association. A long campaign by the National Press Photographers Association, the Radio Television News Directors Association, and the American Society of Newspaper Editors to persuade the bar association to revise its Canon 35 failed when that group reaffirmed its stand in 1963. In 1972 the association replaced Canon 35 with Canon 3A7, equally as restrictive. But by 1978 courts in seven states were working with the media and allowing camera use, without impairment of justice or court dignity.

An important doctrine that has grown up is the doctrine of qualified privilege. This provides that a news medium in reporting the actions of a legislative body or a court is free of the threat of libel suits provided its report is accurate and fair. This doctrine carries with it the implication that the media have an obligation to report legislative and judicial sessions so that the public may know what government and courts are doing. Defamatory statements affecting the reputations of individuals made in legislative sessions and courts may therefore be reported without fear of damage suits.

The right to report is denied more often at the grass roots level of government than at the national level, insofar as legislative bodies are concerned. Boards of education, water commissions, city councils, county boards, and other similar groups often seek to meet in private and conduct the public's business in virtual secrecy. Newspeople wage an unending battle against this practice, without much avail, unless the public demands to know. Some editors and publishers accept the practice and forfeit their right to report the news firsthand, thereby forfeiting their most important right as journalists. Passage of "open meetings" laws in an increasing number of states during the 1950s, at the insistence of various news groups, somewhat improved the access to news at the local level. These laws provide that actions taken in closed sessions are invalid; but they do not force a reluctant legislative group to open the doors wide. By 1975 virtually all states had some form of open meeting law as well as laws guaranteeing opening of public records to reporters needing access to them.

Perhaps the most publicized denial of access to news has been in the national executive departments. This increasing trend—stemming from the necessity for secrecy in limited areas of the national defense establishment and atomic energy research—has alarmed responsible journalists. The American Society of Newspaper Editors and the Society of Professional Journalists, Sigma Delta Chi, have well-organized campaigns demanding free access to news so that people may know the facts necessary to make intelligent decisions.

Appointment in 1955 of a House subcommittee headed by Representative John Moss of California to study the information policies of the government brought some relief. The Moss committee acted as the champion of the people's right to know and the reporter's right of access to news. By publicizing executive department refusals to make information available on public matters, the Moss committee forced some reforms, including passage of the Freedom of Information Act of 1966 giving the citizen legal recourse against arbitrary withholding of information by a federal agency. The law was strengthened in 1974 (details are found in Chapter 6).

Another encouraging sign in the battle for the right to know was enactment by Congress of a Government in the Sunshine Law that took effect in 1977. This law requires more than 50 federal boards and agencies with two or more members to conduct most meetings in the open. The law allows closed meetings for certain specified reasons but requires that the reasons for any closed meetings be certified by the chief legal officer of the agency. In 1978 the House decided to open its debates to daily live broadcast coverage. The body voted, however, to control the broadcast feed itself rather than let a network pool produce it.

But despite such evidences of progress, Washington correspondents say they are fighting a losing battle against administrative orders that forbid federal employees from talking to reporters and that employ other devices to keep an executive department's actions secret unless the administrator deems it desirable to make them public. In this battle, as in others involving the right to report, the reporter's best weapon is the power of the press, which is in turn based on the pressure of public opinion. Reporters who are determined to find out the facts can usually prevail over reluctant public officials.

CHAPTER 4
GROWTH OF THE PRINT MEDIA

THE BASIC EDITORIAL FUNCTIONS

Newspapers, despite their impact on society, have a relatively brief historical tradition. Two hundred and seventy years ago, there was but one struggling weekly in the colonial outpost of Europe that was to become the United States. It was less than 150 years ago, in the 1830s and 1840s, that the "penny press" dailies ushered in America's first era of popular journalism, made famous by James Gordon Bennett and his New York *Herald,* Horace Greeley and his New York *Tribune,* and Henry J. Raymond and his New York *Times.* Bennett taught others how to search out and report the news; Greeley fashioned an editorial page; Raymond put his emphasis upon news interpretation. With their contemporaries and successors, they laid the foundations for present-day American journalism.

The basic journalistic principles thus espoused were further advanced before the nineteenth century had ended by such noted publishers as Joseph Pulitzer, Edward Wyllis Scripps, and Adolph S. Ochs. The goals were two in number. The primary goal was ever-increasing concentration of effort on impartial gathering and reporting of the news and its comprehensive display. The other was demonstration of responsible opinion leadership, provided both through an intelligently written editorial page and integrity and zealousness in telling the news.

As even the colonial editor knew, however, there is a third editorial function of the press and that is to entertain the reader, as well as to inform and instruct him. What is called "human interest" news—stories with appeal based on writing skill rather than necessarily upon news value—has always been in great reader demand. Sensational news—stories involving the human passions, crime and violence, and spicy accounts of the doings of the famous—is likewise age-old in its appeal. The newspaper has also always contained a budget of nonnews material: short stories and other literary content (more prevalent a century ago than today), comics and Sunday feature sections (favorites since the 1890s), advice to the lovelorn (highly popular for early eighteenth-century readers), and a host of varying entertainment items.

The responsibility of the mass media has been to strike a balance among the functions of informing, instructing, and entertaining. The newspaper, as it reached out for mass circulation, sought to fulfill the first two functions in more popularized ways: a more readable writing style, skillful use of human interest elements in news, better makeup and headline display, effective pictures, color. Such popularizing, in the interests of appealing to the entertainment desire, need not detract from the newspaper's social usefulness. There is no reason why the "hard news" of political and economic importance should not be presented as interestingly as possible and in company with other less important, but more attractive, ingredients. But there is a line to be drawn. Over-emphasis on sensationalism at the expense of news and a lavish dressing up of purely entertainment features are merely cheapening, not popularizing.

How well American newspapers have responded to these basic principles over the decades is a matter of judgment. One thing is certain; they responded differently, for there is no such thing as a "typical newspaper" to analyze any more than there is a typical magazine, television or radio station, or book publishing house. What can be measured is the response made by the leaders in different historical periods, as they reshaped their journalistic products to fit the demands of their times and the desires of their audiences. As the sociologist Robert E. Park put it:

The newspaper has a history; but it has, likewise, a natural history. The press, as it exists, is not, as our moralists sometimes seem to assume, the willful product of any little group of living men. On the contrary, it is the outcome of a historic process in which many individuals participated without foreseeing what the ultimate product of their labors was to be. The newspaper, like the modern city, is not wholly a rational product. . . . it has continued to grow and change in its own incalculable ways.

THE COLONIAL PRESS

Early Concepts of News

Reporting, as defined today, means gathering information of interest to other people and presenting it to them accurately in a way that makes them understand and remember it. This definition is broad enough to fit all media of information and comprehensive enough to provide a measuring stick for present and past performance.

The first newspaper publishers were primarily printers, not editors. The majority had a sense of what interested people, but only a few had

THE [N° 58

New-England Courant.

From **M O N D A Y** September 3. to **M O N D A Y** September 10. 1 7 2 2.

Quod eſt in corde ſobrii, eſt in ore ebrii.

To the Author of the New-England Courant.

S I R,
[No XII.

T is no unprofitable tho' unpleaſant Purſuit, diligently to inſpect and conſider the Manners & Converſation of Men, who, inſenſible of the greateſt Enjoyments of humane Life, abandon themſelves to Vice from a falſe Notion of *Pleaſure* and *good Fellowſhip.* A true and natural Repreſentation of any Enormity, is often the beſt Argument againſt it and Means of removing it, when the moſt ſevere Reprehenſions alone, are found ineffectual.

I WOULD in this Letter improve the little Obſervation I have made on the Vice of *Drunkenneſs,* the better to reclaim the *good Fellows* who uſually pay the Devotions of the Evening to *Bacchus.*

I DOUBT not but *moderate Drinking* has been improv'd for the Diffuſion of Knowledge among the ingenious Part of Mankind, who want the Talent of a ready Utterance, in order to diſcover the Conceptions of their Minds in an entertaining and intelligible Manner. 'Tis true, drinking does not *improve* our Faculties, but it enables us to *uſe* them ; and therefore I conclude, that much Study and Experience, and a little Liquor, are of abſolute Neceſſity for ſome Tempers, in order to make them accompliſh'd Orators. *Dic. Ponder* diſcovers an excellent Judgment when he is inſpir'd with a Glaſs or two of *Claret,* but he paſſes for a Fool among thoſe of ſmall Obſervation, who never ſaw him the better for Drink. And here it will not be improper to obſerve, That the moderate Uſe of Liquor, and a well plac'd and well regulated Anger, often produce this ſame Effect ; and ſome who cannot ordinarily talk but in broken Sentences and falſe Grammar, do in the Heat of Paſſion expreſs themſelves with as much Eloquence as Warmth. Hence it is that my own Sex are generally the moſt eloquent, becauſe the moſt paſſionate. " It has been ſaid in the Praiſe of ſome Men, " (ſays an ingenious Author,) that they could talk " whole Hours together upon any thing ; but it " muſt be owned to the Honour of the other Sex, " that there are many among them· who can talk " whole Hours together upon Nothing. I have " known a Woman branch out into a long extempo-" re Diſſertation on the Edging of a Petticoat, and " chide her Servant for breaking a China Cup, in all " the Figures of Rhetorick. "

BUT after all it muſt be conſider'd, that no Pleaſure can give Satisfaction or prove advantageous to a reaſonable Mind, which is not attended with the Reſtraints of Reaſon. Enjoyment is not to be found by Exceſs in any ſenſual Gratification ; but on the contrary, the immoderate Cravings of the Voluptuary, are always ſucceeded with Loathing and a pal-

led Appetite. What Pleaſure can the Drunkard have in the Reflection, that, while in his Cups, he retain'd only the Shape of a Man, and acted the Part of a Beaſt ; or that from reaſonable Diſcourſe a few Minutes before, he deſcended to Impertinence and Nonſenſe ?

I CANNOT pretend to account for the different Effects of Liquor on Perſons of different Diſpoſitions, who are guilty of Exceſs in the Uſe of it. 'Tis ſtrange to ſee Men of a regular Converſation become rakiſh and profane when intoxicated with Drink, and yet more ſurprizing to obſerve, that ſome who appear to be the moſt profligate Wretches when ſober, become mighty religious in their Cups, and will then, and at no other Time addreſs their Maker, but when they are deſtitute of Reaſon, and actually affronting him. Some ſhrink in the Wetting, and others ſwell to ſuch an unuſual Bulk in their Imaginations, that they can in an Inſtant underſtand all Arts and Sciences, by the liberal Education of a little vivifying *Punch,* or a ſufficient Quantity of other exhilerating Liquor.

AND as the Effects of Liquor are various, ſo are the Characters given to its Devourers. It argues ſome Shame in the Drunkards themſelves, in that they have invented numberleſs Words and Phraſes to cover their Folly, whoſe proper Sgnifications are harmleſs, or have no Signification at all. They are ſeldom known to be *drunk,* tho they are very often *boozey, cogey, tipſey, fox'd, merry, mellow, fuddl'd, groatable, Confoundedly cut, See two Moons,* are *Among the Philiſtines, In a very good Humour, See the Sun,* or, *The Sun has ſhone upon them* ; they *Clip the King's Engliſh,* are *Almoſt froze, Feavouriſh, In their Altitudes, Pretty well enter'd,* &c. In ſhort, every Day produces ſome new Word or Phraſe which might be added to the Vocabulary of the *Tiplers :* But I have choſe to mention theſe few, becauſe if at any Time a Man of Sobriety and Temperance happens to *cut himſelf confoundedly,* or is *almoſt froze,* or *feavouriſh,* or accidentally *ſees the Sun,* he may eſcape the Imputation of being *drunk,* when his Misfortune comes to be relared.

I am S I R,
Your Humble Servant,

SILENCE DOGOOD.

FOREIGN AFFAIRS.

Berlin, May 8. Twelve Pruſſian Batallions are ſent to Mecklenburg, but for what Reaſon is not known. 'Tis ſaid, the Emperor, ſuſpecting the Deſigns of the Czar, will ſecure all the Domains of the Duke of Mecklenburg. His Pruſſian Majeſty, to promote the intended Union of the Reformed and Lutherans in his Dominions, has charged the Miniſters of thoſe two Communions, not to make the leaſt mention in the Pulpits of the religious Differences about ſome abſtruſer Points, particularly the Doctrine of Predeſtination, and to forbear all contumelious Expreſſions againſt one another.

Hamburg, May 8. The Imperial Court has order'd the Circles of Lower Saxony, to keep in Rea-

The front page of the *New-England Courant*, the American colonies' first good newspaper. An essay on drunkenness by Benjamin Franklin, under the pseudonym "Silence Dogood," occupies most of the page.

real reportorial instincts. Only a few, too, were good enough writers to tell their stories in an interesting way. Since their access to news was severely limited, and inadequate transportation and communication facilities made the collecting of news a very haphazard business, they scarcely could be expected to be either complete or accurate in their reports. But even so, very few made any move to go out and find the news; they ran what came over their doorsteps or what could be gleaned from other newspapers and periodicals, particularly those coming from London. None had local news reporters as we know them today. Nevertheless, what meager news and entertainment they offered were eagerly devoured by their readers, who had little other choice.

James and Benjamin Franklin were early publisher-printers who were also journalists. James, in his *New-England Courant,* gave Boston readers of the 1720s the first readable and exciting American newspaper. He printed news, despite the opposition of Puritan political and religious authorities, and covered local issues in a dramatic and crusading fashion. He and his contributors, including his younger brother Ben, wrote well; and the paper, modeled on the successful "essay" papers of Joseph Addison and Richard Steele in England, had high literary qualities. Personality sketches, feature stories, and human interest material lightened the pages. Benjamin Franklin carried on the traditions in his *Pennsylvania Gazette,* editing his meager scraps of news more cleverly than his rivals and offering more substance.

During the Revolutionary War period, publishers such as Benjamin Franklin and Isaiah Thomas of the *Massachusetts Spy* were alert to forward the patriot cause, but even as well-to-do a publisher as Thomas did not attempt to have his own correspondent with Washington's army. The paper nearest to the scene of an event covered it; other papers copied the report or relied upon official announcements, messages sent to their local authorities from military and governmental headquarters, and reports of travelers.

The Political Pamphleteers

Throughout the eighteenth century, the political pamphleteer was more important than the editor-printer. Three examples from the years preceding the American Revolution are John Dickinson, Samuel Adams, and Thomas Paine—all well known in the pages of American history, and all of whom used the newspaper of their day as a vehicle to reach the public.

John Dickinson of Pennsylvania, an articulate spokesman of the colonial Whigs, wrote his "Letters from a Farmer in Pennsylvania" for the *Pennsylvania Chronicle* of 1767–1768. Dickinson was opposed to revolution and was actually a spokesman for the business class and its Whig philosophy rather than for the agrarian class. But he and the colonial Whigs could not afford to let the British Whigs impose commercial restrictions that were harmful to American interests. The mercantile system, which prevented development of colonial industry and trade, and taxation measures imposed by a Parliament in which the colonial Whigs were not directly represented were threats Dickinson could not ignore. His forceful arguments for home rule helped swing Americans of his economic group to the revolutionary cause after it became apparent that compromise was no longer possible.

Samuel Adams, the great propagandist of the revolution, belonged to the Radical party. Only briefly an editor himself, he worked with the group of Boston patriots assembled in the office of the Boston *Gazette* that included the publishers, Benjamin Edes and John Gill, and the engraver, Paul Revere. Sam Adams was called the "master of the puppets" and the "assassin of reputations" by his enemies, and undoubtedly he was both. He wrote tirelessly for the columns of the *Gazette,* twisting every possible incident or administrative action of the British into an argument for revolution. When the news was dull and the fires of dissatisfaction needed fanning, he "blew up" minor scrapes into events of seemingly major import. When a crisis arose, such as the passage of the Stamp Act or the imposition of the tax on tea, Adams worked with others to fire up resistance throughout the colonies. His Committees of Correspondence, organized in 1772, kept the word moving among Patriot editors. When British rifles fired in Boston to restrain a street crowd, the *Gazette* called the affair the Boston Massacre. But a year later the *Gazette* was reporting on a memorial service held for the massacre victims, consisting of a propagandistic display in the windows of Paul Revere's house. Such touches as this were the work of Sam Adams, who knew how to stir the popular emotions.

Tom Paine, the political philosopher, arrived in the colonies from England in time to make two great pamphleteering contributions to the patriot cause. His *Common Sense,* which sold 120,000 copies in three months in the spring of 1776, was a hard-headed, down-to-earth argument for independence that the common man could understand. That December, when Washington's discouraged army was camped on the Delaware river across from Trenton, Paine was drafted to write the first of his *Crisis* papers for a Philadelphia weekly:

These are the times that try men's souls. The summer soldier and the sunshine patriot will, in this crisis, shrink from the service of their country; but he that stands it NOW, deserves the love and thanks of man and woman. Tyranny, like hell, is not easily conquered; yet we have this consolation with us, that the harder the conflict the more glorious the triumph. What we obtain too cheap, we esteem too lightly; it is dearness only that gives every thing its value. Heaven knows how to put a proper price upon its goods; and it would be strange indeed if so celestial an article as FREEDOM should not be highly rated.

Paine's words lived to be broadcast to occupied Europe during World War II; at the time they helped to spur the first American victory of the war.

PRESS OF THE NEW REPUBLIC

In the early years of the new nation, two types of newspapers were developing. One was the mercantile paper, published in the seaboard towns primarily for the trading and shipping classes interested in commercial and political news. Its well-filled advertising columns reflected the essentially business interest of its limited clientele of subscribers— 2000 was a good number. The other type was the political paper, partisan in its appeal and relying for reader support on acceptance of its views, rather than upon the quality and completeness of its news. Most editors of the period put views first and news second; the political paper deliberately shaped the news to fit its views. In the struggle over the adoption of the Constitution and the establishment of the new federal government, these party papers played a key role.

The *Federalist Papers,* written for the newspapers of New York state and reprinted throughout the country, were largely the work of Alexander Hamilton, brilliant leader of the pro-Constitution party that took its name from the series of eighty-five articles. Written for mass consumption, they still rank as one of the best expositions of political doctrine ever conceived. When Hamilton's party assumed control of the new federal government, Hamilton directed the editorial opinion of the Federalist party papers he helped to establish. He dictated his ideas to his editors, who, with their Jeffersonian opponents, developed a briefer, one-argument form of editorial writing.

Ranged on the anti-Federalist side with Thomas Jefferson were his personally sponsored poet-editor, Philip Freneau of the *National Gazette,* and other masters of partisanship like Benjamin Franklin Bache of the *Aurora.* Editors on both sides attacked each other with biting sarcasm and bitter invective. Their political sponsors were also viciously treated; the climax came when Bache accused Washington of being a "front man" for the Federalists and said, "If ever a nation was debauched by a man, the American nation has been debauched by Washington." William Cobbett, most fiery of the Federalist editors, retaliated in his *Porcupine's Gazette* with a classic character sketch of Bache in which the kindest word was "liar."

The American press survived the excesses of the 1790s and the dangerous effort at repression of press freedom through the Alien and Sedition Acts. But the traditions of partisan journalism lived on in the political party press of the nineteenth century. Particularly was this true of the frontier papers that supported Andrew Jackson and the Democratic party. The *Argus of Western America* of Frankfort, Kentucky, was one of these grubby but virile sheets that helped to spark the Jacksonian revolution. Amos Kendall and Francis P. Blair, two of its editors, graduated to Jackson's "kitchen cabinet," where Kendall served as postmaster general and journalistic adviser to the president and Blair as editor of the hard-hitting administration paper, the Washington *Globe.* The tradition of an administration organ in Washington had begun with the *National Intelligencer* of Jefferson's day; but none was edited with more single-minded driving purpose than Blair's *Globe.* "Give it to Bla-ar," Jackson would say, and Blair would pass the word along to the party faithful. The Whigs had their strong editors too, like Thurlow Weed of the Albany *Evening Journal.* The attitude of the political paper was well expressed by the pro-Jackson New York *Evening Post,* which advised its readers to buy a Whig paper if they wanted the other side of the argument of the moment. This was the spirit of the pamphleteer rather than that of the true journalist.

The political papers were much more important in the story of the development of the opinion function. The mercantile papers, however, played a role in the development of the news function concept. Even though their primary interest was in shipping news and digests of foreign news taken from European newspapers arriving in American ports, the leading mercantile papers took pride in excelling in their specialties. And as the struggle between the Federalists and the Republicans for control of the national government intensified, news of Hamilton's fiscal policies and Jefferson's moves became important to the business community. Competition was tough, too; in 1800 there were six dailies in Philadelphia (twice as many as in 1978), and five in New York. The weekly publishers had been forced into the daily field to meet the competition of the coffee houses, where the London papers were filed as soon as ships arrived with the latest issues and where news was freely exchanged.

So the individual papers began to go out after the news. Correspondents covered sessions of the Congress in Washington as early as 1808 and were well established by the late 1820s. Seaport dailies hired boats to meet the incoming ships out in the harbor so their editors would have a headstart on digesting the foreign news. The leading New York mercantile papers, the *Courier and Enquirer* and the *Journal of Commerce,* set up rival pony express services between Washington and New York to get presidential messages and congressional news faster.

What the mercantile papers did not do, however, was widen the appeal of their news columns to satisfy the demands of a new reading audience that was emerging from what is now called the Jacksonian revolution. More widespread education, extension of the right to vote, increased interest in politics by a growing laboring class, and other socioeconomic factors were operating to pave the way for a more popular and responsive journalism that was destined to overwhelm the older types of newspapers.

THE PENNY PRESS

Between 1833 and 1837, the publishers of a new "penny press" proved that a low-priced paper, edited to interest ordinary people, could win what amounted to a mass circulation for the times and thereby attract an advertising volume which would make it independent. These were papers for the "common man" and were not tied to the interests of the business community, like the mercantile press, or dependent for financial support upon political party allegiance. It did not necessarily follow that all the penny papers would be superior in their handling of the news and opinion functions. But the door was open for some to make important journalistic advances.

The first offerings of a penny paper tended to be highly sensational; human interest news overshadowed important news, and crime and sex stories were written in full detail. But as the penny paper attracted readers from various social and economic brackets, its sensationalism was modified. The ordinary reader came to want a better product, too.

Popularized style of writing and presentation of news remained, but the penny paper became a respectable publication that offered significant information and editorial leadership. Once the first of the successful penny papers had shown the way, later ventures could enter the competition at the higher level of journalistic responsibility the pioneering papers had reached.

This was the pattern of American newspapers in the years following the founding of the New York *Sun* in 1833. The *Sun,* published by Benjamin Day, entered the lists against eleven other dailies. It was tiny in comparison; but it was bright and readable, and it preferred human interest features to important but dull political speech reports. It had a police reporter writing squibs of crime news in the style already proved successful by London papers. And, most important, it sold for a penny, whereas its competitors sold for 6 cents. By 1837 the *Sun* was printing 30,000 copies a day, which was more than the total of all eleven New York daily newspapers combined when the *Sun* first appeared. In those same four years, James Gordon Bennett brought out his New York *Herald* (1835) and a trio of New York printers who were imitating Day's success founded the Philadelphia *Public Ledger* (1836) and the Baltimore *Sun* (1837). The four penny sheets all became famed newspapers.

Bennett and News Enterprise

James Gordon Bennett can serve as the symbol of the penny press news enterprises. He had been a Washington correspondent, reporter, and editor for other dailies before he launched the *Herald* in 1835. Disillusioned by a previous venture with a political paper, he kept the *Herald* relatively free of political ties. He more than matched the *Sun* with sensational coverage of crime and court news, on the one hand, and challenged the more sober journals with detailed coverage of Wall Street affairs, political campaigns, and foreign news, on the other. As profits from his big circulation and extensive advertising piled up, he spent money on news coverage. He matched his rivals in establishing pony express services to carry the news from Washington and other points. One *Herald* courier service stretched all the way from Newfoundland, carrying European news by pony rider, boat, and train to the first telegraph point. Bennett was among the first to use each of the new means of communication as they burst upon the scene in the 1830s and 1840s, hiring locomotives to race presidential messages from Washington and utilizing the telegraph as soon as Samuel F. B. Morse's invention proved itself in 1844 and wires were strung from city to city. He personally toured the country with presidential candidates and sailed to London on the newest steamship to arrange for better coverage of foreign news. By the 1850s he had made the *Herald* the leading news-gathering paper and the richest in advertising.

Bennett's competitors were not being left in the dust. The New York *Sun,* Philadelphia *Public Ledger,* and Baltimore *Sun* were all in the race for news. So were such older New York papers as the *Courier and Enquirer, Journal of Commerce,* and *Evening Post.* So were two new competitors, Horace Greeley's New York *Tribune,* founded in 1841, and Henry J. Raymond's New York *Times,* founded in 1851. Greeley shunned the sensationalism that had helped the *Sun* and *Herald* to their initial circulation successes and concentrated instead on building up an editorial page and offering news interpretation, but he also covered the running news. His managing editor, Charles A. Dana, directed a reportorial staff of high quality, although perhaps not as slambang as the *Herald*'s group. By the time Raymond entered the New York field with the *Times,* the lines of staff organization were fairly well defined. The owner might still be editor-in-chief, but he had a news executive and a business manager operating the day-to-day business. Raymond concentrated on foreign coverage and editorial policy, seeking to give his reports more depth and meaning in the pattern of the *Times* of London.

The coming of the telegraph speeded the gathering of news, but it also increased the cost. In 1848 six New York morning papers formed the Associated Press of New York, forerunner of the modern press association of the same name. They did so to share the costs of telegraphing digests of foreign news from Boston and of routine news from Washington. Soon other papers asked to share in this common news report, and the New York papers began selling it. Papers in the interior of the country could now, with the telegraph, get the news as rapidly as their eastern metropolitan competitors. The excitement of the Mexican War and of the political crises leading up to the Civil War spurred attention to the need for better mass communications.

The Civil War called for great efforts in news enterprise. The *Herald* sent its own small army of correspondents into the field; other leading papers followed suit. Printing advances of the previous two decades— the flat-bed cylinder press, the type-revolving press, and stereotyping— were needed to handle increased circulations. Sunday editions of daily papers came into being. The illustrated periodicals, *Harper's Weekly* and *Frank Leslie's Illustrated Newspaper,* led the way in using woodcut illustrations and maps, and newspapers followed suit as best they could. By the time the guns finally ceased firing, the traditions of news enterprise and emphasis upon the news function had been well established.

Greeley and the Editorial Page

Horace Greeley is recognized as one of the most influential editors in the history of American journalism. His New York *Tribune,* which he founded in 1841, was the first American newspaper to develop an editorial page that was the product of the thinking of a group of individuals. Not that it was the well-tailored, coherently organized page many newspapers publish today. Orderly departmentalization had not yet come to newspapers in Greeley's day, and in any event methodicalness and consistency were not part of the Greeley temperament. But what the *Tribune* printed represented a dramatic change from the tradition of the pamphleteer.

Greeley was deeply conscious of his responsibility to the reader. He knew the *Tribune* had to be enterprising in reporting the news if it was to compete successfully for readers. But he felt it his responsibility to be just as enterprising in seeking to influence public opinion by devoting much space to serious discussion, editorial argument, and interpretation of events. The *Tribune* examined issues and debated ideas; it did not follow a set party line or insist that there was only one solution to a problem. True, it advocated some of its opinions as vehemently as did the pamphleteer, but in sum total it illuminated the social and economic issues of the day, from differing viewpoints, far more than any other paper had.

Unlike Bennett's *Herald,* which minimized the opinion function while concentrating on news enterprise, Greeley's *Tribune* made the opinion function the key to its popular acceptance. And popular it was. His weekly edition, in which the best of the daily news and opinion was reprinted for mail circulation (a practice of some bigger papers of the period), had the largest circulation of any contemporary publication. It was called the "Bible of the Middlewest," where many of the 200,000 copies went. "Uncle Horace," as Greeley as called, was as well known as any American of his time—only Lincoln, of the men of the period, has had more books written about him. Greeley lived through a period of momentous events and of great social change and, like Lincoln, was able to give expression to the aspirations and hopes of less articulate countrymen.

To many, the activities of Greeley and the *Tribune* must have appeared strangely inconsistent. The editor was greatly concerned with the impact of the industrial revolution on society and the social ills unrestricted capitalism produced. He was willing to examine and debate any seemingly reasonable experiment in social reform or economic theory, in the hope that it would give workers and farmers a more equitable share in the accumulating wealth. So the *Tribune,* ostensibly a Whig newspaper, advocated a form of collective living called "associationism" and ran many columns of material written by the Socialist Albert Brisbane and the Communist Karl Marx. Few of Greeley's readers were won over to socialism, but they enjoyed the debate. Greeley's fight for free land in the West to which people in the slums could emigrate was more popular—but that stand was inconsistent with Whig political principles. Eventually his stand on the slavery issue led him into the Republican party, and he ended his career by running unsuccessfully for the presidency in 1872 as the candidate of the Liberal Republicans and the Democrats against General Grant, candidate of the Whig-minded Republicans.

The Personal Editors

Greeley belonged to the group of editors of the middle nineteenth century called the "personal editors," men who were as well known to their readers as were their newspapers, in contrast to the much more anonymous editors of modern corporate journalism. Some of Greeley's farmer readers were surprised to keep getting the *Tribune* after his death; they assumed the paper would quit publishing, so much did he seem to be the newspaper itself.

William Cullen Bryant, who joined the New York *Post* staff in 1825 and remained to edit it for a half-century, also fell into this category of the personal editor. His journalism was much more reserved than Greeley's and his thinking more logical, but through Bryant's personal editorial opinion, the *Post* exercised considerable influence. He supported Jacksonian democracy and, like Greeley, he showed sympathy for the worker. During the Civil War, he was one of the most effective interpreters of Lincoln's policies. Henry J. Raymond, founder of the New York *Times,* played a personal role outside the newspaper office as a leader in the Republican party, although he tried to make the *Times'* editorial columns calmly interpretive in character.

There were editors outside New York City who made their influence felt during the Civil War period. One was Samuel Bowles III, publisher of the Springfield *Republican* in Massachusetts, a daily of just 6000 circulation. Bowles' editorial ability was so great that his weekly edition of 12,000 copies rivaled Greeley's 200,000 circulation in reputation and did much to unify the North and Middle West in the pre-Civil

War years. Another was Joseph Medill, builder of the Chicago *Tribune,* who was one of Lincoln's firmest supporters. The abolitionist editors, William Lloyd Garrison of the *Liberator* and the martyred Elijah Lovejoy, should be noted too, although they were agitator-pamphleteers.

In the post-Civil War years, the name of Edwin Lawrence Godkin stands out. Godkin founded the *Nation* magazine in 1865 and succeeded Bryant as the driving force of the New York *Post* in 1881. British-born, Godkin decided the United States needed a high-grade weekly journal of opinion and literary criticism similar to those in England. His distinctive style of writing and skill in ironic analysis made the *Nation* a favorite of other intellectuals. William James, the philosopher, said of him: "To my generation his was certainly the towering influence in all thought concerning public affairs, and indirectly his influence has assuredly been more pervasive than that of any other writer of the generation, for he influenced other writers who never quoted him, and determined the whole current of discussion." This was high accomplishment for the editor of a weekly magazine with a circulation of no more than 10,000.

THE NEW JOURNALISM

Between 1865 and 1900, the dynamic capitalism of an expanding America, utilizing vast natural resources and the new machines of the industrial revolution, transformed the national economy. Industrialization, mechanization, and urbanization brought extensive social, cultural, and political changes: the rise of the city, improved transportation and communication, educational advances, political unrest, and the rise of an extensive labor movement. The mass media could not fail to go through great changes along with the society they served. In the world of newspapers, the era is known as that of the "new journalism," a designation used by the men who lived through that time to describe the activities of the master editor of the period, Joseph Pulitzer.

In the thirty-five years between the close of the Civil War and the turn of the century, the population of the country doubled, the national wealth quadrupled, and manufacturing production increased sevenfold. It was the period of the coming of the age of steel, the harnessing of electricity for light and power, and the mechanizing of production processes. National growth and increased wealth meant cultural progress in literature, science, and the social sciences; a great stirring in scholarship and a rapid increase in the number and size of universities; and sharp increases in public school attendance and adult interest in popularized knowledge. Growing social and economic interdependence could be measured by two statistics for the year 1900: A third of the population was urban and 62 percent of the labor force was engaged in nonagricultural work.

Communication facilities expanded in this period of the nationalization of the United States. Telegraph lines and railroad tracks reached near-saturation points; the telephone, coming into use in the 1870s, provided direct communication through intercity lines that covered the country by 1900. The federal postal service greatly extended free carrier service in the cities and instituted free rural delivery in 1897. The low postal rate for newspapers and magazines of 1885 opened the way for cheap delivery of publications. By 1900 there were 3,500 magazines with a combined circulation of 65 million an issue. Weekly newspapers tripled in number between 1870 and 1900, reaching a total of more than 12,000. During the same thirty years, the number of daily newspapers quadrupled and their total circulation increased almost sixfold; the figures for 1900 were 1,967 general circulation dailies selling nearly 15 million copies each day. It was this tremendous increase in the circulation of the printed mass media that was the impetus for inventions such as the rotary press, the typesetting machine, photoengraving, and color printing, which transformed the newspaper into its modern form.

Obviously a new journalism would emerge for this new society. Again, as in the penny press period, there was a new audience: More people were interested in reading; the labor class increased rapidly; and there was a heavy concentration of immigrants in the rapidly growing eastern cities (New York City residents, who increased 50 percent between 1880 and 1890, were 80 percent foreign-born or of foreign parentage). Such readers, stirred by political and social unrest in a period when reform movements sought to readjust the economic balance to bring relief to the worker and farmer, looked for aggressive editorial leadership and opinion-forming crusading in their newspapers and magazines. But they also wanted impartial and thorough coverage of the news. The newspaper that appealed to them was also low-priced, easily read, popularized in content, and bright in appearance. Particularly in the big cities, the entertainment ingredient had to be high, and for the really new readers a new cycle of sensationalism was the major attraction.

Pulitzer and the News

Joseph Pulitzer serves as the symbol of the new journalism era. An immigrant himself, he served his apprenticeship as a reporter before founding the St. Louis *Post-Dispatch* in 1878. In the next five years, Pulitzer built it into the city's leading paper by giving his readers what they wanted. He developed a liberal, aggressive editorial page and gave both the editorial and news columns a fierce crusading spirit. He insisted on accuracy, digging deep for facts, thoroughness of local news coverage, and good writing. One of his famous commands to his staff was "Accuracy! Accuracy!! Accuracy!!!" Another was "Terseness! Intelligent, not stupid, condensation." Still another showed his concern for the lighter side of the news; he reminded reporters to look for both the significant news and the "original, distinctive, dramatic, romantic, thrilling, unique, curious, quaint, humorous, odd, apt to be talked about" news.

In 1883 Pulitzer left the *Post-Dispatch* as his monument in St. Louis and invaded New York City by buying the run-down *World*. Within four years the paper had reached a record-breaking 250,000 circulation, had eclipsed the *Herald* as the leader in advertising volume, and had become the country's most talked-about newspaper.

Pulitzer's success lay in the fact that he had not forgotten the basic news function while he was wooing new readers with entertaining and sensational material. He gave his audience its money's worth in the quality and extent of significant news coverage and presented it in an enlivened style. He plowed money into the building of a competent staff of reporters and editors and he kept pace with mechanical innovations that permitted them to fashion a better product. He combined a popular editorial aggressiveness and crusading spirit with great promotional skill to make the mass of readers feel the *World* was their friend. To attract them to its solid news stories and editorial column, the *World* offered big headlines, human interest stories, illustrations, and other sensationalized approaches. With the advent of color printing in the early 1890s, the *World* added popular Sunday supplements and the comic strip.

Some of Pulitzer's competitors did not sense the total character of his journalistic product and mistakenly assumed that sensationalism alone had made the *World* successful. One of these was William Randolph Hearst, who took over the San Francisco *Examiner* in 1887 and then invaded New York in 1895 by buying the *Journal*. The circulation war between Pulitzer's *World* and Hearst's *Journal* brought the cycle of sensationalism to a new height. Critics who eyed one of the comic strip characters of the times, the "Yellow Kid," dubbed the papers "yellow journals." The yellow journal prided itself on being the crusading friend of the "common man," but it underestimated his interest in significant news and overestimated his capacity for absorbing gaudy, oversensationalized news. The result was a degrading of the news function that reached its climax during the period of the Spanish-American War. After a few years the *World* and other serious-minded papers withdrew from the competition, leaving the techniques of yellow journalism to Hearst and his imitators. Although the yellow journals cannot be held solely responsible for causing the war, their news policies certainly contributed to the war fever of 1898.

There were other notable leaders in the new journalism era. The master teacher of the art of human interest writing was Charles A. Dana's New York *Sun,* which developed many a great reporter and editor. Dana, however, resisted change, and the *Sun* set its face against the general trend of the times. Edward Wyllis Scripps began developing his group of papers, headed by the Cleveland *Press.* They were low-priced, small in size, well-written and tightly edited, and hard-hitting in both news and editorial columns. Melville Stone's Chicago *Daily News* and William Rockhill Nelson's Kansas City *Star* were two more distinctive new papers fashioned in the new journalism pattern. In the South, Henry W. Grady became known as a master news executive for his work with the Atlanta *Constitution,* and because of his own reporting skill.

THE PEOPLE'S CHAMPIONS:
PULITZER, HEARST, SCRIPPS

The rise of the architects of the new journalism in the 1870s and 1880s brought a heightening of attention to the exercise of the opinion function. Joseph Pulitzer, the leading exponent of the new journalism, has been named by his colleagues of this century as the leading American editor of modern times. A memo written by Pulitzer to an editor of his St. Louis *Post-Dispatch* summarizes his idealistic goal for the editorial page:

. . . every issue of the paper presents an opportunity and a duty to say something courageous and true; to rise above the mediocre and conventional; to say something that will command the respect of the intelligent, the educated, the independent part of the community; to rise above fear of partisanship and fear of popular prejudice.

No finer statement of the responsibility imposed upon those who exercise the newspaper's opinion function has ever been written. Those who

Three leaders of the "new journalism" who crusaded for reforms in behalf of all people. *Top to bottom:* Edward W. Scripps, on his yacht; Joseph Pulitzer, as depicted by John Singer Sargent, American portrait and mural painter; and William Randolph Hearst, at the height of his career.

can even occasionally meet such a challenge win the respect of both colleagues and readers.

Pulitzer and his contemporaries developed a growing independence of editorial opinion from partisan pressures. They did not hesitate to support political candidates, but they did not do this automatically as part of a political machine, as did the political press. Most of the leaders were champions of the "common man"—people's champions, doing battle against the trusts and monopolies that characterized big business, the crooked politicians who were "the shame of the cities," the moneylenders and the speculators, and the opponents of reform. The majority supported the political leaders of the Democratic party—Grover Cleveland, William Jennings Bryan, Woodrow Wilson—but they also gave aid to such progressive Republicans as Theodore Roosevelt and Robert M. La Follette. Pulitzer himself believed that the Democratic party best carried out the principles he espoused, but he bolted from the radical Bryan candidacy and gave aid and comfort to such New York Republicans as Charles Evans Hughes in the battles with Tammany Hall. His great editor, Frank I. Cobb, who carried on the traditions of the New York *World* after Pulitzer's death in 1911, was a close adviser to Woodrow Wilson and his solid champion. Cobb, however, insisted that it was part of his job to criticize the administration as well as to defend it. This is part of what is meant by "independence of editorial opinion from partisan pressures."

A distinctive feature of the new journalism paper was its eagerness to crusade in behalf of community welfare. Pulitzer developed the coordinated crusade, using both the news and editorial columns, at the *Post-Dispatch,* and that paper remained famous for its tenacious attacks on wrongdoers in public or business life. These words written by Pulitzer in 1907, which became the *Post-Dispatch* editorial platform, sum up the crusading spirit:

I know that my retirement will make no difference in its cardinal principles; that it will always fight for progress and reform, never tolerate injustice or corruption, always fight demagogues of all parties, never belong to any party, always oppose privileged classes and public plunderers, never lack sympathy with the poor, always remain devoted to the public welfare, never be satisfied with merely printing news, always be drastically independent, never be afraid to attack wrong, whether by predatory plutocracy or predatory poverty.

William Randolph Hearst, in his New York *Journal* and other newspapers, likewise was a crusading champion of the people. His editorial platform at the turn of the century called for nationalization of the coal mines, railroads, and telegraph lines; public ownership of public franchises; the "destruction of the criminal trusts"; a graduated income tax; election of United States senators by popular vote rather than by state legislatures which could be influenced by big business; and extensive new financial support for the public schools. To this he added an active support of labor unions that made them regard his papers as their champions.

One would suppose the liberals of the time would have clasped Hearst to their bosoms. But they did not. They distrusted Hearst's own political ambitions, which extended to the White House; they disliked the bitterness of his editorial attacks upon his opponents. Repelled by the sensationalism and near-cynicism of his news policies, they rejected his editorial page as shallow and insincere. But undoubtedly Hearst had great influence on the ordinary reader of the pre-World War I generation. By the 1920s, however, the Hearst papers were much less progressive in outlook, and by the 1930s their position was almost reversed from the one they had held in 1900. Always strongly nationalistic, in contrast to Pulitzer's support of international cooperation, the Hearst papers became bitterly isolationist by the time of World War I, and remained so even past their founder's death in 1951.

Edward Wyllis Scripps was the third of the great "people's champions" of the new journalism era. Scripps set his circulation sights on the working people of the smaller but growing industrial cities of the country as he developed his chain of newspapers from his headquarters at the Cleveland *Press*. His social goal was to improve the position of the mass of people through better education, labor union organization and collective bargaining, and a resulting reasonable redistribution of wealth. In this way, he reasoned, a peaceful and productive society could emerge in an industrialized America.

Scripps viewed himself as the only real friend of the "poor and ill-informed." He said his newspapers were the only schoolroom the working person had; the public school system did not serve him or her adequately, and other newspapers were either capitalistic in outlook or too intellectual in their appeal. He pictured himself as a "damned old crank" who was instinctively rebellious against the status quo in any field of human activity. He made a point of running small, tightly edited papers that could assert their independence of the business community and resist any attempted influence by advertisers. But he was businessman enough to make a profit on his journalistic ventures, and his employees found him to be cautious in wage policies. Politically, the Scripps papers were strongly liberal; they supported the third-party candidacies of Theodore Roosevelt in 1912 and Robert M. La Follette in 1924, Woodrow Wilson's New Freedom, the right of workers to organize, and public ownership. This liberal pattern continued after Scripps' death in 1926 and until the late 1930s when, under the influence of the late Roy W. Howard, the Scripps-Howard papers became substantially more conservative.

THE OPINION MAGAZINES

Important among the "people's champions" of the reform era at the opening of the twentieth century were the magazines. Dismayed by the bitterness of some of their attacks, Theodore Roosevelt called their work "muckraking," comparing the more sensational writers to the Man with the Muckrake in *Pilgrim's Progress,* who did not look up to see the celestial crown but continued to rake the filth. The magazine men and women, however, considered the appellation a badge of honor.

Magazines had been published since colonial times. Surviving in 1900 were such leaders as the *North American Review,* which began its long career in 1815; *Harper's Monthly,* which appeared in 1850; and the *Atlantic Monthly,* which began in 1857. These literary periodicals were joined by the *Century* in 1881 and *Scribner's* in 1886.

More influential in public affairs were *Harper's Weekly,* edited by George William Curtis and famous for the political cartoons of Thomas Nast; Godkin's *Nation;* the *Independent,* founded in 1848; and the following new arrivals of the 1880s and 1890s: Albert Shaw's *Review of Reviews,* Lyman Abbott's *Outlook,* the *Literary Digest,* and the *Forum.* Three new magazines of the same period that depended upon humor, cartoon, and satire were *Puck, Judge,* and *Life* (the original *Life* featuring the famed Gibson girl drawings).

Entered in the mass circulation field during the 1880s and 1890s were Cyrus H. K. Curtis' *Ladies' Home Journal* and *Saturday Evening Post,* Robert J. Collier's *Collier's,* Frank Munsey's *Munsey's,* S. S. McClure's *McClure's,* and *Cosmopolitan,* which became a Hearst property. Low-priced and popular in appeal, they carried both fiction and nonfiction.

This was an impressive battery of magazines to turn loose during the reform era of the Theodore Roosevelt administrations (all of the public affairs and mass circulation magazines except *Munsey's* and the *Saturday Evening Post* joined in the chase). *McClure's* touched off the major muckraking movement in late 1902 when it offered almost simultaneously Ida M. Tarbell's "History of the Standard Oil Company" and Lincoln Steffens' "Shame of the Cities" series. *Cosmopolitan* countered with "Treason in the Senate," an attack on conservative spokesmen of "the interests" written by David Graham Phillips, a Pulitzer editorial writer. Samuel Hopkins Adams and Mark Sullivan exposed the patent medicines in *Collier's*.

The cream of the writers moved to John S. Phillips' *American Magazine* in 1906, after a break with McClure. In the crowd were Ida Tarbell, Steffens, Ray Stannard Baker, Finley Peter Dunne ("Mr. Dooley"), and a progressive named William Allen White, who achieved primary fame as the highly personal editor of the Emporia *Gazette* in Kansas. They continued to lead the muckraking movement until it dwindled away by the time of World War I.

Coming on the scene in 1914 was the *New Republic,* featuring the writing of Herbert Croly and Walter Lippmann. Shocking American complacency in the 1920s was H. L. Mencken's *American Mercury.* Of all the magazines listed in this account, only the *Nation* and *New Republic* survived as magazines of dissent, joined by *New Times*—and, to their right, by the *National Review. Harper's* and *Atlantic* were the only survivors among the public affairs and literary periodicals; joining them in the quality magazine field that plays a role in opinion formation were the *New Yorker* and *Saturday Review.* Among all the more general magazines mentioned, only the *Ladies' Home Journal* and *Cosmopolitan* are still published. Showing interest in public affairs is the current leader in the general magazine field, the *Reader's Digest.* The news magazines—*Time, Newsweek,* and *U.S. News & World Report*—also exercise the opinion function.

TWENTIETH-CENTURY NEWS TRENDS

Impartial gathering and reporting of the news was generally recognized to be the basic obligation of newspapers by the early 1900s. Some did the job in a much more comprehensive and intelligent fashion than others. But the editor who put views ahead of news, and who tied his newspaper to a political machine, had pretty well gone out of style. Slanting of news to fit the prejudices or political preferences of a publisher was also recognized as a detriment, although some newspapers continued the practice. The Canons of Journalism adopted by the American Society of Newspaper Editors in 1923 contain these two paragraphs, which summarize the aspirations of modern journalistic leaders:

The right of a newspaper to attract and hold readers is restricted by nothing but considerations of public welfare. The use a newspaper makes of the share of public attention it gains serves to determine its sense of responsibility, which it shares with every member of its staff. A journalist who uses his power for any selfish or otherwise unworthy purpose is faithless to a high trust.
Partisanship, in editorial comment which knowingly departs from the truth, does violence to the best spirit of American journalism; in the news columns it is subversive of a fundamental principle of the profession.

No matter how impartial and well intentioned a newspaper's editors might be, they had to expend an increasing effort on comprehensive coverage and display of the news, and its intelligent interpretation, if they were to meet their full responsibilities. Great events of this century made the business of reporting the news far more complex, decade by decade. In the first decade, the story was one of economic and political reform in the United States. In the second decade, it was World War I. In the third decade, it was the world's effort at postwar readjustment. The fourth decade brought the Great Depression and a collapse of world order. The fifth and sixth brought World War II, the atomic era, and the cold war, which rose to the climactic crises of Korea and Vietnam.

The mass media made a reasonable effort to fulfill their increased responsibilities for interpreting the news of events that all but overwhelmed the world. Professional standards had to be raised to meet the challenge. Better-trained and more knowledgeable men and women came to occupy key reportorial assignments and news desk posts. The range of subject matter with which a Washington correspondent had to be familiar in the 1920s was narrow indeed compared to the complexities of Washington news in the 1970s. And since all news tended to become "local" in its impact with the narrowing of geographic barriers in the atomic age, every general assignment reporter had to know far more about such areas as international affairs, science, and economic trends than did his or her predecessors. The modern press associations, particularly, were put under heavy pressures. Newspapers were stimulated by the appearance of new competitors: radio, television, and the news magazine. Radio and television challenged the newspaper both in providing spot news coverage and in news analysis. The news magazines competed with the newspapers by giving the reader background information and point-of-view interpretation. Together, the print and electronic media offered a persistent reader-listener-viewer a sizable amount of information about the swirl of events that virtually engulfed even the most conscientious citizen.

The New York Times

The editors of the New York *Times* built what is generally conceded to be the greatest single news machine of this century, publishing what was called by its admiring competitors a "newspaper of record." The story of the growth of the *Times* since Adolph S. Ochs rescued it from bankruptcy in 1896 illustrates the trend in acceptance of the news function responsibility, even though it is the story of an atypical journalistic leader. For what the *Times* did in its methodical completeness was done at least in part, and in some respects as successfully, by other responsible newspapers.

Ochs told his readers in 1896: "It will be my aim . . . to give the news impartially, without fear or favor. . . ." He also promised them all the news, in concise and attractive form, and a paper that would be "a forum for the consideration of all questions of public importance, and to that end . . . invite intelligent discussion from all shades of opinion." He made no attempt to match the sensationalism of the yellow journals of the time, and he shunned many of the popularized entertainment features of most newspapers, including the comic strip. His Sunday magazine featured articles of current news significance and became, with its more than 1 million circulation of today, an important fixture in the magazine world. His book review section became the best known in the country. His coverage of financial and business news soon matched that of any older competitor. His editorial page, if quieter and more cautious than that of Pulitzer, was intelligently directed.

What made the *Times* great, however, was not so much these accomplishments as its persistence in gathering and printing the news in all its varied aspects. One of the great managing editors, Carr V. Van Anda, was given control of the *Times* newsroom in 1904 with the understanding that he should do whatever it took to do a comprehensive job with the news. Ochs was willing to spend money to get the news; Van Anda was willing to do the spending, and he knew how to get the news. World War I gave Van Anda an opportunity to show his ability. Using the cables and wireless almost with abandon, the *Times* added the reports of its own correspondents to those of the press associations and syndicates. It reported in detail not only on military operations, but on political and economic developments in the European capitals. War pictures were carried in a rotogravure section added in 1914. Most important, the paper began to publish the texts of documents and speeches. The Treaty of Versailles filled eight pages—more than any other American paper was willing to give that important document. This policy, combined with the publication of the annual *New York Times Index,* made the *Times* the leading newspaper for librarians, scholars, government officials, and other newspaper editors.

If there was any complaint to be registered against the *Times* of the Van Anda period, it was that the paper presented a voluminous amount of news without sufficient interpretation or screening for the average reader. The objective fashion of reporting was considered the best, if impartiality was to be achieved, as late as the 1920s. But Van Anda did a goodly share of interpreting the news, and the editors who followed him did more. The Washington and foreign staffs built by the paper ranked with the best, and during the following decades they came to offer interpretive analysis along with factual reporting.

The Daily News

One more wave of sensationalism was to precede the "era of interpretation," however. The 1920s were known as the Jazz Age, and the papers that catered to a new group of readers won the dubious honor of being identified as Jazz Journalism. Their sensationalism was accompanied by the two identifying techniques of the period: the tabloid format and great emphasis on photography.

Leading the sensational tabloids was the New York *Illustrated Daily News,* founded in 1919 by Joseph Medill Patterson, cousin of Robert R. McCormick and partner with him in the publishing of the Chicago *Tribune.* Patterson, unlike his ultraconservative Chicago cousin, was unconventional in his socioeconomic beliefs—socialistic, his wealthy friends said. He wanted to reach and influence the lowest literate class of Americans and was attracted to the tabloid format by the success Lord Northcliffe was enjoying with it in England. The *Daily News* appeared with a photograph spread across its front half-page and was well stuffed with pictures, human interest stories, and entertaining features. By 1924 it had the largest circulation of any newspaper in the country, a position it continued to hold by a wide margin from that time on.

The tabloid format, it should be noted, did not have to be equated with sensationalism. It was used by other papers that were similar to the dailies of conventional size in all respects save that of the half-fold style.

Interpretive Reporting

This type of more skillful, yet impartial, handling of the news was not unknown before the 1930s. But by then the socioeconomic revolution known politically as the New Deal, coupled with the impact of international crises, forced editors to emphasize "why" along with "who did what." Old-style objectivity, which called for the reporter to stick to a factual account of what had been said or done, did not give the reader the full meaning of the news. The new concept of objectivity was based on the premise that the reader needed to have a given event placed in its proper perspective if truth really was to be served. Also discarded were older assumptions that such subjects as science and economics could not be made interesting to a mass readership. Reporter-specialists who could talk both to their subjects and to a popular reading audience emerged to cover politics, foreign affairs, business, science, labor, agriculture, and urban affairs.

E. W. Scripps' Science Service began blazing one trail in 1921, along with such reporters as William L. Laurence of the New York *Times* and Howard W. Blakeslee of the Associated Press. In labor news, two pioneers were Louis Stark of the *Times* and Edwin A. Lahey of the Chicago *Daily News*. The 1960s saw the rise of urban and architectural specialists like Ada Louise Huxtable of the New York *Times* and Wolf Von Eckardt of the Washington *Post*. Examples of successful interpretive writers in Washington are Jack Nelson, Los Angeles *Times* bureau chief; David Broder, Washington *Post* political columnist; Elizabeth Drew, the *New Yorker*'s political correspondent; and syndicated columnist Mary McGrory of the Washington *Star*.

ANOTHER NEW JOURNALISM

In the late 1960s the literature of the mass media began to herald a New Journalism that at least borrowed the title of the innovations of the 1880s. Its reportorial and writing techniques were variously described as tell-it-as-you-see-it, impressionistic, saturation, humanistic, investigative—and even interpretive. Its second and more controversial characteristic was described as advocacy, activist, or participatory. The latter trend merely reflected the widespread frustration of the era and the demand that the conservative establishment give heed and power to others—youth, minorities, women. The mass media should be used, the argument ran, to further such reforms.

Perhaps the leading spirit of this new journalism was Tom Wolfe, although he viewed his efforts as a revolt against old-fashioned book writing rather than news writing. Other major figures were Truman Capote, Norman Mailer, Gay Talese, and Jimmy Breslin. Their work appeared in *Esquire,* the *New Yorker, Harper's,* and the fast-rising *New York.* Those magazines, the old New York *Herald Tribune,* and such underground papers as the *Village Voice* served as vehicles for the new style of reporting, perhaps best described as "saturation." Capote's *In Cold Blood,* although a novel, demonstrated intense journalistic research; Mailer's description of the march on the Pentagon was powerfully impressionistic; Talese utilized incredible detail in his account of life at the New York *Times* in *The Kingdom and the Power;* Breslin made his readers feel the crunch of police clubs on their skulls as he wrote of the 1968 Chicago convention riots.

Out of that 1968 crisis came the best-known example of "advocacy" journalism. The *Chicago Journalism Review* was founded in October 1968 in the wake of disillusionment among young Chicago news men and women over management and public reaction to the role of the press in the riots. Edited by Ron Dorfman, the monthly aggressively criticized the city's press and offered a forum for general media criticism and self-improvement until its demise in 1975. Across the country similar publications appeared, among them the late New York review, [*MORE*]. In many city rooms "reporter power" movements developed among young staff members who sought to make their professional contributions more meaningful and also challenged the established system of command. Among the advocacy journalists were Gloria Steinem, Jack Anderson, Seymour Hersh, and Sander Vanocur.

First of the underground papers spawned by the sex revolution and the credibility gap was the *Village Voice,* founded in 1955 and boasting such names as Norman Mailer, Jules Feiffer, and Jack Newfield. Art Kunkin's *Los Angeles Free Press* proved more radical and anti-establishment. Best known of the campus-based papers was the *Berkeley Barb,* founded by Max Scherr as spokesman for the "free speech" movement and a passionate opponent of the older educational order. San Francisco's *Rolling Stone* became highly successful in the mid 1970s. Among other underground papers that enjoyed at least brief fame were Chicago's *Seed,* Boston's *Avatar,* and New York's *East Village Other.*

Combining radical dissent and underground qualities were such pungent political journals as *I.F. Stone's Weekly* (1953–71), the *Guardian* of New York City, the *Texas Observer,* and Bruce Brugmann's *San Francisco Bay Guardian,* a crusading opponent of that city's orthodox press.

SM14170   OCTOBER 25th, 1975/ISSUE NO. 198   85¢UK30p

ROLLING STONE®

THE INSIDE STORY

By HOWARD KOHN AND DAVID WEIR

PATTY HEARST and Emily Harris waited on a grimy Los Angeles street, fighting their emotions as they listened to a radio rebroadcasting the sounds of their friends dying. On a nearby corner Bill Harris dickered over the price of a battered old car.

Only blocks away, rifle cartridges were exploding in the dying flames of a charred bungalow. The ashes were still too hot to retrieve the bodies of the six SLA members who had died hours before on the afternoon of May 17th, 1974.

Bill Harris shifted impatiently as the car's owner patted a dented fender. "I want five bills for this mother."

The SLA survivors had only $400. Reluctantly Harris offered $350. The man quickly pocketed the money.

Minutes later Bill picked up Patty and Emily and steered onto a freeway north to San Francisco. They drove all night —the Harrises in the front seat of the noisy car and Patty in back, hidden under a blanket. They were too tense to sleep, each grappling with the aftershock of the fiery deaths.

They exited twice at brightly lit service station clusters that flank Interstate 5, checking out each before picking what looked like the safest attendant. They made no other

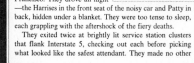

stops and reached San Francisco in the predawn darkness.

The three fugitives drove to a black ghetto with rows of ramshackle Victorians—and sought out a friend. Bill and Emily's knocks brought the man sleepy-eyed to the door. "You're alive!" Then he panicked. "You can't stay here. The whole state is gonna be crawling with pigs looking for you." He gave them five dollars and shut the door. "Don't come back."

The Harrises returned to the car and twisted the ignition key. Patty poked her head out from under the blanket. "What's the matter? Why won't it start?"

The fugitives had no choice —to continue fiddling with the dead battery might attract attention—so they abandoned the car. Walking the streets, however, was a worse alternative.

"C'mon Tania," said Emily. "You better bring the blanket." Bill and Emily both carried duffel bags. Inside were weapons, disguises and tattered books.

A few blocks away, under a faded Victorian, they spotted a crawl space, a gloomy cave for rats and runaway dogs. As Patty and the Harrises huddled in the dirt under the old house, the noise of a late-night party began in the living room above. Patty gripped her homemade machine gun. "The pigs must have found the car!"

"Shhh," came a whispered response. "Shut up, goddamnit. Please shut up!" [Continued on page 41]

14023

A series of exclusive stories helped the *Rolling Stone,* a San Francisco underground newspaper, rise to prominence in the mid 1970s. (Reprinted by permission of the publisher.)

THE BLACK PRESS

Only recently have the American mass media exhibited an understanding interest in the black 10 percent of citizens; even so, the capacity to be sensitive to blacks as readers or viewers was severely limited. There has always been a clear need for a black press.

More than 3000 Negro newspapers—owned and edited by blacks for black readers—have appeared since the first, *Freedom's Journal,* in 1827. But the black community has had few socioeconomic resources to support a press. Historically, the average life span of a black newspaper has been nine years. Henry G. La Brie III, then of the University of Iowa, a research specialist on the black press, found 213 black newspapers were being published in 1974, of which only 11 had founding dates before 1900, as compared to 90 founded since 1960. Total circulation was 4.3 million; only 5 were dailies; only 38 had their own printing equipment. But collectively this struggling press had made its impact on the country.

"We wish to plead our own cause. Too long have others spoken for us," said the editors of *Freedom's Journal,* John B. Russwurm and Samuel Cornish, in 1827. The first black journalist to do that effectively was Frederick Douglass, the remarkable ex-slave who founded *The North Star* in 1847 and became the symbol of hope for blacks of his generation and of today. Douglass helped rally public opinion against slavery and through his writing and speaking helped white men and women to see the degradation of slavery through black eyes. Published in Rochester, New York, *The North Star* reached a circulation of 3000 in the United States and Europe, particularly among influential readers. Renamed *Frederick Douglass' Paper* in 1851, it survived until the Civil War. Douglass then edited magazines for fifteen years. He wrote three autobiographies, tracing the career of an ex-slave who became a skillful editor, polished orator, and inspiring leader.

Ranking in fame with Douglass is W. E. B. Du Bois, who founded *The Crisis* in 1910 as the militant protest voice of the National Association for the Advancement of Colored People. "Mentally the Negro is inferior to the white," said the 1911 *Britannica;* to Du Bois, this belief was the "crisis" that had to be destroyed before discrimination in education, housing, and social status could be overcome.

Just as the standard daily press grew in numbers, circulation, and stature during the new journalism era between 1880 and World War I, so did the black press. Important papers today founded in that period include the largest, New York's *Amsterdam News* (1909); the leading papers in the two most important publishing groups, Baltimore's *Afro-American* (1892) and the Chicago *Defender* (1905); the Pittsburgh *Courier* (1910), Philadelphia *Tribune* (1884), and Norfolk's *Journal and Guide* (1909). Among the major figures in black publishing up until 1910 were Robert S. Abbott of the Chicago *Defender,* John H. Murphy, Sr., of the *Afro-American,* Robert L. Vann of the Pittsburgh *Courier,* T. Thomas Fortune of the New York *Age,* and William Monroe Trotter of the Boston *Guardian.*

In 1970, Abbott's nephew, John H. Sengstacke, was elected to the board of the American Society of Newspaper Editors, the first black to be so honored. Sengstacke was head of the Chicago *Defender* group, which included the Pittsburgh *Courier* and the *Michigan Chronicle* of Detroit. John H. Murphy III headed the *Afro-American* papers.

Out of forty-five efforts to publish dailies in the United States for blacks, as recorded by Professor Armistead Scott Pride of Lincoln University, only the Chicago *Defender* and the Atlanta *Daily World* have published for long periods, the latter since 1932. Its founder, William A. Scott, was murdered in 1934; his successor, Cornelius A. Scott, produced an essentially conservative newspaper. Most of the leading black papers have been moderate in tone, heavily local in news coverage, strong in sports and social news, and occasionally crusading.

Largest in audited circulation in 1978 was the *Amsterdam News* with 65,000 copies. Second was the Los Angeles *Sentinel,* founded in 1934 and edited by Ruth Washington as a mildly sensational and liberal paper. By far the largest in unaudited circulation was *Muhammad Speaks,* voice of the Nation of Islam, reportedly rolling 625,000 copies weekly out of its ultramodern Chicago plant. The *Central News-Wave* group of free circulation weeklies in Los Angeles totaled 233,000 for seven editions. The *Black Panther,* radical left voice, once claimed 100,000 copies. The *Defender* group had circulation claims exceeding 100,000; the *Afro-American* group, some 60,000. Historically, black newspaper circulations peaked during the World War II period, when the Pittsburgh *Courier* achieved a national circulation of 286,000. As the regular press covered stories involving racial issues better, black newspaper readership declined, and community-based weeklies replaced the bigger nationally circulating papers.

If there was a single major voice in black journalism in the 1970s, it was *Ebony,* the picture magazine founded by John H. Johnson in 1945 as a monthly version of *Life.* By 1978 it had a circulation of 1.3 million copies and had outlived its model. Johnson also published *Jet, Tan,* and *Black World,* the latter an outlet for black authors. *Essence,* a New York-based woman's service magazine founded in 1970, had zoomed past 550,000 circulation by 1978. *Encore,* a biweekly news magazine, had 150,000.

THE NEWS MAGAZINES

The news magazines offered a relatively small segment of the population another means of keeping abreast of events. *Time,* the largest in circulation, had 4.3 million subscribers by 1978; *Newsweek* had nearly 3 million; and *U.S. News & World Report,* 2.1 million. Although some issues go to subscribers who use them to bulwark inadequate news coverage by small local newspapers, many go to relatively well-informed citizens who read one or more daily newspapers, listen to television and radio news, subscribe to public affairs magazines, read books, and take one to three news magazines.

Henry R. Luce's formula for *Time* was to organize and departmentalize the news of the week in a style "written as if by one man for one man," whom *Time* described as too busy to spend all the time necessary to peruse the other media. Coverage of national affairs, foreign affairs, science, religion, education, business, and other areas was to be written for this "busy man," not for experts in each of the fields. The magazine developed a big research and library staff, as well as its own good-sized newsgathering organization, to supplement press association services. Begun in 1923, *Time* helped to drive the older *Literary Digest* out of business with this approach. *Newsweek* appeared in 1933, with an almost identical format. *U.S. News & World Report,* which grew out of a combination of two of David Lawrence's publications in Washington, hit its stride in the late 1940s. Two picture news magazines, Luce's *Life* (1936) and Gardner Cowles' *Look* (1937), offered additional news coverage and interpretive articles.

It should be noted that the news magazines offered their readers both news and opinion. *Time* made no attempt to distinguish between the two functions, intermingling opinion and editorial hypotheses with straight news. Its use of narrative and human interest techniques, and overuse of adjectives, added to its editorial bias. *Time* said it wanted to be "fair," not objective or even impartial. The trouble was, some readers mistook *Time*'s "fairness" (opinion-giving) for factual reporting. *Newsweek* injected less opinion into its columns and offered separate editorial opinions written by commentators.

THE PRESS ASSOCIATIONS

The major job of newsgathering beyond the local level is done not by the mass media themselves, but by the two big associations, Associated Press and United Press International. Newspapers, of course, cover their own local communities (although sometimes they even use press association reports about events taking place in their own cities). Some newspapers maintain area or state coverage through strings of correspondents

A typical front page of the Chicago *Defender,* one of America's leading black newspapers.

---

who filter in news to a state desk; this practice varies from one part of the country to another, and many a large paper depends on the press associations for news of events as close as 50 miles from the city room. Only a small percentage of American dailies have their own Washington coverage, and the bulk of this is directed toward stories of regional or local interest, rather than the major news stories of the day. And only a handful of newspapers have their own correspondents abroad. The situation is much the same in television and radio, where the press associations supply virtually all the news for smaller stations, all but local news for many larger stations, and even the bulk of the news for the network-affiliated stations. The news magazines, too, use the press association reports for the basis of their work.

Cooperative newsgathering in this country began, as we have seen, in 1848 with the Associated Press of New York. The telegraph enabled the New York papers that controlled this early AP to sell its news to a gradually expanding group of papers. Opening of the Atlantic cable in 1866 gave the agency better access to European news, which it obtained under exchange agreements with Reuters of Great Britain, Havas of France, and other press services. Regional AP groups formed, the most powerful of which was the Western Associated Press. The dailies outside New York City resented the tight-fisted control of the AP by the New York morning dailies that had founded it; the new evening dailies of the Midwest felt they were being ignored in the supplying of news on the two differing time cycles for morning and evening publication.

A bitter battle broke out among the newspapers in the 1880s. Control of the AP fell to the Western members, headed by Melville E. Stone, founder of the Chicago *Daily News*. Stone drafted exclusive news exchange contracts with the European agencies, cutting off the New York papers from their traditional supply of foreign news, and broke his rivals by 1897. An adverse court ruling in Illinois threatened the membership status of the AP at this same moment, so its headquarters were returned to New York in 1900.

The basis of the AP was its cooperative exchange of news. The members found it necessary to finance a larger and larger staff, however, and that staff took over direction of the flow of news and eventually much of the newsgathering. Its organizational structure was not entirely democratic; the older and larger newspaper members kept control of the board of directors by giving themselves extra voting rights during the 1900 reorganization. Until an adverse Supreme Court decision in 1945, an AP member could prevent the entry of a direct competitor into the group by exercising a protest right that could be overridden only by a four-fifths vote of the entire membership.

Newspapers that could not gain entry to the AP, or that disliked its control by the older morning papers of the East, needed press association service from another source. Edward Wyllis Scripps, possessing both a string of evening dailies and an individualistic temperament that made him dislike monopoly, founded the United Press Associations in 1907 from earlier regional agencies. William Randolph Hearst, whose newly founded papers were denied AP memberships, started the International News Service in 1909. Other agencies came and went, but the AP, UP, and INS survived until 1958, when the Hearst interests liquidated a losing business by merging the INS into the UP to form the United Press International.

The strong men in the AP over the years were Stone, the first general manager, and Kent Cooper, general manager from 1925 to 1948. Builders of the UP were Roy W. Howard, who later became a partner in the Scripps-Howard newspaper group, and presidents Karl A. Bickel and Hugh Baillie. More recently, Wes Gallagher became president and general manager of AP, followed by Keith Fuller, while Roderick W. Beaton became president of UPI.

Unlike the AP plan of organization, the UP and INS had a service to sell to clients. Howard set out to do this job for the young and struggling UP by building up a foreign service, first in Latin America and then in Europe. He embarrassed his agency by sending a premature flash announcing the end of World War I, but both Howard and the UP survived the incident. The enthusiasm and aggressiveness of the "shoestring" UP operation brought it into competitive position with the AP by the 1930s. In 1934 Kent Cooper brought an end to the restrictive news exchange agreements between the AP and foreign news agencies, and the AP joined in the foreign service race more determinedly. The AP also capitulated in supplying news to radio stations five years after UP and INS entered that field in 1935, and made the radio and television stations associate members, without voting rights. The INS, smallest of the three agencies, did not attempt to supply news at the state level except in a few states; it concentrated instead on outreporting and outwriting the other two on major news breaks and features. The UP-INS merger put the United Press International in a position of competitive equality with its older rival and assured the mass media that there would be intense rivalry between two well-managed press associations that serve both in this country and abroad.

SOME CURRENT NEWSPAPER LEADERS

Opinions differ about the quality of individual newspapers; any "list of ten" compiled by one authority would differ to some degree from the listing made by a second competent observer. But news people generally agree that a top-flight newspaper must offer both impartial and comprehensive coverage of the news, as a first prerequisite for national recognition. The second prerequisite for recognition by the craft is a superior demonstration of responsibility in providing community opinion leadership and of integrity and zealousness in protecting basic human liberties. The second prerequisite is much harder to judge than the first.

The United States, unlike many other countries, has no truly national newspapers. It has two dailies without "home communities," however, which have won widespread respect and which circulate nationally with their regionally edited editions. These are the *Christian Science Monitor* and the *Wall Street Journal* (neither of which carries a nameplate that seems to indicate the general-interest character of the paper). The *Monitor,* founded in 1908 by the Church of Christ, Scientist, built a high reputation for its Washington and foreign correspondence and its interpretive articles. Edited by Erwin D. Canham from 1945 to 1970, it serves more than 165,000 readers across the country from its offices in Boston. The *Wall Street Journal's* staff, led by Bernard Kilgore from 1941 to his death in 1967, has seen its readership rise from 30,000 to 1.4 million to make the paper one of the nation's largest. It is produced in eight regional plants through satellite transmissions from the New York office. It won its position on the basis of its excellent writing, coverage of important news, and specialized business reporting.

The New York *Times,* generally recognized as the country's leading daily and "newspaper of record," also has a sizable national circulation, particularly for its Sunday edition. It clearly has been the leader over a period of time in developing its own Washington and foreign staffs, whose stories are also sold to other papers. Publisher-owner Arthur Hays Sulzberger ably carried on the duties of his father-in-law, Adolph S. Ochs, after Ochs' death in 1935 and maintained a remarkable news institution to which many staff members—editors and reporters—contributed leadership. His son, Arthur Ochs Sulzberger, succeeded to power in the late 1960s and favored the judgments of reporter-columnist James Reston and news executive A. M. Rosenthal, who directed the paper's Pentagon Papers publication. In the late 1970s the *Times* added popularized sections—Weekend, Living, Sports Monday, Business Day —to its solid fare in order to maintain its readership appeal.

Across the continent, the Los Angeles *Times* surged forward in the 1960s to reach the top levels of American newspaper journalism. Young publisher Otis Chandler and a competent staff turned the paper to a more progressive editorial outlook than it had exhibited in earlier years, plunged vigorously into civic affairs, and vastly improved the news content. Chandler joined with the Washington *Post*'s owners in establishing a spectacularly successful news syndicate covering the nation's capital and worldwide news centers. The *Times'* editorial page showed intellectual depth, and enjoyed the cartooning skill of Paul Conrad. By the late 1970s the paper had passed one million in circulation and reflected reportorial skill and influence in national and state affairs.

Rising to prominence since the 1930s has been the Washington *Post*. Financier Eugene Meyer and his son-in-law, Philip L. Graham, the paper's publishers, had as their major aim the molding of a vigorous, intelligent, and informative editorial page for capital readers. This they accomplished, with the help of an able staff who could tap Washington news sources for background and interpretation, and the provocative cartoons of Herbert L. Block. Meyer's daughter, Katharine Graham, maintained the *Post*'s quality after the deaths of her father and husband in the 1960s, and pushed the *Post* to levels of news excellence that ranked it with the New York *Times* and the Los Angeles *Times*. The *Post*'s major role in Watergate reporting (see Chapter 6) won it wide public attention and the admiration of others in the media.

The St. Louis *Post-Dispatch*, published by a third generation of the Pulitzer family, continued to offer American journalism an excellent example of the exercise of the opinion function—excelling the standard set by Joseph Pulitzer's New York *World*, which ceased publishing in 1931. A talented *Post-Dispatch* editorial page staff, writing superbly and with a depth of understanding on a wide variety of subjects, made the editorial columns outstanding. The paper continued to win recognition for its crusading zeal and its outstanding Washington bureau.

Known as "Milwaukee's Dutch Uncle," the staff-owned Milwaukee *Journal* has demonstrated editorial page excellence since the days of founder Lucius W. Nieman. The *Journal* has paid close attention to city and state affairs and has cultivated both good writing and a wide grasp of political and human affairs on the part of its good-sized group of editorial writers. The same characteristics have been exhibited by the Louisville *Courier-Journal*, owned and edited by Barry Bingham. Both these papers enjoy local and regional news reporting of excellent depth.

Moving up in rankings by media peers are the Miami *Herald* and the Boston *Globe*. The *Herald*, emerging as the most dynamic paper in the South, was started on its way by Lee Hills, later executive editor of all Knight newspaper group dailies, who built its Latin American area coverage. Boston's century-old *Globe*, guided by sons of earlier executives, publisher William Taylor and editor Thomas Winship, won attention for 1970s investigative reporting, political writing, and community leadership in a long school desegregation controversy.

A change of style and outlook from the ultra-conservative stance given it by owner Robert R. McCormick and maintained through the 1960s brought the Chicago *Tribune* an enhanced national reputation and improved circulation in Chicago. Editor Clayton Kirkpatrick played a guiding role in reducing controversial activities and in encouraging revitalized reporting that won three Pulitzer prizes for local investigative work and one in international reporting before 1978.

Among other papers of high quality, those respected for their news skills include Long Island's *Newsday,* the Baltimore *Sun,* Philadelphia *Inquirer,* and Toledo *Blade* in the East; the Chicago *Sun-Times,* Minneapolis *Star* and *Tribune,* and Kansas City *Star* in the Midwest, the Atlanta *Constitution,* Charlotte *Observer,* and Memphis *Commercial Appeal* in the South; and the Denver *Post* in the West. Another dozen could be named with almost equal justice to such a list of current leaders in exercising the news function.

Although all these newspapers have capable editorial pages, some have won particular attention. When one turns to newspapers that have won top recognition for their editorial leadership and for their aggressiveness in defense of basic liberal principles of a progressive democracy, the names of four are readily apparent: the Washington *Post,* the St. Louis *Post-Dispatch,* the Milwaukee *Journal,* and the Louisville *Courier-Journal.* Examples of effective conservative opinion are found in the editorial columns of the Los Angeles *Times,* the *Christian Science Monitor,* the Chicago *Tribune,* and the *Wall Street Journal.*

As Gerald Johnson once said, "The greatest newspaper is as difficult to identify as the greatest man—it all depends upon what you require." Certainly an intelligent, honest, and public-spirited editorial page is as much an essential of an effective newspaper as is comprehensive and honest reporting and display of the news.

CHAPTER 5
GROWTH OF RADIO, TELEVISION, AND FILM

NEWS TAKES TO THE AIR

Public interest in news made it natural for men and women to use any new medium of communication—the telegraph, the telephone, the underseas cable, the wireless, the motion picture film, radio broadcasting, telecasting, and the communications satellite—to hurry the news to waiting eyes and ears, or to bring news events directly to distant audiences.

The telegraph, the telephone, the cable, and the wireless were nineteenth-century inventions that could speed the transmission of messages to waiting newspaper editors and printing presses. The motion picture film became a competitor that could bring to audiences in theaters a visual portrayal of such an exciting event as the Corbett-Fitzsimmons heavyweight prize fight of 1897—the first news event so shown. Soon excerpts of films of news events were put together into newsreels, which were a part of the standard fare of the movie palace of the 1920s. But the time lag before a newsreel could be shown kept it from being more than an incidental competitor for the newspaper. Interpretive films like Time, Inc.'s *The March of Time* of the 1930s and the development in that decade of the techniques of the documentary film—*The Plow That Broke the Plain* and *The River* were notable examples—foreshadowed the impact film would have on other news media once it had the direct way to reach the public that television provided. In the meantime, news took to the air through the magic of radio.

The first news broadcast in the United States is generally credited to Dr. Lee De Forest, who in 1906 invented the vacuum tube that made voice broadcasting possible, the next step beyond Marconi's wireless telegraphy of the 1890s. On November 7, 1916, the New York *American* ran a wire to De Forest's experimental station at High Bridge, New York, so that the "father of radio" could broadcast to a few amateur radio enthusiasts the returns from the Wilson-Hughes presidential election. Like the *American* and other newspapers misled by the early returns from that closely contested election, De Forest signed off with the statement that "Charles Evans Hughes will be the next president of the United States."

The inventive and engineering resources of wireless and radio were needed for military purposes during World War I, and private broadcasting was banned until 1919. Even then few saw the possibilities of mass radio listening. One who did was David Sarnoff, son of a Russian immigrant family who got his start as a Marconi wireless operator. When three big companies of the communications and electric manufacturing industries—Westinghouse, General Electric, and American Telephone & Telegraph—pooled their patent rights interests in 1919 and formed the Radio Corporation of America, Sarnoff became RCA's sparkplug and the eventual head of both it and its subsidiary, the National Broadcasting Company. His active career extended to 1970.

It was a Westinghouse engineer, Dr. Frank Conrad, who offered the first proof of Sarnoff's contention that people would listen to radio. His broadcasts of music in Pittsburgh in 1919 stimulated sales of crystal sets and led Westinghouse to open KDKA on November 2, 1920, as the first fully licensed commercial broadcasting station. The featured program consisted of returns from the Harding-Cox presidential election, one whose outcome was more easily predictable. The station got its vote results from the obliging Pittsburgh *Post.*

Other newspapers were more directly involved in broadcasting. One, the Detroit *News,* broadcast news regularly beginning August 31, 1920, over an experimental station that was to become a regular commercial station in 1921, WWJ. Others quick to establish stations were the Kansas City *Star,* Milwaukee *Journal,* Chicago *Tribune,* Los Angeles *Times,* Louisville *Courier-Journal,* Atlanta *Journal,* Fort Worth *Star-Telegram,* Dallas *News,* and Chicago *Daily News.* By 1927 there were 48 newspaper-owned stations, and 97 papers presented news over the air. The publishers thought radio newscasts stimulated sales of newspapers—and subsequent events proved them correct.

But despite these evidences of concern for news, radio's pioneers were more intent on capturing the public's interest by entertaining it than by informing it. Dramatic news events and on-the-spot sports coverage combined both objectives. News summaries themselves remained infrequent in the 1920s because they excited little advertiser interest, because radio itself did not collect news, and because news merely read from the newspaper sounded awkward and dull on the air. Meanwhile, KDKA broadcast accounts of prize fights and major league baseball games in 1921. The next year, American Telephone & Telegraph's New York station, WEAF (now WNBC), used phone lines to bring its listeners the Chicago-Princeton football game from Stagg Field. By 1924 an estimated 10 million Americans heard presidential election returns; there were 3 million sets that year, and the number of stations had grown from

30 in 1921 to 530. Twenty-one stations from New York to California joined in a March 1925 hookup to broadcast President Coolidge's inauguration.

The development of networks was vital for radio's progress. In early 1924 the Eveready Battery Company bought time on a dozen stations for its Eveready Hour performers—the first use of national radio advertising. By 1925 AT&T had organized a chain headed by WEAF with twenty-six outlets stretching as far west as Kansas City. RCA, Westinghouse, and General Electric had a competitive chain led by WJZ, New York, and WGY, Schenectady. In 1926 the big companies reached an agreement under which AT&T would retire from the broadcasting business in favor of RCA, and in return would control all forms of network relays. RCA, Westinghouse, and General Electric bought WEAF for $1 million. They then formed the National Broadcasting Company as an RCA subsidiary. The station chain organized by AT&T and headed by WEAF became the NBC Red network at the start of 1927, while the chain headed by WJZ became the NBC Blue network. Regular coast-to-coast network operations began that year. Sarnoff emerged in full control of RCA and NBC in 1930 when Westinghouse and General Electric withdrew under pressure of an antitrust suit.

Only 7 percent of the 733 stations operating in early 1927 were affiliated with NBC. Some rivals organized a network service with the support of the Columbia Phonograph Record Company in 1927; financially reorganized the next year under the control of William S. Paley, it became the Columbia Broadcasting System. CBS bought WABC (now WCBS) in New York as its key station and by 1929 was showing a profit. In 1934 it had 97 station affiliates, compared with 65 for NBC Red and 62 for NBC Blue.

Passage of the Radio Act of 1927 strengthened the two big networks, since the number of stations on the air was reduced by the new Federal Radio Commission to avoid interference in receiving programs, and a group of some fifty powerful "clear channel" stations was authorized. By 1938 all but two of the clear channel stations were either network-owned or affiliated. And although only 40 percent of the 660 stations then in operation were network-affiliated, they included virtually all those licensed for nighttime broadcasting. The two independent clear channel stations, the Chicago *Tribune*'s WGN, and WOR, New York, formed the loosely organized Mutual Broadcasting System in 1934 but found competition difficult. Mutual's complaints to the Federal Communications Commission (the regulatory body was renamed in the Communications Act of 1934) brought about the sale by NBC in 1943 of its weaker Blue network to Edward J. Noble, who renamed it the American Broadcasting Company in 1945.

The growth of the networks after 1927, and their success in winning advertising revenues, made radio a more disturbing challenger to the newspaper industry. So did radio's increasing interest in broadcasting news and public affairs. In 1928, Republican Herbert Hoover and Democrat Alfred E. Smith took to the air, spending a million dollars on campaign talks over NBC and CBS networks that reached many of the nation's 8 million receiving sets. That year the press associations—Associated Press, United Press, and International News Service—supplied complete election returns to the 677 radio stations. Radio's success in covering that bitter presidential election whetted listeners' appetites for more news broadcasts. In December, KFAB in Lincoln, Nebraska, responded by hiring the city editor of the Lincoln *Star* to put on two broadcasts daily of what it called a "radio newspaper." Other stations developed similar programs, and as the Great Depression deepened after October 1929, the public became even more interested in news. By 1930, KMPC in Beverly Hills, California, had put ten reporters on the Los Angeles news runs.

A bitter war then broke out between radio and newspapers over broadcasting of news. Newspaper advertising revenues were sharply contracting as the nation moved toward the 1933 depression crisis. Radio, however, as a new medium was winning an increasing, if yet small, advertising investment. Why let radio attract with news broadcasts listeners who would become the audience for advertisers' commercials, asked some publishers. This argument gave more weight to public interest in news than it deserved, considering the demonstrated interest in listening to such entertainers as Amos 'n Andy, Jack Benny, Walter Winchell, the Boswell sisters, Rudy Vallee, Kate Smith, and the stars of the radio dramas. But after both 1932 politicial conventions were aired on coast-to-coast networks, and after the Associated Press furnished 1932 election returns to the networks to forestall the sale of United Press returns, the American Newspaper Publishers Association cracked down. The press associations should stop furnishing news to radio; broadcasting of news should be confined to brief bulletins that would stimulate newspaper reading; radio program logs should be treated as paid advertising. There were dissenters to this approach, but after a majority of AP members voted in 1933 for such restrictions, all three press associations stopped selling news to stations. Radio now had to gather its own.

The Columbia Broadcasting System set up the leading network news service with former newspaperman Paul White as director. He opened

Left, Edward R. Murrow, highly regarded radio and television news commentator. He later directed the U.S. Information Agency.
Right, Hans Von Kaltenborn, first American radio commentator. His translations of Hitler's fiery speeches and his analyses of war-torn Europe were heard by millions of people.

---

bureaus in leading U.S. cities and in London and developed a string of correspondents. Hans Von Kaltenborn and Boake Carter, already CBS commentators, did daily news broadcasts. Kaltenborn, a former Brooklyn *Eagle* managing editor, had started broadcasting in 1922 and had joined CBS in 1930 to become the first of a long line of radio commentators. NBC organized a less extensive news service. Local stations got their news from the early editions of newspapers, despite AP court suits to stop the practice.

A compromise was soon proposed. This was the Press-Radio Bureau, which would present two five-minute newscasts daily on the networks from news supplied by the press associations. Bulletin coverage of extraordinary events would also be provided. In return, the networks would stop gathering news. The bureau began operating in March 1934, but was doomed to quick failure. Stations wanting more news bought it from five new agencies that jumped into the field, led by Transradio Press Service. A year later UP and INS obtained releases from the Press-Radio Bureau agreement and began selling full news reports to stations. UP began a wire report written especially for radio delivery, which AP matched when it began to sell radio news in 1940. The Press-Radio Bureau stopped functioning in 1940; Transradio succumbed in 1951.

Radio meantime was developing a blend of entertainment and news. The trial of Bruno Hauptmann in 1934 for the kidnap-murder of the Lindbergh baby attracted more than 300 reporters, including many with microphones. Listeners were bombarded with more than 2000 Press-Radio Bureau bulletins. President Roosevelt's famed "fireside chats" and the presidential nominating conventions and campaigns were major events. In December 1936, the entire world listened by shortwave broadcast as Edward VIII explained why he was giving up the British throne for "the woman I love." Kaltenborn hid a CBS portable transmitter in a haystack between the loyalist and rebel lines in Spain to give his American audience an eyewitness account of the Spanish Civil War. Kaltenborn, Boake Carter, Lowell Thomas, Edwin C. Hill, and Gabriel Heatter were the public's favorite news commentators. Ted Husing and Clem McCarthy were the leading sports announcers. America's top radio entertainment favorites in 1938 were Edgar Bergen and his dummy Charlie McCarthy, Jack Benny, Guy Lombardo and his orchestra, Kate Smith, the Lux Radio Theatre and "One Man's Family" dramatic shows, Burns and Allen, Eddie Cantor, Don Ameche, Nelson Eddy, Bing Crosby, and announcer Don Wilson. But before the end of the year it was Kaltenborn who stole the laurels as the world stopped all else to listen to news of the Munich crisis, which brought Europe to the brink of war.

RADIO NEWS COMES OF AGE

Radio fully met the challenge of diplomatic crisis and world war that began with Adolf Hitler's annexation of Austria and ultimatum to Czechoslovakia in 1938. Beginning with a patched-together but impact-producing coverage of the Munich crisis, the radio networks expanded their news reporting and technical facilities tremendously during World War II. At the station level, newscasts took a place of prime importance.

Network news staffs had continued to develop on a modest scale after the 1933 cutoff of press association news. NBC's Abe Schechter placed staff men in London and Paris, in Geneva for the disarmament conference, and in Shanghai for the Japanese invasion of China. G. W. Johnstone of Mutual was financially handicapped but had reporters in the major news centers. CBS news director Paul White had developed the largest organization for both U.S. and foreign coverage, but its staff was stretched thin.

In 1937 CBS sent a then-unknown Edward R. Murrow to Europe as news chief. For an assistant he hired William L. Shirer, who had been working for the just-closed Universal Service, a Hearst-owned press association. Like the others, they did human interest stories and cultural programs for shortwave broadcasts that were rebroadcast by U.S. stations. Then came Hitler's invasion of Austria and the *Anschluss*. Murrow hustled to Vienna. On March 12, 1938, the first multiple pickup news broadcast in history went on the air. Shirer spoke from London, Murrow from Vienna, and newspapermen CBS had hired gave their impressions from Berlin, Paris, and Rome. The pattern was set for radio's coverage of the fateful twenty days in September beginning with Hitler's demand that the Czechs cede him the Sudetenland and ending with the Munich Pact. Key staffers like Murrow (who went on to become television's best-known commentator and director of the United States Information Agency) and Shirer (author of *Berlin Diary* and *Rise and Fall of the Third Reich*) bore the brunt of the effort, reinforced by the cream of the U.S. newspaper and press association correspondents.

American radio listeners heard news broadcasts from fourteen European cities during the Munich crisis period. Beginning with the plea for support made by President Eduard Beneš of Czechoslovakia on September 10 and Adolf Hitler's challenge to the world two days later from Nuremberg, listeners heard the voices of Chamberlain, Goebbels, Mussolini, Litvinoff, and Pope Pius XI. Such broadcasts were not new, but the intensity of coverage was. CBS devoted 471 broadcasts to the crisis, nearly 48 hours of air time; of these, 135 were bulletin interruptions, including 98 from European staffers. NBC's two networks aired 443 programs during 59 hours of air time. On climactic days, these efforts kept the air alive with direct broadcasts, news summaries, and commentaries by the news analysts.

In his "Studio Nine" in New York City, Kaltenborn spent the twenty days catnapping on a cot, analyzing the news reports, and backstopping the CBS European correspondents with hours of analysis and commentary. It was Kaltenborn who provided the translations of Hitler's fiery oratory before the Nazi rallies, and who later predicted what diplomatic steps would follow. He made eighty-five broadcasts, many of them lengthy commentaries, during the three weeks. A few times he carried on two-way conversations with Murrow, Shirer, and other European corre-spondents. The CBS "European News Roundup," usually a 30-minute show from three or four points, was matched by NBC after two weeks. Heading NBC's European effort was Max Jordan, who had a 46-minute beat on the text of the Munich Pact, which he broadcast from Hitler's radio station. He relied especially on M. W. Fodor of the Chicago *Daily News* and Walter Kerr of the New York *Herald Tribune* in Prague, Alistair Cooke in London, and leading press association reporters. Mutual had only John Steele in London and Louis Huot in Paris, and used their occasional broadcasts, cabled news, and shortwave pickups to augment the regular press association news flow.

American listeners felt the brutal impact of Hitler's demands when Jordan and Shirer spoke from microphones inside the Berlin Sportpalast against a background of hysterical oratory and frenzied Nazi crowd reaction. They were grave when they heard Murrow describe war prepa-rations in London, relieved when Kaltenborn predicted that Chamber-lain, Daladier, Mussolini, and Hitler would find a peaceful solution at Munich. Although they devoured columns of type, it was radio that brought them a sense of personal participation in what they realized was the world's crisis, not merely Europe's.

By the summer of 1939 Murrow had a four-man staff: himself, Shirer, Thomas Grandin, and Eric Sevareid, a young newsman who also was to become a leading television commentator for CBS. When German troops marched into Poland, Americans tuned in their radios to hear Prime Minister Chamberlain announce that Great Britain was at war. Bill Henry of CBS and Arthur Mann of Mutual became the first front-line radio reporters. Radio news staffs expanded, and eyewitness broadcasts made history. James Bowen of NBC described the scuttling of the German battleship *Graf Spee* off Buenos Aires. Shirer of CBS and William C. Kerker of NBC reported the surrender of the French to a strutting Hitler in the railroad car at Compiègne. Radio brought news of Dunkirk, of the fall of Paris, Winston Churchill's stirring oratory. And in August 1940, Murrow's "This Is London" broadcasts made the Battle of Britain come alive for his American audience. His graphic descrip-tions of bomb-torn and burning London, delivered in a quiet but com-pelling manner, did much to awaken a still neutral United States to the nature of the world's danger.

The first news of Pearl Harbor reached Americans by radio bulletins that shattered the Sunday quiet of December 7, 1941. A record audi-

Three of America's most popular broadcast comedians. *Top to bottom:* Bob Hope, Jack Benny, and Fred Allen. (Photos courtesy of the National Broadcasting Company.)

ence listened next day to President Roosevelt's war message to Congress. Radio newsmen, using mobile units and tape recordings, joined the coverage of American forces in the Pacific and Europe. There were many memorable broadcasts: Cecil Brown of CBS reporting the fall of Singapore; Murrow riding a plane in the great 1943 Berlin air raid and describing it the next night; George Hicks of ABC recording a D-Day broadcast from a landing barge under German fire. Network reporters made broadcasts and recordings, filed cables, and competed on equal terms with press association and newspaper correspondents.

The demand for news seemed inexhaustible. In 1937, NBC had devoted 2.8 percent of its total program hours to news; in 1944, the figure was 26.4 percent. CBS in 1945 spent 26.9 percent of its network time on news and sports. Variety shows still ranked highest in audience size— those of Jack Benny, Fibber McGee and Molly, Bob Hope, Edgar Bergen and Charlie McCarthy, and Fred Allen. Dramatic shows and popular music were next. But four of the leading programs in listenership in 1944 and 1945 were news shows: CBS commentator Lowell Thomas, the "March of Time," Mutual's emotional Gabriel Heatter with his human interest commentaries, and the irrepressible Walter Winchell. As the war drew to a close, radio expressed the sorrow of the people by devoting three days of programing to solemn music and tributes to a dead President Roosevelt.

RADIO'S POSTWAR EXPANSION

The war years were exceedingly prosperous ones for radio. Total annual revenue more than doubled between 1937 and 1945, and income on revenues increased from 20 percent to 33 percent. When the FCC returned to peacetime licensing procedures in October 1945, there were 909 licensed commercial standard (AM) radio stations. Sixteen months later there were approximately 600 new stations either on the air or under construction, and the FCC had 700 more applications pending. These mainly were for smaller stations; the number of communities with radio stations nearly doubled in those sixteen months. By 1950 there were 2086 AM radio stations on the air and 80 million receiving sets.

Frequency modulation (FM) broadcasting, done experimentally beginning in 1936, was represented by 30 stations on the air in 1942, when wartime necessity brought a freeze in new construction and licensing. In the postwar years many AM stations took out FM licenses, and the number of FM stations on the air in 1950 reached 743, a figure that proved to be a high for the ensuing decade. Few of the FM stations were operating independently and giving audiences the selective programing that later was to characterize FM broadcasting.

Radio newsmen, somewhat to their surprise, found listener interest in news sustained during the postwar years. Sponsors, who by 1944 had pushed news and commentaries into third place behind dramatic and variety shows in sponsored evening network time, kept up their interest in news at both network and local levels. The established stations had in many cases developed their own newsrooms during the war, with personnel to prepare both general news summaries and local and regional news shows. The newly licensed stations, often without network affiliation, found news one area in which they could compete. Indicative of the trend was the founding in 1946 of an association of radio news directors, now known as the Radio Television News Directors Association.

Among the network commentators, Edward R. Murrow began his "Hear It Now" program for CBS, where he was joined by his wartime associate Eric Sevareid. H. V. Kaltenborn, who left CBS in 1940, became NBC's leading commentator. Radio listeners who sat glued to their sets all night in 1948, wondering whether President Harry Truman had upset Thomas E. Dewey in the presidential voting, found Kaltenborn one of the first to realize that Truman's popular vote lead would hold up in electoral college totals. ABC had Raymond Gram Swing, one of the finest of the war era commentators. It also obtained Elmer Davis, who had replaced Kaltenborn at CBS before becoming director of the Office of War Information. Davis won high praise for his postwar reporting, his dry humor and telling barbs, and his ability to get at the heart of complex and confusing issues. NBC scored with public affairs programs from the United Nations during 1946 and 1947. The networks and some local stations also offered documentary programs that analyzed important social issues in a semidramatic format.

But television was casting its shadow over radio. Television's "breakthrough" year was 1948, the one in which the value of time sales for the national radio networks reached an all-time high. Competition among the four networks already was intense, and the vogue for program popularity ratings as a means of snaring sponsors led to such devices as the "giveaway" program featured by 1948 radio. The smaller stations found plenty of local advertising revenues in newly exploited markets, fortunately, and after 1947 radio had more revenue from local advertisers than from network advertisers. The networks were already shifting their attention to television, and station owners were seeking television licenses until the FCC instituted a four-year freeze so that comprehensive plans for television broadcasting could be worked out. In the meantime, CBS forecast the fate of network radio when it made its famed 1948 talent raid on NBC to capture such stars as Amos 'n Andy, Jack Benny, Burns and Allen, Edgar Bergen, and Bing Crosby for future television shows. While network radio dwindled in favor of music, news, and sports programing, radio continued to expand as an industry. By 1978 there were about 8400 stations—4500 AM and 3900 FM—and an estimated 425 million radio sets.

TELEVISION ARRIVES

Experimental television broadcasting in the United States began in the 1920s. The scientific advances that preceded actual broadcasting stretched back over a century in the fields of electricity, photography, wire transmission, and radio. Early television experimenters used a mechanical scanning disk that failed to scan a picture rapidly enough. The turning point came in 1923 with Dr. Vladimir Zworykin's patenting of the iconoscope, an all-electric television tube. Zworykin, then a Westinghouse scientist, soon joined RCA, where he developed the kinescope, or picture tube. Other leading contributors were Philo Farnsworth, developer of the electronic camera, and Allen B. Dumont, developer of receiving tubes and the first home television receivers.

There were experiments in wire transmission of pictures during the 1920s that were to lead to the founding of AP Wirephoto in 1935. One of the researchers, H. E. Ives of AT&T, sent a closed-circuit television picture from Washington to New York in 1927. The next year General Electric's WGY began experimental telecasting. In 1930 NBC began operating W2XBS in New York; in 1939 it became the first station to offer regular telecasting schedules. Large numbers of people first saw television that year at the New York World's Fair. Commercial broadcasting was authorized by the FCC in 1941, but the wartime freeze left only six pioneer stations on the air. Among them were the first commercially licensed stations, NBC's WNBT in New York, and WCBS-TV in the same city. The two big radio networks thus had their entries in television broadcasting.

Because of postwar equipment shortages and industry uncertainties, it was 1948 before television could achieve a significant place among the media. In the meantime, RCA's image-orthicon camera tube had appeared to enhance the possibilities of live pickups, and AT&T was busily extending the coaxial cables that preceded the microwave relay for transcontinental broadcasting. During 1948 the number of stations on the air increased from 17 to 41, and the number of sets in use neared half a million. Cities with television increased from 8 to 23, and the arrival of the coaxial cable and network programing stirred a city's excitement much like the arrival of the telegraph a century before. Cities along the Atlantic coast from Boston to Richmond saw and heard the 1948 political conventions and the Metropolitan Opera. Television's first great star, Milton Berle, stepped before the cameras for NBC in 1948, as did Ed Sullivan at CBS.

Then, in the fall of 1948, came the FCC's freeze on additional station authorizations, which lasted until June 1952. During that time the FCC worked out a comprehensive policy for telecasting designed to give all areas of the country equitable service. In the interval only 108 stations were eligible for broadcasting. A few failed, but many became firmly established. The number of sets in use rose to 15 million. The transcontinental microwave relay was completed in 1951, and on September 4 the first coast-to-coast audience saw the Japanese peace treaty conference in San Francisco. NBC also offered the first telecast of a World Series and the first regular coast-to-coast sponsored program, the "NBC Comedy Hour."

The FCC's 1952 plan called for more than 2000 channel assignments to nearly 1300 communities. To do this, the FCC extended telecasting from the established very high frequency channels (numbered 2 through 13) to 70 more ultrahigh frequency channels (numbered 14 through 83). There were more than twice as many UHF as VHF assignments, and in addition 242 channels were reserved for educational television stations. But different equipment was needed to tune a set to UHF and VHF stations, and the established pattern of set making and broadcasting was VHF. The FCC did not require set makers to include both UHF and VHF tuning until 1964; in the meantime, UHF languished. In a 1953 decision, the FCC ended a long controversy over color telecasting in favor of the RCA compatible system permitting reception in either black-and-white or color.

Television's great "gold rush" came in 1952–53 with the end of the freeze. Among the networks, NBC and CBS were well along in their transition from emphasis on radio to emphasis on television. ABC merged with Paramount Theatres in 1953 and took a third-ranking position in television. Mutual did not attempt to enter television; a Dumont network gave up the attempt to compete nationally in 1955. That year there were 439 stations on the air and 33 million receivers.

By 1960 there were 533 stations and 55 million receivers. In 1978 there were 727 commercial stations on the air (211 of them UHF), plus 259 educational stations. There were 120 million sets covering 97 percent of U.S. homes. Television surpassed radio and magazines by 1955 in total advertising revenues and a year later passed newspapers as the number one national advertising medium, although newspapers continued to lead in total advertising thanks to their top-heavy position in the field of local advertising.

TELEVISION AND THE NEWS

Television's first efforts at news shows too often consisted of newsreels supplied by the United Press and Acme Newspictures and still pictures shown while the on-camera announcer read the script. But television newsmen, equipped with mobile units and magnetic tape, gradually overcame the problems of developing news shows with live film and sound. During the first decade of telecasting, they did far better with on-the-spot broadcasts of major news events, public affairs programing, and documentaries.

In 1951 Edward R. Murrow turned from "Hear It Now" to "See It Now" for CBS. NBC's early morning "Today" show with Dave Garroway, a mixture of news and entertainment, opened in January 1952. That year network viewers saw an atomic blast at Yucca Flats, the political conventions, and a heavyweight championship prize fight. An estimated 60 million Americans saw President Eisenhower inaugurated in 1953. Television audiences next followed live broadcasts of the McCarthy-Army hearings, which resulted in the Senate's censure of the Wisconsin senator, and watched a parade of gangsters before Senator Kefauver's crime subcommittee. Crucial United Nations sessions went on camera. At least 85 million Americans saw one of the "Great Debates" between John F. Kennedy and Richard M. Nixon in 1960, with the presidency at stake. President Kennedy opened some of his news conferences to live telecasting in 1961, and used television extensively at the height of the Cuban crisis in October 1962. An estimated 135 million saw some part of television's coverage of John Glenn's 1962 first manned orbital flight.

If proof were needed of television's ability to report great events, it came on November 22, 1963, when President Kennedy was assassinated

Barbara Walters, whose skill as an interviewer brought her national fame on the NBC "Today" show, became a coanchor for the "ABC Evening News" in 1976, and also did special interview shows, for $1 million annually. (Photo courtesy of National Broadcasting Company.)

in Dallas, Texas. Within minutes the networks began a four-day vigil ending with the burial at Arlington. Many heard the first bulletins on radio, then rushed to watch the unfolding drama and hear news summaries on television. An audience study for New York City homes showed that TV viewing rose from 25 percent to 70 percent on Friday after the assassination reports became known. Viewers saw the new president, Mrs. Kennedy, and the casket returning to Washington. They went with the cameras into the White House, saw the Sunday ceremonies at the Capitol. Sunday viewers on NBC (the only network "live" at the precise moment) saw Jack Ruby lunge forward in a Dallas police station to shoot fatally the alleged assassin, Lee Harvey Oswald, and heard reporter Tom Pettit describe the incredible event. Viewership in New York homes jumped to 80 percent as all the networks ran and reran their film. On Monday the funeral of President Kennedy drew a 93 percent viewership figure, the highest known level in television history. The nation agreed that both television and radio had reported the four days magnificently.

With full involvement of American troops in Vietnam after 1965, the ugliness of the indecisive war there was brought into American living rooms by television news crews. Public reaction against the war led to President Lyndon Johnson's decision to retire from the 1968 election race—an announcement made "live" to a Sunday evening television audience. There were even greater public shocks in 1968: the assassinations of the Rev. Martin Luther King and Senator Robert F. Kennedy, and the turmoil and rioting accompanying the Democratic convention in Chicago. In each event television played a major news coverage role.

Happier was the role played in July 1969 by television when it brought to a worldwide audience the flight of Apollo 11 and direct transmission of pictures of man's first steps on the moon. Viewers saw black and white pictures originating from the moon for five hours, including two hours with the astronauts on the moon's surface. Some 125 million Americans saw the climactic nighttime broadcast, and a satellite network carried the pictures to an eventual audience estimated at 500 million. Truly a "See It Now" triumph of immediacy, the pictures from the moon gave all viewers a sense of participation in a great feat of exploration.

After Murrow left the CBS screen in 1958, Walter Cronkite became that network's leading personality. A United Press war correspondent, Cronkite joined CBS in 1950 and became the star of many of its documentaries, including "Eyewitness to History," "The Twentieth Century," and "CBS Reports." He took over the major CBS news program from Douglas Edwards and transformed it into a 30-minute dinnertime show in the fall of 1963, with Eric Sevareid as commentator. Mike Wallace, Dan Rather, and Morley Safer made the documentary "60 Minutes" a "top ten" show. Other leading CBS correspondents included Roger Mudd, Hughes Rudd, Charles Collingwood, Daniel Schorr, Charles Kuralt, Bernard and Marvin Kalb, Lesley Stahl, Bob Schieffer, Ed Bradley, Sharon Lovejoy, Phil Jones, Heywood Hale Broun, Bruce Morton, and Susan Peterson.

NBC's top stars were two seasoned newspapermen, Chet Huntley and David Brinkley, whose mixture of news and comments between 1956 and 1970 made them a top-ranking television team. When Huntley retired in 1970, John Chancellor emerged as the chief NBC newscaster. Frank McGee, Barbara Walters, and Tom Brokaw were hosts of the morning show in turn. Morgan Beatty and Merrill Mueller had major newscasts. Other NBC correspondents included Joseph C. Harsch, Irving R. Levine, and Elie Abel in Europe; Pauline Frederick at the UN; Hugh Downs, Ray Scherer, Tom Pettit, Aline Saarinen, Sander Vanocur, Edwin Newman, Herbert Kaplow, Marilyn Berger, Judy Woodruff, Don Oliver, Bob Jamieson, David Burrington, John Hart, and Garrick Utley. "NBC White Paper" was the network's major documentary, along with "First Tuesday" and "Weekend."

With fewer resources, ABC kept pace with such commentators and news anchorpersons as John Daly, Frank Reynolds, Howard K. Smith, and Harry Reasoner, who came from CBS in 1970. Barbara Walters came from NBC in 1976. Leading correspondents were Edward P. Morgan, William H. Lawrence, John Scali, Robert Clark, Peter Jennings, Peter Clapper, Nancy Dickerson, Ann Compton, Tom Jarriel, Sam Donaldson, Ted Koppel, Sylvia Chase from CBS, and Catherine Mackin from NBC. Marlene Sanders produced the "ABC Closeups" documentaries with Smith as the main narrator. Reasoner and Walters did "ABC News Reports" and special interviews. The network scored with such programs as "The Soviet Woman" and "Women's Health: A Question of Survival."

Westinghouse's Group W (eleven television and radio stations headed by KDKA, Pittsburgh; WBZ, Boston; and WJZ, Baltimore) had its own news organization with Jim Snyder as national news director. Mutual radio had Bob Moore as news director.

News by satellite became television's most sensational achievement of the 1960s. The successful launching of AT&T's Telstar on July 10, 1962, permitted the first live transmissions between the United States and Europe. These were "staged" shows of a few minutes' duration while the signals could be bounced off the satellite, but they thrilled TV audiences. RCA's Relay carried pictures of events surrounding the Kennedy assassination to twenty-three nations. Howard Hughes' efforts to launch a satellite that would achieve a fully synchronous orbit (an orbit and speed that keep the craft directly over one point on earth) met success with Syncom III in 1964. Four such satellites, equally spaced around the world, could provide television coverage to all inhabited portions of the planet. The Communications Satellite Corporation, formed by Congress in 1962 to unify the U.S. effort, put Early Bird into synchronous orbit in 1965, then followed with the Intelsat II series in 1966 and 1967 and the larger Intelsat III series in 1968 and 1969. After the Intelsat IV satellites followed in 1971–1973, no fewer than 150 ground facilities located in 80 countries were connected to a greatly expanded television facility whose social-political use remained to be determined.

TELEVISION AND ENTERTAINMENT

The period from the end of World War II to the present has been one of turmoil and indeed revolution in the world of visual entertainment. Television's sudden emergence as a major home entertainment medium affected all other media, but particularly radio and motion pictures. In the years after 1948 the aerial became a fixture atop almost every roof; inside the living room the TV screen grew from 7 inches in width to 12, to 17, to 21, and in some cases to 24 inches. During the first years of television's popularity, at least, the presence of such free entertainment had a profound effect on American social habits. Some families planned their day's activities so that they could be at home for favorite programs; that gastronomical phenomenon, the TV dinner, was marketed to be eaten by families sitting in partially darkened rooms with eyes focused on the screen. Gradually audiences became more selective, but the average set still remained on for more than six hours each day.

Having captured a very large portion of the entertainment-seeking audience, television too found many serious problems. Program directors discovered that, operating as they did many hours a day, the television stations devoured good program material faster than it could be created. The writing and producing talent drawn into the television industry simply could not conceive enough fresh material of broad general appeal to fill the stations' program time.

As a result, the mass of television programing offered to the public was uneven in quality. Much of it was trite, inane, and repetitious. The critics denounced it vehemently, with good cause. Yet every week, at least during the winter months, a selective viewer could find many hours of literate, provocative, informative, and frequently very entertaining programs. Some of the best were the "spectaculars" or "specials" originated by Sylvester (Pat) Weaver for NBC to break the monotony of regularly scheduled series. The cost of these lengthy and star-studded productions also could be spread to several sponsors.

Television programing suffered from two major difficulties: (1) the tendency of many program directors and sponsors to underestimate the

Three famed network personalities. *Top to bottom:* Walter Cronkite, CBS; Tom Brokaw, NBC; and Howard K. Smith, ABC. (Photos courtesy of the Columbia Broadcasting System, National Broadcasting Company, and American Broadcasting Company.)

intelligence of the audience and (2) a severe case of overexposure—
too many hours of program time in relation to the amount of good-
quality program material, even when old Hollywood movies were added
to the fare.

New program ideas quickly attracted imitators. The public was subjected to cycles of entertainment, a number of programs similar in nature.
For two or three seasons in the late 1950s quiz programs were extremely
popular; these gave away fantastic amounts of money to contestants who
made the correct replies to many kinds of questions. But the public
began to grow weary of these giveaways, and when revelations of unethical assistance to some contestants were made, most of the quiz programs
disappeared from the air. Western programs, a modification of the
Western movie or "horse opera" that long was a standard item in the
motion picture industry, came into vogue. Soon the obvious tales of the
Old West were exhausted, and producers took to exploring many ramifications of life, translated into a Western setting. In some cases they
took classic fiction plots and reworked them as Westerns. At the peak of
the Western craze, so many of these "oaters" (as the industry called such
horse pictures) were being shot around the overcrowded Hollywood
outdoor locations that the casts of competing shows had to wait in line
for turns to perform their heroics before the camera.

Milton Berle was television's first great star, going on the air for NBC
in 1948. During the medium's first decade, the top audience ratings went
to variety shows and comedies. Holding steady places for several years
each were Berle, Groucho Marx, Ed Sullivan, and Arthur Godfrey. "I
Love Lucy," starring Lucille Ball, held first-place rating for five years.
Then, in 1958, came the Westerns, led by "Gunsmoke," and in 1959
half the "top ten" were action-filled, bullet-punctuated tales. "Wagon
Train" took top honors for four years, then gave way to "Bonanza."
A public outcry against violence contributed to a decline of the Westerns
in the late 1960s and the rise to number one ratings of the "Smothers
Brothers Comedy Hour" and "Laugh-In." Situation comedies like "Go-
mer Pyle," "The Andy Griffith Show," and "Julia" ranked high. Peren-
nials like Bob Hope, Dean Martin, and Lucille Ball kept their ratings.

The 1970s saw the demise of the Westerns ("Gunsmoke" in 1975)
and the rise of family programs, led by "All in the Family" and "The
Waltons." Shows featuring minorities also appeared, such as "Chico
and the Man" (Chicano) and "Sanford and Son" (black). "M*A*S*H"
kept the Korean war years green. The "Mary Tyler Moore Show" and

Carroll O'Connor, as Archie Bunker, tackles an unfamiliar task in this scene from "All in the Family." (Photo courtesy of Columbia Broadcasting System and Tandem Productions.)

Mike Farrell, *left*, as Captain B. J. Hunnicutt, gets into the swing of off-duty life in the 4077th Mobile Army Surgical Hospital under the tutelage of Radar (Gary Burghoff), *center*, and Hawkeye (Alan Alda) in this scene from "M*A*S*H." (Photo courtesy of Columbia Broadcasting System and Twentieth Century-Fox Television.)

its spinoffs were comedy successes, along with veteran Carol Burnett. ABC finally got top rating with "Laverne & Shirley," "Happy Days," and the Fonz, the 1976 Olympics, and a 1977 smash hit, "Roots," tracing black history for eight nights for a new top audience of 130 million.

But not all television entertainment was keyed to audience ratings. The educational program "Omnibus" was a rewarding contribution of the 1950s; so was "Playhouse 90." There were such artistic productions as "Peter Pan" and "Victoria Regina." Leonard Bernstein and the New York Philharmonic orchestra played for appreciative television audiences. Walt Disney's "Wonderful World of Color" even made the "top ten" lists of the 1960s. Such shows, combined with the news and documentary programs, gave television some claim to a role more socially useful than the casual entertainment role identified by critics as a "vast wasteland."

CHANGES IN THE MOTION PICTURE

The motion picture preceded radio as a medium. The genius inventor Thomas A. Edison used some of George Eastman's earliest Kodak film in inventing the Kinetoscope in 1889, but Edison was more interested in his phonograph and let the motion picture project lag. One of his assistants projected the highly popular *The Great Train Robbery* for the Nickelodeon era viewers of 1903, the first motion picture to tell a story. The first great milestone in motion picture art was David Wark Griffith's *The Birth of a Nation,* completed during 1914–1915.

Early motion pictures had to depend on sight and occasional printed titles; the arrival of the sound motion picture in 1926 put the industry on its modern basis. The electronic sound recording and reproduction process, developed by Warner Brothers, was a by-product of telephone and radio technology. The first synchronized music was heard in *Don Juan* in 1926; the first dialog, in *The Jazz Singer* in 1927. Technicolor was the next step forward in making motion pictures; the first three-color feature appeared in 1935. Cinerama, hailed as the most important development since the introduction of sound in 1926, ushered in the wide-screen vogue in 1952. Magnetic sound arrived with Cinemascope in 1953; magnetic strippings were used to put the sound on the same film with the pictures. The wide-screen development was exploited by the motion picture industry to help offset the inroads of television.

The changes in Hollywood's film output were equally drastic. The theme for the major producers became "fewer and bigger pictures," many of them filmed in Europe because of tax considerations and a favorable labor market. The producers found their market for the routine Class B drawing room drama and adventure tale taken over by the televised half-hour show, which the home audience could watch free. So the major studios turned to producing pictures of epic proportions in color, shown on gigantic screens. Here was sweep and grandeur the TV screen could not match, qualities sufficiently alluring to draw the viewer away from his easy chair and the admission fees out of his pocket.

A segment of the film industry went off in another, less desirable direction in pursuit of ways to draw the viewer from television. These filmmakers tried to achieve shock value with material that was too grotesque, socially daring, or close to obscenity for the home TV screen.

One result of the film industry's struggle for survival was a breakdown in the self-imposed censorship code by which the producers policed themselves. This had been adopted in reply to outcries by organized religious and social groups against a too-liberal treatment of sex in some films. For years some producers grumbled that the code was unrealistic in many respects, but generally it was respected and obeyed. Then, in the late 1950s, certain producers intentionally violated its strictures. Sensing a more liberal attitude among the citizenry, and arguing that they were dealing with socially significant subjects which had been forbidden unwisely, these filmmakers plunged ahead. One of these "breakthrough" efforts was Otto Preminger's picture on the previously banned topic of narcotics, *The Man with the Golden Arm*.

In the 1960s, numerous films were released by European and Hollywood producers that would have been taboo a decade earlier. Some of these rightfully could be credited to a more adult and open attitude toward social problems and were sponsored by men willing to fight against censorship barriers they believed to be outdated and unreasonable. Certain legal decisions hitting at film censorship practices in some states, such as that permitting the showing of the controversial British film, *Lady Chatterley's Lover,* broke down the barriers even further. These developments created a more friendly atmosphere for such films as the British *A Taste of Honey,* the American *The Graduate* and *Lolita,* and psychological studies like the Swede Ingmar Bergman's *Through a Glass Darkly* and *Wild Strawberries.* Unfortunately they also opened the way for pictures that had no social purpose but that blatantly exploited the market for crime and sex films. The history of photography is related to Chapter 15, and detailed film developments may be found in Chapter 14.

PART III

CRITICISMS AND CHALLENGES

CHAPTER 6
CRISIS OF CREDIBILITY

GOVERNMENT AND PRESS:
A CREDIBILITY DUEL

The mass media during the decade closing in 1975 came under the most severe attacks from the public and the federal government since the days of the Revolution and the Civil War, when patriots eliminated the newspapers they did not like by destroying the printing offices where they were published. The public, frustrated and bewildered by rapidly changing social and technological conditions, an unpopular war, and the emotional bombardment caused by near-total and near-instant mass communication, tended to blame the mass media for many of their problems. The federal government, always an adversary because of the constitutional role of the press in a democratic society, capitalized on the growing feeling of disenchantment with the media and engaged in a credibility duel characterized by both frontal and indirect assaults.

It was a situation ripe for demagogues. A cult of disbelief had grown steadily since the days of Senator Joseph McCarthy's treason charges and the Republican party's 1952 election slogan of "Communism, Corruption, and Korea." A credibility gap betwen president and public developed for John F. Kennedy, and widened dramatically for Lyndon Johnson and Richard Nixon.

But another credibility gap, between the media and the public, emerged. There was much bad news people did not want to believe, much reality they did not want to have exist: the Bay of Pigs, the Berlin Wall, the assassination of a president, the Vietnam War, racial riots in big cities, college campus riots, the assassinations of Robert Kennedy and the Rev. Martin Luther King, Jr., the collapse of victory hopes in Vietnam, Cambodia, My Lai, Kent State, long hair, sex and four-letter words in the open, and an inflation-depression. Blaming the source of the bad news—the press—became popular.

Some people did not believe the president; some did not believe the press; some believed neither. And both the president and the press encouraged people not to believe the other. In late 1972 Richard Nixon appeared to have the upper hand. Reelected with 61 percent of the vote, the president stood triumphant. But the ever-widening political conspiracy known as Watergate had already begun its course. At first dismissed by the White House as "a third-rate burglary," it developed into a major constitutional crisis. When it was over, 61 individuals and 19 corporations had been charged with violations of federal laws; 18 members of Nixon's administration had pleaded guilty or been convicted, including two cabinet members and four of his closest Oval Office associates; and the president had resigned in disgrace, joining his vice-president, who had resigned a year earlier rather than face bribe-taking charges.

The credibility of the media had been substantially restored, along with that of the government and its Congress and courts. "A President has been deposed, but the Republic endures," wrote one editor. Obviously, however, the long duel between press and government had been costly to both institutions. The cult of disbelief was still strong. It is important to understand how the governmental process could have been so brazenly subverted, and to appreciate why some media leaders took desperate gambles to expose the unlawful conspiracy known as Watergate.

VIOLENCE AND WAR

All peoples resort to violence and war. But few welcome the use of violence in their own social situations and neighborhoods, and nothing is more frustrating to a nation than an unsuccessful, costly war. Americans in the decade 1965–1975 were subjected to violence at home and stalemated war abroad; both widened the public credibility gap.

Vietnam, Cambodia, and Laos
Few Americans knew where these countries were when the first U.S. military advisers arrived in Saigon in 1955. Step by step, America descended into what David Halberstam of the New York *Times* aptly called a quagmire, which was to swallow up one president and help destroy another.

By 1963 the most perceptive of the U.S. press corps in Saigon were challenging the assumptions of the American intervention, but they were prophets without honor in their own country. The assassination of strong-man Ngo Dinh Diem opened the door to U.S. domination of South Vietnamese affairs; the "advisers" had grown to 16,300 in number at the time of President Kennedy's death. Lyndon Johnson responded to the Gulf of Tonkin incident by instituting bombing of North Vietnam and sending 180,000 more troops during 1965. The number rose to more than half a million, but no victory was forthcoming. Instead, the Vietcong humiliated the U.S. command with its Tet offensive of early 1968, which reached the gates of the American embassy.

Public confidence in the war leadership collapsed. President Johnson, before he retired from public life, instituted peace talks in Paris that were to drag on for five years. Antiwar sentiment surged through American youth and spread more widely. President Nixon's plan for "Vietnamization" of the war also included its divisive 1970 widening into Cambodia. By the end of 1971, more than half the U.S. military force had been withdrawn, but there were 50,000 U.S. dead. The country was on dead-center in its attitude toward the war, which eventually would end in total victory for those the U.S. had opposed.

The press, which had to report these events and analyze American policy and strategy, heavily supported the war until 1968. Then many more voices were raised for peace. Television, which had for the first time brought the battles and the brutalities of war into the family living-room, was not thanked for its effort. Americans did not want to hear about or see search-and-destroy missions, burnings of villages, My Lai, and saturation bombings. The majority wanted Nixon's "peace with honor," and the tragedy continued to unfold.

City Riots and the Kerner Report

Television was caught up in another credibility gap in the 1960s. It has been considered by many observers to be a primary cause of the so-called revolution of rising expectations among America's disadvantaged peoples. Both the programs and the commercials aired on television held out a better way of life for minority groups without changing their own real worlds. Unfulfilled expectations built up angry frustrations that erupted into the ghetto riots of Los Angeles, Newark, Detroit, and other cities. America's affluence, of course, was also reflected in movies, radio, newspapers, and other media; undoubtedly, too, there were other factors contributing to the social unrest. But television, the medium most often seen by minority groups, had made an impact that could not be denied. Before big-city riots, television had covered the suppression of civil discontent in the South, principally at Little Rock; Selma, Alabama; and Oxford, Mississippi. A new level of awareness and indignation had spread throughout the rest of the country.

Many public officials criticized television for its thorough coverage of the disturbances and threatened the network news services with new investigations. Critics maintained that black leaders Rap Brown and Stokely Carmichael had no real followings until television and radio provided almost daily platforms. It was alleged that the mere arrival of a TV camera crew on the scene of a demonstration often set off crowd action that had not occurred before. Moreover, public opinion polls disclosed a widespread feeling that the news media incite the violence they report merely by being present during riots and reporting on them.

The National Advisory Commission on Civil Disorders, with Governor Otto Kerner of Illinois as chairman, criticized the news media, including television, for incidents in which it felt bad judgment had been displayed and material treated sensationally. But on the whole, the commission found, the media had tried hard to present a balanced factual account of the riots in Newark and Detroit in 1967. Errors in many cases were attributed to false police reports. This was also true in 1971, when false official statements were made that the prison guards at Attica in New York state had had their throats slashed. Actually they had been shot by their would-be rescuers. A coroner and persevering media reporters forced a prompt retraction of the false statements in fairness to the black convicts.

The Kerner Commission indicted the mass media for failing to communicate to their predominantly white audience "a sense of the degradation, misery, and hopelessness of living in the ghetto" as well as "a sense of Negro culture, thought, or history," thus feeding black alienation and intensifying white prejudices. With few black reporters and fewer race experts, the report charged, the media had not seriously reported the problems of the black community. Pointing out that fear and apprehension of racial unrest and violence are deeply rooted in American society, coloring and intensifying reactions to news of racial trouble and threats of racial conflict, the commission asserted that those who report and disseminate news must be conscious of the background of anxieties and apprehension against which their stories are projected.

The news media soon developed guidelines and expertise with the aim of reporting demonstrations as faithfully as possible. It was generally admitted that the media had not properly prepared the American people for an understanding of social unrest. Through television documentaries, radio and TV "talk" programs and interviews, in-depth newspaper and magazine articles, and the like, the media explored the issues thoroughly and sought solutions. Efforts were intensified to recruit black and other minority reporters. But public support of the black movement dwindled.

Student Demonstrations

As student unrest spread across the nation with disruptions at the University of California at Berkeley, Columbia University, and Kent State, coverage of the disorders by the mass media was criticized both by proponents of "law and order" and by the protesters themselves. A large segment of the public, greatly disturbed by what it saw and read, complained that television was being "used" by the demonstrators for purposes of propaganda. Furthermore, it was alleged, news coverage of the occupancy and burning of buildings and especially of counteraction by both civil and campus authorities provoked similar disturbances on other campuses.

On the other hand, student militants and their supporters complained that the mass media, as part of the establishment they hated, failed to focus on the root problems of the disorders and thus to help the public understand the issues involved. They saw scant evidence that the media were bringing before the public such matters as the universities' tie-ins with the military, their heavy involvement in real estate and other extraneous enterprises, the role of ROTC on campus, the vesting of control of some institutions in boards composed of such "remote" groups as wealthy businessmen and lawyers, the alleged depersonalization of campus life, and the often blocked channels of communications between college administrations and student bodies.

Student militants had observed the unprecedented media attention given to the problem of black employment and representation of blacks on the screen as a result of the civil rights protest movement and the later riots. Many now sought to direct nationwide attention to what they considered the ills of society as reflected in the universities. A hard core of militants obviously sought to tear down the entire structure, whereas most students merely desired changes in some patterns of university life.

The mass media, as communicators and interpreters of such emotionally upsetting events and issues, were caught in the middle. Never before, in this and the other disrupting social issues of the times, had such heavy demands been placed upon the media to illuminate and thus help solve the problems that threatened permanent damage to the health of American society.

Politics and Chicago '68

Newspapers were the primary targets of complaints of press coverage of the Johnson-Goldwater election campaign of 1964, largely because of the newspapers' overwhelming editorial support of Johnson. In 1968, however, most of the complaints were leveled at television. Supporters and nonsupporters of third-party candidate Governor George Wallace of Alabama felt that he had been treated unfairly on television. Objections were raised to the almost daily TV reporting of the heckling that disrupted speeches by Wallace and Vice-President Hubert Humphrey, the Democratic nominee. Some suspected that the legacy of frigid relations between Richard Nixon and the press, coupled with the alleged "Eastern establishment" orientation of television newscasters and commentators, led to occasional uncomplimentary and subjective judgments relating to the Nixon campaign for the Republican party.

Charges of bias and distortion were leveled at the television networks over coverage of the Democratic National Convention in Chicago. Proponents of law and order declared that the film coverage showing police assaults in the streets and parks upon youthful dissenters, largely anti-Vietnam War supporters of Senator Eugene McCarthy in his presidential bid, failed to include provocations which led to many of the beatings and that too much attention was paid to the demonstrators. Network news executives replied that restrictions on the movement of camera crews prevented a more balanced coverage. They pointed out that only about 1 percent of network time was devoted to violence during the week.

Strong-arm tactics employed against some TV reporters at the convention site itself, coupled with reports of assaults on reporters in downtown Chicago and a conviction that convention proceedings were unduly controlled, led to strongly voiced expressions of resentment by TV news anchorpersons. In the words of one observer, "TV lost its cool."

Democratic party officials objected to what they considered a disruption of proceedings and biased reporting caused by constant interviewing by TV camera crews on the convention floor.

Altogether, it was an almost unbelievable, tension-filled four days of events without precedent, as one TV network described them, "either in the history of American politics or in the experience of American journalism." Thousands of viewers wrote and sent telegrams to network and congressional offices. A federal grand jury, the Department of Justice, the Senate Subcommittee on Communications, and the House Interstate and Foreign Commerce Committee investigated television's convention coverage. The Federal Communications Commission ruled, over strong protests, that the coverage was indeed protected by the Constitution's freedom of the press clause.

The Walker Report

The National Commission on the Causes and Prevention of Violence asked Chicago attorney Daniel Walker to study the convention disturbances. Walker's staff took statements from 1410 eye-witnesses and participants and had access to more than 2000 interviews conducted by the FBI. The report described both provocation and retaliation. The provocation "took the form of obscene epithets, of rocks, sticks, bathroom tiles, and even human feces hurled at police by demonstrators," some planned, some spontaneous, and some provoked by police action.

The retaliation was "unrestrained and indiscriminate police violence on many occasions, particularly at night," with reporters and photographers singled out for assault, and their equipment deliberately damaged. The final report of the commission in December 1969 said the Chicago police used "excessive force not only against the provocateurs but also against the peaceful demonstrators and passive bystanders. Their conduct, while it won the support of the majority, polarized substantial and previously neutral segments of the population against the authorities and in favor of the demonstrators."

Although the Walker Report disclosed that no fewer than seventy broadcast and print reporters and cameramen suffered injuries at the hands of the police, scant attention was paid to this fact by a disturbed public. In the words of TV news executive William Small, the public, rather than accept reality, will prefer "to kill a messenger." (Small wrote a book with that phrase as its title.) CBS anchorman Walter Cronkite, angered when he and the TV audience saw floor guards slug CBS correspondent Dan Rather to the floor, later found himself virtually apologizing to Chicago Mayor Richard J. Daley. CBS correspondent Eric Sevareid found the public's reaction obvious:

Over the years the pressure of public resentment against screaming militants, foul-mouthed demonstrators, arsonists, and looters had built up in the national boiler. With Chicago it exploded. The feelings that millions of people released were formed long before Chicago. Enough was enough: the police **must** be right. Therefore, the reporting **must** be wrong.

THE GOVERNMENT ATTACKS

It was in this setting of a frustrating war, big-city riots, student demonstrations, radical militancy, and sex-drugs-pornography permissiveness that Richard Nixon became president. Beaten narrowly in 1960, apparently out of politics after losing the California governorship in 1962 and telling the press "you won't have Dick Nixon to kick around any more," he had rebounded into the political vacuum caused by the Goldwater debacle of 1964, Lyndon Johnson's retirement, and the assassinations of John and Robert Kennedy.

Hubert Humphrey, his campaign left in shambles by the Chicago convention, which alienated both conservative-minded voters and the antiwar intellectuals, made a hard race but failed because he lost all the southern and border states except Texas. Nixon received 43.16 percent of the popular vote; Humphrey, 42.73; and Wallace, 13.63. The Democrats won both houses of Congress; indeed, Nixon was to become the first American president never to carry at least one house with him.

Richard Nixon's personality remains to be fully dissected, but he was clearly a "loner," instinctively distrustful of others, suspicious of motives of individuals and social groups, an advocate of the theory that the ends justify the means, and a hard-nosed politician who nursed resentments into hates and insisted upon taking revenge. This proved to be his undoing, as he seemed to recognize in his final comments as president: "Always remember, others may hate you, but those who hate you don't win unless you hate them. And then you destroy yourself."

The roots of the Watergate conspiracy extend back to 1969. Nixon, feeling intense political isolation and determined to win reelection in 1972, assumed he had to attack his enemies, especially the media. He would coalesce his conservative support by continuing the Vietnam War until peace could be won "with honor," by blunting the black movement through the issue of school busing, and by taking roundhouse swings at those he hated—political radicals, student militants, advocates of social permissiveness, and the intellectuals known as the Eastern establishment.

Nixon had enjoyed the editorial-page support of a solid majority of the country's dailies, but he had been opposed by some of the most influential ones. Among the 125 largest dailies, he had been supported by 78 (down from 87 in 1960) to 28 for Humphrey. The dissenters, who also often opposed the war and were regarded as "soft" on social issues by Nixon and his White House staff advisers, had to be dealt with—key newspapers, news magazines, and liberal elements in television.

The president asked his top aides twenty-one times in one month in 1969 (mid-September to mid-October) to counter what he regarded as unfavorable media coverage, according to an internal White House memo made public in 1973 by a Republican member of the Senate Watergate committee, Lowell Weicker. The memo, written by presidential aide Jeb Stuart Magruder, argued that a "shotgunning" approach was not the best way "to get the media." Magruder recommended harassment of unfriendly news organizations by the Internal Revenue Service and the antitrust division of the Justice Department.

Attached to Magruder's memo was a log of Nixon's twenty-one requests to his aides to register complaints or "take appropriate action" against the media. The president's ire had been raised by "biased TV coverage of the administration over the summer," and the memos covered CBS, NBC, and ABC. One singled out Dan Rather, CBS White House correspondent. Among other targets were political columnist Jack Anderson, *Time, Life,* and *Newsweek.* Nixon's associates proved responsive to his antimedia mood.

The Agnew Criticisms

The spark for a steadily growing conflagration of public debates, pressures against the media, and proposed and actual regulatory action by numerous agencies of government was touched off by Vice-President Spiro Agnew in November 1969. In two speeches, he declared that the networks and newspapers with multiple media holdings exercised such powerful influence over public opinion that they should vigorously endeavor to be impartial and fair in reporting and commenting on national affairs. Specifically, Agnew criticized network managements for employing commentators with a preponderant Eastern establishment bias and for failing to provide a "wall of separation" between news and comment. A similar liberal bias, he inferred, affected the policies of the Washington *Post* and its other media holdings, and those of the New York *Times.* Because Agnew referred to the dependence of broadcast stations on government licensing, although disclaiming any thought of censorship, some observers saw in his remarks an implied threat to the freedom of broadcasters to report and comment freely on public affairs.

Never before had a high federal official made such direct attacks on those reporting and commenting on the news. A research study by Dennis T. Lowry comparing random samples of newscast items reporting administration activities for one-week periods in 1969 and 1970 bore out the contention that the Agnew-generated criticisms had significantly affected the newscasts in the direction of "safe" handling.

The Pentagon Papers

When the New York *Times* began to publish in June 1971 a series of news articles summarizing the contents of a forty-seven volume study of the origins of the Vietnam War, the "Pentagon Papers case" erupted. The study had been ordered by Defense Secretary McNamara, as a "History of the U.S. Decision-Making Process on Vietnam Policy" and had been made by a group from the RAND Corporation and other researchers.

The study was historical and revealed no military secrets or strategy, but it was highly explosive in terms of political and diplomatic interest.

As a Supreme Court justice put it, the Pentagon Papers were also highly embarrassing (to Kennedy, Johnson, and Nixon administrations alike).

Executives of the *Times* decided it was in the national interest to report the documentary evidence that had come to their hands, even though it was stamped "top secret," as was the widespread custom in the government. A team of *Times* staff members led by managing editor Abe Rosenthal and reporter Neil Sheehan labored for three months to prepare the series.

When the first story appeared, Attorney General John Mitchell asked the *Times* to stop the series. The newspaper refused, and the Nixon administration went to court to seek a prior restraint order forbidding further publication. The government obtained a temporary restraining order but was refused a permanent one. It engaged in a second duel in the courts with the Washington *Post* and met increasing resistance from the Boston *Globe* and other newspapers dismayed that prior restraint had been invoked.

The case finally reached the Supreme Court, which by a 5 to 4 order continued the temporary prior restraint order, a shocking setback to the free press concept. The newspaper lawyers then avoided a historic showdown on the absolute nature of the constitutional ban on prior restraint, and argued only that the government could not prove any involvement of national security in the banned publication. To this, the Supreme Court agreed, 6 to 3. Its members disagreed widely, however, on the ethics of the newspapers in printing documents stamped "secret" and on the nature of the prior restraint concept.

Subsequent alterations in the composition of the court, including the death of free press champion Justice Hugo Black, made it appear likely that the court would rule in a future case that it would be possible for the government to show justification for the imposition of prior restraint, even though the court said, "Any system of prior restraints of expression comes to this court bearing a heavy presumption against its constitutional validity." It was hoped that, as with the John Peter Zenger case, the Pentagon Papers case would not be repeated. That is, no president would again seek to impose a prior restraint upon the press, as had been done in 1971 for the first time in the history of the Republic. The political sensitivities of the case made the Nixon administration pause in seeking criminal indictments against any newspaper editors or reporters involved in the Pentagon Papers disclosures, although it moved against Daniel Ellsberg, accused of taking the secret papers from the files.

Why did Nixon and his staff pursue this issue so relentlessly? Because the New York *Times* and Washington *Post* were involved; because Ellsberg represented the liberal intellectual element; because the majesty of the executive branch of the government and the presidency had been challenged in an issue they called "national security." And because, as FBI director William Ruckelshaus testified in May 1973, Nixon had instituted a wiretapping search to plug what he termed "security leaks" to the press as early as May 1969. Between then and February 1971, the FBI had wiretapped the telephones of four reporters and thirteen government employees, mostly members of the National Security Council (this episode involved Secretary of State Henry Kissinger). One of the wiretaps recorded Ellsberg's voice.

When the FBI finally balked in 1971, the tapes were delivered to White House aide John Ehrlichman. Nixon then set up his own special investigative group, the infamous White House "plumbers," who were to implicate the CIA in their efforts. One of their jobs was to "get Ellsberg," and in July 1971 the White House unit obtained CIA "logistical support" in planning a September break-in at the office of Ellsberg's Los Angeles psychiatrist.

All this proof of White House subversion of the FBI and CIA came to light in May 1973 at the Los Angeles trial of Ellsberg and Anthony J. Russo for the Pentagon Papers theft. The CIA director admitted the facts in a memorandum to the U.S. district court, and Judge W. Matthew Byrne dismissed the case against Ellsberg and Russo, citing government misconduct. Nixon's zeal thus ensured Ellsberg's escape from prosecution. And in July 1974, four members of the White House staff (Ehrlichman, Charles Colson, Egil Krogh, and Gordon Liddy) and two ex-CIA men were to be convicted on conspiracy charges or for the actual break-in.

CBS and "The Selling of the Pentagon"

Of the networks, the Columbia Broadcasting System especially drew the hatred of the Nixon staff. Dan Rather, White House correspondent, dueled with the president throughout the entire Watergate period and endured Nixon's sarcasm. Daniel Schorr and Marvin Kalb were harassed by White House-inspired investigations. Kalb was one of those wiretapped. (So was columnist Joseph Kraft; and joining these newsmen on the celebrated White House "enemies list" were columnist Mary McGrory and the managing editor of the conservative Los Angeles *Times,* Ed Guthman.)

It was not surprising, then, that CBS and its then president, Dr. Frank Stanton, should be involved in a major freedom of the press case in 1971. The program was "The Selling of the Pentagon," which had aroused ire both in the White House and in the Congress. At issue was Congress' right to legislative inquiry versus broadcasters' rights under freedom of the press. The case was sidelined in July 1971 when the House of Representatives returned to committee a proposed contempt citation against CBS and Stanton.

The citation was recommended by the House Commerce Committee when the network refused to supply all its "out-takes," or unused pieces of film and tape, used in the production of the controversial documentary. The award-winning investigative report contended that the Department of Defense spends millions of dollars promoting both its activities and political points of view and that, moreover, it had stopped none of its promotions despite a presidential directive to executive agencies to end "inappropriate promotional activities" and curtail "broadcasting, advertising, exhibits, and films."

Critics, including Vice-President Spiro Agnew and high-ranking congressmen, assailed the documentary, one terming it a "professional hatchet job." It was charged that CBS News edited some answers selectively and out of sequence and in one disputed case made it appear that a Marine colonel was expressing his own views when, for two sentences, he may have been quoting someone else. Other allegations of error and distortion also were made.

In reply to a subpoena, Stanton testified before the House Special Subcommittee on Investigations, but declined to produce the out-takes of the program—those edited from the finished product. Pointing to the "chilling effect" not only of the subpoena but of the investigation itself, Stanton stated: "If newsmen are told that their notes, films, and tapes will be subject to compulsory process so that the government can determine whether the news has been satisfactorily edited, the scope, nature, and vigor of their newsgathering and reporting activities will inevitably be curtailed." He said the vital question was whether news and editing judgments shall continue to be made independently by a free press— and whether the letter and spirit of the Constitution could possibly contemplate distinctions between print and broadcast journalism.

On the contrary, contended Committee Chairman Harley Staggers. "Fraud and deception in the presentation of purportedly bona fide news events," he said, "is no more protected by the First Amendment than is the presentation of fraud and deception in the context of commercial advertising or quiz programs." He said the committee needed the out-takes to determine whether the network was "giving viewers an erroneous impression that what they were seeing has really happened, or that it happened in the way and under the circumstances in which it is shown."

The FCC studied the issues and concluded that the CBS editing decisions were a matter of journalistic judgment into which it should not inquire. The FCC also ruled that the network had fulfilled its responsibilities under the fairness doctrine by providing significant opportunities for contrasting viewpoints to be heard.

The House, by a vote of 226 to 181, declined to cite Stanton and the network for contempt. The dean of the Congress, Emanuel Celler, chairman of the Judiciary Committee, reflected the sense of the majority: "The First Amendment," he said, "towers over these proceedings like a colossus and no *esprit de corps* and no tenderness of one member for another should force us to topple over this monument to our liberties; that is, the First Amendment . . . There may be no distinction between the right of a press reporter and a broadcaster. Otherwise, the stream of news may be dried up."

Nixon's Effective Use of Television

There was a positive side to Richard Nixon's involvement with the media. In the wake of his disastrous 1960 television debate with John Kennedy, he assiduously studied the medium. He loosened up, learned to joke about himself in televised interviews, and whenever possible utilized staged situations (convention press conferences with selected members asking questions, political speeches before controlled small audiences, person-to-person interviews) rather than rough-and-tumble news conferences with the "pros."

Most effectively of all, he used television in live news-making situations in which no journalists were interposed between him and his audience. His visits to the Soviet Union were a television success. And his imagination-catching trip to mainland China was a triumph. Americans were seeing China for the first time in twenty-five years; they were also seeing Nixon clinking glasses with surprised Chinese in the Great Hall, striding about the Great Wall, and acting like a tourist. These foreign policy achievements shot his political stock upward.

Such was Nixon's style. He did not like the regular White House press conferences. Franklin Roosevelt had held eighty-three per year; Truman, forty-two; Eisenhower, twenty-four; Kennedy, twenty-two (but with live television for the first time); and Johnson, twenty-five. Johnson also held many impromptu conferences for the White House "regulars" and worked hard to please the press. Nixon averaged only eleven press conferences a year his first two years, and held only three in his final year, 1974.

Instead, Nixon relied upon prime time requests for direct talks to the television audience. During their first year and a half in office, according to one careful count, Eisenhower had made three such requests, Kennedy four, and Johnson seven. Nixon made fourteen his first eighteen months, and his final talk from the Oval Office the night he resigned the presidency was his thirty-seventh, which was also his ranking on the list of presidents, a fact he noted.

Nixon's use of television in the 1972 campaign was faultless. He selected controlled audiences for backdrops, avoided confrontations with his Democratic opponent, and capitalized on his foreign affairs leadership. The luckless George McGovern, plagued with controversies over his running mate and supported only by a loose confederation of political minorities—women's rights advocates, big-city intellectual liberals, blacks, young people—caught the media criticism while the Nixon campaign rolled on toward a nearly clean sweep of electoral votes.

WATERGATE AND THE MEDIA

If the president and his Oval Office advisers had been able to see ahead, they would not have become involved in Watergate. But they had assumed since 1969 that they would be fighting for their political lives in 1972 as minority party leaders against a strong Democratic party candidate—a Kennedy, a Muskie, a Humphrey. And they had put in motion a plan that could not be halted when a hapless McGovern appeared on the scene.

That plan involved the harassment of the media, the creation of an "enemies list," the raising of a $60 million fund for the Committee to Reelect the President that often involved illegal pressures upon corporations, the creation of a "dirty tricks" group that sabotaged Democratic presidential candidates (notably Senator Muskie), and the use of the IRS, FBI, and CIA to discourage political opponents and check on possibly vulnerable Democrats (notably Edward Kennedy).

It also had involved the creation of the White House plumbers group, whose talents were used against Ellsberg in 1971 and who now were to bring the Nixon administration to disaster. It was June 17, 1972; the target was the offices of the Democratic National Committee in the Watergate building complex, including that of Chairman Lawrence O'Brien; the apparent goals were to find interesting materials and to "bug" the O'Brien office in hopes of developing compromising tapes that could be used against the Democrats if they mounted a strong campaign threatening Nixon's reelection.

Disaster struck. The five men on the job bungled it; a watchman called the police; within two or three days the trail was leading from the plumbers back to their White House sponsors. The Washington *Post* assigned two youthful reporters, Carl Bernstein and Bob Woodward, to follow that trail. More experienced men might have faltered, but instinctively executives of the *Post* and its still obscure team of reporters sensed an incredible story was in the making.

What the Tapes Finally Revealed

The twists and turns of the Watergate story can best be understood by first knowing the ending. What became referred to as "the smoking gun" —positive proof of President Nixon's participation in the Watergate conspiracy and consequent criminal obstruction of justice—did not publicly emerge until 780 days after the break-in. Four days later, Nixon was on his way to exile in San Clemente.

The president's entire defense had been built around his claim that he had not known about the Watergate problems until March 21, 1973, when his counsel, John Dean, told him there was "a cancer on the Presidency." Many dents were made in this defense, and Nixon's impeachment had been voted by the House Judiciary Committee, but the "smoking gun" was missing until the story's end.

It was the tape for June 23, 1972, conversations in the Oval Office. Why Nixon had taped his private conversations, and why the tapes survived to bring down his administration, remain subjects for speculation. From the time a presidential aide revealed their existence in July 1973, a tense struggle developed over them. An incredibly detailed presidential daily diary, recording minute-by-minute his conversations and with whom, had readily been made available to investigators and the media. It proved to be the key to the tapes. There were three conversations listed for June 23 between the president and H. R. Haldeman, his chief of staff.

After losing a Supreme Court decision on custody of the tapes, Nixon had no recourse but to release the June 23 tape on August 5, 1974. As the impartial and authoritative research publication *Congressional Quarterly* summarized the event in its 1040-page detailed documentary review, *Watergate: Chronology of a Crisis,* "Nixon acknowledged in an accompanying statement that he had withheld the contents of the tapes from his staff and his attorneys despite the fact that they contradicted his previous declarations of non-involvement and lack of knowledge of the Watergate coverup." Six days after the break-in, the tape related, Nixon and Haldeman had developed and put into operation a plan to

★WANTED★

NAME: WALTER CRONKITE, CBS NEWS.
ALIAS: JOHN CHANCELLOR, DAVID BRINKLEY, TOM BROKAW, NBC;
ERIC SEVAREID, DAN RATHER, DANIEL SCHORR, CBS;
HARRY REASONER, ABC.
CHARGED WITH REPORTING: WATERGATE BREAK-IN AND COVER-UP;
OBSTRUCTION OF JUSTICE; COMPILING ENEMY LIST; FAKING OF
STATE DEPT CABLES; PERJURY (NUMBER OF COUNTS UNDER
INVESTIGATION); WIRETAPPING; SECRET CAMPAIGN FUNDS;
THE ITT SETTLEMENT; GOVERNMENT FUNDING TO IMPROVE
HOMES AT SAN CLEMENTE AND KEY BISCAYNE; NUMEROUS
RESIGNATIONS OF WHITE HOUSE STAFF; FINANCIAL DEALS
AND RESIGNATION OF SPIRO AGNEW; JUSTICE DEPT RESIGNATIONS.
ARMED AND DANGEROUS WITH MICROPHONES AND CAMERAS.

• NOTIFY •
PROSECUTOR RICHARD M. NIXON
OR
LOCAL COMMITTEE TO REELECT THE PRESIDENT

(By permission of Paul Conrad, Los Angeles *Times*.)

---

have top CIA officials tell the FBI to stay out of investigations of the
Watergate break-in for national security reasons. Thus the employees
of the Nixon reelection committee and White House staff members involved might escape detection.

There were other tapes, made public either late in the investigation
or at the later 1974 trial of the coverup participants, that proved the
depths of the Watergate conspiracy and Nixon's involvement. One was
the tape of June 20, 1972, missing 18½ minutes of Haldeman-Nixon
conversation when it was turned over to a federal court in late 1973.
Curiously, it showed the president entirely unconcerned about the break-
in even though his staff was holding an emergency meeting. On March

17, 1973, the president had urged John Dean to "cut" the Watergate scandal "off at the pass" by getting together a story that would exonerate Nixon. And on June 4, 1974, Nixon and his press secretary, Ronald Ziegler, had engaged in this conversation, typical of the vulgarity and shallowness of the tapes (the transcript was released by the House Judiciary Committee six days before it voted to impeach Nixon):

President Right. What I was saying about this crap is that it's reassuring up to a point, but in fact, uh, at least, in this whole business we, we sat there and we conspired about a coverup (unintelligible) or not. We did talk about it on the twenty-first. That's a tough conversation. Unless Haldeman explains it—which he will. (Sighs) But I think we can survive that, too.
Ziegler Yes, sir.
President Do you?
Ziegler Yeah, absolutely. We'll survive it all.

It was that kind of incredible confidence in the ability and power of the White House to withhold evidence, block investigations, and defy truth-seeking opponents which led to the preservation of the tapes that were to become the "smoking guns."

The attitudes of the Nixon administration toward the media were also revealed in the tapes. The Washington *Post* obtained this censored portion of the September 15, 1972, tape from the House Judiciary Committee:

President The main, main thing is the **Post** is going to have damnable, damnable problems out of this one. They have a television station—
Dean That's right, they do.
President And they're going to have to get it renewed.
Haldeman They have a radio station, too.
President Does that come up too? The point is, when does it come up?
Dean I don't know. The practice of non-licensees filing on top of licensees has certainly got more . . .
President That's right.
Dean . . . more active in the, this area.
President And it's going to be goddamn active here.

Three months later, four application challenges had been filed against two Florida television stations owned by the *Post* interests by a number of Nixon friends and supporters. As Kenneth Clawson, White House communications officer, put it to the Los Angeles *Times* later: "I separate out TV from the print media when it comes to criticism. Newspapers are privately owned, but we all have a piece of TV's ass and we're entitled to do something—although I'm not sure exactly what—if it offends us."

Coverups by the White House

Government investigators of the caliber of Archibald Cox and Leon Jaworski, Watergate special prosecutors, and John Doar, Judiciary Committee counsel, were long aware of many of the events concealed in the Nixon-held tapes. Federal Judge John J. Sirica similarly suspected the wide ramifications of the conspiracy and helped to pry out the truth. Those media reporters who became deeply involved in the Watergate story also knew how it was going to end—if proof could be obtained.

It was therefore almost unbearably frustrating to those individuals, and to members of the public who held the same views, to be confronted with two years of false statements by the president, his White House staff, and those who came to his support gratuitously. For the media, engaged in digging out the truth about the conspiracy and seeking to root out of public life those guilty of felonies, it became a touch-and-go contest between themselves and the president as to who would win enough public support to emerge victorious. A confused public, loath to believe their president would tell them lies, could easily believe that what the media was reporting constituted lies. The White House did little to disabuse those who came to that conclusion.

Here, in brief, are some of the public statements of President Nixon and his associates that confounded the job of the media and promoted a credibility gap with the public:

August 29, 1972: Nixon said in his news conference that the FBI, Department of Justice, and General Accounting Office had, at his direction, the total cooperation of the White House and all government agencies. "What really hurts in matters of this sort is not the fact that they occur, because overzealous people in campaigns do things that are wrong. What really hurts is if you try to cover it up." (June 23 he and Haldeman had planned to use CIA pressure to block FBI investigators seeking the source of "Mexican-laundered" cash given the break-in team.)

October 5, 1972: Nixon said at his news conference, "The FBI assigned 133 agents to this investigation. It followed out 1800 leads. It conducted 1500 interviews. . . . I wanted to be sure that no member of the White House staff and no man or woman in a position of major responsibility in the Committee for Re-election had anything to do with this kind of reprehensible activity." (Eventually eighteen pleaded guilty or were convicted despite efforts to shield them.)

May 22, 1973: Nixon issued a 4000-word statement denying any personal complicity in the Watergate scandal. He admitted there had been a White House coverup, yet asserted he was innocent of any planning or knowledge of it. As **Congressional Quarterly**'s massive chronology comments, in view of the Nixon voice on the June 23, 1972, tape, several statements of May 22 were false: "At no time did I attempt, or did I authorize others to attempt, to implicate the CIA in the Watergate matter."

November 17, 1973: Nixon, at the Associated Press Managing Editors convention, said, "I am not a crook."

Others added their voices. In October 1972, Nixon campaign manager Clark MacGregor replied to the Washington *Post*'s story revealing Donald Segretti's "dirty tricks" assignments from the White House: "Using innuendo, third-person hearsay, unsubstantiated charges, anonymous sources and huge scare headlines—the *Post* has maliciously sought to give a direct connection between the White House and the Watergate—a charge which the *Post* knows—and half a dozen investigations have found—to be false." (Segretti and presidential appointments secretary Dwight Chapin were convicted in federal court on the "dirty tricks" charges.) After another *Post* exclusive (October 25) linked Haldeman with the secret White House cash fund for payments to conspiracy participants, press secretary Ronald Ziegler accused the paper of "character assassination" and "the shoddiest kind of journalism." (Haldeman was convicted on five counts in the coverup trial; Ziegler later apologized to the *Post*.)

When the Washington *Post* was awarded the Pulitzer Prize gold medal for meritorious public service in May 1973, the paper, as predictable, was attacked by Vice-President Agnew. But it also was castigated by Democratic Senator William Proxmire for "the McCarthyistic destruction of President Nixon that is now going on with increasing vehemence daily in the press." Proxmire said Nixon "is being tried, sentenced, and executed by rumor and allegation" because the press was quoting John Dean as saying Nixon was involved in the Watergate coverup. He was joined in this gratuitous attack on the *Post* and other newspapers by Democratic Senator Mike Mansfield and Republican Senator Hugh Scott, the two floor leaders. Both denounced "rumor and innuendo."

How the Media Fared with the Watergate Story

The Washington *Post* had led in Watergate coverage from the beginning. Its reporting team, Carl Bernstein and Bob Woodward, was backed by publisher Katharine Graham, executive editor Benjamin Bradlee, managing editor Howard Simons, and District of Columbia editor Barry Sussman (it started as a local police story). The *Post* was first to uncover the CIA connection; first to link the break-in culprits with White House sponsors; first on August 1 to print the proof that a $25,000 check donated to the Committee to Re-Elect the President had ended up in the Watergate conspirators' defense fund (Haldeman had informed Nixon about this slipup on June 23). On October 10 the *Post* broke its major story, identifying the Watergate affair as one of massive political spying and sabotage. It followed with two more October stories linking Dwight Chapin and H. R. Haldeman with the operation.

But few were following in the *Post*'s footsteps. Press critic Ben Bagdikian calculated that of 433 Washington-based reporters who could in theory have been assigned to the Watergate story when it broke in the fall of election year 1972, only 15 actually were. Of some five hundred political columns written by Washington pundits between June and Election Day, fewer than two dozen concerned Watergate.

Media critic Edwin Diamond found that during the seven-week pre-election period beginning September 14, CBS devoted almost twice as much evening air time to Watergate as its competitors (CBS, 71 minutes; NBC, 42; ABC, 41). More than one-third of NBC coverage came on two nights, reporting the indictment of the Watergate break-in team September 15 and the *Post*'s October 10 sabotage story. Half the NBC and ABC stories were less than a minute in length; CBS dealt so routinely with a major political story only five times. John Chancellor of NBC took honors in reporting the October 10 sabotage story fully; CBS ended its efforts with two special reports on Watergate the week preceding Nixon's reelection. George McGovern protested the general lack of interest in vain. Because of media inattention, the Gallup Poll found in October 1972 that only 52 percent of Americans recognized the word *Watergate*.

The Watergate break-in trial began in Judge Sirica's court in January, and attention increased with guilty pleas and convictions. A bombshell burst in March when James W. McCord wrote Sirica a letter saying he and the other six arrested men were only agents for higher authorities. The Los Angeles *Times* contributed its first major newsbreak, linking John Dean and Jeb Magruder to the break-in; the *Post* followed with the names of John Mitchell and Charles Colson (all four eventually pleaded guilty or were convicted of conspiracy).

Watergate was now the consuming news story. Seven out of ten

Americans listened on April 30 as President Nixon announced the resignations of Haldeman, Ehrlichman, Dean, and Attorney General Kleindienst; 41 percent gave him a positive rating, 36 percent, a negative rating. Gallup now found 83 percent had heard of Watergate, but more than half thought it was "just politics." The Senate Watergate Committee with Sam J. Ervin, Jr., as chairman began televised hearings May 17; soon "Senator Sam" became a household character. Magruder and Dean made confessions and major charges against the White House in June testimony. At first the public split evenly (38 to 37 percent) on whether to believe Nixon or Dean; by April 1974, it found Dean more believable (46 to 29 percent).

The Weather

The Washington Post

Index   112 Pages
                  1 Sections

97th Year   No. 247   FRIDAY, AUGUST 9, 1974   Phone (202) 223-6000   15c

Nixon Resigns

The climax of the credibility duel waged between the White House and the press. Huge newspaper headlines of this nature heralded President Nixon's resignation throughout the nation and the world.

Vice-President Agnew's October 10 resignation after pleading no contest to a charge of income tax evasion, based on a court-submitted record of extensive bribe-taking, shocked the country. Attorney General Elliot Richardson accepted plea bargaining because the Watergate crisis pointed to the need for a new vice-president—Gerald Ford. The Washington *Star,* a rock-ribbed Republican paper, took honors on the Agnew exposé.

The crisis over the tapes now began to consume the Nixon administration. Judge Sirica's demand for their surrender had been upheld by the court of appeals; Nixon countered with a plan to submit transcripts only. Special prosecutor Archibald Cox was summarily fired when he objected, and Elliot Richardson and William Ruckelshaus resigned from the Justice Department in what became known as the "Saturday night massacre." A spontaneous wave of protest swept the country; Nixon hastily appointed a new special prosecutor and handed over the requested tapes. But some of them were missing and one had the famed 18½-minute gap blamed on secretary Rose Mary Woods' "stretch" for the telephone (Sirica found it was a deliberate erasure).

When Nixon had issued his May 22 denial statement, the *Wall Street Journal* had commented editorially, "The context can only add to the impression that the President is acting like a man with something to hide." The Washington *Star* openly doubted him; the Washington *Post* and New York *Times* rejected him.

The ultraconservative *National Review* and the Detroit *News* ran November editorials calling for Nixon's resignation in the wake of the Saturday night massacre and the tapes scandal. They were joined by Time Inc., whose magazines had three times endorsed Nixon for president; by the Denver *Post,* and by the New York *Times.* Nixon had not helped his cause with his conservative supporters by angrily attacking television (and particularly CBS correspondent Dan Rather) in a televised press conference October 26: "I have never heard or seen such outrageous, vicious, distorted reporting in 27 years of public life," he said of the Cox-firing coverage.

Public opinion, as reflected in the Gallup and Harris polls, also began to shift. Everybody had now heard about Watergate; the number who believed Nixon's story that he had no knowledge of the break-in or coverup had dwindled to 15 percent. In September 1972, 76 percent said Nixon was a man of high integrity to 13 percent negative; now in November 1973 it was 46 percent negative and 39 percent still endorsing the president's integrity. Harris found in December for the first time that more Americans thought Nixon should resign than wanted him to stay (47 to 42 percent), as compared to 28 to 63 percent in August. But half the population still thought it was all primarily "just politics" rather than "corruption."

The indictments for the Watergate coverup conspiracy came on March 1, 1974. The grand jury gave Judge Sirica a sealed envelope about Richard Nixon; on June 5 his longtime supporter, the Los Angeles *Times,* revealed the president had been named an unindicted co-conspirator with Haldeman, Ehrlichman, Mitchell, and others. Some of their defense attorneys had been intimating the same. (The trial ended with four convictions on January 1, 1975.)

The story now came to a rapid end. Nixon released a massive mound of tape transcripts on April 29. The Chicago *Tribune* flew advance copies supplied them by the White House home in an airplane; had its editorial board read them; published them in full; and editorially announced, "We are appalled." The *Tribune* then called on Nixon to resign or be impeached.

The House Judiciary Committee opened its impeachment hearings on May 9 under chairman Peter Rodino and with the guidance of counsel John Doar. On July 24, it began its televised debate on the impeachment articles; that day the Supreme Court in an 8 to 0 decision read by Chief Justice Burger ordered the president to turn over all tapes requested by the special prosecutor, including the fatal June 23, 1972, recording.

The Judiciary Committee hearings were conducted at the highest levels of democratic processes and did much to reassure the huge television audience that honesty and decency could still prevail. All thirty-eight members had their say. There were twenty-one Democrats (three of them from southern conservative ranks) and seventeen Republicans. A "fragile coalition" of the three southern Democrats and six to seven of the Republicans joined the remaining Democrats to seal Nixon's doom. On July 27 the committee voted 27 to 11 to impeach the president for obstruction of justice; it followed with two more articles charging abuse of presidential powers and contempt of Congress. Its report was still before the House when the President resigned on August 9, but became a permanent record.

The editorial words of the Los Angeles *Times* on August 7, written in the wake of reading the June 23, 1972, transcript, offer a fit closing:

No one can read those conversations between Richard Nixon and H. R. Haldeman without anger—anger at these men whose arrogance let them, with such apparent ease, abuse trust, pervert the system of government and breach the law in a voracious bid for more power. . . .
Mr. Nixon has brought dishonor to the Presidency—dishonor and disgrace. He has broken his oath of office. By his own admission, he has committed felonious crimes. He is not fit to remain the President. . . .
We ourselves especially feel the betrayal of Mr. Nixon. This newspaper has supported him in his candidacy through a political career that we have more often cheered than criticized. As recently as 1972 we had supported his bid for reelection.

Too few newspapers were as forthright and candid as this conservative leader of American journalism in enlightening their readers. While much was said by critics about such liberal media as the New York *Times* and Washington *Post, Newsweek* and *Time,* and CBS spearheading what was called an attack on Nixon, one must rank the Chicago

Tribune and Los Angeles *Times*—rockribbed conservatives—high among those that helped to illuminate the truth. As the evidence piled up, middle ground and conservative papers made it bipartisan, just as seven of the seventeen Republicans on the House Judiciary Committee joined in the same search for truth, once they had seen the "smoking gun."

What of the reporter heroes? Bernstein and Woodward became wealthy writing the best seller, *All the President's Men,* and a movie was made of it starring Robert Redford. Dan Rather made less money with his book *The Palace Guard,* left the White House, and became a CBS commentator and weekend anchorman—voluntarily, he insisted.

What of the public's thanks to the press? Generally the press came out ahead. It could thank the House Judiciary Committee for so handling its hearings that public belief in the charges against Nixon—and in the media which had reported those charges—had been greatly enhanced. The polls showed in August 1974 that only 33 percent of Americans thought Nixon should be granted immunity (as he was the next month by President Ford), while 58 percent said he should stand trial. But in June 1974, in answer to a question asking opinion about the amount of space and time devoted to Watergate, 53 percent said "too much," as against 30 percent "about right" and only 13 percent "too little." The messenger was still only sometimes appreciated.

Aftermath: Ford and Carter

"Our long national nightmare is over. Our Constitution works." Thus Gerald Ford spoke as he took the oath of office the day President Nixon resigned. With a friendly smile and down-to-earth manner, Ford quickly won public support and the praise of a press corps tired of daily warfare with the administration. But the era of good feeling ended only a month after it began, when Ford hurriedly appeared on television to announce he was giving Richard Nixon a full presidential pardon for any offenses he may have committed, before all investigations had been completed. Ford was subjected to heavy criticism and the pardon issue became a major reason given for his 1976 election defeat. The White House press secretary resigned; he was replaced by Ron Nessen of NBC.

Ford held 39 regular press conferences during his term, for an average of 16 a year. This was markedly better than Nixon's average of 7 a year, but below the records of other recent presidents: Eisenhower, 24, Kennedy, 22, Johnson, 25, and Carter, 26. Ford labored under the onus of the Nixon pardon, the winding down of the war in Vietnam, and a high inflation rate. He stubbornly maintained his conservative credentials, and spoke bluntly and plainly at news conferences. But he was credited with restoring to the White House a humility it had lacked.

Jimmy Carter was rated an unlikely prospect to win the presidency, but he and his advisers correctly gauged the temper of the times. Carter entered all 26 Democratic party primaries, astounding the experts with early victories. He became known as a fresh new leader who had never been to Washington, and predictions of victory, made by the news media, became a fact on primary balloting days. There were ups and downs but Carter had his delegates in advance of the convention, while Ford had to fend off Ronald Reagan. In the end, Carter won by two percentage points.

Carter walked down Pennsylvania Avenue, opened the doors of the White House, held press conferences every two weeks, and put on a two hour "phone-in" with Walter Cronkite screening the calls. The religious-minded Carter dedicated himself to total honesty; the press held him to his idealistic statements when he ran into problems, such as the unconventional banking habits of his budget director. Carter's standing in the public opinion polls fell to a low level during 1978.

PUBLIC CREDIBILITY OF THE MEDIA

While many Americans in the last decade viewed the mass media as "too liberal," despite their predominantly conservative ownerships, liberals and young activists saw the media as unresponsive, obtuse, and largely irredeemable as instruments for illuminating the root issues of social unrest. As a result, they turned to underground newspapers, discovered ways in which to "use" the media for their own ends, and increasingly sought government intervention with which to gain access.

Many intellectuals viewed the mass media with disdain for catering to mass tastes. Public officials generally resented the press' role of "watchdog" for the public's interests. Specialists in most fields complained that reporting of their activities often was oversimplified or erroneously stated. Many persons felt that the media conspired with other elements of the establishment in withholding the truth of events. And many newspeople themselves dissented through publication of at least twenty critical journalism reviews. In addition, the media were caught in the public mood of distrust for almost all institutions, including business corporations, the church, educational institutions, and government.

A number of groups and individuals took up Vice-President Agnew's assault against what was considered to be biased and often inaccurate reporting of national issues and events, primarily by the Washington press corps, the New York *Times,* the Washington *Post, Newsweek, Time,* CBS, NBC, and, to a lesser extent, ABC.

Among them were two "nonpartisan, nonprofit" organizations, Accuracy in Media, Inc., and the American Institute for Political Communication. AIM investigated complaints of serious error in news reporting, such as those alleged in the CBS documentary, "The Selling of the Pentagon"; statements on defense spending made by NBC newsman David Brinkley; and New York *Times* articles about the Vietnam War. Congressmen inserted a number of AIM's studies in the *Congressional Record,* prefaced with highly complimentary remarks. The American Institute for Political Communication in 1971 began a series of studies on the relationship of the Nixon administration and the media. One survey, it reported, revealed "a significant degree of bias" in television news coverage of the 1972 Democratic presidential primary ("pro-McGovern") and the Vietnam War ("anti-Nixon").

A third organization, the Institute for American Strategy, which conducts seminars in Virginia for reserve officers, as well as military, industrial, and educational conferences, issued in 1974 a study called "TV and National Defense: An Analysis of CBS News, 1972–1973." It claimed "CBS news and public affairs programs are shockingly biased" in favor of "weakening our foreign policy and cutting our defenses." CBS replied that the sample had been inadequate since it covered only the Cronkite evening news program, not all CBS programing, and had used prejudgments to arrive at desired conclusions.

In addition to numerous magazine articles and newspaper columns, a spate of books appeared with similar contentions of "media pollution." They included Edith Efron's *The News Twisters;* Arnold Beichman's *Nine Lies About America;* and James Keogh's *President Nixon and the Press.*

In reaction to the criticism, the networks commissioned extensive studies of their own news practices and specifically examined the programs that were the subjects of the Efron and AIPC charges. Independent scholars in each instance questioned the methodology and the objectivity of those studies.

A Freedom of Information Center report in May 1972 analyzed the major attitudes toward the media by their most avid critics in comparison with those of media workers. Under scientific scrutiny, the attitudes of this group fell under six categories: The revolutionary, espousing minority rights and opposing "corporate tyranny and media irresponsibility"; the pro-media critic, defending the media while pointing to their failures; the silent majority, distrusting the media's liberal tendencies; the critical intellectual, wanting the press kept free but favoring some government regulation; the traditional journalist, defending newspapers but skeptical of broadcasting; and the staunch defender, desiring both newspapers and broadcasting to be kept free of governmental control. Overall, the study found that the seeds had been planted for an era of stricter governmental control of the media.

A *Newsweek*-Gallup poll found little support for a public inquisition of American journalism. A *Time* Magazine-Louis Harris poll discovered that, although Americans are quick to criticize the way news is handled, underlying trust in the nation's press and its constitutional safeguards remained strong. Another Gallup poll disclosed that the public was fairly closely divided on the question of the fairness of news coverage by the nation's newspapers, although a slightly greater proportion of people said newspapers "favor one side" than held this opinion about television networks.

Summarizing these surveys, and others, the American Newspaper Publishers Association concluded:

Most Americans believe that newspapers are doing a good job of balanced, objective, and informative reporting. This is particularly true for local news coverage. . . . There is, however, a suspicious minority who claim that the press is guilty of partiality, distortion, and inaccuracy—and some believe that there is a strong imbalance between the coverage of undesirable and sensational type events and the good things that should be reported.

A study of public attitudes toward government control over television made by the Roper Organization for the Television Information Bureau in 1977 showed that those taking the position that government should have less control constituted the largest group, 36 percent of the total, but this was down from 41 percent in 1974. Those desiring more control rose from 15 to 24 percent during this period, while those believing the present amount of control is about right totaled 34 percent, down from 36 percent in 1974. An increasing polarization of opinion in this regard is evident in the fact that, since the question was first asked in 1963, those wanting more control had increased by 50 percent while the group wanting less control also had increased—by 33 percent.

POLITICAL BIAS

Charges popular a few years ago that newspapers slanted their coverage of election campaigns to help the candidates they favored are heard less frequently today. That is because far fewer newspapers are guilty of the charge now than in the past. With certain glaring exceptions, American newspapers generally try diligently to provide balanced political reporting. Some keep exact measurements of their stories, to be sure that by election day the rivals in each race have had approximately an equal number of column inches and photographs, as well as equal front-page treatment. Responsible editors are careful to remove prejudicial adjectives, verbs, and descriptions from the news copy.

Even so, the goal of total objectivity is difficult to achieve, particularly since editors are placing more emphasis on interpretive reporting in order to give their readers better understanding of the news background. Unless done with skill, interpretation in news columns can involve injection of the writer's personal feelings, or those of the publisher.

The support given by newspapers on their editorial pages to presidential candidates has been another source for charges of political bias. Figures compiled by *Editor & Publisher* magazine explain why. Historically, the majority of daily newspapers giving support to a presidential candidate has been on the side of the Republican party.

In 1976 President Gerald Ford was endorsed by newspapers with 62.2 percent of the polled circulation (lowest for a Republican since 1940 except for 1964). Jimmy Carter's 22.8 percent was the best for a Democrat since 1940 except for 1964. Newspapers with 15 percent of the polled circulation were uncommitted or unresponsive. But President Nixon had the endorsement of 753 daily newspapers in his one-sided 1972 reelection victory, whereas only 56 supported Senator McGovern, *Editor & Publisher* reported. In terms of the percentage of the polled circulation, Nixon had 77.4 percent to McGovern's 7.7 percent, with the remainder making no endorsement. This was Nixon's highest support in three presidential races. McGovern's meager total (representing 3 million circulation) was the lowest recorded for a major candidate since the trade journal began its studies in 1936.

In 1960 Vice-President Nixon was supported by newspapers with 70.9 percent of the polled circulation in his unsuccessful race against John F. Kennedy, who had 15.8 percent. A dramatic reversal occurred in 1964. President Lyndon B. Johnson, who succeeded to the White House after Kennedy's assassination, faced a right-wing conservative Republican, Barry Goldwater. Johnson had the support of dailies representing 61.5 percent of the polled circulation; Goldwater, 21.5 percent.

The trend swung back to the Republican side four years later, when Nixon faced Vice-President Hubert Humphrey, the Democratic nominee. Nixon had the support of newspapers representing 56 percent of total U.S. circulation, to Humphrey's 15 percent. A few papers supported George C. Wallace, the conservative third-party candidate, and the remainder either did not reply to the questionnaire or remained uncommitted.

THE REPORTER AND NEWS SOURCES

Government and press collide in many areas as reporters seek to gather information for the public. Some of these involve the extent to which government should keep public documents secret; the issuing of subpoenas by courts to force reporters to reveal their sources even though these are deemed confidential, and the imposition of "gag" orders that hamper reporting of court proceedings; and the danger involved when reporters work for the CIA and the FBI and when government agents impersonate news personnel, thereby damaging the media's credibility with the public.

Classification of Public Documents

The Pentagon Papers case produced widespread realization that democratic principles are incompatible with the present sweep of executive privilege and its corollary—the executive practice of classification and withholding information from both the people and Congress. The knowledge that the government had classified the entire history of a foreign policy era, during which secret debate decided not only how but whether to conduct a war, resulted in the most concerted attack ever launched by the press and Congress on the classification system.

New Republic magazine reported that, since World War II, bureaucrats wielding classified labels had consigned 20 million documents to the government's "subterranean empire of buried information." Most of these documents had been classified under the authority of President Eisenhower's 1953 Executive Order 10501, which ruled that official secrecy would be limited to defense matters, under three categories: top secret, secret, and confidential. President Kennedy set up guidelines for declassification in 1961, but very little declassification took place.

After eleven years of wrestling with the problem of the people's right to know the facts of government, Congress passed the Freedom of Information Act in 1966. The law states basically that any person can go to court to gain access to public records, and the burden of proof that secrecy is necessary is upon the government.

In 1972 the House of Representatives and the Supreme Court began separate inquiries into the effectiveness of the FOI law. Samuel J. Archibald of the University of Missouri Freedom of Information Center was commissioned to plot the trend of court interpretation of the act by studying significant cases. His analysis concluded that court judgments have leaned toward the people's right to know. The courts, however, generally have protected "investigatory files compiled for law enforcement purposes," and they have been wary of second-guessing executive decisions about matters that are kept secret "in the interest of national defense and foreign policy."

Declaring that his action was intended to challenge the government's security system, syndicated columnist Jack Anderson in 1972 released secret and sensitive documents which revealed that Dr. Henry Kissinger, the president's adviser on foreign policy, had directed administration spokespersons to support Pakistan against India in the war between those two countries. The fact that the anti-India policy had not been revealed even to Congress aroused further outcries against White House secrecy.

President Nixon established a new system for classification and declassification in 1972. Among other things, the system reduced the number of authorized "top secret" classifiers and made declassification, except for particularly sensitive information, automatic after six to ten years (amended to six years). Media response was mixed. Noting that the Pentagon Papers would have been ineligible for release under the time period, one newspaper editorialized, "If the Congress is to have a voice in war and nuclear testing, it must have quicker access."

Congress moved to strengthen the Freedom of Information Act in 1974, by enacting its amendments into law over President Gerald Ford's veto. Ford argued the amendments were "unconstitutional and unworkable" and a threat to legitimate military and intelligence secrets. The amendments, which went into effect in February 1975, narrowed the scope of exemptions that protected certain categories of government files from public disclosure, such as secrets that affect the national security. Congress also required agencies to answer information requests within ten days of receipt, broadened avenues of appeal and court authority to declassify disputed documents, and established penalty guidelines for wrongful withholding of documents.

Since passage of the law, agencies such as the FBI and CIA have provided copies of thousands of documents about individuals, companies, events such as the Kennedy assassinations, surveillance of known or presumed radical groups, and even, under court order, such items as the transcripts of background briefings and official conversations conducted by former Secretary of State Henry Kissinger. The CIA reported that by the end of 1977, using a hundred full-time employees, it had spent $2 million in searching and reviewing FOIA requested documents, collecting about $10,000 in fees for its work.

Congressional subcommittees continued to review the working of the law, and President Carter drafted proposed changes to reduce the time some documents could remain secret and to clarify the basis for classification. It was an expensive, burdensome process, but at long last the public had greatly improved access to much information considered essential to the proper operation of a democratic society.

Subpoenas, Confidentiality, and "Gag" Orders

The Supreme Court in 1972, by a 5 to 4 vote, decided that news reporters have no special immunity under the First Amendment not to respond to grand jury subpoenas and provide information in criminal investigations, even at the risk of "drying up" their sources.

One broadcast and two newspaper reporters, in separate appeals, urged the court to make it clear that the First Amendment guarantee of a free flow of information gives reporters at least some degree of immunity to government subpoena powers. The appeals from contempt citations were made by Paul M. Branzburg, a Louisville *Courier-Journal* reporter who had investigated the use of illegal drugs; Earl Caldwell, New York *Times* reporter, and Paul Pappas, newsman employed by television station WTEV, New Bedford, Massachusetts, both of whom had investigated Black Panther Party activities.

Justice Byron R. White, writing the decision with the support of four Nixon administration appointees to the court, said: "The Constitution does not, as it never has, exempt the newsman from performing the citizen's normal duty of appearing and furnishing information relevant to the grand jury's task."

Justice Potter Stewart, in an opinion in which he was joined by Justices William J. Brennan and Thurgood Marshall, said the decision "invites state and federal authorities to undermine the historic independence of the press by attempting to annex the journalistic profession as an investigative arm of government." He added: "The full flow of information to the public protected by the free press guarantee would be severely curtailed if no protection whatever were afforded to the process by which news is assembled and disseminated . . . for without freedom to acquire information the right to publish would be impermissibly compromised."

In his own dissent, Justice William O. Douglas wrote: "If [a reporter] can be summoned to testify in secret before a grand jury, his source will dry up and the attempted exposure, the effort to enlighten the public, will be ended. If what the court sanctions today becomes settled law, then the reporter's main function in American society will be to pass on to the public the press releases which the various departments of government issue."

The justices, however, did leave open some avenues for relief:

1. They acknowledged, for the first time, that the process of news-gathering qualifies for some First Amendment protection. According to Justice White, the First Amendment might come into play to protect a reporter if he or she could show "a bad faith attempt by a prosecutor to harass a reporter and disrupt his relationship with his news sources" (a fact not in evidence in the three cases before the court). Justice White declared that if a reporter does not believe a grand jury investigation is being conducted in good faith, he or she could seek relief from the courts. That eventuality might occur, he said, if the reporter is called upon to give information "bearing only a remote and tenuous relationship to the subject of the investigation" or if he has "some other reason to believe that his testimony implicates confidential source relationships without a legitimate need for law enforcement."

2. The court left the door open for Congress to enact legislation binding on *federal* courts and grand juries.

3. The court said state legislatures could enact "shield" laws preventing reporters from being forced to reveal sources of information to *state* courts and grand juries.

4. The court conceded itself "powerless" to bar state courts from construing state constitutions so as to recognize a reporter's privilege of some type.

"Shield" laws were enacted in a number of states. Many journalists, however, declined to support campaigns to persuade Congress and the states to pass protective legislation, on grounds that the First Amendment guarantee of press freedom would be endangered by such action.

In recent years numerous reporters and editors have been jailed on contempt of court charges for failing to reveal sources of information. The most celebrated case was that of William Farr, a Los Angeles reporter who, since the early 1970s, has been in and out of courts and served 46 days in jail for protecting his sources for a story concerning the Charles Manson murder trial.

Countless subpoenas also have been issued in both criminal and civil cases in which the protection of sources was not involved. In some cases news people have testified or given depositions; in others the media have provided clippings and tearsheets; and in still others the subpoena has been successfully refused, denied, or withdrawn.

Despite a landmark Nebraska case decided by the Supreme Court in 1976 against restricting press access to trials, such "gag" orders continued to plague the press. Judges frequently barred both the public and the press from pretrial criminal proceedings and also enjoined the principals from discussing cases with the press.

The Supreme Court ruled in 1978 that the First Amendment provides the press no special protection from police searches, and police do not first have to obtain a subpoena, although a search warrant is required. The case stemmed from a police search of the Stanford University student daily newspaper offices. Press groups considered the ruling a major setback.

The Journalist As Government Agent

The public's faith in the journalist as an independent gatherer and interpreter of the news, free from any connection with government, was diminished in 1977 with revelations that many American news personnel, in the decades after World War II, had served as salaried intelligence operatives for the Central Intelligence Agency while also performing their duties as reporters.

Watergate reporter Carl Bernstein, after an extensive inquiry, said more than 400 American journalists had secretly carried out assignments for the CIA. The New York *Times* said between 30 and 100 journalists were paid for such work.

The *Times* reported that more than 50 news organizations, owned or subsidized by the CIA, had spread pro-American views as well as propaganda and lies in ways that often made Americans and foreigners the victims of misinformation. In addition, the *Times* reported, at least 12 full-time CIA officers had worked abroad as reporters or non-editorial employees of American-owned news organizations, in some cases having been hired by the news organizations whose credentials they carried.

Executives of the networks, newspapers, magazines, and wire services cited by Bernstein generally denied the charges affecting their organizations, on the basis of their own knowledge or of extensive investigations. Some reporters freely acknowledged that they had exchanged information with the CIA, maintaining that, during the era of the Cold War with the communist world, cooperation between journalists and the CIA represented both good citizenship and good craftsmanship.

CIA officials, who saw nothing untoward in such relationships, said the agency had cut back sharply on the use of reporters since 1973, primarily as a result of pressure from the media, but Bernstein insisted that some journalist-operatives were still posted abroad.

A House Intelligence subcommittee conducted hearings on the matter in 1978. The chairman, Representative Les Aspin, said the hearings were intended to give the committee an idea of what kinds of relations with the press intelligence officers consider useful and what kinds of relations the media consider harmful or unethical. A chief concern expressed was the extent to which misinformation planted abroad finds its way back into the American press.

A similar threat to the integrity of the newsgathering process occurred during the Vietnam War era when law enforcement agents masqueraded as reporters and cameramen in order to obtain information, primarily about dissident groups. The Twentieth Century Fund Task Force on the Government and the Press in 1972 reported that Army agents both in the United States and in Vietnam, as well as intelligence units of local police agencies, had posed as reporters. The FBI reportedly did not permit its agents to pose as news personnel, but placed journalists on the payroll when they initiated the move.

Fred P. Graham, in a background paper prepared for the Task Force, pointed out that government may need stratagems to determine the intentions of some militant organizations and prevent or anticipate acts of violence such as bombings. "The penetration of such groups by undercover agents is nothing new," Graham said, "but the use of newsmen as agents is relatively new—and hazardous. By making journalists suspect, the practice threatens to cut off the flow of information needed to enable the public to make sensible judgments about dissident groups. Conversely, a free press that can be trusted to report on dissident groups fairly may well defuse extreme militancy. The press is a safety valve for dissent that protects both the public interest and the right of legitimate social criticism."

CHAPTER 7
THE MEDIA AND SOCIAL ISSUES

SOME BASIC QUESTIONS

Violence and sex, poverty and crime, "computerized man" and the "forgotten" man—these were some of the social problem areas confronting the mass media and the American public during the 1970s.

Since virtually every home had television and radio and the average family spent almost nine hours daily watching and listening, the broadcast media were unavoidably involved in the nation's search for solutions—and often accused of exacerbating its problems. Newspapers, magazines, books, and movies likewise were caught up in the reexamination of values that swept American society. All helped determine the nation's agenda of discussion of current issues and strongly influenced public opinion and action.

Recognizing the impact of the media upon their lives, Americans sought the answer to questions such as these:

1 *Are the seeds of violence and crime being nurtured by the media?*
2 *In today's permissive society do the media help degrade standards of good taste and conduct?*
3 *To what extent should the media be permitted to infringe upon the rights of the individual citizen?*
4 *Are the points of view of minorities and special interest groups given adequate attention?*
5 *Can business meet consumer demands for fairness and accuracy in advertising?*
6 *Can the various media improve their own performance so as to avoid further controls?*

These and other issues require constant examination if the media are adequately to fulfill their roles in today's society.

VIOLENCE

Effects of Televised Violence

A dispute about the effects of viewing acts of violence on television by the American public, particularly by children, other young people, and the emotionally disturbed, has raged for a number of years. The late

Senator Estes Kefauver held hearings on the subject as far back as 1954, and testimony was heard again in the Senate in 1961. As the rate of violent crime in America grew, an increasingly large number of critics pointed to television as one of the possible causes. The assassinations of Senator Robert Kennedy and the Rev. Martin Luther King, Jr., and the attempted assassination of Governor George Wallace of Alabama, combined with civil disturbances and riots at universities, all focused attention on the violent behavior of Americans, forcing them to ask what kind of people they are.

In 1972, the twelve-member Scientific Committee on Television and Social Behavior, appointed by U.S. Surgeon General Jesse L. Steinfeld, completed a two-year, $1 million study to determine whether there is a causal relationship between television programs that depict violence and aggressive behavior by children. Summarizing its five volumes of research encompassing twenty-three projects, the committee reported that the study "does not warrant the conclusion that televised violence has a uniformly adverse effect nor the conclusion that it has an adverse effect on the majority of children." However, continued the report, "the evidence does indicate that televised violence may lead to increased aggressive behavior in certain subgroups of children, who might constitute a small portion or a substantial portion of the total population of young television viewers." The difficulty of finding evidence, the group reported, "suggests that the effect is small compared with many other possible causes, such as parental attitudes or knowledge of and experience with the real violence in our society." In addition, "the sheer amount of television violence may be unimportant compared with such subtle matters as what the medium says about it: Is it approved or disapproved, committed by sympathetic or unsympathetic characters, shown to be effective or not, punished or unpunished?"

Despite the qualified nature of the report, Surgeon General Steinfeld later told the Senate Subcommittee on Communications that, in his opinion, the causal relationship between televised violence and antisocial behavior was sufficient to warrant "appropriate and immediate remedial action"—on the part of the networks and stations, however, and not through government intervention.

In response, the networks insisted that program producers reduce the senseless mayhem on Saturday cartoon shows and also decrease depictions of violence on other programs, in accordance with the industry's Broadcast Standards. And in 1975 the networks began devoting the first hour of prime time (8 to 9 P.M. on the East and West coasts, an hour earlier in the Central time zone) to programs considered suitable for family viewing.

These efforts met with only limited success, however, and public criticism, bolstered by numerous research studies, continued to swell. A foremost critic was Dr. George Gerbner of the University of Pennsylvania, whose decade of research produced a "violence profile" for all programing. In 1977 the Chicago *Sun-Times* interviewed scores of researchers and reported that the majority agreed that watching violence on television and movie screens made some children more violent. The Parent-Teachers Association, American Medical Association, and numerous church and activist groups helped swell the anti-TV-violence movement and began applying pressure on national advertisers. Many companies set their own standards for programs on which they would place advertising. Concern was expressed that some of the violence would be replaced by the excessive portrayal of sex and other subjects in poor taste (such as that found in "Soap," a TV series satirizing daytime "soap operas").

Despite the anger expressed by activist organizations, the House Communications Subcommittee, after a series of hearings in 1977, voted 8–7 to support the Steinfeld committee's finding that a precise cause-and-effect relationship between televised violence and aggressive behavior had yet to be proved. The report concluded that, while the networks were chiefly responsible for the level of televised violence, some of the blame must also be assumed by affiliated stations, program producers, advertisers, and the viewing public—the latter representing the consumer demand that prompted the supply. Six of the seven dissenters, however, assailed the report as unduly protecting the networks, which they held chiefly to blame for TV violence. They urged an FCC inquiry into the market structure of television in which the networks are the major purchasers of programs.

Violence in Newspapers

Because of the nature of the medium, the reporting of violent crimes in American newspapers has drawn less criticism than its display in television and films. However, through the years many readers have objected to the sensational treatment of murders, rapes, and other such crimes, often in the form of detailed front-page stories and photographs published under large headlines. Some have felt that newspapers glorified violent activities, in effect making heroes of criminals. Objections have also been expressed against mayhem in the comic strips (although comic books were more severely criticized on this account) and against the reporting in some papers of almost every minor crime that occurred in the community. Newspaper stories of violent actions, however, have a minimal impact compared with that which is televised and shown in movie houses.

In 1947 the report of the Commission on Freedom of the Press, chaired by Robert Maynard Hutchins, at that time chancellor of the University of Chicago, decried sensationalism. Although written three decades ago, before television entered most American homes, the commission's list of society's five requirements of the mass media remains pertinent today. They are: (1) a truthful, comprehensive, and intelligent account of the day's events in a context which gives them meaning; (2) a forum for the exchange of comment and criticism; (3) the projection of a representative picture of the constituent groups in the society; (4) the presentation and clarification of the goals and values of the society; and (5) full access to the day's intelligence.

In a statement about sensationalism, the commission commented:

To attract the maximum audience, the press emphasizes the exceptional rather than the representative, the sensational rather than the significant. Many activities of the utmost social consequence lie below the surface of what are conventionally regarded as reportable incidents: more power machinery; fewer men tending machines; more hours of leisure; more schooling per child; decrease of intolerance; successful negotiation of labor contracts; increase of participation in music through the schools; increase in the sale of books of biography and history.

In most news media such matters are crowded out by stories of night-club murders, race riots, strike violence, and quarrels among public officials. The Commission does not object to the reporting of these incidents but to the preoccupation of the press with them. The press is preoccupied with them to such an extent that the citizen is not supplied with the information and discussion he needs to discharge his responsibilities to the community.

The press, however, has matured since those days; newspapers depending upon sensationalism for their circulation have, for the most part, been replaced by those like the Washington *Post* and the Louisville *Courier-Journal,* which subordinate crime news of this sort to stories treating criminal activities in a sociological manner. One reason is that, since the advent of radio and television, single-copy street sales constitute only a minor part of most newspapers' circulation; most copies are delivered to homes. For such sales, so-called screaming headlines and breathtaking accounts of crime are no longer necessary. Another reason is that most readers today, more educated than in the past, want their news in a different form. And the better newspapers are inquiring into the causes of conflict and violence, presenting in-depth background stories to throw more light on social problems.

Much of the nation's press, however, played up the 1977 arrest of David Berkowitz, suspected of killing six persons in New York City, in what critics called "a highly irresponsible manner" reminiscent of coverage of the noted Hall-Mills, Charles Lindbergh, and Sam Sheppard cases of earlier eras. Although some network and news magazine coverage was criticized, the charges, including those of exploitation and sensationalism, centered on the New York *Daily News* and on the New York *Post,* the latter owned by Australian publisher Rupert Murdoch, noted for sensationalism.

The "Son of Sam" case, as it was termed, raised such thorny questions as 1) the degree to which constitutional guarantees of press freedom imply unstated responsibilities, 2) the difference between reporting and exploiting the news, 3) the propriety of reporters' becoming part of the story they are covering, 4) the conflict between the public's right to know and the defendant's right to a fair trial, 5) the question of reporters' violating the law to obtain information, and 6) the ethics of the media's paying for information.

OBSCENITY

Pornography in books, magazines, and films became big business in the 1960s and 1970s as sexual mores changed and a new permissiveness in regard to individual conduct permeated American society. At the same time, serious works of art increasingly dealt with so-called adult themes and explicit sexual acts of every nature. The right to read and view what one desired conflicted with the opinions of those who felt that society had the innate right to proscribe such activities.

Obscenity generally is defined in terms of whether the materials are lewd, lascivious, prurient, licentious, or indecent. After almost two decades, however, the U.S. Supreme Court has been unable to draw firm legal lines as to what is obscene and what is not. Virtually each of the nine justices has had his own definition ("I know it when I see it," declared Justice Potter Stewart), and until 1973 a majority could not agree on any one approach. Yet the court maintained that certain materials are not protected by the First Amendment and that the government can suppress those materials. Recognizing the importance of safeguarding constitutional freedom, the court in each decision has attempted to limit severely the kinds of materials that can be suppressed as obscene. The problem has remained, however, that fundamental First Amendment values have been encroached upon, and are in constant jeopardy, because all the court definitions are, as three justices wrote in 1973, "so elusive that they fail to distinguish clearly between protected and unprotected speech."

In *Roth* v. *United States* (1957), the Supreme Court ruled that the standard for judging obscenity is "whether, to the average person, applying contemporary community standards, the dominant theme of the material, taken as a whole, appeals to the prurient interest." The court ruled that obscenity is not within the area of constitutionally protected expression, declaring that "All ideas having even the slightest redeeming social importance . . . have the full protection of the [constitutional] guaranties . . . but implicit in the history of the First Amendment is the rejection of obscenity as utterly without redeeming social importance."

To limit suppression of materials, the court also declared: "Sex and obscenity are not synonymous . . . the portrayal of sex . . . is not itself sufficient reason to deny material the constitutional protection of speech and press. Sex, a great and mysterious force in human life, has indisputably been a subject of absorbing interest to mankind through the ages; it is one of the vital problems of human interest and public concern."

In *Memoirs* v. *Massachusetts* (1966), involving the celebrated eighteenth-century novel, *Fanny Hill,* the court set forth a new definition of "obscene" wherein three elements must coalesce: "(1) that the dominant theme of the material taken as a whole appeals to a prurient interest in sex; (2) the material is patently offensive because it affronts contemporary standards relating to the description or representation of sexual matters; (3) the material is utterly without redeeming social value." The court stressed that material must be "utterly"—unqualifiedly—worthless.

In *Miller* v. *California* (1973), however, the court, in a 5 to 4 vote, revised its definition to "(1) whether the average person, applying contemporary community standards, would find that the work taken as a whole appeals to the prurient interest; (2) whether the work depicts or describes in a patently offensive way, sexual conduct specifically defined by the applicable state law; (3) whether the work taken as a whole lacks serious literary, artistic, political, or scientific value."

The new Miller decision differed from the previous Memoirs test in three significant areas. First, community standards, as opposed to national standards, are to be used. The court did not, however, specify what area it meant as "community." Second, the "utterly without redeeming social value" test became "lacks serious literary, artistic, political, or scientific value." This omits religious, entertainment, and educational genres and leaves more materials open to attack. Third, each state must specifically define the types of sexual conduct prohibited. Chief Justice Burger gave as an example: "(a) patently offensive representations or descriptions of masturbation, excretory functions, and lewd exhibition of the genitals; (b) patently offensive representations or descriptions of ultimate sexual acts, normal or perverted, actual or simulated."

In *Jenkins* v. *Georgia* (1974), the court, ruling that the film *Carnal Knowledge* was not obscene, declared that "community standards" may be those of the state but do not necessarily have to be representative of any specific geographical boundary; they may be the jury's "understanding of the community from which they come as to contemporary community standards." On the other hand, the court said juries do not have "unbridled discretion in determining what is 'patently offensive' " and can therefore be overruled on appeal (as here the decisions of the local and supreme courts of Georgia were reversed). The court said nudity alone is not obscene and prohibitions apply only to "public portrayal of hardcore sexual conduct for its own sake."

As a result of this and another 1974 decision, the legislatures of almost every state set about reviewing their own obscenity laws. They did so in the light of the sexual revolution of the last ten years or so and the controversial 1970 report of the distinguished Commission on Obscenity and Pornography, established by Congress. Concerning the effects of pornography, the commission declared:

The conclusion is that, for America, the relationship between the availability of erotica and changes in sex-crime rates neither proves nor disproves the possibility that availability of erotica leads to crime, but the massive overall increases in sex crimes that have been alleged do not seem to have occurred. . . . In sum, empirical research designed to clarify the question has found no evidence to date that exposure to explicit sexual materials is a factor in the causation of sex crime or sex delinquency.

In contrast to its recommendations affecting adults, the commission did recommend "legislative regulations upon the sale of sexual materials

Performer Liza Minelli, in a scene from an NBC television special. Although her "bumps and grinds" were torrid, they were adjudged appropriate for the production and were not cut. (Photo courtesy of National Broadcasting Company.)

to young persons who do not have the consent of their parents." The commission believed, however, that only pictorial material should be legally withheld from children.

In 1977 Larry Flynt, publisher of *Hustler* magazine, was convicted on a misdemeanor charge of pandering and on a felony charge of "engaging in organized crime" by a Cincinnati, Ohio, jury. He was sentenced to

25 years in prison and fined $11,000. Because *Hustler*'s content openly exceeded the limits set by competing sex-oriented magazines, many civil libertarians found it difficult to oppose the decision. A survey of the editors of men's and women's magazines disclosed that more than three out of four considered the conviction a threat to their magazines' First Amendment rights.

SEX AND GOOD TASTE

Television

Not only violence, but also lesbianism and other sexual deviations, nudity, explicitly portrayed seductions, daring feminine fashions, innuendos, and gutter language—and more—have become common in the mass media and American society during recent years, pleasing some but offending others. The result is what sociologist and columnist Max Lerner has described as a sort of "Babylonian society," where almost anything goes.

Whereas magazines and books are directed to select audiences, mostly adult, and the audiences viewing motion pictures and plays in theaters may largely be controlled, television enters practically every home and, of course, is viewed by young and old alike. Accordingly, the television industry has developed its own Television Code of Good Practice and seeks, with only mixed success, to follow its tenets. Adhering to the code, on a voluntary basis, has been the primary responsibility of individual stations and networks.

The department of broadcast standards of each network seeks to ensure that nothing is broadcast that exceeds generally accepted standards of public taste as represented by their huge national audiences. During a typical season, editors of each network make judgments on more than 2000 program outlines and scripts. They look at a variety of potential problems, including language, treatment of crime, use of narcotics, religious sensitivities, attitudes toward gambling and drunkenness, depiction of physical handicaps, the image of minorities, treatment of animals, and theatrical motion pictures and how they adapt to television. By far the most sensitive subjects are sex and violence.

Sexual subject matter is acceptable to most viewers when it is presented with taste and at times when children ordinarily are not watching. Much concern was expressed in 1977 over such sex-oriented shows as ABC's "Soap" and "Three's Company" and the double entendres and premarital sex situations built into other shows. One survey found that people worry most about sexual themes that seem to impinge on the welfare of their children or their own concepts of normal family life. Child exploitation and homosexuality were most objected to. Four out of five respondents, however, wanted to retain sex-related material on TV but at times when children were not watching, and with parents assuming responsibility. Few favored censorship, either by government or advertisers. The latter found themselves the objects of pressure applied by several organizations. Identified as among the leading sponsors of sex-oriented shows on television in 1977 were American Home Products (Anacin), Ford Motor Co., and Sears, Roebuck & Co.

Given the fact that television is constantly trying to please most of the people much of the time, without giving them more than they want, the medium has shown remarkable growth in intellectual freedom in recent years. Much of the maturation has gone virtually unnoticed because television has endeavored to keep pace with the reality of the nation's social growth. Twenty years ago such subjects as homosexuality, abortion, venereal disease, illegitimacy, and adultery were unheard of in television drama. Today they are the focus of many substantial and sensitively done dramatic programs.

"Those of us in network television particularly do not wish to see a slowdown in the legitimate expansion of programing boundaries," said Herminio Traviesas, vice-president in charge of broadcast standards for NBC-TV. "For while we do hear from our more conservative viewers, we also hear from the more liberal elements of our audience and, lest we forget, from the progressive people in the creative community. In a sense we are like Indians with our ears to the tube instead of to the ground. We are among the first to hear and witness new calls for greater freedom of expression. At the same time we are hearing complaints that television is going too far, too fast."

Radio

"Profanity, obscenity, smut, and vulgarity" are forbidden under the National Association of Broadcasters Radio Code, to which most radio operators subscribe. The Federal Communications Commission maintains a watchful ear for such aberrations from good programing and calls station managements to account at license renewal time if matters of sex and good taste have been violated.

During recent years, as controversial "call-in" shows have multiplied, a few stations encouraged late-night listeners openly to discuss their sex lives. This became known as "topless radio." Society's new permissive attitudes caused many listeners to accept such programs with equanimity;

others were shocked. The industry in general and the FCC in particular, however, criticized instances of extreme verbal candor to such an extent that the practice has largely been abandoned. One station, WGLD-FM, Oak Park, Illinois, was fined $2000 for a "Femme Forum" call-in show on oral sex. The use of a device that delays the broadcast of telephoned observations for seven seconds, giving announcers time to delete offending remarks from listeners, has been a major help with "call-in" shows.

Station WBAI-FM, New York, was disciplined by the FCC in 1978 for broadcasting George Carlin's "seven dirty words" comedy routine. The Supreme Court ruled that broadcasters do not have a constitutional right to air "obscene" words that apply to sex and excretion.

Highly suggestive sexual lyrics on records ("Do It to Me, Baby," "Do It Till You're Satisfied," "Can't Get Enough") have long been a part of the rock music scene. Fortunately for adults easily shocked, such records are heard almost entirely by the young, who seem to accept almost every suggestive lyric as a natural part of life. Adults and some youths, however, have strongly protested the airing of the worst of these songs. The matter came to full public attention in connection with lyrics that seemed to invite the use of drugs ("Sail on, silver girl . . . Like a bridge over troubled water I will ease your mind," which to some meant a hypodermic needle). Many groups recorded such songs, but at one time the Beatles drew the most wrath: "The Beatles are the leading pied pipers creating promiscuity, an epidemic of drugs, youth class-consciousness, and an atmosphere for social revolution," said one educator. "What the Beatles begin is imitated, and often expanded upon, by literally hundreds of other groups who in turn reach tens of millions of people."

The FCC, although it had no jurisdiction over the recording industry, warned broadcast stations that they would be held accountable for knowing the content of songs played on the air. Because of the ambiguity of certain references and the changing nature of youthful jargon, the policing of records to be played proved no easy task. The broadcasters sought to fix the blame on the recording industry, which in turn declared its innocence. The airing of antidrug records and commercials only partially alleviated the problem.

Films

For many years, criticism of commercial motion pictures focused on the artificial world they created. The vision of life presented in Hollywood films was far from everyday reality. It had excitement, glamour, romance, and comedy, but rarely paid attention to the squalid, perplexing problems of life. The filmmakers were selling noncontroversial entertainment featuring stars who had been blown up bigger than life by astute publicity. The major Hollywood studios, which dominated the market, had developed a successful formula and rarely deviated from it. Before television, they had no important rivals in presenting visual entertainment.

A limiting factor against realism on the screen was the highly restrictive censorship code, conceived and enforced by the producers' association as a result of scandals that besmirched some silent film stars in the 1920s. Pressure from the Catholic Legion of Decency and other policing groups strengthened enforcement of the code.

The taboos went to such extremes that a husband and his wife could not be shown together in the same bed. Mention of narcotics was forbidden. Criminals could not emerge as victors, although Hollywood made millions of dollars with gangster pictures full of violence by having the criminal lose at the last moment. A frequently heard claim that movies were aimed at the mentality of a twelve-year-old had much evidence to support it.

Shortly after World War II, Hollywood's attitude began changing. The postwar world wanted more realism. Television's rapidly developing lure was keeping potential moviegoers at home. Filmmakers realized that they needed to alter their approach. More daring producers started making films that dealt with narcotics and contained suggestive sex scenes. They placed their products in theaters without the supposedly essential code seal of approval and drew large audiences.

Eventually enforcement of the code broke down completely. The growing permissiveness of American society emboldened the filmmakers; the increasingly frank films they released in turn contributed to the trend. Several U.S. Supreme Court decisions greatly broadening the interpretation of what was permissible under the obscenity laws speeded up the process. So did the success of uninhibited films imported to this country, especially from Sweden. Although they were shown mostly in metropolitan "art" theaters, their impact on American filmmaking was intense.

The second half of the 1960s saw swift acceleration of boldness on the screen. Nude scenes became commonplace. Sexual situations that had been only hinted at a few years earlier were shown explicitly. An imported Swedish film, *I Am Curious (Yellow),* broke a barrier by showing actual scenes of sexual intercourse. Actresses and actors casually used language in films that was taboo in polite conversation a decade earlier. Films dealt with such themes as homosexuality, lesbianism, sadism, and other deviations from accepted norms. Greater liberality in these fields brought no reduction in the amount of violence shown, a major source of complaint by Europeans against American films. The complaints against motion pictures thus were reversed: Instead of being accused of sugar-coated blandness, they were charged with undue frankness. But with all its boldness, was American filmmaking being realistic? Many critics said no. They contended that, although such problems as homosexuality obviously existed, film producers were putting too much stress on them in order to cash in on shock value at the box office, and still were not coming to grips with the broader social problems of the country. They accused Hollywood of forcing moral looseness upon its audience, often to the embarrassment of theater patrons.

Anxious to preserve their profits from this new freedom and to prevent any government censorship moves, the Motion Picture Association of America adopted a new rating plan. Starting in 1968, each new Hollywood film was released bearing a code letter. This was to inform potential viewers what kind of picture to expect. The letter ratings were: G—for general audiences; M—for adults and mature young people (parents should decide if their children should attend); R—restricted, those under sixteen must be accompanied by a parent or adult guardian; X—those under sixteen not admitted.

Many producers quickly found it profitable to make films that barely stopped short of the X label, getting an R so the pictures could be shown to youth under sixteen when chaperoned. Some producers welcomed an X rating to reach an audience they found to exist for such material. Theater operators reported difficulty at times in finding an adequate supply of good-quality G films.

Largely because of misunderstanding as to the meaning of the word "mature," the M rating was changed in 1970 to PG—all ages admitted, parental guidance suggested. In addition, the age limit for the R category was raised from sixteen to seventeen, and the same change was made for the X category. In some areas, the age limit may vary, according to choice of theater owners.

Jack Valenti, president of the Motion Picture Association of America, has attempted to explain what determines each individual rating:

G: General audiences. All ages admitted. This is a film which contains nothing in theme, language, nudity and sex, or violence that would be offensive to parents whose younger children view the film. . . . No words with sexual connotation are present in G-rated films. The violence is at minimum. Nudity and sex scenes are not present.

PG: Parental guidance suggested; some material may not be suitable for pre-teenagers. . . . There may be profanity in these films but certain words with strong sexual meanings will vault a PG rating into the R category. There may be violence but it is not deemed excessive. Cumulative man-to-man violence or on-the-screen dismemberment may take a film into the R category. There is no explicit sex on the screen although there may be some indication of sensuality. Fleeting nudity may appear in PG-rated films, but anything beyond that point puts the film into R.

R: Restricted, under 17's require accompanying parent or guardian. . . . This is an adult film in some of its aspects and treatment of language, violence or nudity and sex. . . . The language may be rough, the violence may be hard, and while explicit intercourse is not found in R-rated films, nudity and lovemaking may be depicted.

X: No one under 17 admitted. . . . This is patently an adult film and no children are allowed to attend. It should be noted, however, that X does not necessarily mean obscene or pornographic. Serious films by lauded and skilled filmmakers may be rated X.

By using the new code, the filmmakers placed the responsibility of censorship upon the audience, rather than upon themselves. They seemed to have discovered a profitable solution to the competition from television, which because of its home audience was more cautious in selection of material than theater operators were. Many newspapers, however, either refused to print advertisements for X-rated movies or placed severe restrictions upon their content.

Undoubtedly the revolution in American films had made them better related to the realities of life, more experimental and stimulating, and more influential in shaping the country's social patterns, especially among people under thirty. Independent producers now were better able to get their films, often uncommercial by the old standards, before the public. Whether the latent resistance among many Americans would curb the extremes to which some filmmakers were going was still uncertain.

THE MEDIA AND THE INDIVIDUAL

Free Press, Fair Trial

The reporting of arrests and trials, especially in crimes of a sensational nature, came under attack from the American Bar Association (ABA) and certain civil rights groups during the 1960s. This development coincided with an increasing concern by the U.S. Supreme Court about the rights of defendants. Editors were accused by their critics of "trying the case in the newspapers" and printing or airing material prejudicial to the defendant.

In 1968, the ABA house of delegates adopted guidelines prepared by a special committee to restrict the reporting of crime news. The guidelines are known as the Reardon report, after the committee chairman, Associate Judge Paul C. Reardon of the Supreme Judicial Court of Massachusetts. Newspaper people protested that the attorneys had overstepped their role and were trying to sabotage freedom of the press. Eventually a press-bar committee, set up through the American Society of Newspaper Editors, resolved much of the conflict. Under court and ABA pressures, the newspapers grew more cautious about what they printed concerning a crime and the suspects before the matter reached trial. Broadcast newspeople took similar precautions. In addition, the police now became reluctant to disclose the facts of a crime to reporters—information ordinarily given freely in the past. And with the enactment in 1975 of federal Law Enforcement Assistance Administration regulations restricting public release of arrest records, charges, and many types of court records and criminal history data, law officers began to withhold even more information.

For many years courts have forbidden the reporting of trials by print photographers, television cameramen, and radio newspeople operating tape recorders. In order to improve public awareness of legal procedures, however, courts in seven states—Alabama, Colorado, Florida, Georgia, Kentucky, New Hampshire, and Washington—in the latter half of the 1970s began permitting TV and still photo coverage of trials. In Florida, the practice began when television covered the trial of Ronny Zamora, 15, whose attorneys unsuccessfully argued that the youth had been driven to kill a woman through insanity induced by "involuntary subliminal television intoxication"—a lifetime spent in viewing violence on TV.

In nontrial settings, numerous state legislatures have authorized television coverage, the House of Representatives has opened its doors to radio and television under controlled conditions, and network officials have urged the Supreme Court to follow suit.

Libel and Slander

One constant challenge confronting the comunications media is to avoid libeling or slandering individuals or easily identifiable groups. Laws designed to protect persons from unfair and damaging attacks create well-defined limits as to what may be broadcast or printed without risking legal action and possibly heavy financial losses.

Defamation is communication that exposes people to hatred, ridicule, or contempt; lowers them in the esteem of their fellows; causes them to be shunned; or injures them in their business or calling. Its categories are libel, mainly printed or written material; and slander, mainly spoken words. In some states broadcast defamation is considered libel and in others slander; material read from a script generally is considered libel and that which is extemporaneous is usually held to be slander.

Some defamation is considered privileged, such as statements made on the official record during court trials and public meetings of government bodies. For example, council member Jones may call council member Smith "a liar and a thief" during an official session, and the allegation may be safely broadcast or published because it is privileged by law. However, if Jones should make such a statement about Smith in the corridor after the meeting adjourns, the newspaper or broadcast station that reports it would risk a libel or slander suit from Smith unless it could prove that the charge was true.

The basic defenses in a defamation action are truth, proof of privilege, that the statement constituted fair comment and criticism, that the publication was made innocently and without malice, and the publication of a retraction. A retraction actually is an admission of guilt, but its publication generally lessens the amount of any money awarded as damages to the plaintiff.

Historically, the libel and slander laws have protected individuals or small groups of easily identified persons, but not large, amorphous groups. There is pressure now to enlarge protection to cover broader groups, such as ethnic minorities, but the difficulty in writing such laws has discouraged their adoption.

A landmark case in broadening the media's right to comment was the Supreme Court ruling in *New York Times* v. *Sullivan* in 1964. The court held that a public official cannot recover damages for a defamatory falsehood relating to his or her official conduct unless he or she proves that the statement was made with actual malice. This and related rulings have broadened the interpretation of "public official" to include relatively minor public employees and even "public figures" such as former officeholders and prominent personalities.

The Supreme Court in *Rosenbloom* v. *Metromedia* in 1971 extended the Sullivan ruling to include a private person involved in an event of public interest. However, in *Gertz* v. *Welch* in 1974, the court seemed to reverse its position. In a 5 to 4 decision, the court held that a "private person," regardless of involvement in a public event, might recover such actual damages as could be proved for injury or harm resulting from publication of a defamatory falsehood, without proof of actual malice by the libeler, but with proof of negligence as determined by a state standard. The Colorado Supreme Court in 1975 became the first state high court to accept the ruling. Using the "reckless disregard" standard, the judges reviewed seven articles published in the Colorado Springs *Sun* and awarded an antique dealer actual and punitive damages for allegations that he had purchased stolen merchandise.

In *Firestone* v. *Time Inc.,* the Supreme Court ruled in 1976 that the wife of Russell Firestone III, scion of a prominent industrial family, was not a "public figure," even though she was a pillar of Palm Beach, Florida, society and held press conferences during her celebrated divorce trial. She won a $100,000 libel suit against *Time* magazine for incorrectly reporting that her husband had been granted a divorce from her on grounds of extreme cruelty and adultery.

The decision unnerved news media executives and lawyers, occurring as it did during a period when more than 500 libel suits were being filed each year and juries seemed willing to compensate plaintiffs for their injuries with large judgments. With expenses ranging up to $100,000 or more per case, even when won, fears mounted that the threat of such high costs would make the news media more timid in the pursuit of news.

Right of Privacy

Closely allied to libel and slander is the question of which is more important, the privacy of the individual or the privilege of the press? The right of privacy, perhaps the most cherished right of all, is guaranteed, but more and more it is coming into conflict in the courts with the First Amendment right freely to report news.

As previously discussed, public figures such as politicians, entertainers, and athletes give up their right to privacy in return for being public figures. But how much right to privacy does a person who is not a public figure have when that right conflicts with the rights of the press? Such privacy rights have been obtained through a series of judicial rulings in this century.

An individual's privacy may be violated by depicting that person in a "false light," an action that is close to but separate from libel law, and by publicly disclosing private facts about private persons. In a 1975 case pertaining to the latter, the Supreme Court struck down a Georgia law that made it a misdeameanor to print or broadcast the name of a rape victim. Following a court hearing for six youths accused of raping a seventeen-year-old girl who subsequently died presumably from rape-related trauma, an Atlanta television station used the girl's name in a newscast. Claiming serious disruption of the family's privacy, the girl's father filed suit. The Georgia courts upheld the father as a matter of law, and the TV station appealed.

Although the Supreme Court found in favor of Cox Broadcasting Corporation, it would not go so far as to make truth an absolute defense in invasion of privacy cases. The court held that "once true information is disclosed in public court documents open to public inspection, the press cannot be sanctioned for publishing it." The court then dampened the ruling somewhat by stating that it was confining its judgment to "the narrower interface between press and privacy" involved in printing the name of a rape victim rather than "the broader question whether truthful publications may ever be subjected to civil or criminal liability."

Despite the ruling, Georgia editors and broadcast news directors were quick to point out that they would continue to exercise great care in deciding whether it was necessary to report the names of rape victims.

Media lawyers hope that eventually the court will permit the publication of any and all information about individuals unless clear and convincing proof can be shown that such information is false and that the communicator either knew it was false or acted in "reckless disregard" of the facts—the test laid out in the *New York Times* v. *Sullivan* case.

The Privacy Act of 1974 stipulated types of information about individuals that could not be disclosed by federal agencies and provided means whereby persons could determine the nature of information about themselves in official files. A Privacy Protection Study Commission, created by the act, undertook a two-year study of the application of the law and submitted a 654-page report to President Carter in 1977. The report listed five "competing social values" that must be taken into account in protecting personal privacy: First Amendment, freedom of information, and law enforcement interests; the cost of privacy protection; and federal-state relations.

The commission recommended no action be taken that would affect the ability of the press to request or obtain information. The body did suggest, however, that medical records be kept strictly confidential and that it be considered a crime to seek such information through misrepresentation or deception.

Further restrictions on the news-gathering function of the media were imposed when the federal Law Enforcement Assistance Administration decreed in 1975 that, effective December 31, 1977, if a state or community wanted federal money for collecting, storing, or disseminating criminal history records, policies would have to be enacted limiting the release of such information. That meant that about the only information available to the public and the media would be police station "blotter" lists that are organized chronologically. The only way to obtain noncurrent records would be to have available the name of the person and the date of the arrest or court record.

The restrictions brought strong protests from media organizations and, in 1976, the LEAA decided to leave the matter up to individual states. Some states have adopted restrictive or modified policies; others have liberal dissemination plans, usually because an open record or "sunshine" law covers criminal history or arrest records; and some, with no plan, must follow the LEAA revised policies calling for open release of conviction data and restricted release of nonconviction information.

Copyright

On January 1, 1978, a comprehensive copyright revision law, described by Congressional leaders as "the greatest advance in copyright legislation in our nation's history," went into effect.

For more than two decades Congress had endeavored to revise the amended copyright law of 1909, which rapidly became outdated by advances in technology. The development of modern photocopying machines, cable television, and the computer had raised serious and complex problems primarily affecting authors, performers, book and magazine publishers and distributors, libraries, educational institutions, cable television broadcasters, and motion picture and other audiovisual program suppliers.

Copyright is the exclusive right to reproduce, publish, and sell the matter and form of a literary, musical, or artistic work. Designed to encourage the creation and dissemination of original works to the public, copyright was originally established by statute in England in 1556. Prior to that time, the only protection was under common law. The United States had recognized common law copyright, which protected works before publication. The new law, however, established a single system of copyright protection for all copyrightable works, whether published or unpublished.

The law extended copyright protection from the present maximum of 56 years to the life of the author plus 50 years. For works made for hire and copyrighted by others, as well as anonymous material, the new term is 75 years from publication or 100 years from creation, whichever is shorter.

The measure provides for the payment, under a system of compulsory licensing, of certain royalties for the secondary transmission of copyrighted works on cable television systems. The fees are based on the amount of distant nonnetwork programing carried and on subscriber receipts. The assessments are paid to the Register of Copyrights for later distribution to the copyright owners by a newly established copyright royalty tribunal.

The law permits archives and libraries, such as Vanderbilt University's TV news archives, to copy news programs for lending to researchers. The borrowers are restricted from using copies for profit or politics. An American TV and Radio Archives was established in the Library of Congress for collecting, cataloging, and lending broadcast news and entertainment programs.

Noncommercial transmissions by public broadcasters of published musical and graphic works are subject to a compulsory license, thus eliminating the paperwork and legal costs of negotiation for the rights to such broadcast material. Public broadcasters are urged to negotiate their own royalty rates.

One section of the law recognizes the principle of "fair use" as a limitation on the exclusive rights of copyright owners. Within certain prescribed limits, copies may be made for purposes such as criticism, comment, news reporting, teaching (including multiple copies for classroom use), scholarship, or research. Libraries are permitted to make single copies of copyrighted works, also under stringent limitations.

The new law retains the provisions added to the former law in 1972 that accord protection against the unauthorized duplication of sound recordings. Compulsory licensing is provided for the recording of music.

The law removes the former exemption for performances of copyrighted music by jukeboxes. It substitutes a system of compulsory licensing based upon the payment by jukebox operators of an annual royalty fee to the Register of Copyrights for distribution to copyright owners.

Copyright secures only the property right in the manner and content of expression. Facts and ideas recited, or systems and processes described, are made freely available to the public. Although news itself is in the public domain and uncopyrightable, news accounts per se—that is, their particular literary arrangement—may be copyrighted, especially when they bear the mark of individual enterprise and literary style. "The Evening News With Walter Cronkite," for example, is copyrighted. Feature stories, editorials, columns, series of articles, cartoons, maps, photographs, and the like may be copyrighted. Newspapers generally copyright entire editions, by issue or weekly or monthly, in order to protect their advertising from piracy, although the copyright of an advertisement created solely by the advertiser may be retained by that person or company.

For infringement of copyright, courts may award statutory damages ranging from $250 to $10,000. In addition to or instead of a fine, conviction for criminal infringement carries a sentence of up to one year in prison.

Copies of the new statute are available free of charge from the Copyright Office, Library of Congress, Washington, D.C. 20559.

ACCESS TO THE MEDIA

The role of the mass media in influencing important public policy decisions, in maintaining or changing the status quo of our society, and in general in providing outlets for all types of views is enormous. So great is the impact of the media today that it has become common, though it is ungrammatical, to use the plural word "media" in the singular ("The media does this"). Gaining access to such a powerful force is the goal of innumerable business firms, ethnic organizations, labor leaders, consumers, government officials, and other special interest groups. All realize that much can be gained or lost through what is printed or broadcast in the nation's communications media.

Because of the theory that "the airwaves belong to the people," special interest groups have met with greater success in obtaining access to radio and over-the-air and cable television than to the print media.

Newspapers
In 1969 Jerome A. Barron, law professor at George Washington University, proposed a new concept of the First Amendment in relation to newspapers. Pointing out that in the *New York Times* v. *Sullivan* case the Supreme Court had created a new relative freedom from libel for newspapers by the way it had interpreted the First Amendment, Barron said similar techniques could be used to fashion a right of access to the press for the public:

If this approach does not work, then a carefully worded right of access statute which would aim at achieving a meaningful expression of divergent opinions should be attempted. The point is that we must realize that private restraints on free expression have become so powerful that the belief that there is a free marketplace where ideas will naturally compete is as hopelessly outmoded as the theory of perfect competition has generally become in most other spheres of modern life.

In 1974 the Florida Supreme Court, in *Miami Herald Co.* v. *Pat L. Tornillo,* upheld a state law requiring that newspapers give "right of reply" space to political candidates criticized by newspapers. The U.S. Supreme Court, however, unanimously overturned the decision, its opinion reading in part as follows:

The Florida statute fails to clear the barriers of the First Amendment because of its intrusion into the function of editors. A newspaper is more than a passive receptacle or conduit for news, comment, and advertising. The choice of material . . . the treatment of public issues and public officials—whether fair or unfair—constitutes the exercise of editorial control or judgment. It has yet to be demonstrated how government regulation of this process can be exercised consistent with First Amendment guarantees of a free press as they have evolved to this time.

Newspaper editors long have sought to obtain replies from possibly maligned individuals, companies, and institutions both before and after the printing of controversial stories. Letters to the editor columns traditionally have been open to all readers. A number of newspapers have solicited articles from the public to run in the columns opposite their main editorial pages.

Recognizing the pressures for greater access to their publications, however, many newspapers more recently have employed ombudsmen or assigned certain staff members to consider complaints; have endeavored to establish local and state press councils and given support to the recently established National News Council; and have hired reporters and editors from minority groups who bring with them the special attitudes of their communities. But the editors insist that the final decision as to what is printed must be theirs alone. Others call attention to the fact that today's technology permits persons with only limited capital to start their own newspapers.

About the only infringement upon publishers' prerogatives in recent years has been the federal requirement that in classified advertising male and female notices may no longer be kept separate.

Broadcasting

By contrast, broadcasters have had to contend with a multiplicity of efforts to gain access and influence what is aired: the fairness doctrine;

threats by minority groups and others to take over their licenses; the necessity every three years (broadcasters want to extend this period to five years) to prove that they have ascertained community interests and have been operating for the public good; bans on cigarette, postal service, and armed forces advertising; "countercommercials," the airing of viewpoints replying to commercial spots; attacks on television documentaries; demands by citizen groups to provide special programing; network antitrust suits; efforts to reduce televised violence and children's advertising and to maintain good taste in programing; the control of prime-time program segments; access to cable channels; the staging of demonstrations and other "pseudo-events" to gain news attention ("Just do your thing; the press eats it up. Media is free. *Make news,*" proclaimed Yippie Abbie Hoffman). It is small wonder that the broadcaster is harried, but that is the price that must be paid for the prestige, pride in community involvement, and substantial profits that are attained in the broadcast world.

During the last decade, minority groups have applied consistent pressure against station managements in efforts to achieve more programing of special interest to them, to have minorities presented favorably in existing programs, and to have greater ethnic representation on station staffs. These groups obtain agreements from individual stations and they also seek policy changes from the FCC and Congress, in part because of commission and federal court encouragement over the years and in part from an increasing awareness that broadcasters and the government often respond to pressure. Action before the FCC consists principally of participation in license renewal procedures, either as petitioners to deny or as parties to agreements that head off litigation. Many such groups form local coalitions in dealing with broadcasters,

Other special interest groups, such as Accuracy in Media (AIM), join in suits against both the networks and individual media in efforts to promote their causes if voluntary action to alter programing practices cannot be obtained. A discussion of the threats action groups make to the economic security of broadcasters is provided in Chapter 8.

Cable television and public broadcasting are the avenues most open to individuals and special interest groups. More than 20 percent of the cable systems originate some local programing and they welcome community participation.

The assurance that diverse viewpoints will have access to the media and the removal of all barriers to the introduction of new communications technology were among the goals set by Lionel Van Deerlin, chairman of the House Communications Subcommittee, in the committee's efforts, begun in 1977, to accomplish a "basement-to-penthouse" rewriting of the Communications Act of 1934, considered outmoded by modern developments.

The Fairness Doctrine

For many of the nation's broadcasters, one specific legal requirement—the "fairness doctrine"—has had the effect of discouraging coverage of many important social issues. Since 1949, broadcasters had been obligated to offer reasonable opportunity for opposing sides to respond to the coverage of controversial public issues. This statutory requirement to be "fair" was based on two legal philosophies not relevant to print media: (1) the airwaves are public property; and (2) broadcasters are licensed to operate in the "public interest, convenience, and necessity." Public interest is served, the Congress and the FCC have ruled, if the airwaves are made accessible to many differing viewpoints.

Most broadcasting leaders took issue with the fairness principles, charging that the doctrine abridged freedom of speech and press traditionally applied to electronic media by forcing the presentation of various sides of an issue, even when the views may be unfounded, untrue, or hard to identify in a local community. Even more annoying to broadcasters was the "personal attack" clause of the fairness doctrine. This clause said that if an individual is attacked in an editorial or program, a script or tape of the attack had to be sent to him or her, with an offer of a reasonable opportunity to reply. Furthermore, if the licensee endorsed or opposed legal candidates for office in an editorial statement, the same notice and offer of time had to be made within twenty-four hours after the program was aired.

The industry considered the clause unconstitutional, a violation of freedom of the press. Its effect would be to curtail meaningful discussion of issues because of the expense involved in offering time for reply and because the licensee would avoid controversial issues if uncertain about the freedom to comment.

The Supreme Court did not agree with the broadcasters; in 1969 it held the personal attack rules constitutional, noting that "it is the right of the viewers and listeners, not the right of the broadcasters, which is paramount" in such instances. If broadcasters were not willing to present representative community views on controversial issues, Justice Byron White of the court wrote, the granting or renewal of a license might be challenged. To make this threat of a license loss, he continued, "is consistent with the ends and purposes of those constitutional provisions forbidding the abridgement of freedom of speech and freedom of the press." In law circles, this became known as the "Red Lion" decision (*Red Lion Broadcasting Co. v. Federal Communications Commission*).

The Federal Communications Commission has been confronted with fairness questions covering a wide spectrum of material ranging from news and public affairs programs to commercials and political broadcasts. Its rulings have raised serious questions concerning the criteria for fairness. What is reasonable balance in the presentation of opposing views? How does a government agency determine whether a viewpoint is favorable, unfavorable, or neutral? In what amount of time, at what hour, and to what audience should an opposing viewpoint be presented? And the larger question: Should the government be involved in such matters at all? and, if so, how extensively?

Broadcasters have continued to oppose the doctrine as inhibiting the free flow of ideas, and measures have been introduced in Congress to eliminate the requirement. Many who now favor the doctrine have expressed the viewpoint that, once an abundance of electronic channels permits the airing of many viewpoints on controversial issues, the requirement should be eliminated.

Countercommercials

The reinterpretation of the First Amendment establishing the right of access to the airwaves by viewers and listeners resulted in a movement to require the running of countercommercials presenting points of view opposing those expressed by advertisers. The groundwork was laid when the FCC in 1967 decided that cigarette advertising came under the fairness doctrine and stations had to carry enough antismoking messages to counterbalance cigarette commercials. Congress banned all cigarette commercials in 1971, but some antismoking messages continued.

The ecology-oriented Friends of the Earth and other consumer groups then reasoned that, if cigarette commercials could be banned, why not also extend the fairness doctrine to include commercials for other products they considered deleterious to society? The networks replied that commercials for cigarettes were a special case since they had been determined by the Surgeon General to be dangerous to health and linked by numerous studies to such diseases as lung cancer and heart damage. To extend the fairness doctrine to include advertising of products ranging from detergents to gasoline would mean, the networks said, branding most areas of commercial selling as qualifying for debate as public issues. Advertisers would withdraw their advertising, and if a

Women and minority group representatives have risen to prominence in the mass media in recent years. Among them are Connie Chung, Los Angeles correspondent for CBS-TV; Judy Woodruff, White House reporter for NBC-TV; and Carl Rowan, syndicated columnist and television panelist. (Photos courtesy of Columbia Broadcasting System, National Broadcasting Company, and Field Newspaper Syndicate.)

number of counteradvertisements had to be provided free of charge, the networks and individual stations could not survive financially.

Nevertheless, the Federal Trade Commission asked the FCC to force radio and TV stations to offer time—even free time—to almost anyone who wanted to challenge the contents of commercials. Consumer groups asked the FCC to require stations to run "right to reply" messages countering commercials that touched on controversial "public issues," such as pollution. The FCC, however, agreed with the broadcasters that requiring countercommercials would violate the anti-censorship provision of the Communications Act.

Employment of Minorities and Women

In 1967 the National Advisory Commission on Civil Disorders charged the news media with failure to communicate the complex problem of race relations in America (see Chapter 6). Among several suggested remedies, the commission urged that more black journalists be hired and promoted to policymaking positions.

More than a decade later, despite efforts by media managers, less than 1 percent of the newspaper and 3 percent of the broadcast media staffs were minorities, a University of Michigan researcher reported. The news profession has been "shockingly backward" in seeking out, hiring, training, and promoting blacks, according to Robert Maynard, a member of the Washington *Post*'s editorial board. The American Society of Newspaper Editors' committee on minorities found the newspaper situation "deplorable"—both in the employment of minorities and in the reporting of minority activities.

Concerted efforts were made by almost all the media during the early 1970s to employ more minority persons. In the mid-1970s the Federal Communications Commission reported the rate of increase per year by broadcast media at about 9 percent, and the Office of Communications of the United Church of Christ reported that commercial television appeared to be hiring women and minority group members as replacements for whites and men who left their jobs. Recent studies, however, indicate a leveling off of minority employment. And, despite determined efforts, the proportion of minorities enrolled in university journalism courses had not yet reached 4 percent.

In the newspaper field urban newsrooms have employed the most blacks; in 1977, for example, the Washington *Post* had 34 black professionals, about 10 percent of its staff, as compared with 18, representing

5.7 percent, in 1972. However, most small newspapers, the traditional training ground for journalists, were adding comparatively few minority professionals. And on newspapers of all sizes few minority journalists held middle- and top-management positions. Only one daily white newspaper, the Akron, Ohio, *Beacon-Journal,* employed a black managing editor in 1977.

The FCC has been applying equal-opportunity pressures to broadcast stations, but the U.S. Commission on Civil Rights, in a 1977 report entitled, "Window Dressing on the Set: Women and Minorities in Television," said the commission had not been pushing hard enough. The report charged that women generally play dependent, subservient roles in TV programs and that minorities appear primarily in ethnic settings or as "tokens" in all-white shows. The FCC replied that it could not deal with such a complex and subjective concept as stereotyping without becoming deeply involved in a review of broadcast programing.

The problem of minority ownership of broadcast stations also has been adjudged acute. With only a few stations owned by blacks, the House of Representatives considered a bill to permit the Small Business Administration to exceed its $500,000 limit in loans to minority interests for the purchase of broadcast stations and cable systems.

Women have made substantial inroads into the work force of newspaper newsrooms. During one recent 5-year period, it was estimated that the number of women in such news jobs rose 65 percent. More than four of every ten writers, editors, and supervisors in the New York *Times'* Sunday department are women. However, a 1977 Indiana University survey revealed that the daily newspaper industry appears to rank behind other employers in the proportion of women employed as managers— about one woman manager per newspaper. Salaries for women also were found to be lower than those for men.

McLUHAN'S "HOT" AND "COOL" MEDIA

A new level of confrontation between print and electronic media developed in the 1960s as the theories of Marshall McLuhan, a professor of English and director of the Center for Culture and Technology at the University of Toronto, evoked widespread attention and controversy. His books, *The Gutenberg Galaxy* (1962), *Understanding Media* (1964), and *The Medium Is the Massage* (1967), coupled with extensive lecture and television appearances, projected McLuhan as the prophet of a new age of electronics in which the medium, in his opinion, is more important than the message and conventional values less relevant than "depth involvement."

In his work McLuhan has carried forward explorations of various earlier observers. Among them was the late Harold Innis, whose *Empire and Communications* (1950) and *The Bias of Communication* (1951) analyzed the relationship of media to power structures, beginning with those of ancient times.

McLuhan declares that each new medium alters our psychic environment, imposing on us a particular pattern of perceiving and thinking that controls us to an extent we scarcely suspect. For example, the written language, mass-produced by print, became the main cultural transmission belt for many generations. Knowledge and ideas were necessarily processed into the linear, one-step-at-a-time form required by the medium. Man was thus pushed into sequential habits of thinking that are quite unlike the complexity and richness and all-at-onceness of face-to-face communication, and without the resonance of the human voice.

Today, however, the electronic media have restored the resonance (radio) and reintroduced the complexity and all-at-onceness (film, television), and have done it on a scale that gives the world potentially a tribal unity. McLuhan sees modern men and women in a state of shock, unable to adjust to the rapidly changing state of communication and clinging to linear habits in an all-at-once world. Given to puns and a measure of flippancy, McLuhan insists not only that "the medium is the *message*" (that is, more important in itself than what is transmitted) but also that "the medium is the *massage*" (that is, it "roughs up and massages" our senses, altering the environment of our preelectronic world).

Two key terms in McLuhanese are "hot" and "cool." The cooler the medium, the more information must be supplied by the audience, and that is why wide-screen movies are "hot" and a fuzzy television picture is "cool." The more information the audience supplies, the more involved it becomes, and television has given its audience a sense of "depth involvement" more far-reaching than any previous medium, McLuhan believes. "When you go to the movies," he states, "you are the camera, but when you watch TV, you are the screen. The image is not projected from you, but charges at you. The movies were an extrovert orgy, but television is a depth experience." Movies were hot when

Humphrey Bogart made them, but television cools them down into an art form, he insists.

Since television demands involvement, children carry the habit of participation away from the TV set and into the classroom. Accustomed to incomplete and even chaotic images on television, children are quick at making connections on the basis of partly sensed patterns. They are busy "data processing," and may be the hardest-worked generation in history. In watching TV, they form the habit of looking for the reaction, not the action, and they find the step-by-step method of classroom teaching a bore. "Today's children are reluctant to interrupt their education by going to school," McLuhan declares, picking up an observation attributed to the late George Bernard Shaw.

McLuhan's disciples believe that his theories explain the insistence of much of today's youth on becoming involved in solving social problems rather than merely preparing for jobs and traditional life roles; on actively seeking to alter customary methods of education, such as the lecture; and on refusing (or being unable) to categorize individuals by race, religion, economic and social condition, and the like (since all peoples are bound together by instant communication, the family circle has widened, and we have extreme concern about everyone else's lives).

Critics charge that his theories are confusing, illogical, mystical, and lacking in documentation. They deplore his "pop-art intellectualism," his puns, and his seeming call for a return to the jungle, for the abandonment of print-based civilization as we have known it. McLuhan retorts that he is merely an investigator and explorer of ideas trying to persuade us to think about the changes in our environment caused by successive mass media, and that he sees no need to offer logical explanations.

By the 1970s the excitement generated by McLuhan's far-reaching theories had died down somewhat, but his ideas were still being reviewed in mass communication classrooms and in scholarly circles in many countries.

CRITICISMS OF ADVERTISING

The powerful consumer movement in the United States has drawn a sharp bead on advertising within the last several years and sought federal sanctions against what it considers to be social ills encouraged by many industry practices. Through advertising, it is maintained, companies enjoy a virtual monopoly on the kind of information available to consumers. Consumers are not exposed to contrasting viewpoints and are deprived of the diversity of opinion necessary for informed choices.

This imbalance puts human and social interest second to private and political interests. Moreover, it is alleged, much advertising is deceptive and untruthful.

Under particular attack has been the advertising of cigarettes ("harmful to health"), over-the-counter drugs ("encouraging serious drug abuse"), gasoline, automobiles, soap and detergents ("making misleading environmental claims"), and products used by children, such as toys and breakfast cereals ("misleading and falsifying").

The Federal Trade Commission was given vast new powers to regulate business conduct with enactment of the FTC Improvement Act of 1975. Already the FTC had moved against what it termed "unfairness" in advertising, thus extending its powers to the more subjective area of the impression created by an advertisement rather than its literal truth. Its first citations were made against advertising in behalf of Wonder Bread, Lysol spray disinfectant, and Bayer, Anacin, and Excedrin analgesics. Consent agreements that "corrective" notices would be incorporated in advertisements were obtained against such products as Profile Bread and Ocean Spray cranberry juice. Under another consent agreement, six major cigarette manufacturers agreed to place conspicuous health warnings in their advertising. FTC orders requiring the public documentation of advertising claims were directed against manufacturers of such products as automobiles, air conditioners, toothpastes, and cough and cold remedies.

The FTC asked the Federal Communications Commission to require broadcast stations to run counteradvertising requested by public interest groups, but the FCC declined to do so, contending that such action would amount to "a tortured or distorted application of fairness doctrine principles." Nevertheless, the FTC in 1978 was considering pressing harder for countercommercials, particularly those, aired during viewing times popular with children, that would tell them how sweet foods can injure teeth.

Such countercommercials were among several actions contemplated by the commission in response to a petition by Action for Children's Television seeking an outright ban on commercials for products that many persons consider harmful to children's health, notably candy and presweetened cereal. In 1976, acting on another ACT petition, the FTC had issued a consent order barring Hudson Pharmaceutical Corporation from advertising its Spider-Man brand vitamins in comic books or on TV programs aimed at children. The commission said the use of the popular Spider-Man figure "can induce children to take excessive amounts of vitamins which can be dangerous to your health."

In its deliberations the FTC was mindful of a Supreme Court decision in 1976 overturning a Virginia ban against prescription-drug advertising and flatly asserting First Amendment protection for "commercial speech." "Speech is not stripped of First Amendment protection merely because it appears in the form of a paid advertisement," wrote Justice Harry Blackmun. The landmark decision, in *Virginia State Board of Pharmacy* v. *Virginia Citizens Consumer Council,* meant that all government restraints on advertisers would be subject to court reappraisals.

After children's advertising came under strong consumer attack, the broadcast industry instituted reforms, which the FCC incorporated into a policy statement. Satisfied with this action, broadcasters indicated they would resist any further FTC restrictions involving children's advertising on television.

Meanwhile, the advertising industry established a National Advertising Review Board and 20 local boards to examine complaints of possibly misleading or fraudulent advertising. In addition, the Council of Better Business Bureaus established its own National Advertising Division and required companies to substantiate advertising claims.

In numerous governmental hearings, industry leaders strongly defended the social and economic values of advertising. They warned that imposing broad restrictions on all advertising because of the misleading or deceptive content of some would destroy the integrity of the marketing process and the need to foster public confidence in the free enterprise system— which some saw as the real target of the most militant consumer advocates. The House of Representatives blunted the consumer drive in 1978 when it defeated a bill to establish an Agency for Consumer Representation.

Other criticisms of advertising have been made. Some of the more common complaints and the replies that have been made to each are these: (1) *Advertising persuades us to buy goods and services we cannot afford.* Persuasion is present, but never coercion; it is up to each of us to exercise self-control and sound judgment in our purchases. (2) *Advertising appeals primarily to our emotions rather than to our intellect.* Since all of us are motivated largely by emotional drives, it is only natural that advertisers should make such appeals. Again, a cautious buyer will avoid obvious appeals to his or her emotions. (3) *Advertising is biased.* This, too, is natural; all persons put their best foot forward in whatever they say or do. Being aware of this bias, we can discount some of the superlatives used in advertising. (4) *Advertising involves conflicting competitive claims.* But advertising is "out in the open," never hidden as are some forms of propaganda, and we can decide for ourselves. (5) *Advertising is unduly repetitious.* That is because the public is essentially a passing parade, not a mass gathering; there are always new users whom the appeal has never reached. And slogans like "It Floats" have sold goods successfully for generations. (6) *Much advertising is vulgar, obtrusive, irritating.* Actually, only a handful of advertisers employ poor taste in their appeals; their excesses damage the higher standards of the many. And the very nature of radio and television, whose commercials cannot easily be turned off, accounts for much irritation; this complaint is seldom voiced in relation to printed advertising, which can be ignored.

There are still other criticisms relating primarily to the role of advertising itself rather than to its content. Certain economists, especially those who nourish the vision of a planned, controlled society, have charged that advertising is wasteful and unnecessary, adding to the cost of goods and services. This is true when business uses the advertising tool foolishly or for the purpose of maintaining an inflexible high price on a product. But as a general criticism, it is answered with the statement that advertising serves a socially desirable purpose.

Other criticisms are directed at advertising by those who fear that their very lives are being manipulated by clever and unscrupulous Madison Avenue word-wizards whose only objective is to sell goods and ideas regardless of the social consequences. These critics are generally intellectual men and women who resist classification among the masses at whom the communications media are directed. Their intense desire to think and act of their own volition in an increasingly monolithic world leads them to attack advertising—"mass" by its very nature—at every turn, with little thought of the inevitable consequences of a society in which advertising became unduly shackled.

Many opinion leaders consider advertising to be almost wholly devoid of ethics. Frederic Wakeman's 1946 best seller, *The Hucksters,* spawned a series of anti-advertising novels. Advertisers and the broadcast industry shared blame for the rigged quiz shows and the disc jockey payola scandals of the late 1950s, the latter emerging again as a problem in the mid 1970s. The image of the earnest young man-about-Madison-Avenue complete with gray flannel suit, attaché case, sincere smile, and lavish expense account is not one to inspire confidence. Set against the background of yesterday's patent medicine quackery, extravagant advertising, and the laissez faire doctrine of *caveat emptor* and today's allegations of misleading drug and socially harmful cigarette advertising, the bill of indictments is devastating.

Add to this the question of good taste in broadcasting—the jarring loudness of some commercials, the so-called insulting and obnoxious advertisements, the cramming of too many commercials into segments of broadcast time, and the clutter and length of some TV program credit crawls—and it is perhaps understandable that critics of advertising have grown so heated in their denunciations. "TV is a series of tasteless and endless interruptions," cried one critic. "The people are tired of being screamed at, assaulted, and insulted by commercials," exclaimed another.

In addition to the Federal Trade Commission, more than twenty other federal agencies, including the Internal Revenue Service and the Securities & Exchange Commission, have taken some steps to regulate advertising. More than a dozen states have instituted taxes on advertising. The federal government's interest in protecting consumers from business and advertising abuses has been particularly strong in recent years. The Fair Packaging and Labeling Act of 1966 covered food, drug, and cosmetics packages, and the amount of label revision was enormous. A Commerce Department program to stem the proliferation of package sizes followed. In 1968 came the so-called Truth in Lending Act requiring disclosure of the annual interest rate on revolving charge accounts. It was still all right to use the phrase "Easy Credit" in an ad, but if specific language such as "$1.00 down and $1.00 a week" were introduced, the annual interest rate had to be stated. In 1971 Congress banned the broadcasting of cigarette commercials.

Morton J. Simon, Philadelphia lawyer and author, has cited six principal reasons for the current unfavorable government attitude toward advertising: (1) *Advertising is a horizontal industry.* It cuts across almost every business and service, so an attack on any industry almost always includes advertising. (2) *Advertising represents a lot of money.* It spends billions of dollars annually, and some persons view these funds as apparently untaxed and outside the grip of the government. (3) *Advertising lives in a glass house.* By its nature it cannot hide its sins. (4) *The gray flannel suit image is pervasive.* Many consider that advertising people live lavishly and improperly on tax-deductible expense accounts. (5) *Advertising is not constitutionally protected.* Some in government believe that advertising is somehow tainted by its commercial purpose and therefore is not protected by the First Amendment; its legal status in this regard has not been made clear. (6) *Advertising has rarely lobbied.* Unlike most other major segments of the economy, advertising has maintained a Washington lobby only in recent years.

Although bowing to many of the demands of the present consumer movement, the industry insists that restrictive government actions will not ensure the improvement of advertising practices. The answers, spokesmen contend, lie in advertising's own progress toward the achievement of high professional standards and in involving advertising fully, as a partner with other segments of society, in the search for solutions to the vexing problems confronting the American people.

EFFORTS TO IMPROVE

It is generally agreed that government can play only a minor role in efforts to improve the mass media, if they are to remain free. This means that efforts at improvement must come from within the media themselves or be generated by groups outside the media that represent the general public. In each of the media there are groups and individuals who are contributing to the efforts to meet the challenges raised by society.

One group is composed of the various trade associations. For newspapers there are the American Newspaper Publishers Association, representing the dailies; the National Newspaper Association, for weeklies and small dailies; and two subsidiary national daily groups, the International Circulation Managers' Association and the International Newspaper Advertising Executives. There are also strong regional associations—Inland Daily Press Association, Southern Newspaper Publishers Association, New England Daily Newspaper Association, Western Newspaper Foundation, Northwest Daily Press Association—and state associations (usually emphasizing the problems of weeklies).

The trade associations for other media include the National Association of Broadcasters, the Magazine Publishers Association, the American Book Publishers Council, the American Educational Publishers Institute, the Motion Picture Association of America, the American Business Press, Inc., the American Association of Advertising Agencies, and the American Advertising Federation.

Each trade association speaks for its industry in affairs of general interest to the members. The staffs represent the industries when necessary at congressional hearings and before other government bodies. The associations develop promotional materials for their media and operate central offices that act as clearinghouses for information about the industries. The daily newspapers organized a Bureau of Advertising that promotes their media; the Magazine Advertising Bureau, the Radio Advertising Bureau, and the Television Information Bureau do the same in their fields. The National Association of Broadcasters, the Motion Picture Association of America, and the American Association of Advertising Agencies have developed codes of conduct. Although they are primarily concerned with business matters, many of the associations sponsor discussions aimed at improving their media and encourage individual activities aimed at raising the standards of members.

There are also groups of editors and writers. Most prominent is the American Society of Newspaper Editors, limited primarily to editors, editorial page editors, and managing editors of dailies of 50,000 or more circulation. The ASNE formulated the Canons of Journalism in 1923 and attempted to regulate the professional conduct of its members but found it could not expel an accused editor. The code was rewritten in 1975. ASNE's convention proceedings are reproduced in book form in the *Problems of Journalism* series. The monthly ASNE *Bulletin* analyzes problems confronting editors and the press.

The National Conference of Editorial Writers meets annually in sessions featuring small-group critiques of editorial pages. It publishes a quarterly, the *Masthead,* and has a code of principles "to stimulate the conscience and the quality of the American editorial page." The Associated Press Managing Editors Association constantly studies the AP news report, publishes the APME "Red Book" reporting on committee findings and convention sessions, and has drawn up a code of ethics. The International Society of Weekly Newspaper Editors meets annually and presents a Golden Quill award for outstanding work in the weekly field.

The Radio Television News Directors Association is the equivalent organization for the electronic media. It has sought to elevate standards through adoption of a code of principles and has been instrumental in advancing the position of news and public affairs broadcasting in the industry. Among magazine people, the International Association of Business Communicators sets standards of performance and holds annual sessions for men and women who edit company publications. The Public Relations Society of America requires practitioners to pass written examinations before they may be certified as accredited members of the organization. All of these groups issue magazines for their members.

The American Academy of Advertising brings together educators and practitioners in annual meetings and publishes the *Journal of Advertising.* The Business and Professional Advertising Association is an example of other groups active in this field.

The American Newspaper Guild has done much to improve the standards of the newspaper business through the raising of salaries and has attempted to carry out programs of self-improvement. Its publication is the *Guild Reporter.* Membership is limited primarily to workers in larger daily newspapers and the press associations. Its role as a trade union is discussed in greater detail in Chapter 9.

There are other groups: the Society of Professional Journalists, Sigma Delta Chi and Women in Communications, Inc., both more than sixty years old and both operating chapters for working journalists as well as on campuses; Pi Delta Epsilon, honorary collegiate journalism fraternity; Kappa Tau Alpha, journalism scholastic society; AAF/ADS, professional advertising society; Pi Alpha Mu, professional fraternity for men and women in the publishing, advertising, and journalistic management fields; Di Gamma Kappa and Alpha Epsilon Rho, professional broadcasting organizations; and the Public Relations Student Society of America. Most of them issue publications, the *Quill* of the Society of Professional Journalists being the best known.

The Nieman Fellows, consisting of reporters and editors who have been given a year of study at Harvard University under the Nieman Foundation program, issue a quarterly, *Nieman Reports.* The *Columbia Journalism Review,* published by the Columbia University Graduate School of Journalism, offers a quarterly analysis and criticism of media performance. Media practices are examined by a dozen or more publications produced by critical reporters and editors, often with the support of journalism educators. A few metropolitan radio and television stations have instituted programs designed to criticize press coverage, and some metropolitan underground newspapers do likewise. Publications of the Freedom of Information Center at the University of Missouri School of Journalism monitor developments in the mass media. A number of university journalism schools and departments publish periodicals containing media appraisal, among them being the *Montana Journalism Review,* of the University of Montana School of Journalism, and the *Iowa Journalist,* of the University of Iowa School of Journalism. Other roles of journalism educators and the cooperation extended to them by the mass communications industries are discussed in Chapter 20. Articles in *TV Guide* assess industry practices, and other magazines frequently print articles dealing with the media. The Gannett Company, Inc., issues *Gannetteer,* a monthly magazine.

In a broad-based program designed to increase the number of highly competent journalists, the Ford Foundation since 1965 has granted millions of dollars for postgraduate journalism education. The projects include an urban journalism program through the Northwestern University

Medill School of Journalism, expansion of the Nieman program bringing young newspeople to Harvard University for a year's study, further development of the Graduate School of Journalism at Columbia University, a public affairs reporting program in cooperation with the American Political Science Association, a variety of study and seminar programs for journalists of the South in cooperation with the Southern Regional Education Board and the Southern Newspaper Publishers Association Foundation, and a Nieman-like program of study for experienced journalists at Stanford University.

The Newspaper Fund, supported by Dow Jones and Company (publisher of the *Wall Street Journal, Barron's* financial weekly, the Dow Jones News Services, and Ottaway Newspapers, a wholly-owned subsidiary that publishes newspapers in twelve cities) has spent more than $4.4 million since 1958 in attracting talented young people to newsroom careers. The fund's program revolves around six major areas: providing a clearinghouse for career information, summer study on college campuses for high school and junior college journalism teachers, summer intern programs with scholarships for college students, recognition to high school teachers for outstanding performances, programs for minority high school students, and an editor-in-residence program to bring working news men and women to college campuses in cooperation with the American Society of Newspaper Editors.

With the financial aid of the Don R. Mellett Fund of the American Newspaper Guild, community press councils were established in the late 1960s in California, Oregon, Illinois, and Colorado. The councils, composed of both public and media representatives, were intended to provide a forum for public criticism of the media and to enable editors and managers to respond. The idea, however, met with only limited success. Today the strongest councils are a state organization in Minnesota and a regional body in New England.

Backed by eight foundations, the National News Council, with headquarters in New York City, was established in 1973 to serve the public interest in preserving freedom of communication and advancing accurate and fair reporting of news. Similar bodies have long been active in Europe.

The council investigates and considers complaints by the public against those newspapers, magazines, news services, and TV and radio networks considered to be national media. It consists of 18 public and press members. The council has no power of enforcement over the media beyond public release of its findings; its only strength is the force of public opinion.

Media reaction to the council's establishment was mixed. The AP, UPI, CBS, PBS, *Time, Newsweek, Wall Street Journal,* and *Christian*

Science Monitor agreed to cooperate with the council. The New York *Times* News Service declined to do so, and many media organizations took no position. Proponents maintained that the council would enhance media credibility and deal with public complaints before they could translate themselves into a push for governmental controls harmful to the First Amendment. Opponents argued that the media already were criticized sufficiently by readers, viewers, and professional groups and that such a council might be a forerunner of governmental control.

During its first four years of financially shaky existence the council received almost 500 complaints against media practices. The networks drew the most charges, with newspapers second. Of 125 complaints considered by the full council during that period, 73 were held to be unwarranted, 25 were upheld in whole or in part, 26 were dismissed, and 1 was withdrawn.

The findings were fairly well reported in professional publications but only in limited fashion by the news media. In 1977 the *Columbia Journalism Review* began publishing council findings in full, and a monthly newsletter to the media was begun.

William B. Arthur, former editor of *Look* magazine, serves as executive director of the council. In 1977 Norman Isaacs, an activist journalist and former president of the American Society of Newspaper Editors, was named chairman. It was anticipated that the council would expand its functions to include all media, both national and local, and to serve increasingly as a mediator in controversies between the press and the bar, the press and government, and the press and other groups.

In 1977 the ASNE ethics subcommittee voiced its strong approval of the council's operation. Further support came from industry leaders, including William S. Paley, chairman of the board of CBS.

CHAPTER 8
ECONOMIC PROBLEMS OF THE MEDIA

THE MEDIA AS BIG BUSINESS

The most important economic fact about the mass media in the United States is that they are operated for profit by private business. They do not receive subsidies from government. The only significant exceptions to these general statements are the financial subsidies granted to educational television stations and national public radio; even these outlets seek supplementary grants from private corporations and contributions from the public.

Most of our entertainment and information reaches us through printed, broadcast, and spoken sources that would go out of business if they failed to earn a profit. This competition in the marketplace is a great strength of the media, because the challenge of survival stimulates initiative, goads media people into fresh thinking, and promotes vigorous action.

All the media are big business. For example, a person or organization trying to buy a metropolitan radio station could expect to pay about $15 million for it, and perhaps $4–5 million for a big-city FM station with limited audience and range. A major television station might cost around $50 million. For a medium-sized newspaper, the price tag would be $10 to $40 million, and for a top-ranking metropolitan newspaper, at least $75 million.

With such sums at stake, critics of media operations under the free enterprise system argue that broadcasting stations, newspapers, and other print outlets are so concerned with profits that they sacrifice the standards of excellence the critics visualize for them. Enough misuse of media power occurs to give these foes ammunition. Generally, critics focus more on abuses of the private enterprise system in the media than upon urging the alternative, government ownership or subsidy, with the control of content it implies.

NEWSPAPER MONOPOLY

The predominance of "one-newspaper cities," brought about by the death of second newspapers through economic attrition, has raised concern about news monopolies. Critics fear that, in a city with one daily newspaper, the publication will print only the news it wants its readers to see, leaving out or deemphasizing stories that might embarrass the publisher and his or her friends, or run contrary to the newspaper's political position. On the other side, there are frequent cases in which a monopoly publisher, sensitive to vulnerability to the charge, has made extra effort to provide the city with more extensive and deeper news coverage than was previously available in a competitive situation.

Closely connected is the charge that advertisers dictate a newspaper's coverage, or at least exercise veto power over certain kinds of stories that might damage their trade. This charge is especially important in cities with only a single newspaper. Again, there are numerous episodes to document this complaint. Stories have gone unreported because an advertiser requested them killed. Yet there are many cases in which newspapers have defied such pressures. Usually the readers do not hear of the latter.

An example of rejected pressure occurred in a middle-sized city when its only newspaper published a series of stories advising teenagers how to buy a used car. The writer explained the tricks used by "fast buck" dealers to cheat the purchasers. After the first article appeared, the local automobile dealers angrily demanded that the publisher stop the series. He refused. The series was published in full. In retaliation, the dealers cancelled all their advertising in the newspaper, costing it thousands of dollars in revenue. Eventually, the dealers resumed advertising.

Publication of columns called "Action Line" or some similar name, in which the newspaper acts as its readers' problem-solving agent in their dealings with commercial firms and government agencies, often causes it to print facts that show its advertisers in a poor light. The completeness of a newspaper's coverage of controversial issues and sensitive stories depends largely upon the moral courage and journalistic integrity of those who run it.

Fewer than 5 percent of daily newspaper cities and weekly newspaper towns have competing newspaper ownerships. This figure, often quoted by critics, is in one respect misleading. Far more competition for news and advertising exists in these "one-paper towns" than the statistics indicate. The small-city dailies extend their coverage into the "weekly" towns with local news correspondents and advertising solicitors. In turn, the larger daily newspapers frequently make heavy inroads into the small daily cities with news bureaus and regional news pages designed for these cities. It is a matter of intense pride for a small city newspaper staff not to be beaten by the "intruder" on a story in its own backyard.

The chief immediate reason for the disappearance of newspapers is the constantly rising cost of production. The wages of those who write and print the papers, taxes, the cost of newsprint and of gasoline for the delivery trucks, and the news and picture services—these and a hundred other expenses have become higher and higher. The cost of newsprint has increased more than sixfold in the past thirty years, for example, but the price at which most newspapers are sold to the public has not risen at the same pace. Nor has the cost of an inch of advertising. Competition from television and radio for the advertiser's dollar has given the publisher another thorny problem.

In many cities in which two newspapers were competing for advertising and circulation and both were struggling to stay solvent, the two owners saw the financial advantage of combining forces into one publication. One sold out to the other, or they made a partnership arrangement of some sort. The city was left with only one newspaper. There is reason to worry about this trend. Competition between two or more newspapers to cover the news usually gives readers better assurance of being kept fully informed about what is happening in their community.

There is a substantial argument on the other side, however. One strong newspaper in a city, if the publisher and editor are conscientious persons sensible of their responsibilities, often can provide better news coverage and community service than two weak ones. Also, a financially strong paper sometimes is more willing to attack entrenched and harmful interests in a city because it is able to absorb the financial retaliation its foes aim at it by trying to undercut its advertising and circulation income. A paper that is weak financially is usually a timid paper editorially.

Concurrent with the reduction to one newspaper in many cities is the rise of local news coverage by television and radio stations. Thus in many cases citizens do have an alternate source for local news. In the event that a newspaper attempts to ignore or twist a local news situation for a policy reason, an attitude much less frequent than the more vehement press critics claim, the news coverage by television and radio stations can expose this irresponsible action.

In their struggle against rising costs of operation, some competing publishers sought to maintain a semblance of independence by putting out separate newspapers but for economy combining their mechanical departments and even such front-office departments as advertising. This raised protests of restraint of trade. After watching the merger trend dubiously, the federal government moved into the situation. It filed antitrust charges against the Los Angeles *Times* when that powerful newspaper purchased the San Bernardino *Sun-Telegram,* a successful daily newspaper within the *Times'* circulation zone. The government was victorious in the trial, and the *Times* was ordered to sell the San Bernardino newspaper; it was also forbidden to purchase other newspapers that might help it obtain unfair dominance in southern California.

A measure called the Newspaper Preservation Act was passed by Congress in 1970 after lively controversy within the newspaper industry. The law created exemptions to the antitrust law, so that a financially troubled newspaper might join forces with a healthy publication in the same city. The newspapers are allowed not only to operate joint production facilities, but to combine business departments and have joint advertising and circulation rates. Their editorial departments remain separate. An argument for the measure is that it will preserve a second "voice" in the city. Publishers who testified against it, especially those from aggressive suburban newspapers, asserted that it would increase the trend toward monopoly.

Federal antitrust prosecutors also have taken action against the syndicates that sell features to newspapers, such as comic strips and political columnists. These suits have sought to break up the practice by some syndicates of selling exclusive territory. It works this way: A metropolitan newspaper that circulates through a large area purchases a popular feature from a syndicate for a high price. The syndicate grants the newspaper exclusive rights to publish the feature in a broad territory. This prevents other newspapers in the territory from buying the feature, and gives the large paper a monopoly on it. Once widely practiced, the sale of exclusive territory has dwindled because of government pressure.

No magazine may have a "monopoly" in the sense of the newspaper published as the single daily in a community, but the disappearance of many prominent magazines has restricted the reading choice of citizens. Most new magazines in recent years have been aimed at specialized audiences. The deaths of *Look* in 1971 and *Life* in 1972 were preceded by those of the two weekly general interest magazines, *Collier's* and the *Saturday Evening Post.* The disappearance of these organs of popular readership left a void that could be filled only partially by the *Reader's Digest.*

Generally speaking, the magazine world offers "pairs" to the reading audience: *Time* or *Newsweek, Harper's* or *Atlantic, Nation* or *New Republic, McCall's* or *Ladies' Home Journal.* There are some notable "singles": *Reader's Digest, National Geographic, Playboy, Esquire, National Review,* and the *New Yorker.* Thoughtful critics say only a handful of the magazines named live up to their potential.

GROWTH OF GROUPS

After many decades in which family owners controlled most newspapers, the past ten years have seen a tremendous transfer to group ownership. This financial control by absentee owners is a topic of spirited debate within the newspaper industry. Advocates of group operation contend that a large organization with ample management, financing, and material resources can improve an independently owned newspaper. Opponents of the group ownership phenomenon argue that out-of-town corporate ownership robs a newspaper of its local "heart," even when the same editors are left in charge after the takeover, and puts too much emphasis on profit by forcing local management to achieve financial goals laid down by the corporation's central office.

A study published in *Editor & Publisher* in the late 1970s showed that more than 1000 of the country's approximately 1750 daily newspapers were owned by groups; this represented 71 percent of total daily newspaper circulation. While many of the 167 groups it listed were small, controlling only a few newspapers, some groups (they don't like to be called chains) have grown to spectacular size. By 1978, Gannett Newspapers owned 75 daily newspapers, Knight-Ridder Newspapers 34, and Newhouse Newspapers 29. In terms of circulation, Knight-Ridder was largest, in excess of 3.5 million copies.

The spectacular expansion of the acquisition-hungry groups was rooted in economics. The problem of paying inheritance taxes after a publisher's death caused many family ownerships to sell out, often at inflated prices that the publishing groups could afford because of their ability to make advantageous tax arrangements.

Most group ownerships today emphasize the local identity of the newspapers they operate, rather than rigid conformity in physical appearance and content to a group formula, such as was widely enforced by the newspaper chains of earlier days. At one time, for example, a Hearst newspaper was identifiable immediately, no matter what its city of publication.

OWNERSHIP ACROSS THE MEDIA

Ownership by corporate groups extends far outside the newspaper industry. Many groups own broadcasting stations as well, and some are conglomerates that also control magazines, book publishing firms, and other diversified interests. This intermedia ownership developed in a society whose economic atmosphere encourages mass production, big enterprises, and diversification of corporate investments. Since intermedia competition has replaced internewspaper competition in most American cities, the fact that corporate groups have ownerships in several media camps simultaneously has created concern about concentration of too much control in the hands of a relatively few individuals who operate these intermedia giants (see Table 8.1).

Table 8.1
EXAMPLES OF GROUP NEWSPAPER AND CROSS-MEDIA
OWNERSHIP IN THE LATE 1970s

	Knight-Ridder Newspapers	Gannett Newspapers	Newhouse Newspapers	New York Times
Daily newspapers	34	75	29	10
Weekly newspapers	14	8		
Television stations	1	1	6	1
Radio stations	2	2	4	1
Cable TV systems			22	
Magazines			6	4

Two graphs show the trends in internewspaper competition and intermedia competition since 1880. They summarize analyses of the problem made by Professor Raymond B. Nixon, using data from *Editor & Publisher International Year Book, Broadcasting Yearbook,* and other sources. In Figure 8.1, the number of dailies published in the United States rises from 850 in 1880 to a peak of 2200 in 1910, then declines to a plateau figure of 1750 after 1945, plus or minus a few as stops and starts of dailies fluctuated.

Figure 8.1 also shows the steady increase in single-daily cities from 509 (42 percent) in 1910 to 1284 (85 percent) by 1969. Another 171 cities were being served by 342 dailies published in morning-evening combination ownership situations or joint printing operations. That left 123 dailies in 45 cities where competition between separate ownerships still existed. These represented 3 percent of the 1500 cities with daily newspapers. In 1910 there had been 689 cities (57 percent of 1207) with two or more competing dailies. Before leaving the daily newspaper,

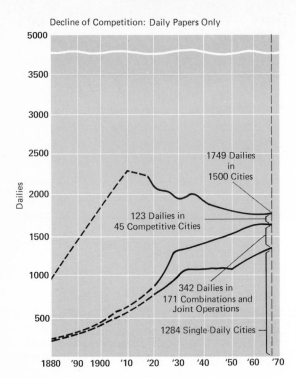

Decline of Competition: Daily Papers Only

1749 Dailies
in
1500 Cities

123 Dailies in
45 Competitive Cities

342 Dailies in
171 Combinations and
Joint Operations

1284 Single-Daily Cities

FIGURE 8.1

however, we should note that the drop in numbers of daily newspapers from the 1910 peak has been only 20 percent and that the circulation of the survivors has increased from 22 million to approximately 63 million.

Figure 8.2 shows a new concept: "media voices" replaces "daily newspapers" as the criterion for competition. By a media voice is meant any separate ownership in the field of local mass communication; "competition" means there are two or more separately owned newspapers, radio stations, or television stations in any combination. Thus the 1500 cities with daily newspapers had a total of 5081 media voices. Of these, 4879 were competing voices in 1298 cities. Only 202 were single-voice cities, and these were nearly all suburbs so close to central cities that outside voices are readily available, Professor Nixon reported. In addition, 1447 other cities had a local broadcast station. So the total of U.S. communities with daily mass communication was 2947.

An example of what cross-media ownership does to control of media voices is found in Minneapolis. The citizens of that city can find Cowles

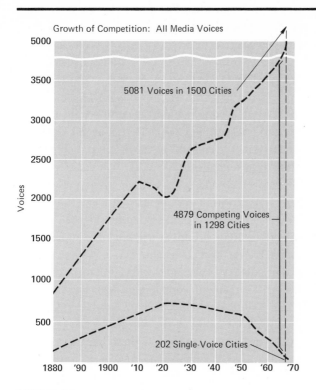

FIGURE 8.2

family members in ownership situations affecting both their morning and evening newspapers, the leading radio station, the CBS-affiliated television station, and their subscriptions to *Harper's* magazine. All these media outlets are operated independently of each other, but there is still the influence of ownership philosophy.

The Federal Communications Commission took action to check the movement toward intermedia ownership early in 1975, when it adopted a rule barring future acquisitions that would place a newspaper and any broadcast station in the same city under common ownership. It left untouched existing combinations, except in sixteen American cities in which one company owned the only daily newspaper of general circulation and all or most of the broadcasting stations. These companies were ordered to divest themselves either of the newspaper or a station by

January 1, 1980. If a company owned the only newspaper plus AM and FM stations, it was allowed to keep one of the stations along with the newspaper.

This order was a compromise, and therefore less sweeping than what was advocated by those who wished to wipe out single ownership of a newspaper and broadcasting station in any market. Nevertheless, the action drew vehement protests from some of the groups affected. The cross-ownership issue reached the United States Supreme Court, which in 1978 unanimously upheld the FCC order, overruling a Circuit Court of Appeals decision. This assured continuation of existing joint owner-ships in most cities. The FCC also formulated a restriction on common ownership of a cable television system and a television station in the same market; this likewise drew a challenge.

Despite the large numbers of broadcasting stations, the networks re-main the most important forces within the industry. In entertainment, in public affairs, and in news, the viewer relies mainly on NBC, CBS, and ABC. Federal restrictions limit group ownership of stations to a handful. But cross-ownership has been constant, and newspapers and magazines are associated in common ownership with 25 percent of com-mercial television stations, 7 percent of commercial AM stations, and 9 percent of FM stations. Regional groups such as Cox Broadcasting and Westinghouse are a significant factor in the market.

Regardless of intermedia ownership, control of the other mass media has always been limited. In magazine publishing, ten large firms have dominated the field, and competition in subareas such as news maga-zines, women's magazines, picture magazines, and quality journals has severely declined. In book publishing, two dozen firms account for two-thirds of the business each year. Eight large studios historically domi-nated the film industry, although their influence has been diminished by independent production by stars and the influence of television. The news media have their choice of two U.S. press associations, the Asso-ciated Press and United Press International. Certainly tendencies toward domination of the limited numbers of units within these fields by com-mon ownerships cutting across the media constitute a challenge to society.

LICENSE RENEWAL THREATS

A decision of the U.S. Court of Appeals for the District of Columbia Circuit in 1971 sent shock waves through the broadcasting indus-try. In the case of *Citizens Communications Center et al. v. Federal Communications Commission,* the court reversed and declared illegal an

FCC policy statement issued in January 1970. That statement had declared that if, in a license renewal contest, the licensee could demonstrate "substantial" past performance without serious deficiencies, all other applications would be dismissed without a hearing on their merits.

Indicating that the FCC must choose the applicant who would provide the best service to the public and who would ensure the maximum diffusion of control of the mass media, the court ruled that the Federal Communications Act places the licensee on renewal in the same position as an initial applicant. Each must make the best case possible on the basis of program offering, integration, diversification, past performance, and any other matters the parties might ask the FCC to consider as pertaining to licensee fitness. Each broadcasting station must have its FCC license renewed every three years.

Although at one time *average,* and later *substantial,* performance by the station has been sufficient to maintain its license, now, the court ruled, only *superior* performance should be considered a plus of major significance in renewal proceedings. The court suggested that anyone involved in *superior* programing would (1) eliminate excessive and loud advertising, (2) deliver quality programs, and (3) reinvest to a great extent the profits on the license to the service of the viewing and listening public. The court pointed out that this decision would permit new interest groups and hitherto "silent minorities," as they emerge in our society, to be given some stake in and chance to broadcast on radio and television frequencies. The court concluded that its decision restored healthy competition by repudiating an FCC policy unreasonably weighted in favor of the licensees it regulates, to the great detriment of the listening and viewing public.

Chairman Dean Burch of the FCC, informed of the decision, declared, "If this decision stands, it is the end of multiple ownership." *Broadcasting* magazine previously had editorialized, "Nothing less than survival is at issue." Broadcasters viewed the decision as designed to restructure the broadcasting industry so as to eliminate all absentee ownership and all multiple ownership. Few broadcast licensees, it was contended, could meet the test of a carefully contrived application; those who could would not be able to buy a second station because then, under these criteria, both would be lost. The value of broadcast facilities would be diminished if not destroyed, it was contended, and all stations sooner or later would be confronted with an expensive, time-consuming renewal hearing and the possible loss of their licenses to groups assembled for the purpose of obtaining a valuable franchise at a low price. The decision affected all stations including those owned by the networks (although not the networks themselves).

Broadcasters had been virtually secure from challenge as a result of the WBAL, Baltimore, decision in 1951 and the Wabash Valley verdict in 1963, wherein programing performance was weighted heavily against the uncertainty that the challenger could carry out his proposals. Only WLBT-TV, Jackson, Mississippi, had lost its license, on grounds of discrimination against blacks. In 1969, however, the FCC denied renewal of the license of station WHDH-TV, Boston, and awarded it to a competing applicant. The unprecedented decision rocked the broadcasting industry, since it seemed to signal a new FCC policy under which renewal applicants with other media holdings, like WHDH-TV (which was owned by the Boston *Herald-Traveler*), were vulnerable to challenges by applicants that had no other media interests. The commission endeavored to establish this as a unique case, but broadcasters remained apprehensive. The *Herald-Traveler,* which had been supported financially by the TV station, ceased publication in 1972.

The Boston decision encouraged the filing of competing applications against a number of major licenses. The fears of broadcasters, especially those with other media holdings, were eased temporarily when the FCC adopted a policy statement asserting that it would favor an incumbent broadcaster over rival applicants if in a comparative hearing it could be shown that the station's programing "has been substantially attuned to the needs and interests" of the community. The statement also made clear that the FCC would not deny renewal of a license simply because the company had other media interests.

When the Court of Appeals' 1971 decision reversed this FCC policy, however, broadcasters renewed their efforts to obtain relief from Congress. Numerous bills, designed both to lengthen the renewal period from three to four or five years and to give the renewal applicant preference over the challenger for substantially living up to its license commitments, were introduced. By 1978, however, no such bill had been enacted. Although few challenges had been successful, many broadcasters continued to fear that they might not be able successfully to defend their practices at license renewal time.

PRESSURE FROM MINORITIES

Blacks, Chicanos, and other minority groups have brought strong pressures to bear against the media in recent years. They allege that racism has been rampant in employment, news coverage, and programing practices. They charge that the media have been engaged in a conspiracy—conscious or unconscious—to prevent the public from learning that blacks and the poor are exploited by media advertisers. They maintain that some commercials and dramatic programs on television and radio depict false, stereotyped images of minority individuals, particularly Mexican-Americans and American Indians.

Actual or threatened challenges to broadcast license renewals have been the principal means of breaking down the barriers. The first assault, on grounds of racial discrimination, cost the operators of WLBT-TV, Jackson, Mississippi, their license in 1969. Next, KTAL-TV in Texarkana, Texas, succumbed to black demands. The station agreed to employ two black reporters to appear on camera, to consult with substantial community groups to determine area needs, and not to preempt network programs of interest to any substantial community group without prior consultation. In Atlanta, twenty-eight area stations agreed to black demands in areas of programing, employment, and service to minorities. Numerous other stations acceded to similar demands.

The Time-Life, Inc.–McGraw-Hill agreement in 1972 set a precedent in the buying and selling of television stations in blocks by multistation owners. When McGraw-Hill proposed to buy five stations from Time-Life, Inc., Chicano groups in each city protested the sale on grounds of violation of the FCC policy prohibiting a single licensee from acquiring more than two VHF and one UHF stations in the fifty largest television markets without making a compelling public interest showing. Although the FCC approved the sale, threatened court action resulted in McGraw-Hill's decision not to buy WOOD-TV in Grand Rapids, Michigan. In addition, the company agreed to the establishment of a minority advisory council to act as consultants in program planning and production and in the recruitment and training of minorities for station employment. A national coordinating council was established to review these actions. Moreover, provision was made for one-minute public-access, public-service announcements; the appointment of a national minority affairs coordinator; the goal of 15 percent employment of minorities within three years; assistance to minority businessmen; substantial minorities programing; and a continuous program of ascertainment of community needs.

Ownership or control of broadcasting outlets by blacks remains low. A recent check showed only 51 radio stations and three commercial television stations in black hands; two of the latter are in the American

Virgin Islands. The FCC and the National Association of Broadcasters are seeking technically and financially qualified minority owners for stations.

Accelerated effort is evident in the hiring and programing practices that numerous broadcasters had voluntarily adopted during the 1960s in recognition of minority needs. Successive surveys by the Office of Communications of the United Church of Christ disclosed that an increasing number of minority employees were being hired. President Nixon appointed the first black, Benjamin L. Hooks, to the FCC. Despite these gains, minority groups, aided by a congressional black caucus, continued to press for additional reforms in network and station hiring and programing practices.

Women's rights organizations also exerted strong and increasingly successful pressure on the media for sexual equality in staff hiring and equal opportunity for women employees in decision-making positions, and for equitable distribution of choice assignments between men and women. By the late 1970s, the number of women reporters on the air had increased noticeably; so had women's bylines in newspapers and magazines. Progress into media administrative positions was less rapid because of the seniority built up by men before the full impact of the women's movement was felt. FCC pressure on stations to meet standards set by the federal Equal Employment Opportunity program accelerated improvements in the broadcasting field.

AUDIENCE RESPONSES AND PREFERENCES

Newspapers, radio, and television come close to being universal media in the United States. Nine out of ten American adults see a daily newspaper regularly; of those who do not, a majority read a weekly newspaper. Radios are found in 99 percent of homes, television sets in 97 percent. Again, the adult audiences come close to the total potential.

Magazines rank next in appeal; the best available survey figures show that 60 to 70 percent of adults read at least one magazine regularly. Approximately 30 percent of adults, when asked, say they have attended a movie during the previous month; 25 percent say they have read a book.

These figures constitute both a tribute and a challenge to the mass media. Public support, it might be said, becomes an embarrassment for those who must produce publications, programs, and films for such a diverse and overwhelming mass audience. One can hope to have more than 18 million subscribers to a magazine, like *Reader's Digest;* sell 10 million copies of a paperback like *Valley of the Dolls*; produce a smash hit film like *Star Wars;* or have a TV audience like that for the Super Bowl professional football playoff game. But usually the problem is to satisfy mass audiences with a heterogeneous product: the newspaper, the daylong programing of television, the patter and music of radio, the general interest magazine—to hold enough audience to earn advertising and circulation revenues.

Readership studies, audience ratings, and other scientific methods determine audience preferences for mass media content. In the print media the final determination is how many copies of one's publication are bought; movies have their box office receipts for measurement. Television and radio must rely upon audience ratings and critics' reactions, since programs are received free. But all these figures do not accurately reflect what people really feel about the media.

One study, repeated since 1963, was made by Roper Research Associates and reported to the sponsors of the study, the television industry. In it, respondents were asked where they usually get most of their news of "what's going on in the world today" (a question minimizing the importance of local news, in which newspapers excel). In 1977 their reply was from television, 64 percent; newspapers, 49 percent; radio, 19 percent; magazines, 7 percent; "other people," 4 percent (some listed more than one principal source). Respondents also were asked how well they felt individual media were doing their job. Seventy percent rated television's job performance "excellent" or "good," compared with 66 percent for churches, 65 percent for the police, 59 percent for newspapers, 47 percent for schools, and 41 percent for local government.

Opposite results were found in an earlier survey by the Louis Harris organization for *Time,* when it asked, "How upset would you be if your main news source were to become unavailable for a month?" The results: 44 percent said they would be "very upset" to lose their newspaper, and 33 percent would be "very upset" to lose their favorite television news broadcast.

Both studies disclosed that the public considers television "most believable" in a situation involving discrepancies between news media. The Roper study results were 51 percent for television, 22 percent for newspapers, 9 percent for magazines, 7 percent for radio, and 13 percent in the category of "don't know; no answer." The Harris study, while it shows a clear majority believing the newspaper is sometimes "unfair, partial and slanted," records only a third with a similar view toward television news.

There were other results in the Harris poll for media workers and scholars to reflect upon. Two out of three adults said they were better informed than they were five years earlier, a vote of confidence for the media. By a clear edge, respondents labeled television news "more full of violence" and "more full of sex" than newspapers. More than nine out of ten said they regularly watched television news: CBS, 35 percent; NBC, 35 percent; ABC, 13 percent. Among publications, Harris reported, *Time* and *Newsweek* were known by half the reading public, the New York *Times* by 30 percent, the *Wall Street Journal* by 28 percent, the now defunct *National Observer* by 14 percent, and the Washington *Post* by 13 percent. It is apparent that the visual impact of television has added an aura of believability to its newscasts, not always justified, that the print media have yet to match.

ECONOMIC PRESSURES ON THE MEDIA

The inflation of the 1970s has created enormous problems for the managers of all mass media in the struggle to operate at a profit, just as it has affected other fields of business. Heavier costs of labor, equipment, and materials must be offset by higher revenue. For the print media, this can be achieved by higher charges to the consumer—15 or 20 cents for a copy of a newspaper instead of 10 cents, higher advertising rates, and larger circulation if that is attainable. In the electronic media, increased advertising rates are the principal source. The danger in this spiral is that the higher charges for the product, or for advertising space in it, will reach the point that they will drive away customers, actually decreasing net revenue and weakening the media.

Because television advertising rates are determined by the popularity of the shows in which the commercials appear, an intense battle for ratings goes on among the three national networks, ABC, CBS, and NBC. After being a chronic third-place finisher in the ratings reports, ABC made a major jump during 1977 and 1978 with frothy new shows. Often it finished first in the weekly ratings. This caused some movement of CBS and NBC affiliates to ABC affiliation.

Astute managers seek to keep price increases to a minimum by enforcing rigid cost controls and by adopting new technology that helps them to produce an equal or improved product while using less manpower. Faced with skyrocketing postal charges, some national magazines such as *Esquire* abandoned their familiar large-page formats for much smaller ones to reduce the weight of each copy. Newspapers followed a similar course by reducing the dimensions of their pages as inconspicuously as possible to cut down newsprint consumption.

For the print media, the most effective route toward lower costs has been the adoption of automated printing production, an electronic revolution that will be discussed in the next chapter. Ironically, interest rates on the money publishers had to borrow in order to purchase the costly new labor-saving equipment were so high that a portion of the potential savings was gobbled up in payments to the banks. At times, it was difficult to borrow money at any price. As will be shown later, automation also entered the radio field.

The pressure of operating costs is responsible to a considerable degree for many shortcomings in media performance. Managers usually are aware of their organizations' shortcomings but contend that they cannot afford the additional staff members, the color television mobile units, the investigative reporting teams, or the purchase of expensive features and films they know are needed to upgrade the product they offer the public. Media managers with few exceptions have pride in their stations and publications; they face a constant conflict between what they would like to give their customers and what they can afford to give in order to operate at a satisfactory profit.

Forty years ago, before television, nearly half the advertising dollars spent in the United States went to newspapers. Today newspapers still receive the largest percentage of those dollars, although that percentage has dropped sharply to 30 percent. Television is a strong second, with 18 percent. Fortunately for all the media, the total expenditure for advertising has soared, so it is possible for a well-managed station or publication to operate with comfortable and in some cases excellent profits, provided the owners remain alert to changing public moods and adopt technical developments within their industries. Many are doing precisely that.

PART IV

THE MASS COMMUNICATIONS INDUSTRIES AND PROFESSIONS

CHAPTER 9
NEWSPAPERS

THE CHANGING NEWSPAPER

If a newspaper editor of forty years ago were to return from the special corner of heaven to which all famous editors assume they are destined and walk into his old newsroom, he wouldn't recognize anything. Women copyeditors would be revising news stories on small television screens. Black reporters would be writing stories. There would be no familiar clatter of Linotype machines from the composing room. Wall-to-wall carpeting would cover the city room floor. Absolutely unbelievable!

All this would baffle the editor enough. Then, picking up a fresh edition of the daily publication he nurtured for so many years as though it were his own child, he would take one look and explode, "See what they've done to my paper!"

Newspapers have undergone a fundamental change in the past two decades. Their traditional goals and styles of news coverage have been redirected. Their methods of production, once so laborious, have now been fitted to the newest technology. Production methods are changing so rapidly in the era of the computer that even the most progressive publishers and editors are uncertain of what further improvements are coming. The switch from printing with lead plates in a system more than a century old to one employing laser beams—and perhaps no printing plates at all—challenges and fascinates the best minds in a business long known for attracting tough, resilient people.

Despite these changes in techniques, however, the fundamental role of newspapers remains unaltered. They continue to be the written record of contemporary civilization. They report in detail events great and small, from the political cataclysm that drove Richard M. Nixon from the presidency to the automobile collision down the street. Despite the handicap of short-range perspective forced on them by the demands of daily, indeed hourly, deadlines, they seek increasingly to evaluate the news as well as report it. The word "perspective" is heard and pondered more among today's editors than it was among those of the past. To achieve balance and significance tests the technical skill and intellectual capacity of editors and writers because they operate under severe time pressures in a society whose standards are in flux. Few absolutes guide their decisions. They work not in the luxury of contemplation, but under the tyranny of the clock.

For the majority of the population, newspapers probably still are the basic news medium. They have been outdistanced by television in speed and visual punch, but they still provide greater depth and variety of reporting than television can, and with more lasting impact. Wise editors recognize the changes television has brought about and seek to focus their efforts on the function they can perform most valuably. Without newspapers, the American public simply could not be well informed.

In this chapter we will look at newspapers in operation. We will observe the roles individuals play in producing them; examine the changes in technology that have swept from the mechanical departments into the newsrooms, intertwining departments that in the old days were often run as antagonistic empires; and discuss the problems that must be solved before the first copies of the latest edition are delivered.

Approximately 61 million copies of daily newspapers are sold each day. The term *newspaper* covers a surprisingly broad range of publications. It includes the small weekly in which every task is done by a handful of people and the huge metropolitan daily with a staff of thousands and a daily circulation of a million copies. Between these extremes are hundreds of daily and weekly newspapers of many sizes and degrees of prosperity.

No matter what their circumstances, all newspapers are alike in the sense that they are made of type, ink, and newsprint. They exist to inform and influence the communities in which they are published, and the men and women who produce them share a common urge to get the news and advertising into print. Into the pages of every newspaper goes an essential but intangible extra ingredient, the minds and spirits of those who make it.

Newspaper work is an adventure, so full of fresh experiences that men and women who have been in it for years still come to work with a subconscious wonder about what unexpected developments the day will bring. It is based upon a firmly disciplined routine, because "getting the paper out" on time is paramount, and this can be done only if a definite work pattern exists in all departments.

The exciting things that can happen within that framework are innumerable. For those in the news department, there is the stimulation of being on the inside of big developments, of watching history being made, and of meeting intriguing people. For those who work in advertising and circulation, there is satisfaction in conceiving and executing ideas that bring in money and influencing people through skill with words. Working on a newspaper is an open invitation to create ideas and put them to work. The newspaper people who succeed best are those who handle the necessary routine meticulously and bring to their jobs an extra spark of creative thinking. Those for whom the atmosphere and work lose their excitement frequently move on to other media or occupations.

As one of the mass communication media, the contemporary newspaper has three fundamental functions and several secondary ones. The basic ones are these: (1) to inform readers objectively about what is happening in the community, country, and world; (2) to comment on the news in order to bring these developments into focus; and (3) to provide the means whereby persons with goods and services to sell can advertise their wares. The newspaper's less vital roles are these: (1) to campaign for desirable civic projects and to help eliminate undesirable conditions; (2) to give readers a portion of entertainment through such devices as comic strips, cartoons, and special features; (3) to serve readers as a friendly counselor, information bureau, and champion of their rights.

When a newspaper performs all or most of these tasks well, it becomes an integral part of community life. Television "sells" its news by developing on-the-air personalities whose mannerisms and aura often have more impact on the viewer than the content of the news they are delivering. Newspapers lack that personality advantage; a familiar byline on a story carries the impress of authoritative knowledge to the steady reader but cannot match the congenial smile or the cynically lifted eyebrow of the TV news commentator. Therefore the newspaper must build a personality of a different sort based upon its complete contents and tailored to its audience. It may be brisk, breezy, and compact like the New York *Daily News,* whose readers often digest its contents while standing in a subway train; gray and consciously stodgy in appearance, and full of long foreign and national stories like the New York *Times,* which aims to create an image of significance and permanence; or in the case of a smaller city newspaper where many residents know each other, filled with local stories on minor police actions, golden wedding anniversaries, meetings of organizations, Eagle Scout awards, and local civic disputes, along with an adequate number of major national and foreign stories. The job of the editor is to give a particular audience what it wants and needs.

The printed word has a lasting power and precision beyond that of the spoken word or the visual image, although it has less ability to startle and shock. Readers can refer to it again and again. Stories may be clipped and saved by readers for many years and be readily examined in the newspaper's files decades later. This fact increases the reporter's feeling of writing history. It contributes to the newspaper's position as a stabilizing, continuing force in the community.

In the self-examination by the newspaper industry brought about by the challenge of television, editors as a whole came to realize that too often the history they were recording was only the surface manifestation of the day's events—there was too much emphasis on who said this or did that, and not enough attention to why this had happened. This has led to an upsurge in investigative reporting, frequently by teams of reporters, in which the newspapers try to report frankly how our complex society is actually working. Reporters are given time to probe into such situations as conditions inside mental hospitals and nursing homes, the devious and sometimes illegal deals between political leaders and contractors, of the manner in which charitable institutions actually spend the money they receive from kind-hearted donors. The possibilities are almost endless, if an editor is sufficiently curious and has a staff large and aggressive enough to carry out his or her instructions.

The frequency of this type of reporting on good newspapers is one of the things that the returning old-time editor would notice first. His paper today would have fewer sensational headlines based on crime and tragedy and more front-page stories looking behind the scenes.

The other great change the returning editor would find in his paper is its physical appearance. For decades, the front pages of most newspapers were eight single columns of news stories, mostly with one-column headlines, broken by an occasional picture or two-column type box, and an eight-column banner headline across the top. The page had a vertical stripe effect. Many newspapers today use horizontal makeup. Stories are wrapped across the page under multiple-column headlines, often with type set in two-column width. A rapidly growing number of newspapers are using six wider columns on each page, rather than the traditional eight narrow columns. Graphics experts are experimenting with other combinations of type and pictures, not only on front pages but throughout the paper, seeking ways to make the pages more eye-catching without complicating production methods so much that the deadlines can't be met.

GENERAL ORGANIZATION OF NEWSPAPERS

Newspapers in the United States can be divided into three categories: weeklies and semiweeklies, serving small areas with limited circulation; small and medium-sized dailies, which comprise the great bulk of our daily press; and metropolitan newspapers whose circulation areas have populations of 1 million or more.

No matter what their size, newspapers have a common organization. Each has five major departments: *editorial,* which gathers and prepares the news, entertainment, and opinion materials, both written and illustrated; *advertising,* which solicits and prepares the commercial messages addressed to readers; *production,* which turns the editorial materials and advertisements into type and prints the newspapers; *circulation,* which has the task of selling and delivering the newspapers to the readers; and *business,* which oversees the entire operation.

The goal of newspaper stories is to present a report of an action in easily understood language that can be comprehended by a mass audience of different educational levels. Simplicity of writing is emphasized. If newspapers are to fill their role of communicating to the mass of the population, they cannot indulge in writing styles and terminology so involved that many readers cannot comprehend them. The best newspaper reporters are those who can accurately present complex situations in terms that are easily understood by the majority of their readers.

Television's ability to give the public "right now" visual reports of events in progress has led newspapers to deemphasize the publication of brief, last-minute bulletins. The day when newspapers published extra editions with huge headlines and two or three hundred hastily written words about a major news development is gone. Yet only a few decades ago, this was the principal method of spreading news around a city. Newspapers today put more emphasis on depth and less on excitement, a change that has opened new fields for the thoughtful, competent writer.

Newspaper advertising is divided into two types, *display* and *classified.* The former ranges from inconspicuous one-inch notices to multiple-page advertisements in which merchants and manufacturers proclaim their goods and services. Classified advertisements are the small-print, generally brief announcements packed closely together near the back of the paper; they deal with such diverse topics as help wanted, apartments for rent, used furniture and automobiles for sale, and personal notices. On almost all newspapers except the very smallest, display and classified advertising are handled by different staffs. Most newspapers receive about three-fourths of their income from advertising and one-fourth from circulation.

The staff setup of all newspapers is also basically the same, although naturally the larger the newspaper, the more complex its staff alignments. The top person is the publisher, who also may be the principal owner of the newspaper. On some papers the publisher's decisions on all matters are absolute; on others a board of directors or newspaper group management may set policy. The publisher's task is to set the newspaper's basic editorial and commercial policies and to see that they are carried out efficiently by the various department heads. On quite a few newspapers, especially smaller ones, the publisher is also the editor.

Usually a business manager or general manager under the publisher administers the company's business operations, which range all the way from obtaining newsprint to the purchasing of tickets as the newspaper's contribution to a community concert series. The heads of the advertising, circulation, and production departments answer to the publisher through the business manager, if there is one. But the editorial department, jealous of its independence to print the news without in theory being subject to commercial pressures, demands and generally gets a line of command direct to the publisher. The titles of executive editor and managing editor are most commonly used to designate heads of the news operations. The associate editor usually directs the newspaper's editorial, or opinion-making, function.

THE EVOLVING NEWSPAPER PATTERN

The American newspaper industry is the third largest industry in the nation. It consists of approximately 1750 daily newspapers and 9400 weekly newspapers, a total that fluctuates slightly from year to year. Although the widely publicized death of long-famous metropolitan newspapers has given a misleading impression, the newspaper industry is in a healthy and expanding condition, despite concern about slow circulation growth. A slightly larger number of daily newspapers are being published than at the end of World War II.

Fewer than a third of the daily newspapers in the United States have a circulation above 20,000. About 125 of these exceed the 100,000 mark. Thus, while the greatest public attention is focused on huge metropolitan newspapers like the New York *Times* and Chicago *Tribune,* their place in the total industry is relatively small.

If there is an average American daily (and the individualistic patterns of publishing make the description of a typical newspaper almost impossible), it has a circulation of not more than 15,000 copies and serves a city of about 30,000 and its surrounding trade area. A typical weekly has a circulation of about 2,000 to 4,000 copies in a small town and its surrounding countryside. Neither has direct newspaper competition in its own community.

Although many of the best-known American newspapers are morning publications, evening newspapers dominate the field, more than four to one. A tabulation in the late 1970s showed approximately 330 morning newspapers and 1440 evening newspapers, some of them twenty-four-hour publications with day and night editions. In some cases, the morning and evening papers are under a single ownership. Morning papers are especially numerous in the metropolitan areas, and are gaining strength there at the expense of the evening papers.

The most spectacular manifestation of the changing American newspaper pattern in the last two decades has been in the great cities. One famous newspaper after another has been forced to quit publication, leading poorly informed observers to the false conclusion that the American newspaper industry was declining. What actually has happened is that newspapers have been heavily affected by the changing patterns of American life. Forty years ago the bulk of metropolitan populations lived within a few miles of the city's center. They did their business and shopping in the downtown area. The efforts of the newspaper in newsgathering, circulation, and advertising were concentrated close in. As the move to the suburbs accelerated, the metropolitan newspaper's problems increased, especially for the evening papers. Operating costs kept rising while the newspaper's audience kept moving farther from its production plant. Newspapers had to be hauled greater distances to readers, through heavy traffic. The downtown stores opened large branches in suburban shopping centers; and new peripheral government agencies were created, which had to be covered for news. The new suburbanites developed loyalties to their outlying communities instead of to the central cities. Because a number of large companies moved their plants and offices to the metropolitan fringes, many suburban residents no longer commuted to downtown. Higher purchasing power and income were concentrated around the fringes, not in the core area.

Quickly, suburban daily newspapers in the largest metropolitan areas were created to serve this new audience. Some were long-time weeklies that went daily. Others were entirely new. Their growth has been one of the major publishing success stories of the last quarter-century. Between

1950 and 1968, the number of metropolitan newspapers in New York was reduced from eight to three; in Los Angeles, from five to two; and in Boston, from seven to four.

The metropolitan morning newspapers weathered the upheaval better than the evening papers, partly because they had less pressure during the night hours to distribute their papers to the outlying areas, and partly because they faced less competition from television as a purveyor of last-minute news and time-consuming entertainment. Most metropolitan newspapers that have survived and adapted themselves to changed conditions have been showing circulation growth.

The local newspaper's greatest advantage over larger "invaders" from out of town, and over local television and radio news broadcasts, is its more detailed presentation of hometown news. Many readers regard this as the most important ingredient in their newspaper.

What Do Readers Want?

Industry leaders awakened during the 1970s to the disturbing fact that fewer Americans were purchasing newspapers than in the past. Between 1969 and 1975, total daily newspaper circulation declined from 62,059,589 to 60,655,431. Population rose during those years; obviously newspapers were not keeping pace with national growth. Why? The problem was intense for newspapers in large cities, with their mobile population.

Editors and publishers subjected their newspapers to searching examination. They sought through polls, seminars, in-depth interviewing and other forms of public contact to discover what contemporary Americans wanted in their newspapers and how to satisfy those desires. Editors were shocked to learn through research that large segments of Americans, especially among young adults and low-income minority groups, felt little or no need for newspapers in their daily lives. Many claimed they received all the news they wanted from television. Some were bored by too much political news—indeed, by the political system that produced it. Others maintained that newspapers were too crime-oriented, too "establishment" in tone, too neglectful of material about the new lifestyles and information that would help them cope with financial and other problems. The "turned off" readers called newspapers dull. The age group from 21 to 35 was especially weak in newspaper readership and became a target for reawakened editors.

In order to reach new readers, the newspapers made changes in their format and content: Magazine-like graphics to brighten pages and tell stories in visual form. More stories about daily living problems and styles. Greater emphasis on personalities in the news. Adoption of concise news summaries, often on the front page, to meet the challenge of television's brief news coverage for persons who thought they didn't have time to read much. More investigative reporting. In sum, briefer, brighter, and more searching newspapers.

Critics argued that some newspapers went too far in this change of direction, becoming "soft" in content and neglecting the hard news that traditionally is the primary function of a daily newspaper. But by the late 1970s, American newspapers as a whole had become more attractive and more relevant to changing social patterns. Their circulation was rebounding, too; not yet up to the pace of population growth, but at least advancing. Jarred out of traditionalism and complacency, editors were doing a better job of producing newspapers with appeal to all ages and interest groups, but still had much to learn about what the American public wants.

OPPORTUNITIES IN NEWSPAPER WORK

Not so many years ago, the newsroom was a white, male haven. The occasional woman who crashed the reporting staff was assigned to emotional feature stories and was dubbed a "sob sister." The only other women on the editorial department payroll worked in the women's department, generally known as "society" or more casually as "sock," where they wrote wedding stories and club reports. The chances of a black or other minority member getting a job on the news staff of a newspaper were close to zero, in part because timid editors were afraid that sending them out on assignment might offend news contacts, as indeed actually occurred in some instances.

Newsrooms were not much different in this respect from many other business operations in the pre-World War II era. A change in attitude became apparent after the war, influenced by the social upheaval accompanying that conflict. A few black reporters began to appear on metropolitan news staffs. Young women hired as city room office "boys" during the wartime manpower shortage in some cases were able through aggressiveness and demonstrated ability to take over reporter jobs.

Change came slowly, nevertheless. Only in the late 1960s and early 1970s did women and minority members, especially blacks, begin to get equal treatment in hiring. Now, in most newspapers they are given equal consideration with white male candidates as job openings arise. Long-overdue changes in social attiudes plus the competent performance of those hired have brought this about, and newspapers are much better for it. Their reporting has a broader outlook and reflects a background more in line with the makeup of contemporary society.

The complaint remains that few women and black staff members hold high editorial posts on newspapers, that they still are regarded as second-line staff members. Although they are still largely not found in decision-making editorial positions, the situation is changing rapidly. Time will bring about the cure. In most cases they have been held back not by prejudice, but by seniority and the well-earned claim of longer-experienced staff members to climb up the ladder as openings occur. Today women are holding city editorships and managing editorships in growing numbers. The *Christian Science Monitor* in 1974 named a woman its chief editorial writer, a distinguished post.

Editors find it easier to find qualified women for their staffs than qualified minority members. Relatively few blacks have been graduated from journalism schools or come out of college with other suitable degrees and shown an interest in journalism. As a result, competition to hire able young black reporters is intense. As soon as one gets experience on a small paper, a larger paper beckons with a bigger salary. Because of this demand, skillful black news men and women tend to gravitate to higher-paying metropolitan newspapers faster than their white counterparts.

Many news jobs open up on American newspapers each year; since some 11,000 publications are in operation, counting the combined total of daily and weekly papers, the turnover in personnel is extensive. Because interest in journalism as a career has been increasing among college students, competition for these jobs is lively. Some college education, preferably a degree, is increasingly being regarded as a prerequisite for a job in a newsroom. Many editors in hiring beginners place the ability to spell and write grammatical English, plus indications that the applicant has a liberal stock of general knowledge and a variety of interests, above the applicant's supply of technical newspaper knowledge.

A growing number of daily newspapers have summer intern programs for college undergraduates with journalistic ambitions to fill the gaps in their staffs caused by vacations. Frequently, a successful summer internship leads to a permanent job upon graduation. Internships are filled quickly, so those desiring them should make initial contacts with possible summer employers early, perhaps during Christmas vacation.

Weeklies and small dailies are the most common places for beginners to get their start. They have personal involvement in more aspects of newspaper work on a small paper than on a large one; the experience acquired on a small paper, and the confidence gained, are important assets when the reporter or advertising representative seeks to step up to a larger newspaper.

News and Editorial

There are two main divisions of newsroom work—*reporting,* which includes gathering and writing news and feature stories and the taking of news and feature photographs; and *desk work,* which is the selection and preparation for printing of the written material and photographs submitted by the reporters, photographers, and the wire and syndicate services. Those who do the desk work are called editors.

This distinction between the newsgatherers and the news processors is quite sharp on large daily newspapers. Some editors will go a year or more without writing a single news story, and metropolitan reporters have nothing to do with the selection of a headline or page placement of the stories they write. On smaller papers, the distinction is less pronounced, and in many cases an editorial staffer spends part of the day as a reporter, photographer, and writer and the other part in selecting and processing the news for publication. The smaller the paper, the greater the need to be the proverbial jack of all trades.

Some men and women find their greatest satisfaction in being reporters all their lives—probing for information, being close to events as they happen, and mingling with the people who make the news. Theirs is the most exciting part of newspaper work when big stories are breaking, and they are the ones the public knows. Few outsiders have any concept of the inside office workers who really put the paper together. Many of the finest reporters in the country abhor the idea of being bound to a desk all day, shuffling paper and fighting the mechanical demands of type and newsprint.

The fact remains, however, that a reporter rarely is promoted directly to a high editorial place on a large or medium-sized daily. The top jobs go to those who have had desk experience. They are the organizers, the planners, the men and women who think automatically of whether a head will "count" and whether all the essential stories for an edition are moved out to the composing room before deadline so the papers will come off the press on time. By the same token, few desk workers are truly successful unless they have had a thorough grounding in reporting, so they can know the problems a reporter faces on a story and can supply useful suggestions.

A beginner may start as a city hall beat reporter for a small daily, or as the telegraph editor, handling the wire and writing headlines. Sticking to the first choice could lead eventually to a metropolitan reporting staff; to the latter, to a large paper's copy desk. Or, in either capacity, the newcomer may remain with the small daily and soon rise to editorial management status.

On most daily newspapers there are specialized editing-reporting jobs, in which the editorial worker gathers news and also helps in preparing it for print. The woman's page, the sports page, the business page, and the entertainment page fall into this category. Some men and women prefer to become specialists and do their reporting in one area. The woman's pages of a modern daily, often broadened in scope under a title like "Family Living," offer many opportunities for stimulating writing. Sports is a magnet for prospective young men reporters and, increasingly, women as well. Business news has become a specialty on many papers, with staffs of as many as six or eight persons assigned to the area. Some metropolitan papers offer opportunities for critical reviewers of films, television, the drama, and books. Varied opportunities also arise to specialize in one of the broader general news areas: politics, science, labor, religion, urban and racial problems, space and aviation, social work, and public health.

A very important area of work is the editorial page. Editorial page staffs run to eight or ten members on metropolitan papers that pride themselves on the quality of their opinion offerings. Some specialize as writers of editorials on international affairs; others specialize in economics and business, or perhaps local subjects. The editorial page director coordinates their work and consults with the publisher on major policy decisions. At the smaller daily level, there may be only one editorial writer, plus a managing editor who may also attempt to comment on the day's news part of the time. Weekly newspaper editors sometimes write regular editorial columns; others prefer to write what they call "personal columns" in a more informal style.

Opportunities to advance on an editorial staff come in many forms. Much depends upon the staff member's temperament, and a bit of luck. As a rule, the management chooses for promotion to the top positions, when an important vacancy occurs, a man or woman with all-around experience and a record of dependability, good judgment under pressure, and creative thinking.

Photography

The newspaper photographer fills a large and growing role on the staff of every daily newspaper, large or small, as the field of photojournalism expands. On a newspaper, the photographer's primary task is to record in a single picture or a sequence, rapidly and factually, the news and feature developments of the day that lend themselves to pictorial treatment. The photographer may take pictures for the news, sports, woman's page, and entertainment editors, as well as for the promotion and advertising departments, so versatility is important. On large staffs employing twenty or more photographers and technicians individuals may develop specialties and work primarily in these fields.

Planning photographic coverage on good newspaper staffs is as meticulous as the arrangement of coverage by reporters. Large newspapers have photo editors who specialize in this work. Memorable news photos usually are the result of having a photographer assigned to the right place at the proper time, plus the photographer's instinct for the climactic moment in a news situation and technical ability to take an effective picture when that moment comes.

Newspaper photography has advanced far from the days when an aggressive copyboy of limited education could be taught the rudiments of a camera and turned loose as an ambulance-chasing photographer. Today many news photographers have college educations or have attended professional photography schools. They look upon photojournalism as a satisfying career and know that their income will increase with their skill. News photography is not a field for a shy person. The photographer must be ready at times to fight for the picture. However, the widely held concept of the photographer as a rough, brash person shoving heedlessly into the middle of things is inaccurate and misleading.

On the larger papers, the photographer's equipment ranges from the 5″ x 7″ Big Bertha camera with a 28″ lens to the 35mm or $2\frac{1}{4}″$ x $2\frac{1}{4}″$ camera. The trend is toward the use of small, inconspicuous equipment. Assignments range from aerial photos to closeups of tiny objects, such as rings. Two-way radio may keep the photographer in constant touch with the editor. Smaller dailies may have only one or two photographers, and the weekly editor often takes his or her own pictures. The reporter who can take photographs, and the photographer who can report, are in special demand on small papers.

Newspaper photographers receive the same salaries as reporters under American Newspaper Guild scales. They frequently supplement their salary checks with overtime assignments and with after-hour jobs such as photographing weddings. Freelance photographers, not on the newspaper payroll, are paid for newsworthy pictures that they submit for publication.

The movement of experienced photographers between media compares to that of writers and editors. A photojournalist may remain on newspapers permanently, move to the photographic staff of a television station or a magazine, or choose to enter the commercial or industrial photographic field (see Chapter 15).

Advertising, Circulation, Management

Although news reporting is the most glamorous and best-publicized part of newspaper work, many other opportunities are available for young men and women in advertising sales and copywriting, circulation, promotion and public relations, personnel, research, production, and general business management.

The advertising department is one of the most attractive for sales-minded persons. A good newspaper space salesperson must be much more than a glib talker. The advertising representative must be able to supply the potential advertiser with abundant and accurate figures about the paper's circulation pattern and totals, the advertising rates, and the kind of merchandising support the advertiser will receive. Knowledge of at least the rudiments of layout and artwork is important. In addition, the representative should be enthusiastic and able to give the merchant ideas about how best to use an advertising budget. Selling newspaper advertising requires the art of persuasion, a briefcase well loaded with facts and ideas, and a strong personal belief that newspaper space will move merchandise off the merchant's shelves.

Advertising work for weeklies and small dailies is an excellent training ground. Some recent college graduates become advertising managers of weeklies, handling all types of business for their papers from classified ads to major local accounts. The same sort of opportunities for diversified experience come on small dailies, although as they increase in circulation the dailies tend to specialize their advertising staff functions. On smaller papers, the advertising representative is likely to be copywriter as well; on larger dailies, there are positions for copywriting specialists and artists.

Many advertising careers begin in the classified department of larger newspapers, where the newcomer deals with many small accounts in a variety of fields. A certain amount of classified advertising comes in voluntarily, but most of it must be solicited. Classified is sold on a day-to-day basis with deadlines only a few hours before publication. Much as on a reporter's beat, sales representatives have territories and detailed lists of accounts to cover.

Classified advertising is closer to the people than any other type. A three-line ad offering a desirable item for sale at a reduced price may cause the private advertiser's phone to ring dozens of times within a few hours after the paper appears. The advertiser is delighted and impressed by the paper's readership. Conversely, the failure of an advertisement to get results may lead the advertiser to grumble, "That paper is no good!" A good classified copywriter seeks to learn the tricks of concise, alluring wording. Readership tests show that classified sections are among the best-read in a newspaper. Recently, newspapers have abolished the practice of listing help wanted advertisements by sex, and now do so only by type of job offered.

The young sales representative is often promoted from classified into the local display department, and later perhaps into the smaller and more select national (or general) department. While classified ad department members scramble to meet daily quotas of lines for the next day's paper, national advertising department members work with manufacturers and distributors of brand-name products, often weeks in advance of publication. Schedules are sold in multiple insertions, sometimes in color. A newspaper's national sales staff works in conjunction with its national newspaper representative organization, which solicits advertising for it in other cities.

The circulation department offers some opportunities for college-trained individuals with organizing ability, promotional ideas, and a liking for detail. Supervisors who have a knack for working with carrier boys and the rapidly increasing number of carrier girls, much like a high school coach, are in demand. Although the top circulation jobs on large newspapers carry high salaries, the number of jobs available in this department for college-trained persons is somewhat less than in editorial and advertising.

On larger dailies, well-paying and interesting jobs exist in such supplementary departments as promotion and public relations, research, personnel, and administration. Some newspapers put out their own institutional publications for employees.

In the production department, which puts the words into type and prints the newspaper, the work is mechanical in nature, requiring technical skill. The work attracts few college-educated persons. Most employees in the department work their way up through apprenticeship programs to journeyman status, and perhaps into supervisory positions. Graduate engineers and those with advanced training in electronics are becoming more frequent in production work. The revolution in printing methods, which we will discuss shortly, recently has drawn women into the nation's composing rooms, long almost exclusively a man's world.

Cost control is extremely important in newspaper production, just as in any manufacturing process. Elaborate accounting sheets are kept showing the cost of setting a column of type, making up a page, printing a thousand papers, increasing the size of an edition by two pages, working a press crew overtime because of a missed deadline, and a hundred other expenses. All these costs are weighed carefully in setting the newspaper's advertising rates. The publisher who pegs space rates too low will attract additional advertising but will lose money by doing so. If a loosely run production department has such large costs that the publisher must charge abnormally high rates to cover them, advertisers will use other media instead.

Most editorial people on large newspaper staffs, it might be added, know little and care less about such production and cost problems. They regard the business aspects of publishing as something remote and of scant concern to them. This is unfortunate, especially if they have thoughts of striking off on their own some day on the small weekly they dream about.

Salaries

Newspaper salaries, although not at the top of the list, compare favorably as a whole with those in other businesses and professions that require a good education and creative thinking. They have improved sharply during the past twenty-five years. The activities of the American Newspaper Guild have been an important factor in this improvement. Organized in 1933 during the Depression when editorial salaries in particular were low, the guild has campaigned as an organized labor union for higher wages and more favorable working conditions. It has called strikes against newspapers to enforce its demands. A rise in newspaper salaries was inevitable, even without the existence of the guild, or the industry could not have held its workers as economic conditions improved. But the activities of the guild speeded the process.

Today the guild has 30,000 members, mainly on larger papers. Its contracts with management cover salaries, vacations, severance pay, and working conditions. The salary levels are minimums, covering all men and women in the categories specified. Some guild contracts cover just editorial departments; others, all nonprinting employees. The basic contract provides a graduated pay scale, with annual steps from the starting minimum through five or seven years to a top minimum. Salary advancement faster than, and beyond the top of, guild scales is by individual negotiation with management. Salaries on newspapers without guild contracts usually are in line with guild papers of similar circulation.

Like pay in other industries, newspaper salaries rose rapidly during the mid-1970s inflation, especially on papers whose contracts included cost-of-living increases. In a handful of metropolitan cities—Washington, for example—they were well above the $400-a-week point in the late 1970s and were approaching the $25,000 annual figure. Many veteran staff members are above guild minimum levels.

Such salaries are paid only in a few cities where living costs are exceptionally high; don't expect that kind of money in smaller cities, where living is more reasonable. Beginning salaries in a great number of cities were well above $150 a week, and rising, in the latter part of the 1970s. Broadly speaking, average newspaper staff members can expect to start at salaries comparable to beginning teachers with the same amount of education, perhaps somewhat higher, but as their years of experience increase, their salary advantage over teachers becomes greater. Most newspaper people can't expect to earn as much as successful doctors and attorneys.

Twenty-five years or so ago, editors hiring young reporters told them, "You won't make much money, but you'll have a lot of fun." The second half of the cliché is still true; fortunately, by and large the first half no longer is accurate.

Newspaper salaries in general are comparable to those paid in broadcasting, but lower than on large magazines and in public relations. This fact often lures the young graduate directly into the public relations field, often an unwise decision because a few years of the discipline and challenging experiences of news reporting generally will make the person more effective in other fields later.

The guild salaries are for 37- to 40-hour weeks, for average people. Superior people get above-minimum salaries. But as in all professions, they must expect to work more than a mere 40-hour week to get extra pay. Any newspaper person can add income by becoming a specialist, or doing outside writing and speaking so long as this work does not conflict with the person's basic employment. Another route to the top pay levels is through skilled desk work, where a pronounced shortage of qualified personnel has existed in recent years, particularly since the introduction of video display terminals.

Although many men and women spend their entire careers in the newspaper business, others move on from it into related fields. Newspapers are a training ground for workers in all mass communications media.

A copyeditor studies a news story she has "called" from the newsroom computer onto her video display terminal for editing. (Photo courtesy of South Bend *Tribune,* South Bend, Indiana.)

THE PRINTING REVOLUTION

The word "revolution" should be used cautiously. By proper definition, it means a complete or drastic change. Thus it is precisely the word to describe the upheaval in the methods of printing newspapers that has taken place during the past dozen years, and is continuing. The changes that have already occurred, and further ones now being developed, soon will make the typical newspaper plant of twenty-five years ago look like a prehistoric metal graveyard. Or as *Gannetteer,* the publication of the Gannett Group, said of its last Linotype machines, "like pterodactyls looking for a tarpit."

By 1900 most of the basic daily newspaper letterpress printing processes that currently are being tossed onto the dumpheap had been developed—the Linotype machine that set lines of hot metal type at the command of an operator's fingers on the keyboard, the makeup of hot metal type into page forms, and the stereotype plates that were locked on the presses. During the next fifty years the United States saw the development of the automobile, the invention of the airplane, radio, and television—yet the techniques for printing the newspapers that reported these events remained static: noisy, slow, and prone to error.

Then, with a slow rumbling, the revolution began. It first involved long rolls of specially treated paper tape, about half an inch wide. Instead of fingering a Linotype keyboard and releasing one matrice at a time, an operator punched the words on a keyboard that perforated the roll of tape. A different combination of holes in the tape represented each letter, figure, and punctuation mark. This was known as TTS, teletypesetting. These tapes were fed through the Linotype or Intertype machines, automatically releasing the matrices at high speed. One operator could monitor two or three machines simultaneously. TTS speeded up the traditional "hot metal" method of creating type but was only a forerunner of greater changes. The real upheaval came when that electronic marvel, the computer, was created for calculation and industrial use, and ways were found to harness it to setting type.

Preparing Type for Newspapers

The goal of electronic typesetting is to reduce keyboarding to an absolute minimum. That is, to eliminate the wasteful duplication of physical effort traditionally involved in transforming a news story from a sheet of copy paper in a reporter's typewriter into corrected type, ready for printing.

Under the old method, the reporter wrote a story and turned it in to the city desk. The city editor marked it up with a copy pencil, then a copy desk editor gave it a further dress-up and wrote a headline for it. Next the Linotype operator typed out the corrected story on his keyboard, changing it into lines of metal type. A proof of the type was pulled and read by a proofreader; errors marked by the proofreader were corrected by having the Linotype operator set replacement lines for the erroneous ones. Sometimes the operator created new errors while correcting the original ones. A printer pulled out the bad lines from a galley of type and put the corrected ones in their place. All too often he carelessly placed the new lines in the wrong spot in the galley, creating a fresh error that appeared in print as mixed-up lines. Finally, another printer placed the galley of type in the page form where an editor had dummied it to appear. The process required many hands, was slow, and was prone to creating errors that were not in the original story.

Contrast that system with the electronic method that is emerging in newsrooms throughout the country. Competing electronic systems have been developed, so that variations are found in different modernized newspapers, but all are designed to achieve the same goal. And that is

The editing nerve center of a daily newspaper with a circulation of 125,000. The city editor is in the foreground with his back to the camera. The copy **desk** is to the far left, the news editor is in the checked shirt, and the men to the city editor's right are the Sunday edition editor and state edition editor. Each desk has a video display terminal. The "Lazy Susan" in the center revolves to distribute material among the editors. (Photo courtesy of the South Bend *Tribune.*)

---

to have a story typed by a reporter go directly into a computer storage bank, from which it is called out by an editor onto a screen by the push of a button, for review and correction; by another push of a button, the computer feeds the story into the phototypesetter, from which it emerges as errorless type on a long sheet of paper with headline attached. It is ready to be pasted onto a page-size sheet of light cardboard; this in turn will be processed into a printing plate for the press. Only one typing effort by the reporter is required. The saving in time and labor, and the reduction in the possibilities of error, are huge.

The key piece of machinery that makes this possible, in addition to the computer itself, is a cathode ray device called the *video display terminal,* or VDT. This is a special electric typewriter keyboard, supplemented with command keys, with a small television screen on top. As the reporter types the story, it appears line for line on the video screen. By pushing certain command keys the writer can move the words around on the screen to make inserts, spelling corrections, and deletions, until the story is considered finished and ready to submit to the editors.

In the old days on a big newspaper the reporter called out "Copy!" and a boy rushed the typewritten page to the city desk. Or, if time wasn't pressing, the reporter carried it to the editor's incoming basket. On the VDT, the reporter pushes a command button and the story is placed in computer storage. A brief memo of its content goes to the city editor. With the video screen cleared, the reporter can proceed to write another story. Portable terminals will enable a reporter out in the field, covering a football game, for example, to transmit the story directly into the home office computer storage.

The editor, when ready for the story, strikes the proper symbol key on the VDT and the words appear on the screen. The editor too can make changes on the keyboard; the story then can be passed to a VDT screen on the desk of a copyeditor, who makes a final check for errors, writes a headline, and indicates the size and column width of the headline by striking the proper symbol keys. Finally, the copyeditor touches the key "Set" and the computer dispatches the story to the phototypesetting machine. Incoming press association stories also flow directly into the computer's memory bank, for similar handling.

The phototypesetting machine is the compact electronic replacement for the old Linotype. It contains a whirling disk of type letters in different faces, or a cathode ray tube device. At the flowing electrical impulse commands of the computer, the phototypesetter records the indicated letters in sequence on fast film; this film produces a positive print of the words on a sheet of coated paper that emerges from the darkroom through a slot, ready for pasteup. This is called "cold type."

Another electronic typesetting machine, often used in conjunction with the VDT. is the *optical character reader,* or OCR. The reporter types a story on a special electric typewriter using hard white paper. The writer and the editor mark corrections on the story pages with a light blue felt-tipped pen to which the electronic eye is "blind" and strike out unwanted words with a heavy black pen. A special operator types in the corrected words in certain positions under the original typed line. The copy sheet is placed face down into the OCR (optical character recognition), or scanner, which resembles an office copying machine. A small electronic "reader" inside scans the copy line for line, inserting the corrections as marked, at tremendous speed. The output can be fed directly into a phototypesetting machine or into the computer storage bank for later callup, or produced as punched tape that can be placed physically into the phototypesetter at a desired time. A "souped-up" Linotype machine in the old days did well to produce ten lines a minute. A phototypesetter can produce as much as five hundred lines a minute.

Because of the delicate machinery involved, the changeover to electronic equipment has been full of "bugs." Nor has it been easy for oldtimers in the newsrooms. Accustomed to pounding out stories on favorite typewriter "mills" whose idiosyncrasies they knew, some found it difficult to remember the "modes" and technical instructions involved in operating the VDT. They discovered, too, that the computer can talk back. It is programed to query steps the operators take and buttons they push that seem inconsistent to its mechanical "brain."

One tale illustrative of the frustrations involved, told around the Gannett organization, involves an operator who typed something into the computer. The machine answered on the terminal screen, "Are you sure?" The irritated reporter typed out, "Hell, no." He didn't know that the first two letters of his mild expletive, *he,* were the same letters as the command, "Help." Whereupon the computer printed out for him a list of all the commands for the entire system.

Other news staffers adapted quickly to the electronic systems as faster, cleaner and, indeed, more fun. After a while, even the reluctant ones admitted that they wouldn't want to go back to the old ways.

An important result of the typesetting revolution has been to break down the ancient barriers between the composing and news rooms. Control of typesetting has been largely moved "up front" into the hands of the editors, away from the composing room. The further the revolution proceeds, the smaller the role of the composing room becomes. The traditional proofreader may disappear, except for small special tasks.

On the near horizon, but still in the experimental stage, is a video terminal arrangement by which an editor can make up an entire news page on a large desk-instrument screen, placing premeasured stories, pictures, and advertisements in the desired positions. Then by punching a button the editor orders the entire page to be photoset swiftly, ready to be transformed into a printing plate for the press. This process is called full pagination. When fully operative, it will put control of page production primarily in the news department's hands. By facsimile transmission, the full page can be moved electronically to subsidiary printing plants miles away.

To many newspaper people, much of this still seems like dream stuff. Because of the heavy investment involved, labor contracts, and disputes as to which commercial systems are best, adoption of the new machinery is uneven. The course has been set, however; within a decade the great

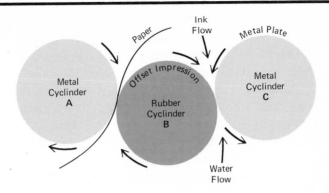

FIGURE 9.1 How offset printing works. The impression on the plate affixed to cylinder C is "offset" onto rubber cylinder B, then printed on paper passing between cylinder B and cylinder A.

majority of American daily newspapers will be using all or most of the methods described above.

Printing the Paper

Traditional printing methods in the pressroom are undergoing a radical change, too, if one that is not quite so spectacular. The heavy lead stereotype plate formed from a made-up page of metal type and locked onto a press cylinder is rapidly becoming a museum piece.

Two systems are replacing it. One is *offset printing,* the use of which began on weekly newspapers and spread rapidly to small and then larger daily newspapers. By the late 1970s, approximately three-fourths of the American daily newspapers were being printed by offset, although the largest ones were hesitant to switch to this method, primarily because of the millions of dollars involved in junking their letterpress presses and replacing them.

Offset printing is based on lithography, an older process in which printing was done from a smooth flat surface of stone. In surface printing, the image is placed on the stone by a greasy substance that has an affinity for ink. The nonprinting surface is covered with a thin film of water that repels the ink. Thus only the image is printed on paper when pressure is applied. The image is transferred from the printing plate cylinder to a rubber blanket attached to a second cylinder. It is then transferred to the paper, which is carried by a third impression cylinder. Development of offset presses capable of printing on a continuous web of paper was a major step in adapting this process to newspaper printing. Newspapers printed by offset are noted for their excellent photographic reproduction and strong, solid black tones.

Newspapers unwilling to discard their traditional presses, because of cost or other factors, have turned to the lightweight printing plate weighing a few ounces as a replacement for the bulky stereotype plates. Several commercial variations of this concept exist. The underlying principle is the same. A thin photosensitive polymer substance is spread onto a page-size aluminum plate. The image of the pasted-up news page in negative form is exposed photographically onto the polymer and the nonprinting surface material washed away. Laser beam techniques also are being developed to transfer the page impression onto a thin plate. The plate is mounted on a lightweight, curved "saddle" and locked onto the press cylinder.

Still in the future, but expected to emerge from the laboratories into daily newspaper pressrooms during the 1980s, is an even more radical system called *plateless printing,* which will eliminate the printing plates. The printed word will be applied to rolls of newsprint by computer-controlled ink jet technology. Some of the country's most imaginative scientists and engineers are working to make this ultimate step in the printing revolution a reality.

Further down the road, but potentially workable, is the "newspaper in the home," transmitted by cable television circuit from an electronic newsroom to a home TV screen. That idea, too, is under serious examination by researchers.

THE WEEKLY NEWSPAPER

A Midwestern weekly newspaper editor recently told a story about the pharmacist in his small county seat city who gave the wrong dosage for a prescription. The boy to whom the medicine was given died, and charges of negligence were brought against the druggist. His attorney obtained a change of venue to have the case tried in another county, so the trial publicity would not be seen in detail locally and damage the druggist's reputation. This offended the editor's principles of reporting the news, so although the extra expense strained his limited budget, he sent a reporter to the other county and covered the trial in detail. The druggist lived across the street from the editor. They saw each other every day. The druggist escaped without imprisonment, but because of the editor's action he still refused to speak to him more than two years after the trial.

This incident illustrates an essential point about weekly journalism—its intimacy. The people about whom the editor writes are neighbors, social acquaintances, fellow members of churches and clubs. They apply pressure on the publisher and editor of the weekly newspaper to conform, to shush up unpleasant news. Although less subject to time pressures than editors on daily newspapers, weekly editors have special problems. A large daily would not publish reviews of high school plays; the weekly is expected to do so, and if the review speaks ill of the performance, the editor can expect phone calls and visits from the actors' parents, accusing the newspaper of painting a false picture of the town's teenagers.

In thousands of American towns, the weekly newspaper is at the core of community life. It is the chief source of information about the activities of individuals and organizations, and the merchants look to its advertising columns as a weekly tool for selling goods. In the files of a small-town weekly are recorded the vital statistics of the town's life—the births and deaths, marriages, social events, and tragedies, and the ludicrous moments that give life zest. Even when it is overshadowed by a big city daily a few miles away, the weekly newspaper often has a secure place in the heart of its community and can continue to thrive. The chief stock in trade it has to offer is names—subscribers reading about their neighbors and about themselves. The larger the newspaper, the less impact the names in news stories have on readers, because they do not know all the people mentioned. This personal link is an advantage the community weekly newspaper has over its larger, more sophisticated city cousin.

The weekly newspaper is editing and publishing in its simplest form, although anyone who believes that putting out a weekly is easy has been badly misled. All the jobs involved in any newspaper must be done: getting news and editing it, selling advertising, handling circulation, and seeing to it that the paper is printed on time. On a large daily many people handle each of these operations, but on a weekly everything is done by a handful of workers. The 40-hour week is only a dream to the editors and publishers of weekly newspapers. After the day's work at the office is finished, the weekly editor covers civic meetings, attends social functions in the hope of getting news, and listens to the complaints of fellow townspeople. Weekly newspaper publishing is a risky enterprise for a person who thinks only in editorial terms; unless the publisher quickly learns the business tricks of obtaining revenue from advertising and circulation, the paper won't live long. Nor does the free time between editions exist in the way envisaged by a metropolitan newspaper worker who dreams of settling down in a small town to the easy life of a weekly editor. The minute one week's edition is out, the editor starts churning out copy for the following week and the publisher starts a new round of advertising solicitation. When the two jobs are embodied in one person, as often is the case, he or she rarely has a free day, even on weekends.

The development of offset printing has changed life on weekly newspapers. In earlier days, most were printed in the newspapers' own small hot metal shops, on aged equipment and a flat-bed press of nineteenth-century vintage. The resulting newspaper was poorly printed, often with miserable reproduction of photographs. Today, a large majority of weeklies are produced by offset, either in their own plants if the paper is large enough to justify the investment, or in a central plant along with several other weeklies. More weekly newspapers are switching over to offset every year.

Most weekly newspapers carry a Thursday publication date, for a sound commercial reason. It is the day on which local merchants want to reach readers with news of their weekend sales. The grocery stores in particular key their merchandise pattern to their Thursday newspaper advertisements, offering special items on sale through Saturday or Sunday. Some weeklies appear on Wednesday, if many of their merchants desire a longer sales span.

A look at the operation of a typical up-to-date weekly newspaper in a small city gives us a picture of what this kind of newspaper life is like. The paper has been in continuous publication, with some changes of name, since 1879. It is published in a city of slightly less than 5000 population whose economy is based on farming and small manufacturing. The newspaper's circulation is 2700, most of it within the radius of a few miles of its downtown office.

A few years ago, the paper closed its old-fashioned printing plant and now is printed offset in a daily newspaper plant 27 miles away. Although this has reduced costs and produced a far more attractive product, the almost-daily delivery trips between towns are a nuisance. Usually its edition is 16 pages, dropping occasionally to 12 or rising to 22. Six persons compose its staff: a general manager who handles business affairs, sells and lays out advertisements, and takes news pictures and prints them in the darkroom; an advertising manager; a general handyman and runner who makes the trips to the printing plant; a woman bookkeeper; a woman all-around staff member who handles subscriptions, helps out at the front counter, writes the "society" news and a chitchat column, and lays out advertisements for merchants who seek the feminine touch; and the editor. The manager specialized in graphics at a two-year college. The editor is a recent journalism school graduate.

Virtually every story and picture is of local origin, except for a weekly handout column from the district congressman and a few public interest publicity releases for organizations like the National Safety Council. No press association or other national news is included. Stories and pictures of weddings and engagements take extensive space; so does high school sports material.

The editorial and advertising staffs must keep a daily flow of material moving to the printing plant. The advertising deadline is Friday noon for the issue that carries a dateline of the following Thursday, although an occasional small ad is slipped in Monday morning. The deadline for news is noon Tuesday. With their final copy in hand, the manager and editor drive the 27 miles to the small daily publishing plant that prints their paper, where the final type is set early Tuesday afternoon and the news pages made up.

Wednesday at the daily newspaper plant is a busy one. It prints three weekly newspapers that morning—one at 9 A.M., "ours" at 10 A.M., and a third at 11 A.M.; then it clears the presses for its own daily edition.

The paper we are examining distributes some of its copies to subscribers by mail, but sells 1200 of its 2800 copies directly to cash customers at stores and at its home office, where people are waiting when papers arrive from the printer's at noon Wednesday. These cash customers are too anxious for the paper to await its delivery by mail the next day.

Three out-of-town daily newspapers, one a major daily from a city 30 miles away, are sold in the town, yet the weekly manager does not consider them direct competition, even though they carry some news from his town.

The range of editorial excellence among weekly newspapers is wide. Splendidly edited weeklies are to be found throughout the United States, along with others that barely qualify for the label "newspaper." Rarely are weeklies of the crusading type, again with outstanding exceptions. Most weekly editors see their role as that of printing constructive, orthodox news without dealing in what often is called sensationalism. In some cases the newspaper's profit margin is so thin that the publisher cannot risk irritating an important advertiser by printing something the person dislikes. Frequently a weekly newspaper, such as the one we have examined, has no editorial page at all. Without resorting to big-city street sensationalism, many weekly editors could serve their communities better if they dealt more bluntly with local problems, despite the pressures not to do so. The American weekly press as a whole is conformist and conservative.

Free Circulation Weeklies

In recent years, especially in suburban areas, some weeklies have changed to a free distribution basis. They give their paper away instead of selling it, delivering it to every home addressed to that faceless creature, Occupant. Those who use this practice prefer to call it "controlled circulation"; their opponents use the derogatory term "throwaway." Some such publications are "shoppers," containing only enough editorial filler to close up the chinks around the ads.

The publisher who gives away a newspaper accepts three financial disadvantages to gain one important advantage. The newsprint bill rises and income from circulation disappears, and if copies are distributed by mail, postal costs rise too. But by convincing advertisers that the town is blanketed with copies of the paper the publisher can obtain a higher advertising rate and more linage. As advertising income rises, so does net profit. Such free distribution methods usually work best in those areas where there is a large concentration of homes.

The next step above the weekly newspaper is the semiweekly, published twice a week, frequently on Monday and Thursday, or sometimes with a Sunday edition. Relatively few semiweekly and triweekly publications exist, because usually a weekly that seeks to expand into broader fields makes the jump directly to daily operation.

THE SMALL AND MEDIUM-SIZED DAILY NEWSPAPER

The great difference in operation between weekly and small daily newspapers is the addition of the element of timeliness. The principle of "today's news today" dominates minds of all daily newspaper staff members. Because the process of assembling and printing the newspaper is done six or seven times a week, thinking must be accelerated.

Working on a daily does not necessarily make a reporter or an advertising solicitor a better worker, but it does tend to produce a faster one. Deadlines take on a fresh, compelling meaning. On a daily, if the copy deadline is 12:40 P.M., any stories sent out to the composing room after that minute may cause a late press start. That in turn can mean missed bus connections and lost street sales for the circulation department.

A substantial overlap exists between the weekly and small daily fields, in the sense that weekly cities sometimes are larger than small daily cities, and some weeklies have more circulation and advertising than small dailies. Yet, given a choice of jobs at identical pay, the majority of staff members probably would choose the daily. They find more stimulation in the faster pace and in having a greater kinship with world affairs through the presence of wire service news in the office.

What, then, causes some towns to have daily newspapers and other larger ones to have only a weekly? Essentially it is a matter of geography, supplemented at times by the commercial audacity of the publisher. When a good-sized town is close to a large city, competition from the big neighboring paper may make successful operation of a small daily financially impossible. Yet there is room for a weekly newspaper to present community news and advertising. A small daily in a relatively isolated region may operate at a profit, whereas the same paper would fail if published in the shadow of a large city.

The primary problem a daily newspaper publisher faces is that the cost of producing the paper is the same every day, regardless of how much or how little advertising each issue carries. A "fat" paper one or two days a week cannot carry all the burden if the other issues have little advertising content. Most newspapers try to average better than a 50:50 ratio between the amount of editorial and advertising content, with the greater weight going to advertising—up to 65 percent or more on some days.

A small daily is excellent training ground for all journalists; many who later attain fame have started on such publications. On the smallest dailies, those in the 5000 circulation range, staff members "double in brass" by doing a little bit of everything. The key newsroom figure on the very small daily is the managing editor, who not only directs a staff of four or five other persons but covers stories, usually night civic meetings, and does most of the desk work that puts the local and national press association news into form for the printers. The managing editor sometimes writes editorials, too. On a larger daily this work would be handled by several persons, but the managing editor succeeds in getting them all done and still gets the paper to press on time.

Usually the managing editor of even such a small daily has a college education and perhaps five years of newspaper experience. The work combines managing editor, city editor, and copy desk jobs into a single person responsible for producing a newspaper that fluctuates in size from 8 to 16, or occasionally 20, pages a day. Typically, the staff under the managing editor includes one or two persons with some college education and some "locals" who have been hired at some time to help out, shown sufficient talent to fill lesser jobs, and become permanent fixtures.

The advertising staff of a very small daily often consists of a business-advertising manager who handles most of the big accounts, another display advertising salesperson, a clerk-secretary, and a classified advertising manager. The circulation manager frequently is a young local person who has come up from the ranks of carriers. There must be a bookkeeper, too, and a proofreader—a very small group, altogether, to produce a newspaper day after day. This is daily journalism at its lowest level.

An important aspect of newspaper work a young journalist learns on a small daily is meeting deadlines. With mechanical facilities limited, the flow of copy must be scheduled closely, giving the beginner a sense of urgency. The editorial newcomer learns to "make do" with the available time and equipment, to cover local stories, to observe the workings of a press association wire, to write headlines. Mistakes in stories are brought home to the writer quickly because of close business and social ties with the news sources. Also, the person breaking into the business has an opportunity to practice photography and to get a taste of photojournalism under realistic operating conditions. If a beginner has that extra spark of creative writing and imagination so sought after by newspapers of all sizes, it will shine forth more quickly on a small daily than almost anywhere else in journalism the young woman or man might work.

Small-Daily Editorial Problems

Perhaps you wonder how a five-person editorial staff can produce enough copy day after day to fill the newspaper. Where does this small staff in a little city find sufficient news and get it all written fast enough to make the daily deadline? The answer is, help from other sources of copy. Part of the allotted editorial space is filled with feature material purchased from newspaper syndicates, and part is filled with wire service stories selected from the global news reports on the AP or UPI teleprinter. Photographs help, too, plus adding to reader interest. Some are local photographs taken by staff members or supplied by commercial photographers; others are purchased from the news picture services. A three-column picture 6 inches deep occupies 18 column inches, almost the equivalent of a full column of type.

Taking a 500-word story from the press association teleprinter and sending it to the composing room is quicker and easier than writing a local story of the same length. Even the smallest daily needs to give its readers highlights of major world developments, but overdependence on wire service copy diminishes the local newspaper's value to its readers. They would prefer to read well-developed local "enterprise" stories and interviews than second-rate telegraph stories. The diligent small-city managing editor, knowing this well, is torn constantly between providing readers with as much of the latter material as the small staff can obtain, and meeting the demands from the mechanical department to get the pages filled by deadline so the press can start on time.

As the circulation of a newspaper increases, so does the staff. With somewhat larger staffs, the tasks performed by the managing editor of the small daily are divided among several persons, and the functional organization that reaches its peak on the staff of a metropolitan newspaper begins to emerge.

The managing editor's primary role is to oversee all the operations. Under that person is a city editor, who directs the work of the local reporters and photographers, and a telegraph editor, who selects and edits stories from the wire. As the staff grows, a copy desk is set up to handle the editing of copy and the writing of headlines. With specialists at work, the result is a better-edited newspaper.

Impact of the Medium-sized Daily

The medium-sized daily—say one approaching the 50,000 circulation point that is sometimes used arbitrarily to mark the start of the "big city" group—often reaches far beyond the city limits because its copies are distributed by truck, bus, mail, and even airplane to surrounding rural areas. A motorist driving along a country road can often judge the impact of the newspaper published in a nearby city by the number of brightly painted tubes nailed on posts outside farmhouses to receive delivery of the daily editions.

Papers of this size are financially strong enough to have editorial staffs of considerable scope, usually with several persons of outstanding ability. Some may eventually move on to metropolitan papers; others are content to spend their working lives in the congenial atmosphere of a

TYPICAL ORGANIZATION OF A MEDIUM-SIZED DAILY NEWSPAPER

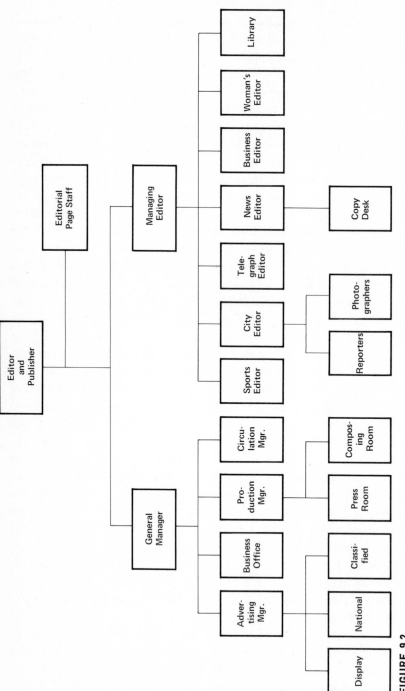

FIGURE 9.2

middle-sized paper in a community sufficiently large to have an urban flavor, yet small enough for comfortable living.

At first glance, the medium-sized daily operating under the shadow of a metropolitan giant would appear at a severe disadvantage. Usually it cannot offer the bulk that American readers too often associate with a desirable product. In fact, frequently the result is just the opposite. The medium-sized daily prospers because it provides the reader with as much, or nearly as much, press association and feature material as desired, and in addition provides detailed news of the local community. Density of population in these fringe areas is sufficient to provide a strong circulation potential. The presence of branch outlets of major downtown stores offers large advertising sources. Most department stores with suburban branches place advertising in the community dailies— advertising revenue that might previously have gone to the metropolitan papers. Metropolitan newspapers in some cities, notably Chicago, have sought to counteract this trend by operating community dailies of their own that concentrate on local news as supplements to their downtown general publications.

The standards of medium-sized dailies in content, policies, and personnel frequently are high. Their salaries, although not equal to the metropolitan levels, are generally good and living costs frequently lower. For a young reporter whose ultimate goal is metropolitan journalism, a period of work on a well-regarded medium-sized daily is an excellent recommendation.

Editors of suburban community dailies keep a keen eye on the news "play" by their metropolitan rivals. They can give their readers later news than the afternoon big-city newspapers can, because the latter are handicapped in distributing their editions through heavy city traffic. By establishing a later deadline, the fringe daily can take advantage of quick delivery within its own community.

Selling the Papers

When it comes to selling the product it has produced, the daily newspaper is unique. It may have millions of dollars of equipment and a staff of experienced professional men and women to create it—yet leave the delivery of its newspapers and much of the selling effort to boys and girls, many of them not yet in their teens.

Management experts consider this a crazy system. Yet it works. Under this carrier system, a large majority of the 61 million daily papers sold in the United States reach their purchasers. Circulation managers have put computers to work in their offices to handle billing, maintain circulation lists, and speed up truck loading, but so far they have not found an electronic replacement for the carrier who brings the newspaper to the subscriber's door—preferably with what is called "pajama delivery," the paper placed so close to the front door that the subscriber can reach it without stepping outside.

Only in very large cities with heavy commuter traffic on public transportation do street sales of papers have the importance they once did. The home delivery carrier collects weekly or monthly for the daily service. Copies of an edition sold on the street, including through vending machines, are called single-copy sales.

Most methods of selling a newspaper are based upon the principle of having the publishing company sell copies to a distributor or delivery agent at a wholesale price several cents below the announced price per copy. The agent, including the home delivery carrier, sells the papers to the public at the published price; the difference between wholesale and retail prices provides the agent's profits.

Single-copy street sales are affected by the weather, traffic, shopping conditions, holidays, and the nature of the main headline. These factors do not influence home delivery sale. Thus home delivery gives a newspaper assured income and a firm circulation figure to quote to advertisers.

A few decades ago, in the fight to win circulation and outdo their rivals, some newspapers resorted to making exaggerated claims about their sales. Since advertising rates are based on circulation figures and on the cost of reaching each thousand readers, this led to many discrepancies and a chaotic situation in which honest publishers were placed at an unfair disadvantage by the unscrupulous operators. To correct this situation, the Audit Bureau of Circulations (ABC) was formed in 1914.

Newspapers that belong to the ABC, as most dailies do, submit detailed reports of their circulation every six months and open their books to a detailed examination by ABC auditors every year. Rigid rules are enforced. The organization puts limits on methods of solicitation, the number of low-cost subscriptions, bulk sales, and other devices used by publishers to inflate circulation figures. Types of circulation that fail to meet ABC standards are disallowed, and others of a somewhat transitory nature are appropriately indicated on the statements published by the ABC about each paper.

In their constant battle to build circulation, some daily newspapers use many kinds of prize contests. Most publishers prefer to build readership more slowly but solidly through their carrier and street-outlet organizations. No newspaper can afford to have its advertisers see that its daily sales are slipping. If that happens, the advertiser demands lower rates and the financial woes multiply. In the recent history of American newspapers there are many proofs of the fact that once a newspaper goes into a prolonged circulation decline, its prospects for survival are slim.

One widely used method of handling home delivery is known as the little merchant system. A carrier boy or girl has a route of several city blocks and is responsible for delivery of papers over that route, as well as for collecting the subscribers' fees. The more new subscribers or "starts" the carrier obtains, the more the carrier's monthly income will be. In effect, the carrier is an independent small merchant. The circulation departments conduct prize contests to stimulate production of new orders, giving rewards such as bicycles, sporting equipment, and trips to amusement centers to carriers who reach specified quotas. The underlying premise in this circulation system is incentive; the paper tries to make it worthwhile for the carrier to give up free hours, or to rise very early each morning, in order to deliver papers.

Changes in our life style are causing problems that earlier generations of carriers did not face. Thousands of families in large cities live in high-rise apartment buildings that have strict security systems. The carrier has difficulty entering the building to deliver and collect; newspapers left outside apartment doors are stolen. With so many women working at jobs outside their homes, nobody is at home to answer the doorbell when the carrier makes a daytime collection round. That means extra work at night to collect.

Then there are the preprints, another rather recent phenomenon. These are advertising sections printed in advance, separately from the basic newspaper, often by a commercial printer outside the newspaper plant. Properly labeled and dated, these are inserted into the newspaper, usually by the carrier. Stuffing machines can assemble such sections in advance in the mailroom of a large paper, but by the late 1970s the goal of developing an "on-line" stuffing machine to insert the preprint sections into the regular papers as fast as they rolled off the press was still unfulfilled. So the final inserting of the preprint sections, either singly or in preassembled groups, falls upon the carrier, who usually receives extra payment for the work. In the past, these advertising sections frequently went to homes as circulars through the mail, but soaring postal rates have made it more economical for merchants to have their preprints inserted into the newspaper (making the edition heavier for the carrier to haul around).

Given proper adult supervision, the carrier system works for newspapers because the product is partly presold. An appetite for news exists, and in most communities the newspaper is a household word. The youthful appeal of the carrier is often the decisive sales factor. Some critics, however, contend that overheavy reliance on juvenile sales representatives has held back newspapers from reaching their full sales potential. Recognizing this, the American Newspaper Publishers Association engaged Massachusetts Institute of Technology management experts to study the newspaper distribution system in search of new ways to do the job. Among the facts uncovered was that it costs more than 10 cents to get a copy of a daily newspaper into a reader's hand from the time it rolls off the press. In many instances, the subscription price of a home-delivered copy is no more than 10 cents. This means that all other costs of writing and printing the paper, plus any profit, must come primarily from advertising sales.

THE METROPOLITAN PRESS

The newspaper as a mass communication medium reaches its highest development in our metropolitan centers. Here the publishers and editors think of readers in terms of millions. If we calculate three readers to each copy of a paper printed, which is a common rule of thumb, a big-city newspaper with a Sunday circulation of a million copies is read by 3 million persons. The impact of a single news story published in such an edition is easy to perceive.

Many newspaper workers in editorial, advertising, and circulation departments look upon a metropolitan newspaper job as the goal of their careers, the sign of professional success. Ironically, quite a few big-city newspaper people in quiet bull sessions between editions talk longingly of escaping the scramble of metropolitan journalism for what they conceive of as the calmer, more orderly and satisfying life on smaller papers. Given an opportunity to break away from metropolitan work, however, many of this wistful brigade either refuse to do so or drift back to the so-called big time. The tempo, adventure, and prestige are alluring.

As stated earlier, metropolitan newspapers are the one group of the American press that has suffered severe attrition in the last quarter-century. Many of those whose names had been household words for decades have ceased publication, amid sentimental scenes of desolation and farewell in newsrooms that have seen the handling of so many dramatic stories in American history. No matter how understandable the underlying social and economic reasons for these deaths, the passing of individual newspapers grieves both readers and staff members. A newspaper is such an ingrained part of public life that its sudden disappearance leaves a painful sense of loss.

Undoubtedly, the best-known newspaper in the country is the morning and Sunday New York *Times.* The *Times,* edited as the country's newspaper of record, publishes lengthy texts of official documents and exhaustive reports on national and international developments. Its circulation—approximately 1 million daily and 1.5 million Sunday—is nationwide. It appeals to readers who want an abundance of government and cultural news. The *Times* is not written for a general mass audience, however, and many Americans find it less interesting than their own more personalized local newspapers. Like all newspapers, the *Times* commits its share of errors and shadings of news coverage. Such missteps are not surprising in a publication of its size, but they underline the point that no newspaper is totally accurate, no matter how great its reputation. Primarily because of its work on the Watergate story, the Washington *Post* also has become a household word nationally.

Few if any stories in a metropolitan paper are read by all who purchase the paper. Every reader chooses selectively, picking a limited number of items from the huge tray of reading delicacies on the basis of personal needs, interests, and whims. Even so, every story in a metropolitan paper, no matter how insignificantly it is displayed, is seen by thousands of readers.

Thus the reporter's writing on a large newspaper is absorbed by a very large number of persons. Yet the very size of the metropolitan region makes it impossible for the reporter to have direct contact with the audience. Except for personal acquaintances and the handful of readers who are either irate or thoughtful enough to report their reactions to an individual story, the metropolitan reporter has little opportunity to determine how stories are received. This is one of the most striking differences between big-city and small-town newspaper work.

The young man or woman looking toward metropolitan papers as a place to work discovers two major differences from smaller cities: greater speed and greater specialization.

Most small dailies have one basic edition a day. Some may supplement this with a street-sale edition in which the front page is remade with larger, flashier headlines and late news bulletins for sale to casual purchasers. Or they may have an early, less complete edition for distribution in rural areas. In contrast, some metropolitan newspapers publish at least five editions within a period of eight hours. Afternoon newspapers are especially burdened with numerous editions because of the fast-changing nature of news during the daytime hours and distribution problems. This requires high-speed work. The edition schedule is an almost sacred document, whose stated deadlines govern the work of several hundred employes. If the press run of a big newspaper starts 15 minutes late, a blunt-spoken post mortem often results in the publisher's office.

The final minutes before the deadline in each newspaper department are a-tingle with concentrated work. When the deadline has passed, and each department in the complicated process knows that it no longer can call back anything it has done or push anything more into the paper, there comes a period of relaxation and waiting for the fresh edition copies to be brought up from the pressroom. Then the buildup process for the next edition begins.

A typical metropolitan deadline sheet has minute-by-minute rules telling when the final story must cross the city desk and the copy desk and move to the composing room; when the last photograph must leave the editorial art department; when the final page must move out of the composing room; and what minute the press must start. A smooth flow of pages through the assembly line is essential. In a huge newspaper plant the production of a daily newspaper is a coordinated effort rarely exceeded in manufacturing, especially when we remember that the primary product fed into this conveyor belt system, news, is an intangible raw material difficult to find and hard to define. Few readers realize the intensity of effort and planning behind the daily newspaper tossed upon their doorsteps. Newspapers have failed to tell their own exciting story well enough.

The young reporter who obtains a metropolitan job right out of school usually considers himself or herself extremely lucky, as having gotten a big jump on classmates who go to work on weeklies or small dailies. Unfortunately, this is not necessarily the case. The big-city novice finds stimulation in associating with skilled veterans and watching exciting stories move through the production line. But too often the novice is shunted into a minor reporting job, like covering the overnight police beat, and is unable to get the all-around experience classmates are absorbing on smaller papers. Years may pass before the newcomer gets an opportunity to work on the copy desk. Seniority plays an important part in assignments on metropolitan staffs, and unless the young reporter is fortunate or shows exceptional talent for writing, advancement is slow.

Many editors and personnel managers of metropolitan papers advise beginners to work on small papers from three to five years before trying the metropolitan field. Often a young person coming to a metropolitan staff with a few years of smaller-city work will advance faster than one of similar age who has spent those same years on the big-city paper. The all-around experience of a smaller paper prepares the young reporter to fill many different jobs as they become available.

How a Metropolitan News Staff Functions

The key figure in the local newsgathering activities is the city editor, who has one or more assistants. Possibly a hundred reporters, even more in a few cases, are deployed at the most productive news sources, held in reserve as general assignment reporters, or organized into investigative teams. The reporters who are placed on specific beats, such as the police department or city hall, are responsible for gathering all news that occurs in their territory and turning it in to the city desk. When time permits, they write the stories themselves. But the urgency of deadlines often makes this impossible, so they telephone their facts to a rewrite specialist. These writers are old hands, hardened under pressure, swift in their writing and quick at organizing a mass of facts into a story that reads smoothly and concisely.

When the story has been written, it is turned in to the city desk. There the city editor or an assistant reads it to catch errors, make sure that it is easily understood, and find "angles" that need further development. Writers and editors concentrate on finding a good "lead" for the story, an opening paragraph that summarizes the situation or entices the reader further into the article.

Much reporting is done by telephone. The reporter assigned to a story calls as many sources as possible to cross-check the facts for accuracy and to obtain the best-rounded story possible. Some metropolitan beat reporters, especially those covering the police, may not write a story a week, even though they have worked on dozens by telephone.

While the city staff is gathering the local news, other groups are putting together other parts of the paper. News from the rest of the country and abroad arrives on the press association machines and from special correspondents. This is edited and coordinated on the telegraph desk.

City news and telegraph stories pass across the news desk, where they are weighed for importance and general interest. The news editor assigns them appropriate sizes of headlines and marks them into position on dummy sheets; it is these sheets that tell the printers how to assemble the mass of stories into the proper pages. The stories then pass to the copy desk for final editing. The appearance of video display terminals in a rapidly growing number of newsrooms is changing the familiar physical routine of copy desk work, but the principle is the same whether copyeditors are working with stories typed in the traditional manner or displayed for them on video screens. The language experts, supervised by the copy desk chief, give the stories a final polishing and write the headlines. From the copy desk the stories are released to the composing room.

The sports department, the woman's or family section, the financial editors, and other special groups are at work filling the pages allotted to them in a similar manner.

The person in charge of the entire news department is the managing editor, just as on the very small daily we discussed earlier. Only instead of doing the detailed work in person, the editor supervises the dozens of men and women who do it. The managing editor's post on a metropolitan newspaper is one of the most demanding and responsible jobs in all journalism.

SUNDAY PAPERS — WORLD'S LARGEST

By far the bulkiest newspapers published anywhere are the Sunday editions of American metropolitan newspapers. These mammoth publications wrapped in sections of colored comics often contain more than 300 pages, nearly 4 pounds of reading matter covering everything from the current world crisis to interior decorating advice, theatrical notices, baseball scores, and weekly television logs.

In the United States there are about twenty such Sunday newspapers with 500,000 or more circulation, and several with more than a million. Even these mammoth figures are greatly exceeded by the circulation of several British Sunday papers printed in London and distributed throughout the British Isles. They do not have the advertising bulk of their American counterparts, however.

The Sunday paper is designed for family reading and is distinguished from the daily editions by two elements: a large feature "package," and bulk retail advertising. As a medium for late spot news, the Sunday paper is less important than the daily editions because relatively less news occurs on Saturday (which it is covering) than on weekdays. Much of the material in the news sections is of a feature or background nature, stories for which no space exists in the smaller daily editions. Many newspapers print part of their Sunday editions well in advance because of the difficulty of printing such huge issues on the available press equipment on the publication date.

The Sunday editions of most newspapers have substantially higher circulation than the daily editions and sell at a price often more than double that of the daily paper. Publishing a Sunday paper is a very expensive operation because of the heavy costs involved in buying the colored comics and nationally syndicated magazine inserts and in preparing the abundance of locally created feature material, such as the weekly TV log and the staff-edited local magazine section. Newsprint costs on bulky papers are enormous. Smaller newspapers find Sunday publishing unprofitable in many instances, especially since they must compete against widely distributed metropolitan editions. As a result, the Sunday field is dominated by big-city newspapers that can afford to enter it: for most of them, it is very lucrative and provides a substantial share of annual profits.

Department stores have found Sunday editions to be one of their most effective selling tools. The paper is read at home in leisurely surroundings, and almost every member of the family peruses at least one part of the edition as it is scattered around the living room floor. So the stores put a heavy share of their advertising budget into the Sunday edition, often taking many pages in the same issue to publicize their wares.

CHAPTER 10

MAGAZINES

THE ROLE OF MAGAZINES

Much communication of ideas, information, and attitudes among the American people is carried on through magazines. Thousands of periodicals fall within this category. They range from the slick-paper, four-color monthly with circulation in the millions down to the small, special interest quarterly that, though virtually unknown to the general public, may have very strong influence within its field.

The magazine exists to inform, entertain, and influence its readers editorially and put before them advertising messages of national or regional scope. With a few exceptions, its outlook is national rather than local. Magazines never appear more frequently than once a week; thus they have more time to dig into issues and situations than the daily newspaper, and consequently they have a better opportunity to bring events into focus and interpret their meaning.

So many different types of magazines exist that making broad statements about their functions and goals may lead to inconsistencies. Some are published solely for their entertainment value and are loaded with material of little consequence. Others deal entirely with a serious investigation of contemporary problems, and many combine entertainment and service material with reporting and interpretation. It is valid to state that magazines have a much better opportunity than newspapers to serve as thoughtful interpreters and analysts of events and trends.

The magazine, with its more durable cover and bound pages, has a semipermanence the newspaper lacks. Magazines such as *National Geographic* often are kept around a home for years, or passed from hand to hand. They are halfway between newspapers and books in this regard and also in content. Broadly speaking, the magazine examines a situation from the middle distances, and the book examines it from the higher ground of historical perspective.

There is another basic difference between newspapers and magazines. A newspaper must appeal to an entire community and have a little of everything for almost everybody. With a few exceptions, like the *Wall Street Journal,* a newspaper cannot be aimed at a single special interest group and survive. Yet hundreds of successful magazines are designed for reading by such limited-interest groups as gasoline station operators, dentists, poultry farmers, and model railroad fans. Therein lies the richness of diversity that makes the magazine field so attractive to many editorial workers. The possibilities for the specialist editor and writer are greater than on newspapers, although the number of editorial jobs on magazines is fewer.

TYPES OF MAGAZINES

Generalizations about the content, style, and appearance of American magazines are dangerous because so many variations exist among the approximately 9500 periodicals now being published. That is the number given in Ayer's *Directory,* as distinguished from listings of newspapers with general circulations. Not all appear in magazine format, however; quite a few are tabloid or regular newspaper size. No more than 600 can be classified as general interest magazines. In contrast, there are 2500 specialized business and trade publications, 1300 in the field of religion, and about 700 agricultural periodicals, to list three major subfields. Not included in these figures are some 9000 industrial, or company, publications designed for employees, customers, stockholders, dealers, and others. Many of these are issued in magazine format. Although all magazines share certain basic problems of production and distribution, their editorial content and advertising are of a hundred hues. Even trying to group them into categories becomes difficult because inevitably there is overlapping, and a few magazines almost defy classification. Most magazines fall into the following general categories:

General Family Interest

Two mass circulation magazines that sell 18 million or more copies each issue lead this group. One is the *Reader's Digest,* begun in 1922 by DeWitt and Lila Wallace as a pocket-size compilation of nonfiction articles. Now the centerpiece of a giant publishing enterprise, it is a well-staffed mass circulation monthly blending informative, inspirational, and entertaining nonfiction. The other, *TV Guide,* appears weekly in regional editions; after a quarter-century of publication by the Annenberg family's firm, it has emerged dominant in its specialized function.

Television's diversion of advertising revenues from general family interest periodicals spelled the doom of such once-great magazines combining nonfiction and fiction as *Collier's* and the *American,* which died in 1956, and the *Saturday Evening Post,* abandoned as a weekly in 1969 (a monthly "nostalgia" edition still appears on newsstands). In the 1970s, for lack of advertising, the enormously successful picture magazines *Life* and *Look* also disappeared (except for occasional special issues of *Life*).

Into the void came the *National Geographic,* published since 1888 as a staid travelog journal, which blossomed out as a slickly edited, superbly illustrated monthly with 9 million circulation. It absorbed some of the displaced photojournalism specialists. Others from *Life* and *Look* found their way to the Smithsonian Institution, whose *Smithsonian* magazine, founded in 1970, zoomed to 1.5 million circulation in a half-dozen years. *Ebony,* founded in 1945 by John H. Johnson as a black picture magazine, had a comfortable 1.3 million circulation three decades later. *Redbook,* with 4.7 million circulation, caters to young adults.

News Magazines

Close behind in general family appeal are weekly publications designed to summarize the news and provide added depth and interpretation that newspapers cannot give. They publish articles on news situations, examine headline personalities, and discuss trends in such diverse fields as religion, labor, sports, art, and the environment.

The present leaders (discussed in Chapter 4) are *Time,* with a 4.3 million circulation; *Newsweek,* near 3 million; and *U.S. News & World Report,* a more specialized journal with about 2 million readers. *Jet* has 600,000 circulation among black readers.

Sophisticated Writing Quality

Possibly the most distinctive of American magazines has been the *New Yorker,* founded in 1925 by Harold Ross and carried on after 1951 by William Shawn. E. B. White long conducted its "Talk of the Town"; it has had writers of the quality of James Thurber, Wolcott Gibbs, A. J. Liebling, and Frank Sullivan; artists like Helen Hokinson, Peter Arno, Otto Soglow, and Charles Addams. It also gives its half-million readers—along with the cartoons, whimsy, and fiction—penetrating "Profiles" and lengthy incisive commentaries on public affairs.

Esquire, founded in 1933 by Arnold Gingrich, ran the top bylines of American writing: Wolfe, Hemingway, Faulkner, Steinbeck, Capote, Mailer, Talese. It had a million readers but faltered and was sold to Clay Felker, who turned it into a sophisticated men's semimonthly in 1978. Felker had just lost control of his successful *New York* and of *Village Voice,* like *Esquire* havens for 1960s-style new journalists. Soon after Felker founded *New West* in Los Angeles, his backers sold to Rupert Murdoch. *New York,* founded in 1968, had such talented writers as Tom Wolfe, Jimmy Breslin, Judith Crist, and Gloria Steinem

(Steinem's 1972 creation, *Ms.,* was born in *New York*'s offices and became the magazine of the women's liberation movement).

Quality and Opinion Magazines

Still enjoying a third of a million subscribers each are the century-old quality literary magazines *Harper's* and *Atlantic. Harper's* veered more toward nonfiction and public affairs in the 1960s. Greatly changed but still viable in 1978 was the *Saturday Review.* Of the more combative magazines of opinion, the widest circulating (100,000 level) are the liberal *New Republic* and William Buckley's conservative *National Review.* More pungent are the 110-year-old *Nation* and *New Times,* founded in 1973 in Washington by George Hirsch.

Women's Interest

Half of the top fifteen magazines in circulation in 1978 fall within the category of periodicals aimed straight at the woman reader. Men who happen to pick up the *Ladies' Home Journal, McCall's,* or *Good House-keeping,* to mention three long-time leaders, feel as though they have accidentally opened the wrong door. The inside of a woman's magazine is a world of food, beauty hints, fashions, homemaking advice, inspiration, frank talks about personal problems, and emotional fiction. During the 1960s the last two categories became the "play" emphases for *McCall's* and the *Journal.*

Their circulations ranged between 7 and 8 million in a fierce editorial battle. By 1978, two sedate women's service magazines distributed in supermarkets, *Woman's Day* and *Family Circle,* had passed the 8 million mark; *Good Housekeeping* was close to 5 million. *Better Homes and Gardens,* the leading "shelter" magazine, had 8 million.

There are many special women's magazines ranging from 500,000 to 1,750,000 in circulation: *Vogue* and *Harper's Bazaar* in fashion; *True Story* and *Cosmopolitan* for entertaining reading; *Glamour* and *Mademoiselle* for the young and *Seventeen* for the even younger; *Essence,* a 1970s service magazine success for black women. *Ms.* tops the women's movement publications, and two newcomers reflecting "woman power" in sports are *Sportswoman* and *WomenSports.*

Men's Interest

Only two magazines aimed at men fall within the top fifteen in circulation—*Playboy* and *Penthouse.* Hugh Hefner's *Playboy,* begun in

1953, approached a 7 million circulation with a mixture of nude photographs, articles and stories, and rather pompous editorials based on a hedonistic philosophy that interested both men and women readers. By 1978 it had declined below 5.5 million circulation, as the more explicit *Penthouse* reached 3.5 million and *Hustler* and *Oui* passed the million mark among the rash of "skin" magazines on the sales rack.

In the men's interest category, but increasingly attractive to women, are several magazines of 1 to 2 million circulation: *Sports Illustrated, Outdoor Life, Field and Stream,* and *Sports Afield; Popular Science, Popular Mechanics,* and *Mechanix Illustrated* in the how-to field; and *True* and *Argosy* for adventure.

Special Interest Magazines

The hundreds of periodicals aimed at special audiences form a very large segment of the magazine industry. Some are little known to the general public because they are infrequently displayed on the newsstands; others fall in major circulation categories.

The latter type includes the "shelter" magazines about family living, headed by *Better Homes and Gardens* and *Sunset;* farm magazines like *Farm Journal* and *Successful Farming;* such science-interest publications as *Scientific American* and *Science Digest;* youth-oriented magazines such as *Boys' Life, Scouting, Junior Scholastic, American Girl,* and the area-associated *Parents' Magazine;* travel guides like *Holiday* and *Travel & Leisure;* and such diverse publications as *Psychology Today, Popular Photography,* and *Outside* (recreation).

The movie and TV fan magazines form still another special interest area. Others include trade and technical journals, professional and scientific publications, and publications aimed at readers with hobbies such as model railroading or stamp collecting. Religious magazine publishing is an influential and important field. There are both denominational and nondenominational publications, the largest of which—*Presbyterian Life, Catholic Digest,* and the *Christian Herald*—circulate to hundreds of thousands of readers. The *National Jewish Monthly* serves 200,000 families.

Sunday Supplement Magazines

Distributed as part of the Sunday newspapers in many large American cities are some large-circulation magazines. Faring badly in the competition for advertising revenues with television, the nationally edited group lost the *American Weekly* and *This Week,* but retained *Parade* with 20 million copies and *Family Weekly* with 11 million in 1978. A black-oriented supplement, *Dawn,* was a 1970s success distributed with black newspapers. Founded in 1965, the black-edited supplement, *Tuesday,* was distributed with conventional dailies. Best known of the Sunday magazines produced by individual papers is that of the New York *Times*.

The Business Press

The fastest growing area in magazine publishing has been that occupied by the nearly 2500 periodicals known as the business press. One small segment includes the general business or business news magazines, headed by *Business Week, Forbes,* and *Fortune,* all above 500,000 in circulation. The rest are identified by the American Business Press, the industry trade association to which most of the larger business publishing houses belong, as "specialized business publications serving specific industrial business, service, or professional business audiences." Nearly half of these business magazines are industrial, followed, in order, by merchandising, medical, export and import and international, financial, educational, and government.

Largest of the U.S. publishing houses in the business field is McGraw-Hill, with thirty-five publications, 800 full-time editors and reporters, a worldwide business news service, and such well-known magazines as *Business Week* and *Electrical World.* The next largest group publishers are Cahners Publishing, Chilton, and Miller Publishing. Some well-known titles are Chilton's *Iron Age,* Fairchild's *Women's Wear Daily,* and *Modern Medicine.* All told, the business press has a circulation of more than 60 million and puts out more than 800,000 editorial pages per year, the work of 14,000 editors.

Company Publications

These are magazines published by corporations for distribution to their employees and customers, usually without charge. Their purpose is to present the company's policy and products in a favorable light and to promote a better sense of teamwork and "belonging" among the employees. They are known also as industrial magazines; the term "house organ," once widely used for them, has fallen into disfavor.

This field of industrial publishing has made large advances as corporations have become more conscious of their public relations. Many of these company publications are edited by men and women widely experienced in general magazine work who have been given ample funds to produce magazines of sophisticated appearance and high-grade editorial content. More and more companies are coming to the realization that they must hire professional people and set their standards to compare with general magazines on a broad basis. As one leading industrial editor, a veteran of general magazine staffs, expressed it, "No longer can the mail clerk or the personnel manager be regarded as an authority in the field of industrial editing. The emphasis definitely is on editing— and on journalism." Some journalism graduates, particularly women, move directly into industrial editing. In many such publications articles of general interest, unrelated to the company's products, are included, and company "propaganda" is kept at a very subdued level. Some large corporations, in fact, publish a number of magazines aimed variously at customers, stockholders, and employees. For example, the International Harvester Company and the Ford Motor Company publish some two dozen employee magazines each at different plants. Some of the more elaborate company publications, intended to reach the public as well as employees, have circulations above a million.

Company publications are of many sizes and shapes, and it is difficult to say at any given time how many of them qualify as magazines. Many appear in newspaper format. One recent estimate put the combined circulation of major company periodicals above 100 million. American business and industry invests more than $500 million a year in these 9,000 publications with some 15,000 editors and staff members.

HOW MAGAZINES ARE MARKETED

The magazine industry rests on twin foundations, circulation and advertising. The general practice is for publishers to sell each copy to the reader for less money than it costs to produce it. They close this gap and make their profit through the sale of national advertising. Failure to attract and hold advertising is fatal.

Since hundreds of magazines, as well as other media, compete for advertising dollars, successful publishers must convince advertisers that the purchase of space in their pages is a good investment. This proof is based largely on circulation figures. Magazines must show either very large mass distribution figures among a general readership or a firmly established circulation among the special interest groups to which their publications appeal editorially.

These economic principles have a powerful influence on the shape of the entire magazine industry. A magazine must be designed for appeal to a well-defined segment of the population, such as outboard boating enthusiasts or members of a fraternal order, or it must possess such broad interest that it will attract huge numbers of general readers.

Approximately fifty magazines have circulations of more than a million. The rising population in the United States makes the big publishers hopeful of even greater circulation figures in the next decade. The death of a half-dozen mass circulation magazines in recent years created the false impression that hard times had hit the magazine field. Circulation figures and other evidence, such as record revenues, show that this is not the case. Individual magazines have suffered because of changing public tastes and marketing conditions, including increased postal rates and the loss of much advertising to television, but the magazine field as a whole is healthy.

Hundreds of small magazines operate profitably year after year by concentrating on their special fields. Since advertising rates are based largely on circulation, many advertisers cannot afford to buy space in magazines with circulations in the millions, on which the rate for a single black-and-white advertising page ranges from $20,000 to $45,000 and for color from $30,000 to $65,000. Instead, they spend their money in publications they can afford and that offer them an audience especially adapted to their products. To counteract this, some large magazines offer advertising space on regional or fractional split-run bases, and this practice accounts for some 20 percent of total magazine advertising revenues.

One of the largest magazine publishers today, in terms of total income, is Time Inc. Started in the early 1920s, when *Time* made its appearance with a new style of news magazine, this corporation grew spectacularly. Its picture weekly, *Life,* held top place among all magazines in gross advertising revenue from the 1950s to its demise in 1972. *Time* now holds that position. The firm also publishes *Fortune,* devoted to the business world; *Sports Illustrated;* and two new ventures, *Money* and *People* (2 million circulation). Given 1978 trials was *Woman.*

The Hearst magazine group is affiliated with that newspaper publishing family's empire. The group includes such large and profitable properties as *Good Housekeeping, Cosmopolitan, Harper's Bazaar, Popular Mechanics, Sports Afield,* and *House Beautiful.* Its group of more than a dozen publications also lists magazines in the motoring, medical, and leisure fields.

Other major groups include the McGraw-Hill trade publications, headed by *Business Week;* the McCall Corporation, with *McCall's* and *Redbook;* Meredith Publishing Company, with *Better Homes and Gardens* and *Successful Farming;* the Johnson Publishing Company, with *Ebony, Jet,* and *Tan;* and the Condé Nast publications, *Glamour, Vogue, Mademoiselle,* and *House and Garden.*

Magazines are sold by two principal methods, single-copy sales on newsstands and mail delivery copies to subscribers. (Some trade publications are distributed free of charge to controlled lists in order to give advertisers a large audience for products.) Circulation is one of the most costly and complex problems a magazine publisher faces. Copies of each issue must be distributed nationwide and must be on sale by fixed dates each week or month. Copies unsold when the publication date for the next issue comes around must be discarded at heavy loss. Newsstand sales of magazines are handled through news wholesalers. Intricate arrangements and "deals" are made to ensure good display at outlets, since many sales are made on impulse as the buyer walks past the colorful array on the racks. This makes attractive cover design and provocative, attention-getting titles and sales catchlines on the covers extremely important. Consumer magazines as a whole probably obtain slightly more than half their sales from subscriptions.

Unlike newspapers, a large majority of magazines do not own their own printing facilities. The editors and advertising staffs prepare each issue in the office and then send the material to a commercial printer who holds a contract to produce the magazine. In fact, a few large printing houses with high-speed color presses do the printing for most of the major national magazines. This freedom from the heavy initial investment in printing equipment enables new publishers to start magazines with limited capital; however, unless the new venture embodies an attractive basic idea or "angle," and is well edited, the printing and circulation bills can soon eat up the adventurous newcomer's capital.

EDITORIAL CONTENT AND OPERATION

The editorial content of American magazines is predominantly nonfiction. About three-fourths of the material printed in consumer periodicals is factual, and the percentage is even higher in the trade and professional journals. Many magazines carry no fiction at all.

Editorial operation of magazines varies greatly, depending upon the size, type, and frequency of the publication. Generally, editorial staffs are relatively small. A magazine selling 4 million copies can be prepared editorially by a smaller staff than the one needed to put out a newspaper that sells a half-million copies. This is possible because much of the material published in many magazines is written by freelance writers, either on speculation or on order from the editors. These writers are paid fees for their work and do not function as members of the staff.

The magazine editor's job is to decide what kinds of material he or she wants to publish, arrange to obtain it, and then present it in a manner pleasing to the reader's eye. Most editors work from a formula; that is, each issue contains specified types of material in predetermined amounts, arranged to give a desired effect. Articles and stories are selected for publication not only on their merit but for the way they fit the formula.

The editor has a staff of assistants to screen freelance material, work with writers, think up ideas, and edit the material chosen for publication. An art director arranges attractive layouts and chooses the covers. A cartoon editor selects such drawings if the periodical carries them. On many magazines a substantial portion of each issue is written by staff members.

The skillful, imaginative use of photojournalism has contributed heavily to the acceptance gained by many magazines in recent years. Combining technical efficiency with an appreciation of the esthetic and the dramatic, the photojournalist is an able communicator with a camera. Most magazines have their own staffs of professional photojournalists, but freelance photographers, often working through agents, provide many striking pictures. Rates range in excess of $300 per page for black-and-white pictures, $400 for color pages, and $500 for cover shots. Charges may be assessed for time taken in shooting the pictures at rates in excess of $200 per day. Picture editors make assignments and select the photos wanted for publication.

A key part of most magazine operations is the editorial conference, a session in which the editors discuss the forthcoming issue, make decisions on the material to be used, examine proposed layouts, and agree upon projects for future issues. Magazine projects frequently are planned months in advance of publication. On some staffs one editor makes the decisions on nonfiction ideas and articles and another on fiction.

The news magazines operate somewhat differently. All their content is written by staff members, who are responsible for designated categories of material and for specific assignments, somewhat like a newspaper. Bureaus around the country submit material ordered from the home office, which then is rewritten and condensed to fit the available space. The magazines also lean heavily on press association material. News magazines operate on a rigid schedule in order to put the latest information on the newsstands throughout the United States.

Most magazines have at their command large amounts of freelance material submitted by writers who hope to "strike it lucky" and sell their work for a substantial sum. As most editors will testify, a relatively small amount of the unsolicited material unloaded on their desks by the mail carrier each day ever reaches print. Not that most of it necessarily is badly written or devoid of fresh ideas, but much of it does not fit the magazine's formula. The problem for the freelance writer is to have the right manuscript in the right editorial office at the right moment—not an easy task. Professional writers usually submit their articles in outline form or as just a brief proposal.

Since editors have found that they cannot depend upon unsolicited freelance material to fit their individual needs, they go in search of what they want. They assign article ideas to writers they know, and then work with them until the manuscripts have the desired flavor and approach. Or the idea might be assigned to a member of the staff and developed in the same manner.

Very few men and women in the United States, perhaps only 250 or 300, make a living as full-time freelance magazine writers. Probably fewer than a hundred of them earn $10,000 a year. Although an established writer may be paid from $1000 up per article, the uncertainties of the craft are many and the number of big money markets is relatively few. Most of these full-time magazine writers work largely on assignment, being commissioned by editors who know and like their work to prepare articles on ideas proposed by the editors or ideas approved by them. In many cases the freelance writers use agents to sell their output to editors on a commission basis. Almost all fiction in big magazines is sold by agents, and many professional article writers use their services. The agent functions to a degree as an adjunct of the editorial staff by channeling worthwhile stories to appropriate magazines. The better-known agents are quite selective about the authors they will handle, and having a well-known agent is a helpful endorsement for a writer.

Much of the contributed material published in magazines is written by men and women who do freelance work on a part-time basis as a sideline to their regular occupation. Newspaper men and women, other mass media people, teachers, attorneys and other professionals, even housewives with a flair for writing try their hands at freelancing with varying degrees of success.

There are hundreds of places where magazine material can be sold. Competition to place articles and fiction in the mass circulation magazines is intense, and the material purchased must be excellently written and extensively researched. Preparation of a major magazine article requires so much skill and time that the work for the major general magazines is done largely by the small group of full-time professionals and staff members. However, the part-time freelancer can hit even the biggest magazines with short material, such as anecdotes, personal experiences, and humor. With a little luck and a large amount of perseverance, a writer can sell numerous articles to smaller magazines and specialized periodicals. However, the pay in these smaller markets is not high; it ranges from $50 for a 2500-word article or short story up to about $500. Rates of payment for the confession-type magazines are 3 to 5 cents a word. At the upper end of the scale, where the competition is intense, the mass circulation magazines pay from $1000 to $3000 or higher for an article. The rates are flexible because the editors will pay extra if they consider that the material is exactly right for them or if the writer has a well-known name worth publicizing on the cover. One of the best ways for the newcomer to break into the market is to submit short-item filler material, for which many magazines pay $10 or more.

JOB OPPORTUNITIES

The magazine industry provides interesting, stimulating, and generally well-paid jobs for thousands of men and women. On some periodicals, the editorial staff members do extensive writing, handling special departments and articles; on others, the editors are engaged largely in selection and editing of submitted material.

Magazines offer greater opportunities for the woman editorial worker than newspapers do. The percentage of staff positions held by women is greater and the opportunity for advancement to high editorial positions is much brighter. Women associate editors, managing editors, and even editors-in-chief are not uncommon.

Although there is no certain formula for the man or woman college graduate to use in seeking a magazine job, the surest way to draw attention is to sell the magazine some articles or stories. The very fact that the editor buys the material shows that he or she approves of the writer's work. Personal contacts developed in this editor-writer relationship sometimes lead to staff positions. In some of the large magazines, young men and women get their start in the research department and other jobs around the fringe of the editorial staff.

Large magazines draw many of their staff members from the trade magazines and company publications, much as metropolitan newspapers hire reporters who have had training on smaller dailies. The mechanical techniques of magazine editing and design are complex and can best be learned by experience on smaller publications.

Industrial magazines are among the finest training grounds for magazine workers. This is a rapidly expanding field, as more and more corporations realize the value of issuing a periodical for customers, employees, salespeople, stockholders, and other groups the management wishes to impress. These are divided into internal publications, for distribution within a company, and external ones, which go to non-employee readers. Many are combinations of these approaches. The type of distribution influences the kind of editorial matter used and to some extent the size of the staff. The best available estimate puts the number of editorial employees on company publications at around 15,000. Although many of these publications are prepared by a single editor, with clerical help, the more elaborate ones have a staff of six or eight editors. They use the same techniques of design, multicolored artwork, and editorial presentation as those employed by the better-known consumer magazines.

External publications usually are published by manufacturers who hope for repeat sales of products of relatively high price. The automobile manufacturers are among the most lavish publishers in this field; magazines like the *Ford Times* and *Dodge News* are widely circulated to maintain contact with users and to promote sales and service.

Many fraternal and nonprofit organizations also publish magazines in order to maintain the bond with their members or supporters. Such periodicals as *American Legion* and the *Rotarian* publish a rather broad range of general articles their editors consider of interest to their readers and interweave promotional and fraternal material about the sponsoring organization.

Work on specialized magazines, both of the industrial magazine and trade varieties, sometimes requires technical knowledge in such fields as engineering, electronics, and chemistry. It is natural for a young man or woman seeking a job to enter whatever trade field holds particular interest for him or her. No matter what technical knowledge may be necessary, however, the fundamental requirement in all magazine work is a sound training in English. With this foundation and a willingness to work hard at learning the rudiments of a specialized field, the aspiring trade journal or industrial editor can progress steadily. A knack for simplifying technical material for the ordinary reader is a desirable asset. College courses in economics are valuable in almost any kind of magazine work because so much of the material printed in magazines deals in some way with the operations of American business. Many schools offer industrial and technical courses to help students prepare for industrial journalism.

Pay scales on magazines are generally attractive and rise to high figures for a small number of men and women in the top editorial positions of the mass circulation magazines. The chief editor of a major consumer magazine receives a salary of at least $30,000 a year, up to more than $100,000 if he or she is a veteran with a proven "touch" or directs the work of a magazine group.

These salaries carry with them a substantial amount of job uncertainty. If a magazine begins to lose circulation or advertising, frequently one of the first corrective moves is to change editors, even though the fault may not lie in the editorial department at all. When a magazine is struggling to work out a new formula to regain readership, it may try several editors before finding one who can do the job. The pay offered to college graduates as beginners is in line with that offered by other media.

Salaries in the trade and industrial magazine fields are somewhat lower but still good, and the job security is better. Recent surveys by the International Association of Business Communicators show that salaries for industrial editors range to $20,000 a year or somewhat higher. The salaries received by editors of farm publications range from $15,000 to $25,000.

Editorial and business offices of most large national magazines are in New York and other eastern cities. Trade publication headquarters are situated throughout the United States, depending in part upon the market being served. There are numerous editorial links between magazine and book publishing, since much magazine material eventually finds its way into book form. This leads to some movement of editorial workers from magazines to book publishing firms and occasionally back in the other direction. Many writers and editors move into magazine work from positions on newspapers, long a journalistic career entry point.

CHAPTER 11
BOOK PUBLISHING

THE ROLE OF BOOKS

Books are a medium of mass communication that deeply affect the lives of all of us. They convey much of the heritage of the past, help us understand ourselves and the world we live in, and enable us to plan better for the future. Books are a significant tool of our educational process. And they provide entertainment for people of every age.

The nation's educational, business, professional, and social life could not survive long without books. Judges and attorneys must examine law tomes continually; doctors constantly refer to the repositories of medical wisdom and experience; governmental officials must remain aware of all the ramifications of legislative fiat. Teachers and pupils alike find in textbooks the vast knowledge of history, philosophy, the sciences, literature, and the social sciences accumulated throughout the ages. Men and women in every walk of life read to keep abreast of a fast-changing world; to find inspiration, relaxation, and pleasure; and to gain knowledge. Books, without doubt, explain and interpret virtually every activity.

Creative writing has been one of the principal hallmarks by which each succeeding world civilization has been measured; the works of Plato and Aristotle, for example, both reflected and refined the quality of early Greek life. Social historians long have examined the creative literature as well as the factual records of a civilization in their efforts to reconstruct the life of the people of a particular time and place. In the United States today the finest published fiction has a reverberating impact upon our society; the ideas and the techniques employed have an enormous effect on the theater, movies, television scripts, and magazine pieces. Many outstanding productions result from the book publisher's enterprise in encouraging and promoting new as well as established authors. Creative writing enhances most of the art forms by which our civilization will one day be judged.

Whether they are paperbacks or hard-cover volumes printed on quality paper, books provide a permanence characteristic of no other communications medium. The newspaper reporter and the radio-television commentator write and speak in the main to an ephemeral audience. Those who write for magazines may anticipate longer life for their messages. Books, however, such as the superb copies of the Bible produced by Gutenberg in the fifteenth century, live always.

For the mass communicator, books and book publishing perform several important functions. They not only serve as wellsprings of knowledge, but through translation and reprinting book publishing may convey vital ideas to billions of people throughout the world. And in the publishing trade itself the journalist may find a rewarding outlet in editing and promoting the distribution of books.

In the writing of books, journalists such as Harrison Salisbury, David Halberstam, Tom Wolfe, John Hersey, Theodore H. White, Bob Woodward, and Carl Bernstein, to name only a few, have vastly increased the size of the audience for their reporting efforts, and each has made the impact on the world of ideas that almost invariably accompanies the creation of a widely read book.

Because of the relative slowness of writing, editing, and publishing a manuscript, books lack the characteristic of immediacy possessed by other media in conveying messages to the public. What may be lost in timeliness, however, is often more than compensated for by the extreme care possible in checking facts, attaining perspective, and rewriting copy for maximum effectiveness. This sustained, systematic exposition of a story or of an idea (with the reader's concomitant opportunity to reread, underscore, and study at leisure) is afforded only by books among all the media of communication.

Unlike most newspapers, but like many magazines, books may have a highly selective audience that makes it not only unnecessary but also undesirable to aim the communication at a fairly low common denominator of reading or listening ability. Nevertheless, authors and publishers definitely are engaged in mass communication, even though their efforts at times may be directed toward only a very small segment of the public.

A COMMON HERITAGE

Newspapers, magazines, and books had a common beginning, and the paths to the attainment of their present central roles in civilization were beset by mutual problems pertaining to printing and distribution. The art of writing itself has been traced well beyond 4500 B.C., when the ancient Egyptians carved hieroglyphic, or pictograph, messages in stone and the Babylonians formed their wedge-shaped, or cuneiform, letters in clay tablets. In China scholars used ink made from tree sap to write on slips of bamboo or wood. The first books may possibly have consisted of a number of these bamboo slips, each about 9 inches long, tied together by a thong. When learned men had to load their bamboo books into several carts to transport them from place to place, it was apparent that a new writing material was needed. The Chinese are credited with the invention of paper, and the Egyptians later developed the first cheap writing material from papyrus plants growing along the Nile.

Europeans, however, did not begin making paper until the fourteenth century. Their books were handwritten and illustrated on vellum or parchment, usually by the monks. Gutenberg's invention of movable type opened the door to the printing of books on paper, of which his famous Bible of 1456 is an example. Several million volumes came off European presses by 1500; this printing of books in large quantities paved the way for the religious reformation and made possible popular education.

Both books and newspapers, which developed as news books and broadsides, were considered threats to the authority of church and state. In England Henry VIII started the control of the press with a list of prohibited books in 1529. The censorship restrictions that continued until 1694 were aimed as much at books and pamphlets as at newspapers. The human target often was the same, for the occupations of bookselling and journalism were closely allied throughout the early period. The bookshop was the center of literary culture; the printer was often also the bookseller; it was he who got out the news broadsides and news books. The heavy emphasis upon book advertising in early newspapers also testifies to the link.

Book and newspaper publishing were also closely identified in early United States history. The first book published in the American colonies came off the Puritans' Cambridge printing press in 1640. Early book publishing in each colony often was religious in tone, but local histories were also produced. Then, as the journalists took over, the horizons widened. Benjamin Harris, who got out one issue of his *Publick Occurrences* in Boston in 1690, was a bookseller importing from London. Editors such as James and Benjamin Franklin had sizable libraries and reprinted literary material in their papers—including Daniel Defoe's *Robinson Crusoe*. The patriot journalist Isaiah Thomas was also an important book publisher; his shop at Worcester produced the first American novel, the first American dictionary, more than 400 technical books, and 100 children's books. Thomas was the first American to publish Blackstone's *Commentaries,* Bunyan's *Pilgrim's Progress,* and Defoe's *Robinson Crusoe* in book form. He himself wrote a two-volume history of American printing.

By 1820 more than 50,000 titles, including books, magazines, and newspapers, were listed as American. Readers were still buying 70 percent of their books from European publishers even though American book publishing was increasing by 10 percent a decade. Names such as Emerson, Thoreau, Poe, Cooper, and Whitman emerged in the realm of American literature, giving both books and magazines a great lift, even though English writers such as Dickens remained favorites. Around 1850 some publishing houses, including Harper's and Scribner's, were active in both the book and magazine fields. Book publishing, however, came to require distinctively specialized equipment and editing knowledge, and the two areas gradually became separate.

The great cultural stirring following the Civil War brought a sharp expansion of both scholarly book publishing and publication of literary and popular books. Works in science, history, and philosophy came from the presses along with millions of encyclopedias and even more dime novels. Free public libraries, spreading across the country after 1880, played an important part in stimulating book publishing and reading. Henry James, Mark Twain, and William Dean Howells became leading names in American literature. At the turn of the century the "muckrakers"—among them Lincoln Steffens, Jack London, Frank Norris, and Upton Sinclair—produced books as well as countless newspaper and magazine articles to expose instances of corruption and greed in American life. Thus the print media continued to share a common background in their use by American writers to discuss the social, political, and economic problems of each generation. Social historians must examine all the print media to gain a full understanding of the development of our civilization.

THE SCOPE OF BOOK PUBLISHING

Today, book publishing is a pygmy among American industrial giants; it makes up only a tiny fraction of the country's more than $800 billion economy. Approximately 40,000 new titles (including more than 30,000 brand new ones) are issued annually by more than 1500 firms. Actually, some 900 publishers bring out nearly all these titles, and the top 100 publishers issue about 60 percent of them. In general (trade) publishing, fewer than 5 percent of hardbound books sell more than 5000 copies in the life of the particular title. Textbook publishing produces over one-third of the industry's annual gross income of more than $3.8 billion.

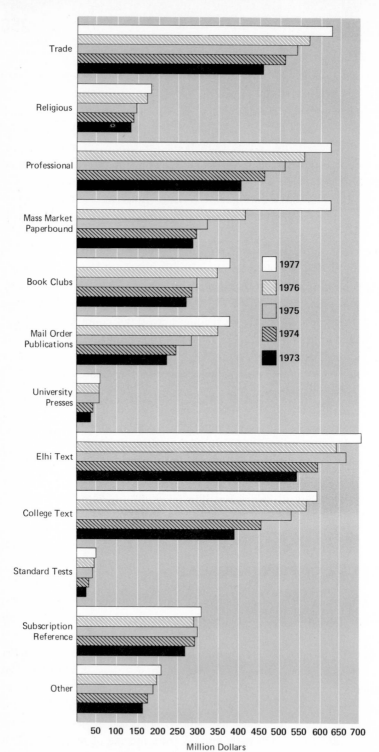

FIGURE 11.1 1973 to 1977 book publishing industry sales by division. (Data courtesy of the Association of American Publishers.)

Book publishing offers a number of intriguing specialties, and Figure 11.1 shows the relative sizes of these various industry divisions. Many publishers concentrate successfully in special areas. Medical, religious, garden, law, music, art, suspense stories, westerns—all may constitute special departments of publishing firms. University press publishing, concerned mainly with materials by and for the use of scholars, attracts many interested in embarking on a publishing career. Subscription-reference book publishing is one of the largest and most remunerative special areas with sales of almost $350 million.

There are more than 6000 outlets for new hardcover books in the United States, including more than 3500 general bookstores, about 80 college stores, and about 450 book divisions of department stores. Around 200 book clubs receive more than $300 million a year from readers. More than 29,000 libraries acquire books. Among them are about 8500 public library systems and more than 5000 branches; 2800 university, college, and junior college libraries; 4000 "special" libraries such as law and medical collections; and around 55,000 libraries in elementary and secondary schools.

The inexpensive paperbound book today is a vital part of every branch of book publishing. In fact, paperbacks have been with us both here and in Europe since the early 1800s, with major growth here taking place in the 1870s and 1880s. In 1885 about one-third of all titles published were bound in paper; the same is true today.

Since World War II the sale of paperbacks in drugstores, newsstands, supermarkets, airports, regular bookstores, and elsewhere has cut deeply into the sale of magazines and second-hand books, but is often deliberately coordinated with the sale of hardcover books. In 1975 paperback sales by publishers were in excess of $339.6 million. The sale of paperbacks to libraries, to elementary and secondary schools, and to colleges and universities has increased dramatically. Printed from rubber plates on high-speed rotary presses, these volumes are to a large extent books that have previously succeeded in the conventional format. Many, however, are brand new titles, some for popular entertainment, some for use in schools and colleges, some for home guidance and instruction. The prices of all paperbacks have risen markedly, but there is still a significant price gap between them and the clothbound books. Publishers generally are pleased that the huge sales of paperbacks have increased reading, proliferated the use of books, and as a result, made all forms of publishing more profitable.

A textbook editor prepares an outline for a new book.

Most leading book publishing firms that started a century or more ago began as either printers or booksellers. Today, with the exception mainly of Doubleday and some university presses, book publishers have removed themselves from the printing field. The temptation to feed the hungry presses and pressroom gangs by taking on inferior and unsalable manuscripts was one of the principal contributing reasons. And only Scribner's, Harcourt Brace Jovanovich, Doubleday, and McGraw-Hill operate bookstores of their own. A merger trend since the 1960s caused the submergence of such separate entities as Macmillan, Appleton-Century-Crofts, Row, Rinehart, World Book, D. C. Heath, Ginn, Thomas Y. Crowell, and D. Van Nostrand.

These consolidations occurred mainly after Wall Street "discovered" the publishing field despite its relatively small size. Beginning in 1959, publishers were offered the chance to "go public," that is, to convert their proprietorship into shares that would be traded and priced on the stock market. More than twenty firms responded. Not only did publishers themselves diversify their product offerings by buying companies that produced materials in other media, but conglomerates and communications firms acquired publishing companies. Many integrated firms, however, ran into trouble, and by 1975 fewer mergers were taking place. Corporate management often was unable to cope with the variety of diversified business and was troubled by something as highly specialized and individualistic as book publishing. It was frequently found better to run an acquired company as a subsidiary, and many acquisitions were spun off as not satisfying growth requirements.

STEPS IN PUBLISHING

All books begin with an idea, germinated usually by the author or by an editor employed by a publishing concern. If the author has the idea, he or she generally prepares a précis and perhaps several sample chapters and submits them to a literary agent or publisher. If it is the editor's idea, he or she seeks out the writer who can best develop the book based upon the concept. Publishing firms vary in the number of editors employed and the duties with which they are charged. In general, however, the editor works closely with an author in the preparation of a manuscript, and also may shepherd the work through various business and production stages. The editor must keep abreast of matters of public taste and interest and be able to anticipate insofar as possible the types of books that will find markets in the months ahead. Reference, technical, and textbook editors, who deal with specialized subject matter, often employ professional readers; trade editors, especially in fiction, are less likely to employ outside advice.

A common fallacy held by each summer's crop of job applicants in book publishing is that a publisher or an editor is simply a person of taste who sits, feet on desk, waiting for hungry authors to arrive with best-selling manuscripts. Book publishing, however, is like an iceberg. The part that shows, namely books that are reviewed in mass media journals and magazines and that are sold in the general bookstores, constitutes only about 8 percent of the overall dollar volume in books. For every editor who breaks bread with a Philip Roth or a Norman Mailer, there are hundreds who are editing reference works or working with college and school textbook authors. For most publishing houses, the unsolicited manuscript is almost never publishable, as many a disillusioned beginning writer can testify.

Accepted manuscripts are turned over to copyeditors, who may often do considerable rewriting as well as search for grammatical, spelling, and punctuation errors; corroborate facts; correct discrepancies in style; and perhaps help cut the copy to a predetermined length. The copyeditor must also coordinate entries in the bibliography with the citations in footnotes (if the book has them); ensure that chapter headings correspond with contents; relate pictures, tables, charts, and the like with the text; query the author if necessary; read the galley proofs including indexes; check corrections made by the author in the proofs; and in general ascertain that the text is as accurate as possible.

The production department, which may consist of from three or four to two dozen or more persons, normally serves as the book publisher's liaison with the printer. Highly specialized employees oversee the designing of the book, obtain art work if necessary, estimate length, select the type and paper, order the typesetting, printing, binding, and supervise preparation of the cover and the jacket. Every book presents an individual problem and every stage of production must be worked out carefully in advance.

Long before the book has been produced, plans are under way for its distribution. The sales department studies possible markets and lays its campaign plans in cooperation with advertising, promotion, and publicity personnel. The salespeople who visit bookstore buyers throughout the country are called in for conferences concerning the entire list of books being prepared for sale. In accordance with the advertising budget established for the book, based on anticipated sales, media are selected and dealer aids such as posters, circulars, or mail enclosures are prepared.

The publicity department writes and mails news releases, arranges author interviews on television and radio and other personal appearances, sends copies to reviewers, announces the book in trade magazines, arranges for exhibits at conventions attended by booksellers, and works on other "angles" to promote the sale of the book. The primary responsibility of the promotion department is to establish a climate of acceptance for the new title by employing every possible means at hand.

The larger bookstores may be called on by the publisher's sales representatives fifteen or twenty times a year. These persons work normally on salary or commission or a combination of the two, and frequently carry the lines of two or more houses. In addition, of course, some sales personnel call on booksellers in behalf of jobbers and other outlet accounts.

There are today more than 600 college travelers and these men and women perform a distinctly different function. Calling on the nation's college professors, they make certain that their clients are acquainted with or have complimentary copies of textbooks appropriate to the courses they teach. Travelers seldom if ever write up bookstore orders themselves. They must hope that the professors they visit, who usually have freedom of textbook selection, will give them their share of business via the local college bookstore. The college traveler also acts as a manuscript scout since most college textbooks are, of course, written by college professors.

The hundreds of school book agents work through state, county, and city adoption systems in selling their wares except where local boards of education, teachers, or superintendents are involved. School textbooks are largely written by staff members of a publishing house working in active collaboration with professional teachers.

Many other ramifications involved in producing and selling books are not covered in this sketch of the principal steps in publishing. It is an intricate business, and many years are required to learn the ground rules.

HOW THE MASS COMMUNICATOR FITS IN

The kinship of book publishing to other mass media activities should be apparent. There are writing and editing to be done; copyediting and proofreading; illustrating and designing; and advertising, publicity and other forms of promotion, printing, and distribution. There must be shrewd insight into what the public is interested in, and why; the newspaper city editor's sense of rapport with readers finds its counterpart in the identification of the book editor with the tastes of various segments of the book-buying population.

It is true, as pointed out earlier in this chapter, that book publishing is a step removed from the operations of the other media that have a genuinely mass audience to deal with continually; books often are read by highly selective groups. Yet, reporting and editing and preparing advertisements for any of the other media can provide an ideal background for the performance of those duties in the book publishing field.

The writer for newspapers, magazines, and radio-television, for example, inevitably gains insights into human life that can be drawn upon to advantage at the book editor's desk. As a student as well as a practitioner of effective writing, he or she can recognize craftsmanship in others and can quickly spot good or poor writing in a manuscript. The editor's experience in rewriting the work of others can help to shore up any weak spots. As a journalist, he or she has learned to respect facts and documentation and will insist upon high standards. He or she knows the principles of style and grammar and can supervise the work of copyeditors and proofreaders. Experience gained in having worked with printers and other craftsmen, including photographers, artists, engravers, and pressmen, will assist in the all-important area of reducing job costs. As a reporter or editor for a newspaper, magazine, or radio or television station, he or she has drawn paychecks from a profit-making organization and has gained an appreciation of sound business methods that helps in dealing with authors who may never have earned bread and butter in the ordinary business world.

The knowledge of typography that the mass communicator learns in journalism school or on the job will be of use in the ordering of printing for a book and the production of its cover and jacket. The advertising staff man or woman can draw upon this same knowledge of typography, as well as other journalistic techniques, in the preparation of direct mail folders, posters, and advertisements for newspapers and magazines. He or she will find that the same principles of copy, layout, illustration, color, and selection of paper and ink apply in the preparation of advertisements for new books.

The man or woman writing news releases and other publicity materials, and contacting the various media, will likely be a former newspaper editorial employee. There is no substitute for such experience in fitting a person for effective promotion, publicity, and general public relations duties.

RUNGS ON THE JOB LADDER

Even the publisher's son or daughter "hits the road" west—or north or south, as the case may be—to learn the business from the bottom up. Traveling to the cultural oases of the nation, to wherever books are bought, sold, and read, is the normal beginning pursuit for those who seek careers in book publishing. The theory (and it has been proved a thousand times) is: You can't become a good editor sitting in a New York or Boston office; you can learn the facts of bookselling life only by intimate acquaintance with a constantly changing market, finding out what will sell and what won't, and getting some idea of "why" in both cases. After three or four years, the traveler may wish to swap suitcase for swivel chair, qualified to serve as an editor or in some other specialized capacity in the home office. Scores of men and women, however, make lifelong careers of being travelers. They enjoy being their own bosses and being free from office routine.

Most travelers are personable, college-trained lovers of books whose starting salaries generally range upward from $8000, depending on age, experience, and potential. All their expenses while on the road are paid. Experienced travelers may net between $15,000 and $25,000 or even more annually. Moving into the office, the travelers most likely will put their road experience to work in the editorial, sales, advertising, or production departments. Eventually, they may become department heads, later perhaps officers and directors of the company with salaries in the $25,000, $35,000, or maybe even the $50,000 range.

Beginners in the editorial offices of book publishing firms often are assigned the task of reading and making initial judgments about the merits of the unsolicited manuscripts that almost every mail delivery brings. As their judgment is corroborated by senior editors, they are assigned greater responsibilities. Some become copy and proof editors and research facts in encyclopedias and other reference works.

Later, as some ascend the publishing ladder as editors, others move into advertising and publicity jobs. They write news and feature copy, prepare advertising materials, compose jacket blurbs, engineer radio and television personal appearances and lecture tours, and otherwise exhibit ingenuity in promoting the sale of books. For these services they may be paid from $10,000 to as high as $25,000 annually. Hundreds of persons freelance as copyeditors and proofreaders at home, earning between $5 and $8 per hour. Proofreaders also are employed by compositors.

In the past decade space-age technology has made inroads into book publishing. Computers are used not only for keeping inventory, computing royalty accounts, and making schedules, but also for complicated typesetting, where they replace the traditional Linotype machine and film eliminates the need for metal characters. Most composition, printing, and binding are done by a few large book manufacturers in the East and Midwest who provide the convenience and speed of an integrated operation. There are, however, hundreds of small printers, compositors, and bookbinders around the country who do an occasional book.

The book manufacturer as well as the publisher employ both men and women as production managers. It is their responsibility to see that all elements of a book are in the right place at the right time; they are the liaison between the manufacturer and the publisher. In addition to the production staff, both publishers and manufacturers employ estimators, designers (both freelance and staff), schedulers, and general management people, most of whom have had special technical school training or printing plant experience.

QUALIFICATIONS

A good education, high intelligence, a love of books, and an ability to keep abreast of the latest trends and developments in all phases of human life but particularly in the area of one's specialization are prime characteristics of a good editor. One need not be a creative writer. Persons with highly individual ideas and taste are unwilling to remain anonymous and to play second fiddle to authors with quixotic personalities. The good editor has the capacity to deal in calm, unruffled fashion with everyone, including the occasional prima donnas whose genius or near-genius may spell the difference between profit and loss in a publishing year.

Whether one wishes to become a general editor, a copy or proof editor, an advertising specialist, or a publicity or promotion person, the college graduate who aspires to a career in book publishing will profit by an education, as well as experience, in mass communications. He or she will seek to acquire a sound background in literature, history, languages, the natural and social sciences, philosophy—in fact, in all areas of knowledge that comprise a liberal education. Professional education will not be overlooked, for the insights, skills, and fundamental knowledge gained in the classrooms and laboratories of a school of communications should prove of inestimable value throughout a career.

CHAPTER 12
RADIO AND RECORDINGS

RADIO IN TODAY'S SOCIETY

When television appeared in American homes three decades ago, the doomsayers snapped off the dials of their radio sets and proclaimed, "Radio is dead." Who would be satisfied merely with listening to something happen when it could be seen actually occurring on the television screen? Radio refused to succumb, however. Today the radio industry is thriving after undergoing a revolution in content and technique that enables it to exist side by side with television, and to share prosperity with its raucous, aggressive cousin, the recording industry.

Radio is everywhere. The homemaker doing the dishes, high school boys and girls cruising in a car, a blind beggar on a city street, workers installing a roof: all have radio sets going in the background. Development of the transistorized set, which transformed radio from a bulky parlor instrument to a tiny portable one, contributed heavily to the survival and growth of radio. Its music and voices are the background accompaniment for millions of Americans who go about their duties and pleasures often hardly aware that they have the radio going, so accustomed are they to it. They absorb radio's messages in words and music while only half realizing that they are doing so. Not only are radio and recordings a major form of mass communication, but they contain a subliminal element that is insufficiently recognized. The United States has become a country that largely abhors silence; is it uneasiness at being alone? Whatever the psychological explanation, radio fills the void.

Approximately 8400 radio stations broadcast daily in the United States, of which about 60 percent are AM (amplitude modulation) and 40 percent FM (frequency modulation) stations. All stations operate under licenses granted by the Federal Communications Commission. The AM stations range in power from 50,000-watt clear channel stations operating twenty-four hours a day with an audience range of several hundred miles to tiny 250-watt stations that are on the air only from sunrise to sunset. The reception range of FM stations is relatively small.

With so many stations broadcasting, especially in large cities, competition among them for an audience and for the advertising dollars that support them is intense. Anyone who twists the dial of a car radio while driving through a metropolitan area realizes what a cacophony of sound

A radio disc jockey on the air. The microphone, clock, control board, rack of tape cassettes, and records are his tools, along with a smooth flow of language. On the small screen in front of him is a radar weatherscope. (Courtesy of the South Bend *Tribune*.)

is emerging from radio transmitters at almost any hour. The Chicago area, for example, has approximately fifty AM and FM stations. In the late 1970s radio stations as a group were receiving about 7 percent of all advertising dollars spent in the United States (newspapers had 30 percent; television, 18 percent).

Before the appearance of commercial television in the late 1940s, radio filled the role that TV does today as the purveyor of general family entertainment. With few exceptions such as foreign language outlets, stations sought to present programs with broad audience appeal. Those with network affiliations offered highly developed 30- and 60-minute comedy, drama, and variety programs built around star performers, comparable to television network programs today but without the visual element.

Television changed that because it could do the general entertainment job more effectively. Radio executives had to create new forms of programing that did not imitate television. These programs had to be produced cheaply, since millions of dollars in advertising budgets were being switched from radio to television. Radio's offerings today are largely recorded music, newscasts, and sports.

Many radio stations make no attempt to attract a broadly based audience, but aim their appeal at limited but specialized and loyal groups. They seek to establish their identity with a special "sound." Stations may concentrate on country and western music, hard or soft rock, jazz, soul music, gospel music, or middle-of-the-road popular melodies supplemented with nostalgia through use of "golden oldies." Often a station employs a format mixing these ingredients. A few AM and FM stations offer classical music. Generally, the powerful AM stations lean toward less strident forms of popular music and general interest programing that will attract older listeners as well as younger ones. Some important stations are all news, offering twenty-four hours a day of continuous newscasts, commentary, interviews, and talk without musical interludes.

The cement that holds recorded musical programing together on many stations is the disc jockey. The deejay introduces recordings, tosses in chit-chat, reads commercials, talks with telephone callers on the air, conducts listener contests, tells the audience what time it is and whether it will rain, and generally keeps the ball rolling during several hours of an on-the-air stint. Usually the segment of air time is called by the deejay's name—the "Jerry Smith Show" or the "Big Wally Show." Often disc jockeys try to project flamboyant, wacky images and distinctive voices that make them stand out from the pack. Few women have yet crashed the barriers of the big-time disc jockey world, although feminine voices are heard on smaller station shows.

Automation of programing is a significant, growing trend among medium and small radio stations. Syndicate producers sell precisely timed, hours-long taped programs of music and talk, including station announcements and spaces for insertion of taped local commercials. The prepackaged program is put on the air by a tape-playing machine supervised by an engineer, eliminating the need for an announcer. By reducing manpower, the station can operate more economically. Automation creates sameness among stations using it and takes away the individuality that live announcers provide. Automated stations resemble broadcasting jukeboxes, with commercials added.

News is a fundamental ingredient of radio formats, but the radio industry as a whole spends little money or staff power in newsgathering. Most smaller stations depend on the press associations for pretimed newscasts that announcers tear off the teleprinters and read on the air. They supplement these with taped on-the-scene news capsules provided by the press association audio services. Network affiliate stations use hourly national newscast "feeds," sometimes following or preceding them with local news highlights, in some instances rewritten from the local newspaper. When a radio station is operated jointly with a television station, the radio news coverage often is better than that provided by independent radio stations, because the television station's news-gathering facilities and announcers are available to the radio station.

Some commercial FM stations are owned by AM stations and operated as adjuncts; others are independents or educational outlets. Large-city FM stations often develop their own programing to lure special audiences. The audience soared during the 1970s, and late in the decade an Arbitron Radio survey showed FM listenership in the 10 largest markets almost equal to that of AM.

Under joint ownership, news broadcasts and some other programs may be aired simultaneously on the AM and FM outlets. Frequently the AM station plays livelier music than its FM counterpart, whose programing may tend toward soothing "beautiful music." When the management owns a TV station as well, its facilities are putting three programs on the air simultaneously, aimed at different segments of the potential audience. Mutual Broadcasting System broke new ground in 1977 by contracting to transmit its network radio programs via satellite for better reception quality.

Although their role has changed drastically, the radio networks continue to hold a significant position. Their programing is concentrated on news, sports, and special events, but from time to time they experiment with other offerings. In the 1970s the Columbia Broadcasting System revived the CBS "Radio Mystery Theater," a late-night series of stories done with eerie sound effects. Radio's use of sounds to evoke images was a device perfected in the pretelevision days and then largely forgotten. The CBS "Mystery Theater" became a hit with those who remembered the old days and those who were intrigued by techniques they had never heard.

THE HISTORY OF RADIO

Various inventions in the nineteenth century paved the way for the perfecting of radio in the twentieth. Guglielmo Marconi's development of wireless telegraphy was followed by an improvement made by Dr. Lee De Forest in 1906 in the vacuum tube that made voice transmission possible. Little interest was shown in the possibility of mass radio listening, however. In 1912 Congress empowered the Department of Commerce to issue licenses to private broadcasters and assign wave lengths for commercial operators, primarily to prevent interference with government point-to-point message communication.

Amateur enthusiasts built their own receivers and transmitters and finally Westinghouse, sensing a new sales market, applied for the first full commercial license for standard broadcasting. Its station, KDKA in Pittsburgh, began operating on November 2, 1920, by broadcasting returns from the Harding-Cox presidential election. An experimental station, 8MK, began daily operations from the Detroit *News* building on August 20, 1920, and in October 1921, the *News* obtained its first full commercial license for what became station WWJ.

The rush was on. Between January 1922, and March 1923, the number of stations increased from 30 to 556. Broadcasting of such events as the Dempsey–Carpentier fight in 1921 and the Army–Notre Dame football game and the World Series in 1923 stimulated national interest. Listeners ran the "cat's whisker" across the crystals of their sets, trying to bring in a station on the earphones; many sets were homemade. On certain nights local stations would remain silent so listeners could tune in distant stations. The introduction of sets with loudspeakers increased the nation's pleasure.

Radio made a spectacular leap forward when the National Broadcasting Company, a subsidiary of the Radio Corporation of America, was formed late in 1926 and extended programing coast to coast in 1927. WEAF was the originating station for NBC's Red network and WJZ for its Blue network. The Columbia Broadcasting System was created in 1927 and grew quickly. In 1934 the Mutual Broadcasting System was organized, primarily to provide network-caliber programs to smaller stations. Regional chains also developed. An order by the Federal Communications Commission led to NBC's sale of the Blue network in 1943 and its renaming as the American Broadcasting Company in 1945.

Under the First Amendment to the Constitution, government is restrained from interfering with the freedom of the press or the freedom of speech. But although anyone with enough money is free to found a newspaper anywhere at any time, there is only a limited number of broadcast channels. The theory is that these channels belong to the people and since they are limited the people must allocate them through Congress. Thus, when stations jumped from one wavelength to another to avoid interference, Congress in 1927 established a five-man Federal Radio Commission, and in 1934 replaced it with a seven-member Federal Communications Commission to regulate the airwaves in the interest of the public. It has been in efforts by the FCC to define "public service" that controversy has arisen, such as Congress's requirement that equal time must be provided for rival candidates for public office. The newspaper can publish what it desires in such matters, whether in the news, editorial, or advertising columns, subject only to public opinion and the laws of libel and obscenity. Broadcasting, however, because of its peculiar physical structure, must be regulated.

Newspaper publishers grew uneasy about radio's growing share of the advertising dollar and feared that radio news broadcasts might hurt newspaper circulation. They attempted for nearly a decade to prevent the major press associations from selling their news reports to radio stations, but eventually capitulated. A Press-Radio Bureau was established in 1933 to provide the stations with two daily news reports and bulletins of "transcendent importance." The public demand for radio news grew, leading to creation of Trans-Radio Press, a newsgathering organization catering primarily to radio stations. In 1935 the United Press and International News Service began service to radio networks and stations with news that could be sponsored; shortly thereafter, the Associated Press followed suit, and the war was over.

Radio developed its own stars, including such attractions of the 1920s as the A&P Gypsies and the Gold Dust Twins. The networks were on the air from 9 A.M. to 11 P.M., eastern standard time, with a melange of humor, kiddie stories, soap operas, variety shows, interviews, poetry, dance bands, and symphony orchestras.

During the depression years of the 1930s radio provided inexpensive home entertainment. President Franklin D. Roosevelt's "fireside chats" helped allay fears and bound the country together. Such personages as Will Rogers, the cowboy comedian-philosopher, with an alarm clock at his elbow that clanged when his time was up, and Eddie Cantor, the banjo-eyed comedian, did their bit to bring Americans out of the economic doldrums. Programs had their own theme songs. Millions of listeners thrilled to "Gang Busters" and "The Lone Ranger." They awaited the daily or weekly visits of "Amos 'n Andy," "Fibber McGee and Molly," Walter Winchell, Jack Benny, and Bob Hope.

On an otherwise peaceful Sunday, December 7, 1941, radio brought the catastrophic news of the Japanese attack on Pearl Harbor. Millions remained close to their radio sets during World War II, listening to such commentators as Elmer Davis, Edward R. Murrow, H. V. Kaltenborn, and Eric Sevareid. Shortly after the war, television arrived.

CAREER OPPORTUNITIES

Success as a performer in radio is heavily dependent upon the kind of voice personality the individual projects. If it is vibrant and distinctive, a voice the listener will remember, the beginning performer has a much better prospect of advancing to the big stations. A performer's physical appearance is not of prime importance, but a lively, friendly personality usually is evident in the person's voice, a fact that is quickly detected by the listener.

Voice is not enough. Professional coaching can improve vocal technique and confidence, but it cannot create intelligence and a good command of English. The most successful radio newscasters, talk show hosts, and disc jockeys have quick minds and an ability to articulate their thoughts smoothly in ad lib situations.

Getting a start in radio as an announcer, newscaster, sportscaster, or record program host usually involves working first at a small station to gain technique. Small-town radio stations resemble weekly and small daily newspapers as starting points for careers. The pay is not high, but the opportunity for all-around experience is abundant. An announcer on such a station may spend several hours on the air, then go out on the street to sell advertising commercials, and also double as a station engineer. The latter job involves at least a rudimentary knowledge of electricity and knowing what meters to read and what switches to turn to keep the station on the air. To do this, the broadcaster must have at least a third-class Federal Communications Commission engineer's license. Keeping the station log and selecting music are other duties sometimes carried out by on-the-air personnel.

The ability to write radio news copy and advertising commercials is an important tool. As in television writing, the basic technique is to compose conversational English that rings true to the ear. Such writing avoids complex and inverted constructions, and uses simple declarative sentences in the manner in which people normally talk. On smaller stations, most newscasters write their own copy or take it from press association teleprinters. Metropolitan stations have staffs of newswriters who prepare copy for the announcers to read and who sometimes go on the air themselves. Newsgathering is under the supervision of a news director at medium-sized and large stations.

When a young broadcaster believes himself or herself ready to move up to a larger station, the usual practice is for the applicant to submit sample tapes along with a résumé of work done and desired. The applicant may then be invited for an interview. The classified advertising pages of *Broadcasting,* an industry trade journal, are an important clearinghouse for job openings. Radio help wanted ads may specify that a station is seeking a personality for a drive time spot (the hours when motorists with car radios are going to work and returning), an experienced "beautiful music" announcer, or typically, "contemporary MOR (middle of the road) jock who can move an afternoon show and do production."

From a middle-sized station, the next step is to a metropolitan major outlet or to a network. The number of network job openings is limited. Or the young broadcaster may discover ability as a salesperson or technician and choose to work up toward station managership by this route.

Generally, radio salaries are comparable to newspaper salaries and are based on experience and station size. "Personality" disc jockeys on metropolitan stations may make exceptionally large salaries, as long as their audience ratings remain high. In some cases, the personality is paid a commission on commercials as a salary supplement. Sports announcers sometimes have the opportunity to earn extra money by making play-by-play broadcasts of games.

The number of women on the air is relatively small still, although increasing. During the mid 1970s the networks took a significant step by using women newscasters on their hourly newscasts. Minority groups too are finding increasing opportunities. Approximately 25 percent of broadcasting station staffs are women.

THE RECORDING INDUSTRY

In the eyes of radio stations and the recording industry, music is merchandise. Radio depends on the recording companies for the flow of new songs to keep its shows fresh, and the latter in turn need radio "play" to introduce their products to potential purchasers. The two industries are closely linked because of this mutual need. Record distributors supply recordings free of charge to the stations.

Through the sale of single records, long-playing albums, and tapes, the recording industry does business of more than $2 billion a year. This comes from the sale of approximately 600 million units, roughly three records or tapes for every inhabitant of the United States. Recent growth of tape cassette sales has increased these figures spectacularly.

The recording industry is highly promotional and emotional in nature, subject to quick switches in the public mood. Those who manage it are constantly seeking new sounds and fresh personalities. When the Beatles came to the United States from England with their lively songs and ebullient personalities early in the 1960s, their concert appearances, record sales, and radio exposure were so spectacularly successful that promoters have been trying to surpass them ever since. Profits are enormous for performers who click. So is the adulation. When Elvis Presley, the so-called "King" of rock music, died in 1977, he had sold more than 300 million recordings; so had the more traditional, older Bing Crosby, who died a few months later.

American preoccupation with numbers and rankings—football's Top Ten, for example—has led to the radio and recording industries' exploitation of the Top Forty songs concept. Weekly charts published by trade publications, especially those in *Billboard*, list the top songs currently being played and sold across the country. Radio program directors watch these charts closely, noting the rise of new songs and adding them to their play lists, dropping others each week to make room.

Unscrupulous record promoters and broadcasters at one time engaged in a conspiracy in which the promoters paid off the broadcasters with cash or valuable gifts to favor certain records on the air. This became known as the "payola" scandal. As the result of an investigation that showed the practice to be widespread, stern measures were taken to punish offenders and halt the abuse. Nothing more was heard of payola for several years, until in 1975 federal grand juries in several cities returned indictments against individuals and companies charged with using the forbidden methods. The search for payola continues.

Recordings are the most potent mass medium of protest and anti-establishment fervor on the American scene. Their messages have challenged traditional values. The rebellion among young Americans against the Vietnam War in the late 1960s and early 1970s found a voice in the folk singers and recording groups—political protest to a rock beat. The mood that resulted in mass outdoor rock festivals, starting with Woodstock, spread through radio and recordings. Sexual frankness (so intense that lyrics by such groups as the Sex Pistols of Great Britain sometimes were banned from broadcast), violence, and praise of the drug culture dominated many rock songs of the 1970s. New slang was circulated by individual singers and groups; the latter tried to outdo each other in garishness, weird names, and wildly throbbing beat. As a channel of communication for the younger population, to which older listeners aren't tuned in, recordings and concerts given by their stars are more potent than persons over thirty realize.

CHAPTER 13
TELEVISION

THE FUTURE OF TELEVISION

During the last three decades television has radically altered the lives of people throughout the world. Now, rapidly evolving technological developments, such as videocassettes and videodiscs, are about to free television viewers from the constraints of the broadcast schedule. Satellite transmission and cable television, including over-the-air and cable pay-TV, are transforming important aspects of the industry. And the introduction of holography, fiber optics, and other exciting and useful innovations is close at hand.

Through the electronic magic carpet of television, millions of viewers worldwide were transported to the scene of the Sadat-Begin peace visits in late 1977 and even witnessed the historic on-the-air decisions that preceded these historic missions. As they do each year, millions more watched the 1978 Super Bowl football game with all its pageantry. Witnessing these events and others, such as the Olympics and the World Cup soccer matches, the Papal Mass at the Vatican at Christmas and the Muslim Hajj, and the investiture of the Prince of Wales, has become commonplace. Americans share all types of experiences by television, making them aware of their diversity but also forging a spirit of unity. Through direct-to-home satellite television, the other nations of the world may well achieve a similar understanding. It is likely that future historians will rank television—the twentieth century creation of the industrial and technological movements of the past two centuries—as the most revolutionary and democratizing medium of our times.

So rapidly is the state of the art advancing that, in the decades ahead, virtually every home, school, and business in the United States can gain access to a nearly unlimited number of channels for a multiplicity of uses: commercial, public, and community television and radio; two-way communications for banking, shopping, responding to opinion polls, and the like; facsimile reproduction; and a host of services involving the storage, transmission, and retrieval of data—all part of the emerging Information and Entertainment Age.

In this emerging scheme of things commercial over-the-air broadcasting will meet the mass audience requirements for news and entertainment. Public broadcasting will fill the varied needs of specialized audiences by providing greater choice, diversity, and enrichment. Cable

both newspapers and broadcast stations, although newspaper owners no longer are permitted by the FCC to purchase broadcast properties in the same city.

The television industry in 1976 made a pretax profit of about 24 percent from more than $5.2 billion in total revenues, with some operations making as much as 30 percent in profits. The profit margin of the networks, set at 8.9 percent in 1963 and 13.2 percent in 1973, was projected to reach 17.9 percent in 1979, according to Wall Street analysts. The average 30-second announcement in prime-time network television costs about $50,000. When more than 86 million persons viewed at least part of the 1978 Super Bowl football telecast, one minute of commercial time was priced at $344,000.

Almost 150,000 persons are employed in television. Although small in comparison with other industries, television and radio are responsible for the livelihood of thousands of persons in related businesses. They include talent agents and managers, program producers and distributors, commercial and jingle producers, business and promotion film distributors, film processing technicians, researchers, consulting engineers, management consultants, brokers, and station representatives, as well as employees of news services, association and professional societies, unions, station finance companies, and public relations, publicity, and promotion firms. A comprehensive summary of television industry statistics may be found in *Broadcasting Yearbook*.

World Television

During the past decade in particular, television has spread to most of the countries of the world. Its impact ranges from heavy use in the more developed nations to reception largely by the rich in the poorest lands. United States citizens possess about half of the world's TV sets. Usage is also high in Japan, the United Kingdom, West Germany, France, Italy, and Canada, in that order, with the emerging nations, such as those in Africa, enjoying the least TV viewing.

The United States exports far more films and videotaped programs than any other country. More than 150 American companies produce and export TV programs, with the nine companies comprising the Motion Picture Export Association of America accounting for about 80 percent of total sales abroad. America's competitive position has been enhanced by the rapid growth of color TV; the trend toward commercialization of TV channels in other countries, providing more money for buyers of American programs; the sales potential of satellite telecasts of special events; and the growing availability of and need for educa-

will complement commercial and public broadcasting by improving its signal and extending its reach and by offering, through an abundance of channels, greater opportunities for specialized programs and nonbroadcast services. Free, subscription, and direct-payment mechanisms will coexist and compete, just as they do in the print media. This is the prediction of the research and policy committee of the Committee for Economic Development. These national leaders point out that coherent and responsive national policies must be formulated soon to permit the orderly development of such a telecommunications system in the United States.

THE SCOPE OF TELEVISION

In the United States

Television sets may be found in 97 of every 100 homes in this country, an apparent saturation level that has changed little in recent years. Three of every 4 homes, however, now have color sets, as compared with only half in 1970. Nearly half of all TV households own more than one set. And better than 1 out of 6 homes are tied into cable systems.

Television is considered the most pervasive medium known to modern man. The average American family devotes more time to watching television—about 6 hours daily—than to any other form of leisure activity. Five of every 7 television stations (there are more than 990 in all) broadcast on the long-established very high frequency (VHF) bands, using channels 2 through 13, and the remainder on ultrahigh frequency (UHF), channels 14 through 83. More than 9 of every 10 home receive UHF programs. Residents of more than 135 cities view the pr gram fare of three or more local stations.

Most commercial television stations are affiliated with one or m of the three major networks—the American Broadcasting Compa Columbia Broadcasting System, and National Broadcasting Com Approximately 100 stations operate on an independent basis. We 100 individuals and companies, including the major networks, o or more television stations. However, Federal Communicatio mission rules limit multiple ownership to seven television st which not more than five may be VHF (and each may owr than seven AM and seven FM radio stations). Many com

tional films produced in the United States. The United Kingdom, France, and the Federal Republic of Germany also export much programing. Mexico produces many programs for Latin American countries. Countries in the Middle East obtain most of their programs from Lebanon and Egypt. Programs produced in socialist countries are used mainly in other socialist countries.

A cultural imbalance is evident, however. According to a survey by Tapio Varis, a Finnish researcher, less than 2 percent of commercial and noncommercial programing viewed in the United States and China is received from foreign sources; in the Soviet Union, 5 percent; in France, 9 percent; and in Japan, 10 percent. By contrast, such countries as Chile, Mexico, Uruguay, Saudi Arabia, Italy, Australia, and Zambia import more than 50 percent of the programs viewed by their citizens— Saudi Arabia, in fact, imports 100 percent. Feature films, series and serials, and entertainment shows comprise the bulk of these programs. British productions such as "Civilisation," "Upstairs, Downstairs," and "Search for the Nile" have been well received in the United States. Most of the imported programs viewed in Great Britain come from this country.

United States investors own stock in stations throughout the world. Most are minority holdings, representing from 10 to 20 percent of total investment. The biggest investors have been the three networks and Time-Life Broadcasting International. American advertisers are taking advantage of the world trend toward the commercialization of television. Only in recent years has advertising been permitted in such places as France, Holland, Hong Kong, Indonesia, West Germany, Italy, and Mexico.

Color telecasts via satellite are viewed worldwide. The Communications Satellite Corporation, a private, profit-making company, was established in 1962 by Congress to own and operate the American segment of this telecommunications system. An eighty-member International Telecommunications Satellite Consortium coordinates the technology and program exchanges. The first INTELSAT satellite, known as Early Bird, became operational in 1965. Four years later the beams of these satellites, positioned above the Atlantic, Indian, and Pacific oceans, covered the whole world. In addition, the Applications Technology Satellites (ATS) serve individual regions and countries on an experimental basis.

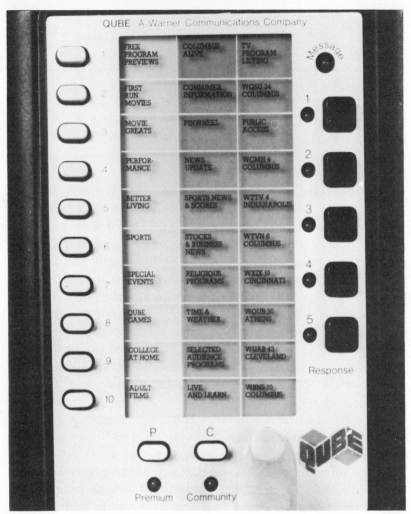

QUBE home terminal unit, introduced in Columbus, Ohio, in 1977, connects to the subscriber's television receiver and enables the viewer to select from 30 channels of programing. Subscribers also may play interactive games, take tests, instantly register their opinions, and participate at home in other television programs and events. Pay-TV programs may be selected on an individual basis and are automatically billed by a computer. The QUBE unit was developed by Warner Cable engineers in collaboration with Pioneer Electronic Corporation, of Tokyo, Japan, a major manufacturer of high-quality electronic products. (Photo courtesy of Warner Cable Corporation.)

CABLE TELEVISION

In order to bring improved television service into geographical areas of the United States with inadequate reception, the first Community Antenna Television (CATV) systems were constructed in 1949 in the hills of eastern Pennsylvania and Oregon. At the end of its first decade, cable television served 550,000 subscribers through 560 systems. By 1969 there were 2260 systems serving about 3.6 million subscribers. By 1977 more than 3800 systems reached 12.5 million subscribers in 17.3 percent of the nation's 72 million households. An estimated 30 percent penetration of U.S. homes by cable is anticipated by the end of 1981.

Only three to five channels were provided originally. Now, however, newer services not only strengthen existing signals but import programs into areas already served by television and often originate programs of their own or lease channels to those who do. Using live, film, or videotape formats, more than 2400 systems originate programing in their own studios, the average for 13.5 hours weekly. Most systems offer between six and twelve channels.

Since the capacity of the coaxial cable, unlike that of the broadcast spectrum, has no inherent limits, future systems are expected to offer forty or even eighty channels. In so doing they could provide not only diverse broadcast services with improved signal quality, but also a wide array of nonbroadcast entertainment and information services, including two-way communications, facsimile reproduction of newspapers and mail, and business, home, health, educational, and municipal services. For example, channels will be available to private users such as banks and motion picture vendors, and open channels to users such as supermarket chains and department stores.

Approximately three-fourths of the cable firms are owned by individuals and companies that have other media interests as well. Approximately 32 percent of the systems are linked with broadcast interests, almost 20 percent with program producers, and 13 percent with newspapers. The operators invest from about $25,000 for a small black-and-white operation to $2 million or more for a color studio. As much as $20 million may be required to establish a system in a large city. The costs of laying cable range from $3,500 per mile in rural areas to $80,000 in metropolitan areas. Users pay an average of $15 to have the system connected to their households and then an average of $6.50 per month for the service.

Advertisers are charged from $5 to $200 per minute on the local origination channels. Total advertising revenues on these channels exceed $3.5 million. Most of a system's revenues, however, are derived from the fees paid by subscribers. The return on investment is slow; it may be ten years or more before an investor realizes a substantial profit. Cable, therefore, is essentially a franchised monopoly in its service area.

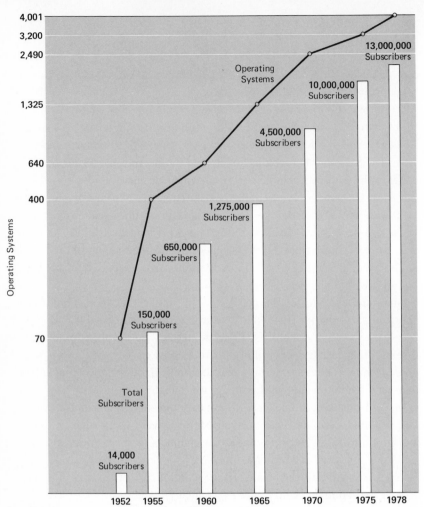

FIGURE 13.1 Growth of the cable TV industry in the United States as of January of each year. (*Sources:* Figures for 1952 to 1974: *Television Factbook,* services vol. no. 44 [1974–1975 ed.]. Figures for 1975: National Cable Television Association. Figures for 1978: *Television Factbook,* services vol. no. 47 [1977–1978 ed.].)

Cable television's commercial success was assured in 1972 when, after a five-year dispute among broadcasters, cable operators, and copyright owners, the FCC for the first time permitted cable systems to operate with distant signals in the top 100 markets. Various restrictions were imposed, however, and cable TV's development also was slowed for several years by lack of venture capital.

Pay TV—the system of providing programs for a fee through a "scrambling" device requiring special equipment and entering the home on a cable or over-the-air—offered the largest economic returns. Commercial broadcasters opposed pay cable television on the ground that any siphoning of programs would result in public deprivation. In 1975 the FCC adopted new regulations placing limits on movies and sports events that could be shown on cable TV. Cablecasters were prohibited, for example, from showing any film between three and ten years old, as well as many major sports events, even those not broadcast by commercial television.

The FCC's so-called antisiphoning rules were overturned, however, when the Supreme Court in 1977 refused to review a landmark decision by the U.S. Court of Appeals for the District of Columbia in *Federal Communications Commission* v. *Home Box Office.* The appeals court found unanimously that there was no evidence pay cable TV would adversely affect either the public interest or over-the-air television; that the FCC had no statutory authority to regulate pay cable TV; and that its restrictions violated the medium's First Amendment right of free speech. The decision lifted a cloud of uncertainty that had hovered over the future of cable TV and held the promise of greater program diversity for the viewing public.

By 1978 more than 450 pay cable systems served 1.2 million subscribers. By the end of 1981 the number of subscribers was expected to range between 3 and 4 million.

Satellite transmission of programs was pioneered in 1975 by Time Inc.'s Home Box Office, followed in 1978 by Showtime, the pay TV branch of Viacom International. Home Box Office serves more than one million subscribers, representing about 80 percent of the pay cable industry. The company produces about 20 percent of its programs in its own multimillion-dollar studio. Showtime buys all its programs and offers about 75 percent films, 20 percent entertainment specials, and 5 percent sports.

The UPI in 1977 began a 24-hour satellite news service featuring a continuous voice commentary over a changing series of still photos. In the same year the American Satellite Network was formed by Digital Communications, Inc., as a new delivery system for CATV. Other satellite services, including those for religious programs, also were started. In all, more than 100 earth satellites were in operation.

An experiment dubbed "Qube," described as a "dramatic leap" in cable TV, began in Columbus, Ohio, in 1977. With an investment of $10 million, Warner Cable Corporation offered Columbus homes thirty channel choices combining conventional television, community channels, premium programing on a pay-per-view basis, and the capacity for subscribers, by pushing five response buttons, to participate in local game shows, vote on referendums, take quizzes, purchase products, and predict the plays of a sporting event.

Cable operators were pleased by the creativity evident in the industry, by the relaxation of controls, by the clarification of regulations involving the use of programs embodied in the new federal copyright law (see Chapter 7), and by new technological developments on the horizon. The latter include the eventual replacement of conventional cable with optical fibers and the use of laser (light amplification) devices as the signal source for the fibers. Major problems were yet to be overcome, but the cable industry seemed at last to have come into its own.

VIDEOCASSETTE AND VIDEODISC TELEVISION

Lending a fifth dimension—convenience—to television's attributes of sight, sound, motion, and color, home videotape recorders (VTRs, or VCRs as they also are known) became a major consumer product in the late 1970s.

Developed primarily in Japan, VTRs enable viewers to record programs and play them back at their own convenience; to view prerecorded cassettes; and to play videotapes made with their own cameras.

Industrywide sales of a million units were predicted by 1979, when the sets were expected to cost considerably less than the original $1000 or more. Industrial and educational sales were substantial, but the home entertainment market was the largest.

Making the various systems compatible was a major problem, but competition was expected to boil down to the Sony and RCA systems. Another obstacle was posed by a copyright infringement unit. The industry tended to discount the suit on the grounds that as long as taped programs are not used for commercial gain, they are within legal bounds, and that taping off the public airwaves is not a violation of copyright, especially since the recording off radio has long been common and unrestrained.

Also available were videodisc systems enabling owners to view programs on their sets by playing discs resembling phonograph records. N. V. Philips of Holland and MCA, Inc., marketed the first sets in 1976, providing 30 minutes of uninterrupted color or black-and-white programing, plus sound. The playback systems were sold initially for about $500 and the discs at from $2 to $10.

Matsuki Electric Company of Japan announced in 1977 the development of two new videodisc systems—one with a 30-minute playing capacity per side and the other with a one-hour capacity per side.

The discs look like records, play like records, and are made like records, and also can produce stereophonic sound.

Together with regular and pay cable TV, electronic cameras, 84-inch Video Beam sets, and the highly popular video games, the VTR and videodisc systems opened a new era of super-TV home entertainment far removed from the earlier years of time-tabled, limited-choice, small-screen television.

PUBLIC BROADCASTING

Public broadcasting has emerged only recently as a major force in television and radio. In seeking to provide alternative programing for the American public, the noncommercial medium offered "The Great American Dream Machine," "Sesame Street," "The Electric Company," news and public affairs programs, and other contributions of merit. An integrated system of national direction, program production and distribution, and local station influence evolved. But its chief problems were how to determine the right mixture of central and federated control, how to determine the appropriate audience, and how to obtain enough no-strings-attached funding. Since politics is public broadcasting's marketplace, strong political winds whirled about the system. Only permanent financing, most public broadcasting advocates argued, could substantially insulate the system from the vagaries of political life and ensure its long-range stability.

The Corporation for Public Broadcasting was established by Congress in 1967, acting largely upon a Carnegie Commission report that declared: "A well-financed and well-directed system, substantially larger and far more pervasive and effective than that which now exists in the United States, must be brought into being if the full needs of the American public are to be served." The commission was referring to National Educational Television, which supplied programs for noncommercial stations licensed almost exclusively to communities, universities, state authorities, and public school systems. Failing to take into account years of notable educational accomplishments, some critics viewed NET educational and public programing as "pedantic, impoverished, noble, and often deadly dull," with negligible audiences.

In 1970 the newly authorized CPB established the Public Broadcasting Service to manage programing production and distribution and station interconnection. Production centers were designated at seven noncommercial TV stations across the country. In addition, the Children's Television Workshop, producer of "Sesame Street" and "The Electric Company," became, in effect, an eighth center, although it was a nonprofit corporation with ties to no one except that it was funded by CPB, the U.S. Office of Education, and the Ford Foundation. National Public Radio, a noncommercial radio interconnection largely exchanging locally produced programs, was created in 1971.

PBS was unlike any other national broadcasting network. With a board of directors dominated by the chief executive officers of licensing organizations, it was far more federated and far more loosely organized. The programs it distributed were produced by the major centers and funneled through the network, but final responsibility for clearance and scheduling rested with the local stations, which could screen programs before airing. NET merged with WNDT-TV, New York, to become WNET, one of the seven production centers.

Public broadcasting gained steadily in favor. Despite the fact that two-thirds of the TV stations broadcast on UHF channels, by 1978 approximately 60 percent of the nation's households viewed public television about three hours each day. And the 203 public radio stations, although reaching fewer than two-thirds of families with radios, attracted millions of listeners.

President Carter submitted to Congress a proposed Public Broadcasting Financing Act of 1978. The bill would authorize $1 billion in matching federal funds over a five-year period beginning in fiscal year 1981 and make drastic organic changes in the system. It would encourage more journalistic independence, including the right of stations to editorialize; seek to resolve organizational conflicts within the system; trim the bureaucratic structure to eliminate waste; enlarge the role of independent producers and the public; strengthen national programing; require the system to raise $2.25 for every $1 received from federal funds; stipulate that stations receiving funds open their meetings and financial records to the public; and increase the participation of minorities and women.

Congressional debate centered on the funding provisions, with a tax on commercial broadcasters suggested as one alternative source. The administration, however, sought to postpone discussion of other sources pending a report of the Carnegie Commission on the Future of Public Broadcasting, expected in January, 1979.

HOW A TELEVISION STATION OPERATES

Unlike the printed media and the commercial motion picture industry, a television station gives its product away. Anyone possessing a television set can watch hour after hour of programs free of charge. Yet the station, of course, must earn money to cover its high cost of operation and return a profit. It does so through the sale of commercial advertising time.

Examination of the operation of an actual successful TV station of medium size affiliated with one of the three major networks shows how American television functions. In most respects this station is typical of scores in the United States, although it has a considerably larger news operation than many of its size.

The station is headed by a general manager. Answering to the manager are four major department heads—chief engineer, program director, news director, and sales manager. The head of the production department reports to the program director. The promotion director is closely linked to the sales department but answers to the general manager.

Although it is on the air eighteen hours a day, the station creates only about three or four hours of programing in its own studios, mostly local news and homemaker offerings. The rest is obtained from the network and from independent suppliers of filmed shows. To do this job, the station has a staff of fifty-five men and women, plus eight to ten part-time employees. Some of the latter are local college students who usually help with live show production. The station offers a full hour of local news, weather, and sports at the dinner hour preceding the evening network news program, and another 30 minutes of news in late evening. During the week it presents other local background news and discussion programs. Fourteen men and women of varying degrees of experience comprise the news staff.

The necessary income with which to operate the station is obtained from three primary sources: the network, national spot commercials the station puts on the air during station breaks, and local and regional commercials. One widely held misconception is that an affiliate station pays the network for the national programs it puts on the air. The reality is just the reverse.

Each of the three major networks has approximately 200 affiliated stations. In addition, the federal government permits each network to own and operate seven stations of its own, five VHF and two UHF. They are known in the trade as O and O's. An affiliate contracts with a network for the exclusive right to broadcast in its coverage area all programs distributed by the network. It also has the right to refuse to broadcast any network program. Rejections occur when the station believes its audience will find a particular program objectionable, or when it prefers to use that block of air time to broadcast a program it originates or obtains from another source. In practice, most affiliates broadcast more than 90 percent of the network programing. When a network plans to present a controversial program, it transmits the show in advance to the affiliates on a closed circuit; the station executives then decide whether to use it. The network also provides advance summaries of all its scheduled programs, letting the affiliates know what to expect on the air.

With certain exceptions, the network pays the station to air a network program; the price is based on the size of the station's market. In our example, the station's average compensation is approximately $700 per hour. The network pays the station 30 percent of its card rate. During an hour-long show, most of the commercials are put on the air by the network, which receives all the income from them. However, station break slots in which the local station inserts its own commercials, either national or local, are left open. It keeps all the revenue from these spots.

Thus it follows that the larger the number of affiliates carrying a show, the larger the network's audience and the greater the amount of money it can charge an advertiser that places a commercial on the show. Television advertising rates are based on the cost of reaching 1000 viewers. That is why the industry became so concerned in 1977 when national ratings services revealed that both daytime and nighttime viewing had declined after almost two decades of an almost continuous rise. Changing demographic patterns of the viewing audience were among several factors cited as the possible reasons for the decline.

To supplement network and local programing, stations obtain programs from other sources as well, under varying financial arrangements. A common form is the syndicated show, such as the Mike Douglas afternoon interview program. The station purchases the show from a syndication firm for a flat, negotiated fee. All commercial time slots are open for local commercials. If the station's sales staff is effective, it fills those spots with well-paying sales messages. A variation is the barter program, of which the Lawrence Welk show is an example. The station receives the program without charge, and the Welk organization does not provide any compensation. Half the spots in the hour-long program are sold nationally by the Welk organization. It keeps all this income, from which it covers the expense of preparing the show. The other half of the commercial slots are reserved for the local station's own commercials.

Still another variation is the network show provided to an affiliate without the usual compensation from the network. Enough local spots are left open during the program for the station to come out satisfactorily from a financial standpoint. The "Today" show and Sunday professional football broadcasts are examples of this arrangement. The audiences for these broadcasts are so high that, in these instances, a local station can afford the noncompensation arrangement.

Occasionally, a station will replace a network program in prime time with a nonnetwork program that it considers exceptionally important or more lucrative. This action often angers followers of the preempted program, so is done infrequently. The Billy Graham evangelistic crusade, for example, will purchase consecutive evenings of prime time, for which it pays the station more than the $700 hourly network rate. This is a good financial arrangement for the station because it receives full income for the hour and at the same time appeals to the portion of the viewing population that finds the Graham message inspiring.

MAJOR FUNCTIONS OF THE TELEVISION STATION

The News Function

The area of news and information is an important, aggressive, and prestige-building division of the television-radio programing structure. Many types of programs are provided. One is the regular newscast, giving 5- to 60-minute or longer summaries of happenings in the community, nation, and world. A second area is the background and interpretation program. It may be a newscaster's straight presentation of facts, a panel discussion, an interview, or a documentary. CBS's "Sixty Minutes," for example, gives a news magazine approach during prime evening time and provides information to groups with both general and special interests.

Another category for journalists in broadcasting is the extraordinary news event, such as the Soviet-American "handshake" in space or the assassination of a prominent figure in public life. During these times, regular commercial programs are dispensed with to permit immediate news coverage. Under strong pressure the reporter must give facts and interpretation instantly, with no opportunity for editing.

Hard-nosed investigative reporting is a basic and exciting function at many stations. Often officials have been indicted, new laws passed, and countless irregularities corrected as a result. Consumer reporting is widespread and growing as newspeople regularly take on malpractices ranging from bait-and-switch advertising to price gouging. Both investigative

A television reporter at a minority housing project is on camera for NBC-affiliate KSTP-TV in St. Paul, Minnesota. (Photo by Irene Clepper.)

and consumer reporting require the firm support of station management because of the possible reaction of advertisers as well as other members of the viewing audience. An increasing number of stations send reporters to cover regional stories and even to distant cities and foreign countries, often sharing their coverage in news-exchange agreements with other stations. Assigning reporters at state capitals either permanently or during legislative sessions is standard practice. Other types of outlying news bureaus also are maintained by many stations.

Electronic news gathering systems, providing live-action coverage, are in widespread use. Generally two technicians and a reporter travel in a van or panel truck equipped with a top-mounted microwave dish. Through the use of a miniature camera and a portable tape recorder, an account of the news event is beamed back to a prominent landmark in the city, atop which four "horns" have been placed to pick up signals from all points of the compass. At the studio, tapes are edited on machines to transfer selected segments from original to final form. Edited news segments may go directly to the air at that point, or be transferred to two-inch tape "carts" for random insertion into newscasts. All tape elements are bypassed, of course, when the story is presented live.

The three networks as well as independent services provide electronically fed color news reports of an international, national, and regional nature daily to stations throughout the country for incorporation into locally produced newscasts. Television and radio alike spend a great deal of time and money to keep their audiences abreast of the news. Election-year coverage is especially costly. To most broadcasters, however, the expense of covering news events is well justified. Stations and networks discovered quite early that news programs rank exceptionally high in public interest and render a public service while building a steady audience and steady revenues. Surveys conducted annually by the Roper Organization, Inc., have shown that since 1963, television has been the source of most news for the American people. In addition, the most recent surveys have revealed that television enjoys an almost 2.5 to 1 advantage over newspapers as the "most believable" news medium.

The revolution in communications technology, while improving the quality of news programing, also has put broadcasters in a better financial position in covering news as well as in other operations. The developments include new videotape technology, high-quality magnetic-strip sound on film, satellite communication, instant-replay techniques, portable film and tape equipment, the use of high-speed jet aircraft to transport tape or film, and efficiently packaged, high-capacity switching gear that simplifies the problem of television pickup from almost any major point in the United States or the world.

In recent years national news consultant companies have been engaged by many television stations to increase the viewership of news programs. Using the techniques of motivational research and sophisticated surveys, these experts have proposed changes in news program formats. But many news directors and reporters have decried the application of techniques designed to please the most viewers as destroying the integrity of the news programs. In one director's words, the result often is "slick, breezy news shows, dispensing glib headlines, socko action films and orchestrated 'spontaneity'—newscasts for people who can't stand television news." Another director accused consultants of becoming absentee news czars: "They dictate who should be on the air, and how the news should be presented, and load up the newscast with show biz."

The consultants' advice to humanize the presentation of news has resulted in numerous "happy talk" programs with newscasters becoming, as one educator termed them, "Charlie Chuckles" and "Nancy Yuk-yuks." The practice of crowding a large number of items into each newscast has been another consequence, as well as the replacement of

Film for use on a local television news program is edited by the news editor and a photographer. (Courtesy of the South Bend *Tribune*.)

some personnel. The principal consultant firms, Frank N. Magid Associates and McHugh and Hoffman, Inc., along with a number of news directors and station program directors, have defended research into audience reactions and the resulting recommendations as essential management tools designed to improve news programs and raise competitive ratings.

Local and regional surveys of this type supplement the long-established national rating systems that determine the life and death of all television programing. The A. C. Nielsen Company bases its ratings on a sampling of 1200 electronically metered homes. Although these reports often are disputed (*"I've* never been called by a ratings service," many viewers complain), the findings are supported by diaries maintained by 800,000 families either for Nielsen or the other major audience-research service, Arbitron, formerly known as ARB. The local and regional surveys often are at variance with the national ratings, but they merely reflect viewing habits of the particular areas involved.

The Editorial Function

Although network newscasts have been accused by numerous individuals and groups of being biased in their presentations, such charges rarely have been made of local station news programs. More than half of the nation's TV stations air editorial viewpoints, either sporadically or regularly, in clearly marked segments of their newscasts. Some stations have introduced a "letters column," in which comments from viewers are read as a part of the newscasts. Others invite viewers to present their views at a certain time each day, arrange panel programs involving local community leaders, and air minidocumentaries and, although the cost is high, regular documentaries on subjects of prime interest.

Owners of stations that editorialize view the action as part of their obligation to serve the interests of their local communities. They regard editorials as making an important contribution to the public's understanding of issues, and at the same time enhancing their station's prestige and helping to build audiences. Stations that do not editorialize cite lack of time or manpower for the extensive preparation necessary to do an effective job. Some owners believe that editorializing is not an appropriate activity for a broadcast station. Surveys have shown that most viewers welcome editorials, feeling that such an expression of views helps them to think and to make up their minds about important issues.

Special editorial personnel or news staff members often require more than five hours to prepare the average editorial for broadcast. In order to ensure that the editorial is received as reflecting the viewpoint of management and to maintain a desirable distinction between news and opinion, the editorial generally is delivered by the station manager himself, usually in two or three minutes of air time. Some stations present editorial cartoons. In order to meet the requirements of the fairness doctrine, the right to reply is offered with each editorial.

Programing and Production

Broadcasting programs are planned and produced by the programing department. On small stations, only a few persons may be employed to make commercial announcements, read news and sports summaries, select and play recordings, and introduce network programs. Large stations, however, may employ seventy-five or more persons to handle a variety of specialized jobs.

Programing policy and scheduling for a large station are handled by the program director. The traffic manager prepares daily schedules of programs and keeps a record of broadcast time available for advertising. The writing and editing of all scripts are the responsibility of the continuity director. Assisting is the continuity writer, who prepares announcers' books containing the script and commercials for each program together with their sequence and length.

The director supervises individual programs, possibly under the supervision of a producer, who handles the selection of scripts, financial matters, and other production problems. At times these functions are combined in the job of producer-director. Program assistants obtain props, film slides, artwork, and makeup service; assist in timing the program; and prepare cue cards. Some stations employ education and public affairs directors who supervise noncommercial programs such as those presented by churches, schools, and civic groups. Many also have community relations directors, who provide liaison with numerous segments of the viewing and listening audience.

Television and radio staff announcers present news and live commercial messages, identify stations, conduct interviews, describe sports events, and act as masters of ceremonies. On small radio stations they may also operate the control board, sell time, and write scripts and news copy. Announcers on small stations often obtain FCC licenses in order that they also may operate transmitters.

Large television and radio stations may employ a librarian to handle the music files, and a musical director to supervise rehearsals and broadcasts. Television stations also have film editors who prepare films and videotape recordings for on-the-air presentation. The station's files of films and tape are maintained by a film librarian.

Television performances that are aired either live or on tape require the services of a studio supervisor, who arranges scenery and other equipment; a floor or stage manager, who directs the movement of actors on the set and relays stage directions, station breaks, and cues; floor personnel who set up props, hold cue cards, and perform other such chores; makeup artists, who prepare personnel for broadcasts; scenic designers, who plan and design settings and backgrounds; and sound effects technicians, who coordinate special sounds. Working with all these programing personnel are the engineers and broadcast technicians, who use their highly specialized knowledge to convert the sounds and pictures into electronic impulses that can be received by the public.

Advertising and Promotion

As has been noted, network national advertising, national "spot" advertising, and local advertising provide the bulk of operating revenue for television and radio stations. Large stations may also receive income from such services as producing programs for clients and making films and tapes. The advertising staffs of the national networks solicit advertising from companies whose products or services are marketed throughout the country. They provide a continuing flow of up-to-date information about the markets served by their affiliates and make contracts both directly with big companies and with the agencies that represent them.

National firms with large staffs of trained solicitors represent individual stations in calling on agencies and companies for business. They sell spot advertising, which may range from a series of brief announcements to full programs originating in the local studios and from commercials to 15- or 30-minute programs. These firms, located strategically in the major cities, make sales presentations for any or all the stations on their lists.

This leaves local advertising to be handled by the station itself. The commercial manager must build a staff of account executives, who often have a triple job to do: sell advertising in general, broadcasting in particular, and their own station specifically. This is true because the local merchant may not be fully aware of the advantages of advertising and may have practically no knowledge of what a carefully conceived television or radio advertising campaign may do for business.

The account executive first learns as much as possible about the prospective client's business. In consultation with the local sales manager and station program director, a suggested plan, involving possibly a regular program and a series of commercial announcements, is prepared. If the plan is accepted, skilled writers prepare the copy and continuity. After the advertiser is convinced that the campaign is selling goods or services, the salesperson seeks gradually to sell the sponsor additional broadcasting.

An important adjunct to sales is the promotion department. The promotion manager may be a staff member with no other responsibilities or may be the general manager, the commercial manager, a copywriter, or a salesperson. In order to attract both audiences and advertisers, the promotion manager prepares station advertisements and publicity stories for local newspapers, for trade publications read by agency and company advertising people, and for use over the station's own facilities. In addition, the promotion manager develops ideas for posters and other outdoor advertising; engages in such public relations activities as delivering speeches, answering station mail, and handling telephone inquiries; and attracts attention to the station and its individual programs through such devices as parades, stunts, and personal appearances by star performers.

OPPORTUNITIES AND SALARIES

Thousands of job openings occur in all phases of broadcasting each year. During the 1970s, however, as a steadily increasing number of journalism and mass communications college graduates poured onto the market, and as an economic recession took place, great perseverance and marked evidence of talent were essential for young people desiring to break into the business. A willingness to begin work with small stations, to move to where job openings occurred, and often to seize other opportunities for employment while waiting for the desired job frequently were necessary.

When openings develop, station managers generally turn to their files of job applicants, many of whom are already employed on smaller stations. For many jobs the graduates of schools with highly developed programs in radio, television, and speech are preferred. These persons already have learned production, programing, and/or news gathering and presentation techniques and thus generally can perform specified chores almost immediately. At times bright graduates of print-oriented schools of journalism, or of straight liberal arts or business programs, are transformed into broadcast personnel.

One of every nine persons employed in television is a member of a minority group, and the number is increasing each year. In fact, a study of FCC data has shown that three of every four new employees hired since 1971 have been women or minority group representatives. Only 13.7 percent of the women employees, however, serve in the so-called image-maker capacities of owner-managers and professionals, as compared with 37.3 percent in periodicals. So, despite the increasing number of women such as Barbara Walters of ABC who have become national and local celebrities in broadcasting, the movement of women into higher echelon positions still lies ahead.

Stations are constantly in the market for competent advertising solicitors and continuity writers. Writing commercials requires a knowledge of selling, and more often than not such a job is filled by a woman. Salaries in these fields compare favorably with those requiring similar talents in the other media. Good promotion men and women with large stations commonly earn $12,000 or more.

Beginning salaries for television and radio news personnel are comparable to those paid newspaper reporters and editors. These range from $7500 to $8500, depending upon the size of the station, regional competitive factors, and the training of the applicant. After three to five years, salaries for radio newswriters range from $9500 to $13,000, while television newswriters on large stations may earn more than $14,000.

Talent fees for those with on-mike and on-camera assignments push these incomes even higher.

Skilled network employees earn much higher salaries. Those who serve as assignment editors and who produce network shows earn additional fees. Newswriters at network originating points and at stations owned and operated by NBC and ABC are represented by the National Association of Broadcast Employees and Technicians. The union's news jurisdiction includes all writing, editing, processing, collecting, and collating of news, including film. The bargaining agent for all CBS writers and for NBC and ABC on-the-air news personnel in New York City is the Writers Guild of America. Those under individual contract with the networks to write and deliver their own news programs are represented by the American Federation of Television and Radio Artists, the union that covers all on-the-air performers. They earn talent fees for newscasts and other air work plus a guaranteed wage. Barbara Walters' $1 million a year as coanchorperson of the ABC Evening News and producer of "specials" is a record salary for a journalist.

As might be expected, personnel employed by large broadcast stations earn higher salaries than those paid by small stations. The range of TV salaries is roughly as follows: General manager, $20,000 to $50,000; station manager, $15,000 to $37,000; commercial manager, $11,500 to $26,500; program manager, $10,000 to $17,500; promotion manager, $8,000 to $15,000; chief engineer, $10,000 to $20,000; and news director, $10,000 to $19,000. Radio station salaries generally are lower. These salaries include fees and commissions, but not fringe benefits. Compensation varies widely according to geographic location, station and market size, program emphasis, and other factors.

QUALIFICATIONS

The television program director must have a comprehensive knowledge of all the production techniques entailed in staging a performance before cameras and microphones, such as sets, graphics, script, makeup, lighting, and music. Mastering detail and knowing how to work with all kinds of people are vital.

The film director must possess the same broad background and also be acquainted with the special characteristics of film and videotape, including camera limitations, sound recording problems, types of emulsions, and lab processing techniques. Often that person must be both a writer and director.

The copy and continuity writer, of course, must be a word person, able to set a mood or epitomize a situation quickly and succinctly. Knowledge of the entire business of television or radio advertising is most helpful.

The promotion manager must develop a continuing plan designed to project a favorable image for the station. Writing news and advertising copy, devising publicity and promotional campaigns, and having some familiarity with typography, layout, editing, public speaking, and general public relations principles and practices are necessary tools of the trade.

Sound training in reporting and editing is essential for success in television newsrooms, and a knowledge of photography and cinematography are valuable adjuncts. The successful news person must have curiosity, persistence, an interest in people, a good educational background and knowledge of current events, an ability to write clearly and speedily, poise under pressure and, if expected to read news copy, a voice of acceptable quality, inflection, and diction.

Other desirable qualifications include the ability to gather news under all conditions; to edit the stories, film, and tape of others, including wire copy; to find local angles in national stories, simplifying complex matters and making them more meaningful; and to recognize feature angles in routine stories. The news person also must be familiar with laws applicable to broadcasting, including copyright, libel, and slander. In the handling of news, an awareness of broadcasting's responsibilities to the public, including the exercise of judgment and taste in selecting news items, is essential.

The qualifications for announcers and disc jockeys are described in Chapter 12.

CHAPTER 14
THE FILM

THE ROLE OF MOTION PICTURES

"It is imperative that we invent a new world language . . . that we invent a nonverbal international picture-language. . . ." So writes Stan VanDerBeek, painter and experimental film maker. As corollary activities, VanDerBeek proposes using present audiovisual devices in the service of such a language, developing new image-making instruments to find the best combination of machines for nonverbal interchange, and establishing prototype theaters called Movie-Dromes to house these presentations—described as "Movie Murals," "Ethos-Cinema," "Newsreel of Dreams," and "Image Libraries."

While VanDerBeek's method is radical, the principle underlying his approach is as old as the motion picture itself. Early in the history of film, its practitioners and advocates recognized that the motion picture was truly an international language. And, while the "image-flow" described by VanDerBeek is as yet imperfectly realized, the desire for "peace and harmony . . . the interlocking of good wills on an international exchange basis . . . the interchange of images and ideas . . ." is as old as tribal man. Although, on the surface, VanDerBeek's "A Proposal and Manifesto" is naive and idealistic, on a smaller, infinitely more conventional scale, the language of motion pictures *is* helping to bridge the gap among the people of different nations.

As motion picture critic Stanley Kauffmann observes, "Film is the only art besides music that is available to the whole world at once, exactly as it was first made." And film, like opera, can be enjoyed despite the viewer's ignorance of the language employed in the dialog or narration. Kauffmann contends, "The point is not the spreading of information or amity, as in USIA or UNESCO films, useful though they may be. The point is emotional relationship and debt." To understand this observation, consider the Russian entertainment film *The Cranes Are Flying* (1957), a romantic drama of life and death, of love and loss, set in the years 1941–1945 and played by Russian actors against a Russian background. If one empathizes with the young lovers, sharing their anguish at war and separation and their desire for peace and reunion, the viewer has been drawn into an emotional relationship with the characters that makes it impossible for him to view all Russians as unfeeling puppets solely committed in thought and deed to advancing the Communist state.

Although the advent of sound tended to nationalize film and reduce film's claim to being an international art as in the days of the silent movie, the current popularity of foreign films in America and the even more widespread distribution of American films in foreign markets demonstrate the primary role played by a film's visual elements, and the lesser importance of language as a communications device. In fact, when a motion picture is subtitled for distribution in a foreign market, the subtitles convey little more than one-third of the dialog. Yet the meaning of the film is seldom, if ever, impaired, and its beauty is often enhanced.

The USIA film *Years of Lightning, Day of Drums* (1964) illustrates the lesser role played by verbal language in motion pictures, even in a nontheatrical film. Approximately 40 percent of the film uses neither dialog nor narration. Designed as a tribute to John F. Kennedy and as a vehicle to bolster confidence that the work Kennedy had begun would continue after his death, the film presents the six facets of the New Frontier, interlacing such programs as the Alliance for Progress, Civil Rights, and the Peace Corps, with sequences depicting the funeral. These funeral sequences are largely wordless, with the sound track carrying natural sound: the heavy footsteps of the marchers, the more staccato hoofbeats of the horses, and the steady, muffled drumbeat. Yet no words are necessary during these sequences. Death and bereavement are not uniquely American experiences. The styles of burial and mourning may vary from country to country, but the loss occasioned by death is a constant. Similarly, the scenes depicting the parades and enthusiastic crowds that greeted Kennedy on his international speaking tours need little narration—save the words spoken by Kennedy himself. The human face is the human face; closeups of Kennedy's face, or of a nameless Filipino's or Costa Rican's, demand no verbal interpretation. Assembled from stock footage, *Years of Lightning, Day of Drums,* by sharing Kennedy's death with the foreign viewer, shares his political achievement and America's aspirations.

A note of warning: Film is probably the most powerful propaganda medium yet devised. As a consequence, its potential for aiding or injuring civilization is enormous. In addition to supplying a verbal message through dialog, narration, or subtitles, the film provides an instantaneous, accompanying visual message—supplying the viewer with a picture to bulwark what has been learned through language. Thus, the imagination need not conjure a mental image to accompany the words; the viewer leaves the theater complete with a concept and its substantiation. If a picture is worth 1,000 words, a picture together with three or four carefully chosen words is worth 10,000 words. Makers of television commercials know this; so does anyone who has ever thought carefully about this compelling and utterly contemporary medium of communication.

In the past, American motion pictures have been associated with Hollywood. Persons desiring careers in the film industry saw and followed one road—and that road led to the golden West. But the situation has changed today. There are many roads leading to important and satisfying work in films, and not all end in Hollywood, as this chapter will reveal.

THE ENTERTAINMENT FILM

Hollywood: 1945–1965

The late 1940s were boom years for Hollywood. At the close of 1946, box office revenues from United States movie theaters totaled a record $1.7 billion—compared with $1.2 billion in 1953, and $904 million in 1963. During 1949, more than 90 million tickets were sold weekly in American movie houses—compared with 45 million paid admissions each week in 1956, and 21 million in 1968. Again during 1949, the major studios—among them Metro-Goldwyn-Mayer, Twentieth Century Fox, Columbia Pictures, RKO, and Warner Brothers—released 411 new motion pictures, compared with 296 released in 1954, 235 in 1959, and 203 in 1963. Administered by the men who had established them, the major companies offered such escapist films as the horror-thriller *The Beast with Five Fingers* (1946) and the slick romantic comedy *June Bride* (1948), along with such provocative and candid films as *The Best Years of Our Lives* (1946) and *Crossfire* (1947) to a receptive and apparently uncritical American audience.

But then several events caused the near collapse of the Hollywood movie empire. First, television rocketed into prominence—almost replacing the motion picture as a medium of mass entertainment. Successful prime-time network television series attract between 30 million and 50 million viewers—a number roughly double that of movie tickets sold weekly in 1968. And second, as a consequence of action taken by the federal government in the early 1950s, the major companies were forced to sell their chains of movie theaters—thus denying the studios an automatic outlet for their products regardless of intrinsic merit. In noisy desperation, Hollywood turned to the wide screen, undertook longer and more expensive film productions with star-studded casts, made use of more "adult" subject matter, advocated increases in ticket prices, started to produce 30- and 60-minute filmed series for television, and began selling already exhibited movies to the television industry. Between 1955 and 1958, Hollywood sold almost 9000 pre-1948 feature films to television, and by 1960 the major studios were vying with each other for sale of films produced since 1948.

The first of these retaliatory measures, the wide screen, has been called the most significant innovation in film technology since the advent of sound. Until the appearance of the first wide-screen motion picture, *The Robe* (a $5 million Cinemascope film produced and distributed by Twentieth Century Fox in 1953), the standard screen shape had been a rectangle 20 feet wide and 15 feet high; this represents a ratio of 4 to 3, or 1.33:1—a proportion determined by the width of the film and going back to Thomas Edison and the Kinetoscope. The new wide screen changed the ratio to anything from 2.62:1 to 1.66:1, with Cinemascope settling at 2.55:1. Regardless of trade name and varying dimensions, however, most new screens are at least twice as wide as they are high.

Initial critical reactions to the wide screen were mixed, with some filmmakers insisting that the new screen size signaled the end of the closeup and rendered established directorial and cutting techniques ineffective. In time, however, the advantages and possibilities of the wide screen became apparent to filmmakers, who have used its inclusiveness to achieve a naturalness and spontaneity, and its new dimensions to experiment with new kinds of visual compositions and new uses of the closeup.

In response to the wide screen and as a further effort to bring the American public back into the movie theaters, Hollywood began to produce longer and more expensive movies with casts of thousands and an abundance of well-known stars. Often, best-selling novels or successful dramas that called for copious action and spectacle provided the "story" for these productions—as in *The Ten Commandments* (1956), *Raintree County* (1957), *El Cid* (1961), and *Cleopatra* (1963).

During these years, the already complex machinery needed to produce a Hollywood picture was becoming even more complex, with producers, directors, writers, actors, cameramen, editors, stunt men and women, script consultants, script personnel, costumers, set designers, wardrobe assistants, prop men, lighting technicians, makeup artists, carpenters, actors' agents, painters, publicists, and gossip columnists composing the Hollywood scene. Overseeing the vast collective enterprise that movie making had become were the studio presidents and executive producers

—men like Jesse L. Lasky, David O. Selznick, Samuel Goldwyn, and Darryl Zanuck, who exercised ultimate authority over script, stars, and budget.

The collaboration and expense involved in a typical Hollywood film are revealed in the following example. A major Hollywood studio made a film that included a scene in a newspaper office. This consisted merely of an office boy tearing a bulletin off a press association teleprinter and rushing across the city room to hand it to the managing editor. The action required less than a minute on the screen and filled barely a page in the shooting script.

For authenticity, the film producers arranged to shoot this brief scene in the city room of a Los Angeles metropolitan newspaper, after the last afternoon edition. Technicians and stage hands brought in lights, sound equipment, and cameras. Lighting experts put masking tape over all shiny articles in the city room to reduce the glare. Desks were moved to make an easier path for the actor playing the office boy role. Clerical assistants, supervisors, and actors arrived. By the time the little episode had been shot, nearly 100 persons had been involved and several hours consumed.

This kind of procedure has made Hollywood films expensive to produce but technically expert. One reason for the huge overhead is the high degree of unionization among motion picture personnel. Few industries are so intensively organized; rigid limitations are enforced upon the duties each worker can perform and the kinds of physical properties he may touch.

A recent breakdown of the average production budget for a Hollywood movie indicates the large percentage consumed by sets and other physical properties, as well as studio overhead:

Story costs	*5%*
Production and direction costs	*5*
Sets and other physical properties	*35*
Stars and cast	*20*
Studio overhead	*20*
Income taxes	*5*
Net profit after taxes	*10*

As a final measure, Hollywood sought to dramatize subject matter once denied film treatment as a result of the Production Code. In 1956, revisions in the code permitted depiction of drug addiction, kidnapping, prostitution, and abortion. Soon, movies treating narcotics addiction, like *Monkey on My Back* (1957) and *The Pusher* (1959), and films involving prostitution, like *Butterfield 8* (1960) and *Girl of the Night* (1960), were released bearing the Motion Picture Seal of Approval. Although the new freedom of subject matter resulted in the creation of a few artistic successes, Hollywood quickly managed to create new clichés from the once-forbidden subject matter at its disposal—proving once again that mere sensationalism is as empty as the most bland "family-type" situation comedy.

Not even the inclusion of such stars as Elizabeth Taylor, Doris Day, Cary Grant, Rock Hudson, Burt Lancaster, and Marlon Brando could remedy the decline in movie attendance. And gradually, Hollywood became aware that the casting of a star meant little in terms of the commercial success of its movie. Further, although selling old movies to television and producing filmed television series were profitable and aided Hollywood's faltering economy, such measures did not strike at the core of what was plaguing Hollywood.

Something was happening to the American movie-going public. It was changing, and although Hollywood was changing too, the movies and their audiences were moving in unrelated directions. What were these changes? It is true that the movie-going public was watching fifteen or more hours of television a week. But what other reasons account for the decline of Hollywood in the mid 1950s and early 1960s? The increased popularity of foreign films, the rise of the American experimental filmmaker, different methods of distribution, and the growth of a visually more sophisticated audience—all these are partial reasons. In its own way, each contributed to the decline of Hollywood and, paradoxically, to its reemergence as a vital force in film production.

THE FOREIGN FILM

Italy

If Hollywood chose to ignore, by and large, the realities of the post-World War II world, that was not true of Italian filmmakers. Responding to the grim reality of a war-torn, impoverished Italy, Roberto Rossellini directed *Open City* (1945)—the first important film shot in a style quickly dubbed by the critics as neorealism. Combining stock newsreel footage with his own film (shot chiefly on the streets of Rome and scratched to resemble newsreels), Rossellini depicted the hardships endured by Italians during the Nazi occupation and their courageous resistance. To heighten the authenticity gained by actual locations and natural lighting, he used only a handful of professional actors whom he encouraged to ad lib, and chose ordinary Roman citizens as supporting players. Although none of these techniques in isolation was new, none had been used so successfully together before; and *Open City* became, as the film historian Arthur Knight has said, "the key film in the entire neorealist Italian revival."

Equally as personal and visually intense, and equally as concerned with social realism, are two early films by Vittorio De Sica. In *Shoeshine* (1946), De Sica portrays the lives of a group of homeless Roman boys involved in the corrupt underworld of the Italian black market. *Bicycle Thief* (1947) treats the relationship between a father (played by a factory mechanic) and his son (played by a Roman newsboy) who together try to beat the apparently insurmountable odds occasioned by unemployment, poverty, and corruption.

Other directors central to this movement are Luigi Zampa (*To Live in Peace,* 1946; *Angelina,* 1947), Giuseppe De Santis (*The Tragic Hunt,* 1947), and Alberto Lattuada (*Without Pity,* 1947). Within a five year span, neorealism began to die out, its force vitiated by postwar recovery and renewed prosperity.

In recent years, amid a rash of conventional and often sensational films, the work of two masterful directors has emerged. Described as "second generation realists," Federico Fellini (*La Dolce Vita,* 1960; *8½,* 1962; *Juliet of the Spirits,* 1965; *Satyricon,* 1970; *Amarcord,* 1974) and Michelangelo Antonioni (*L'Avventura,* 1959; *La Notte,* 1960; *The Red Desert,* 1964; *Blow-Up,* 1966; *The Passenger,* 1975) have little in common except a compulsion to use the surfaces, rituals, and hidden recesses of contemporary existence as theme and subject matter, and a proven ability to use improvisation as an effective cinematic technique.

France

Suffering lack of funds and the shifting patronage of the French government, French filmmakers in the late 1940s and early 1950s were engaged in the production of drab imitations of American gangster films; sensational melodramas; *film noir* (the film of despair, represented by such works as Clouzot's *Manon,* 1959; Clement's *Les Jeux Interdits,* 1952); films based on successful or distinguished fiction

(*Symphonie Pastorale,* 1946; *Devil in the Flesh,* 1947; *L'Idiot,* 1947);
films embodying existential doctrine (*Les Jeux Sont Faits,* 1947;
Cocteau's *Orphée,* 1950); films exploiting sex (initiated by Roger
Vadim's *And God Created Women,* 1956); and a few individualistic
works, such as the comedies of Jacques Tati (*M. Hulot's Holiday,* 1953;
and *Mon Oncle,* 1958) and Robert Bresson's *Les Dames du Bois de
Boulogne* (1944), and *Journal d'un Curé de Campagne* (1951).

But then, in 1958–1959, the New Wave erupted on the French film
scene, with Francois Truffaut's *Les Quatre Cents Coups* and Alain
Resnais' *Hiroshima Mon Amour* winning awards at the 1959 Cannes
Film Festival. Other films that heralded the New Wave are Claude
Chabrol's *Le Beau Serge* (1958), Louis Malle's *Les Amants* (1958),
and Jean-Luc Godard's *Breathless* (1959). Although heterogeneous
and resistant of labels in the manner of all creative artists, these New
Wave directors do share many cinematic ideals as well as an outlet for
these ideals in the influential film journal *Cahiers du Cinema.* Truffaut,
Godard, and Chabrol had been film critics in the early 1950s, and they
continued to write interestingly of the cinema. Describing his own procedures, Truffaut has said,

I start with a very imperfect script, in which there are certain elements that please and stimulate me. Characters that strike some
chord of response in me. A theme that lets me "talk about" something I want to film. As I work I find I am eliminating all the scenes
of story transition and explanation. So it can happen that when the
film is done, it is completely different from what it was proposed
to say in the first place. The shooting of the film is that sort of
adventure.

In *Breathless,* Godard took his camera onto the Paris streets. Using a
hand-held Arriflex and a three-page script outline by Truffaut, Godard
allowed the camera to follow the actions and reactions of Michel (a
small-time gangster, played by Jean-Paul Belmondo) and his American
girl friend (played by Jean Seberg), depicting a life devoid of logic or
purpose.

Although the New Wave has dissipated itself (by 1964, Cannes was
denigrating the very movement it had applauded five years earlier),
these films and their directors have made great and irrevocable contributions to cinema art—in particular, in the imaginative and "free"
camera work that characterizes New Wave films, in the encouragement
of a liberated acting style dependent on improvisation and self-portraiture
rather than on self-conscious or stagey performance, on the fanciful use
of silent film techniques, on the absence of conventional plotting and

continuity, and on a moving away from a cinema grounded in literature and drama to one that uses the strengths of the film medium to make its own powerful, highly cinematic statements.

England

Films like *Blue Scar* (1948) and *The Brave Don't Cry* (1952), both depicting the life of coal miners; *Chance of a Lifetime* (1950), set in a small Gloucestershire factory; and such short films as Lindsay Anderson's *Every Day Except Christmas* (1957), concerning workers at Covent Garden, and Karel Reisz's *We Are the Lambeth Boys* (1958), in which a boys' club in London furnishes the principal locale, prefigure the realism of British theatrical films in the late 1950s.

Room at the Top (1958) was the first in a remarkable series of outspoken realistic films to gain widespread critical attention. Soon, motion pictures like *Saturday Night and Sunday Morning* (1960), *A Taste of Honey* (1961), *The Loneliness of the Long-Distance Runner* (1962), *A Kind of Loving* (1962), *Billy Liar* (1963), *Morgan* (1966), *The Leather Boys* (1963), and *This Sporting Life* (1962) had established the reputations of their directors—Karel Reisz, Tony Richardson, John Schlesinger, Sidney Furie, Lindsay Anderson—and the significance of the British feature film. Describing their work as "free cinema," these directors brought to the screen a penetrating social realism focused on the English working class, preparing the way for the Beatles (who themselves are featured in Richard Lester's *A Hard Day's Night,* 1964; and *Help!,* 1965) and the ascendancy of Liverpool over Pall Mall.

Other Countries

In Soviet Russia, film production is not only nationalized but the work of individual studios like Lenfilm, in Leningrad, and Mosfilm, in Moscow, is closely supervised by a specially designated state committee. Not unexpectedly, therefore, many Soviet feature films have either implicit or explicit social messages, like the strongly chauvinistic *The Turbulent Years* (1960). But there are also films that focus on personal crises and solutions rather than on social problems. Among them are the previously mentioned *The Cranes Are Flying* (1957), *Clear Sky* (1961), *I'm Twenty* (1965), and such adaptations of literary classics as Sergei Youtkevich's *Othello* (1955) and Grigori Kozintsev's *Don Quixote* (1957) and *Hamlet* (1963).

Although the Polish film industry is also nationalized, Polish film-makers have produced a sizable body of sensitive and cinematically expert films. Many, like *The Last Stage* (1948) and *Five Boys of Barska Street* (1954), depict Poland's immediate past (World War II, the Nazi occupation, concentration camps, and the politically troubled postwar years) with a frank and searching realism. Andrzej Wajda's *Ashes and Diamonds* (1958) provides a good example. Set in the late 1940s, the film depicts as its hero a basically apolitical young man who, acting upon orders from a right-wing political group, kills a Communist leader and is killed, in turn, by agents of the state.

A later film by Wajda, *Innocent Sorcerers* (1960), eschews any overt political concern, depicting the aimless, amoral, unsentimental existence of worldly and bored Warsaw young people, and shows the influence of the New Wave in both subject matter and treatment. Other important Polish directors are Roman Polanski (*Knife in the Water,* 1962), Andrzej Munk (*Eroica,* 1957), Jerzy Kawalerowicz (*Mother Joan of the Angels,* 1961), and Kazimierz Kutz (*A Pearl in the Crown,* 1972).

Although, as in Poland, the Czechoslovakian film industry is nationalized, a young group of Czech filmmakers has been producing some significant movies since the early 1960s—like Jan Nemac's *Diamonds of the Night* (1964) and Milos Forman's *Peter and Pavla* (1964) and *The Loves of a Blonde* (1965). But when Soviet intervention put an end to the increasing liberalization of the Czech government in 1968, the much-heralded "new Czechoslovak film" also died. Directors like Forman, Kadar, Barabas, and Taborsky no longer work in Czechoslovakia.

In Sweden, recent filmmaking has been dominated by Ingmar Bergman, who uses film to explore such abstract and eternal problems as the meaning of life and death (*The Seventh Seal,* 1956), the nature of truth (*The Magician,* 1958), and man's tragic inability to communicate (*The Silence,* 1963, and *Cries and Whispers,* 1972).

The Japanese film has become best known to American audiences through the work of Akira Kurosawa. Like Bergman, Kurosawa depicts elemental problems and passions using highly stylized, historical settings to underscore the timelessness of his themes. *Rashomon* (which won the Grand Prize at the Venice Film Festival in 1951) concerns the nature of truth, while *Throne of Blood* (1957), like *Macbeth* after which it is patterned, depicts the breaking down of morality through greed. Also drawing upon Japan's rich history of legend and strict social order, the films of Kenji Mizoguchi (*Ugetsu,* 1953, and *Sansho the Bailiff,* 1954) nevertheless transcend nationality. But Japan has not neglected contemporary settings and subjects, as Kurosawa's *Drunken Angel* (1948), Imai's *Stained Image* (1953), Toyoda's *Wheat Whistle* (1955), and Ozu's *Tokyo Story* (1953) attest.

RECENT DEVELOPMENTS IN THE AMERICAN FILM

American Experimental Filmmakers

While Hollywood in the 1940s and 1950s persevered in its chosen course, determinedly oblivious to innovations in European filmmaking, a segment of the American movie-going public was well aware of their importance. Excited by the new techniques and possibilities for film, dismayed at the impersonality and inanity of most Hollywood movies, and aware that film is as much an art form as the novel, dance, or painting, numerous young Americans turned to film to give shape to their feelings and ideas, as their predecessors (and many of their contemporaries) had chosen the more conventional vehicles of drama, fiction, poetry, painting, or sculpture.

Much of the credit for publicizing and organizing the work and esthetic doctrines of America's experimental filmmakers goes to Jonas Mekas, himself a filmmaker, in addition to being a publisher and editor of *Film Culture,* occasional film critic for the *Village Voice,* and organizer of the Film Makers' Cooperative and Distribution Center. In describing his own work and that of other independent filmmakers, Mekas has said:

Our movies come from our hearts—our little movies, not the Hollywood movies. Our movies are like extensions of our own pulse, of our heartbeat, of our eyes, our fingertips; they are so personal, so unambitious in their movement, in their use of light, their imagery. We want to surround this earth with our film frames and warm it up—until it begins to move.

Of extreme importance to the experimental filmmakers is the unambitiousness and intensely personal nature of their films, as described by Mekas. In many instances, desire and budget dictate that the film be the result of one person who functions as producer, director, cameraman, editor, and often distributor. The actors are often friends, and usually nonprofessionals. Most films are done on 16 mm. And, as in the New Wave films, there is an absence of chronological continuity and carefully plotted story lines, along with considerable use of improvisation and emphasis on spontaneous action and reaction rather than upon stagey performance.

As the New Wave is a convenient rubric that lumps together highly individualistic directors, so the New American Cinema Group—"a free organization of independent filmmakers dedicated to the support of the men and women giving their vision to the filmic art"—is a convenient label, embracing filmmakers with divergent purposes, talents, and methods. But, like the New Wave directors, the New American Cinema Group shares an outlet for its views, the magazine *Film Culture,* and evinces a common hatred and a common enthusiasm. As the French directors rebelled against film's prior dependency on literature and rejoiced in the cinema as an art form with its own esthetic, so the New American Cinema rebels against all that is unimaginative, standardized, and hopelessly phony about Hollywood and celebrates, too, the film as an art form.

Among the more notable experimental filmmakers are Jonas Mekas (*Guns of the Trees, The Brig*), Stan VanDerBeek (*Mankinda, Skullduggery, Summit, Breathdeath*), Stan Brakage (*Dog Star Man, Window Water Baby Moving, Scenes from Under Childhood*), Bruce Conner (*A Movie, Cosmic Ray, Liberty Crown*), Kenneth Anger (*Scorpio Rising, Inauguration of the Pleasure Dome*), Gregory Markopoulos (*Twice a Man, Serenity, Ming Green*), Charles Boultenhouse (*Handwritten, Dionysius*), Shirley Clarke (*The Connection, Skyscraper, The Cool World*), and, of course, Andy Warhol and Paul Morrissey.

Parodying Hollywood's film factories with his own Factory, Hollywood's star system with his own superstars, Hollywood's trumped-up and ultimately phony retailing of sex and sex goddesses in *Screen Test,* and Hollywood's bad guys, good guys and Westerns in *Horse,* Warhol has been enormously and unabashedly prolific and successful. In all his films, whether in the early "documentaries" like *Empire, Sleep,* and *Eat,* or in the later "feature" films, *Kitchen, The Chelsea Girls, My Hustler, Bike Boy,* and *Lonesome Cowboys,* Warhol's constant subject has been the film itself. Even as producer for Morrissey's films, notably the highly successful *Trash,* Warhol's personality and vision dominate. Using a variety of techniques, from a static camera focused on one object for more than eight hours, to cinéma vérité pushed to an extreme, to employing two screens and running two films simultaneously, Warhol has drawn attention through technique and subject matter to the film as product and substance, reveling in and revealing its particular properties as a physical entity.

The many purposes and styles of American experimental films range from social criticism using documentary techniques to embodiments of the subconscious through surrealism and myth to psychedelic experiments with light and color. At their best, the films of the avant garde are exciting, fresh, sensitive, and fully able to transmit their maker's vision. At their worst, they are very bad indeed—as bad as the worst products of any art form—as trivial and boring, for example, as the worst Hollywood movie.

Hollywood: 1965–1978

In 1950, when a consent decree put teeth into a court decision calling for the major motion picture studios to sell their theater chains, a monopoly was broken up that had linked production with distribution and had fostered the exhibition of American motion pictures regardless of quality. And when this blow to Hollywood was followed by the ascendancy of television in the American economy and the American home, Hollywood began to retrench. In addition to cutting back on production, the major studios dropped contract actors, directors, and writers at option time. In 1950, there were 474 actors, 147 writers, and 99 directors under contract to the major studios; in 1955, there were 209 actors, 67 writers, and 79 directors; in 1960, there were 139 actors, 48 writers, and 24 directors. Three studios—RKO, Republic, and Monogram—stopped production entirely. And approximately 6000 movie houses closed their doors.

Into these troubled waters stepped the independent producers. Some of the independent production companies were formed by the stars themselves—among them Burt Lancaster, Frank Sinatra, Kirk Douglas, and Bob Hope. Other independent companies were started by directors—William Wyler, Alfred Hitchcock, Elia Kazan, and Otto Preminger. Some had been producers, like Sam Spiegel and Arthur Hornblow. Still others had been writers, like Richard Brooks, Joseph Mankiewicz, and Robert Rossen. In itself, the independent production company was not a new commodity in Hollywood. But the independent producer had never made any significant inroads in the Hollywood system until the 1950s. At that time, the major studios, having involved themselves in fewer productions, began increasingly to finance and then distribute films made by the independent production company. Gradually, therefore, the studios began to function like United Artists, which had been started in 1919 as a releasing company without studio facilities.

By accepting the lesser role of financier, promoter, and distributor, even at times leasing their own facilities to the independent production companies, the major studios relinquished artistic control over the films they were underwriting. Control passed to the independent producer, creating a situation that allowed a film to have a style impressed on it by those who made it rather than by a studio boss overseeing a dozen or more films simultaneously.

Although not all the motion pictures produced by the independent companies have been artistic or commercial successes, a good many independent productions are of outstanding quality and have increased the prestige of the Hollywood movie both here and abroad. Seven of the nine films winning Oscars as Best Motion Picture of the Year between 1954 and 1962 were produced by independents: *On the Waterfront* (1954), *Marty* (1955), *Around the World in Eighty Days* (1956), *The Bridge on the River Kwai* (1957), *The Apartment* (1960), *West Side Story* (1961), and *Lawrence of Arabia* (1962). Other successful independents have been *The Diary of Anne Frank* (1959), *The Hustler* (1961), *Advise and Consent* (1962), *Guess Who's Coming to Dinner* (1967), *In the Heat of the Night* (1967), *The Graduate* (1967), *Bonnie and Clyde* (1967), *Easy Rider* (1969), and *Rocky* (1977).

And, in turn, the more interesting and stimulating movies have been bringing American audiences back into the movie houses, but with a difference: The Opinion Research Corporation of Princeton, New Jersey, reported that in 1975 persons under 24 years of age comprised approximately 60 percent of the movie audience and that 88 percent of that audience was under 40 years of age. W. R. Simons & Associates reported that 31.7 percent of adult men and 28.8 percent of adult women attended the movies once or more in the average month (defined as "frequent" movie-going) in 1977. Persons who have attended college are more than twice as likely to see movies as those without a high school diploma. This means that movies are less a mass medium than an elitist medium—that is, less a form of mass art than of high art. In the inevitable rearrangement caused by displacement, television has become the mass medium. The two media, however, are intertwined. A recent Gallup poll found that 63 percent of the population is interested in viewing movies at home, 19 percent because they dislike going to theaters.

In the 1970s, however, the Hollywood epic was reborn. As in the 1930s, the public sought refuge from a declining economy in movie theaters. Films such as *Star Wars, Close Encounters of the Third Kind, The Godfather,* and *The Exorcist,* with star-studded casts and big-budget effects, drew crowds in numbers unprecedented since the advent of television. Box office grosses in 1976, for example, amounted to $2.4 billion, the largest ever, although only 186 films were released, far below the average total of 373 films per year in the 1950s and 445 in the 1940s. Ironically, film producers were using television to lure audiences, spending well over $98 million in 1977 for advertising on local and network levels.

To accommodate the new audiences and the new movies, 16,800

movie screens were in operation in the United States in December, 1976. Of this total, 13,000 were in indoor or "hardtop" theaters and 3,800 were in drive-ins. From 1972 to 1976 indoor screens increased by 21.5 percent and drive-in screens by 2.7 percent. In all there were approximately 700 circuits, each with four or more theaters, operating about 53 percent of all movie houses. The remaining movie theaters were owned and operated by 6,800 individuals or companies.

Within the past few years, elaborate movie palaces of the 1920s and 1930s, such as Times Square's Paramount, Roxy, Capitol, and State, have been torn down. Approximately 243 new theaters, both indoor and outdoor, were either opened, announced, or placed under construction in 1976. The day of the multiauditorium theater was at hand. Most were twin-auditorium theaters, but some had three, four, and even six auditoriums. Along with these more ambitious projects were an ever-increasing number of minitheaters, deluxe houses with audience capacities of 150 to 400 persons and relatively inexpensive to construct and operate. Of these 243 new projects, approximately 35 percent were in shopping centers, continuing a trend that had begun in 1962.

At present, American motion pictures continue to dominate the world market, being preferred in most countries to the indigenous product. It is estimated that American films take up 60 percent of the world motion picture playing time, occupying 67 percent of motion picture screen time in England, 55 percent in Italy, 33 percent in France, and as high as 90 percent in other countries with less developed film industries.

The International Movie

Part of the life style that characterizes the new Hollywood concerns the international movie. A step toward internationalization occurred in the 1950s. The independent producers, not being shackled to particular film studios, made movies in Europe and other foreign locations in order to profit from cheaper labor costs and national subsidies, to use actual locales, and to please the movie stars themselves who, by establishing residence in a foreign country, could avoid paying U.S. income tax on money earned while working abroad.

At present, changed tax laws and increased foreign labor costs have reduced the advantages of filming in foreign locations. But the transporting of Hollywood actors, directors, cameramen, and all the assorted personnel connected with movie production continues, and this trans-

Atlantic and trans-Pacific traffic has helped to return movie making to its international beginnings. The new mobility of contemporary movie-makers has been aided tremendously by certain technological developments. Lightweight cameras and sound recording equipment, as well as ministudios capable of being airlifted, are allowing movie producers to set up shooting where whim and geography dictate.

Further, such elements as the directors and writers, as well as the financial backing and distribution arrangements, have done their share to internationalize the industry. For example, *Blow-Up,* which won the 1967 Cannes Film Festival Golden Palm Award, was an English entry, with an Italian director (Antonioni), produced for MGM. *Taking Off,* which won the 1971 Cannes Jury Special Prize, was a United States entry directed by the Czech director Milos Forman. The 1966 Berlin Festival winner was a British entry, *Cul-de-Sac,* made by the Polish director Roman Polanski, who also directed *Rosemary's Baby.* The list could go on and on. Even such an American movie as *Bonnie and Clyde* was almost a French product. Its American writers, Robert Benton and David Newman, wrote the screenplay first for Francois Truffaut. When Truffaut rejected the script (he was then filming *Fahrenheit 451*), Benton and Newman approached Jean-Luc Godard, who was interested but ultimately decided against undertaking the project. And it was only at this time that Warren Beatty began negotiations, finally buying the script for $75,000.

The many film festivals prevalent today are additional evidence of the internationalism of the film industry. Festivals in Cannes, Berlin, Venice, San Sebastian, New York, Moscow, Montreal, Cork, Chicago, and Mexico have provided showcases for films from every nation and a meeting and market place for actors, directors, writers, and producers.

FILM CRITICISM

As film's potential for personal and artistic expression was realized, and as its capability for being more than a cheap entertainment medium for the illiterate was understood, an accompanying esthetic developed to explain and analyze the form and content of motion pictures. Vachel Lindsay's *The Art of the Moving Picture* (1915) and Rudolf Arnheim's *Film* (1933) are early examples of enlightened film criticism.

Good film criticism, like good literary criticism, serves two functions: (1) It explicates the work at hand, and (2) it elevates the public taste. The first function is the more obvious. As film techniques have become more complex, as film has probed deeper into human sensibility and experience, and as films have become identifiable as the work of a particular director who uses personal symbols in the manner of contemporary poets and novelists, effective film criticism seeks to explain this heightened complexity by clarifying techniques, images, and relationships of time, place, and character.

The second purpose is perhaps best explained by Walt Whitman's oft-quoted remark that great audiences make great poets. An audience knowledgeable about film history and techniques is in a position to recognize the second-rate, the false, the vacuous, the film that appears to be saying something but in reality says nothing, and the slick directorial tricks that attempt to hide the untrue. Great audiences make great poets (filmmakers) because they provide a need and a receiving ground for great poetry (films); they inspire the poet (filmmaker) to do his best by giving him a reason for being that transcends his physical identity. Advances in film technology and subject matter have occurred and will continue to occur because film artist and film audience have become knowledgeable together.

At its best, good film criticism is informative, expanding the reader's knowledge by relating the film at hand to other works of a particular filmmaker, or to other films of similar or dissimilar genre; it respects the film and glories in its potential realized; it bears the stamp of its creator's mind by possessing a distinctive style; it bridges epochs and nations by linking past with present achievement regardless of country of origin.

In all this, the film critic must be distinguished from the film reviewer, who serves a reportorial function. Whereas the film critic seeks to analyze and explain, the film reviewer seeks to ascertain the merits of a particular film with the intention of warning his audiences against an inferior, boring, or morally degrading film, or touting those films with a high entertainment value. Gene Shalit has served this function in his frequent reviews on NBC's "Today" show. For the most part, movie reviewers write for the daily papers, previewing and describing films for their readers; they seldom go beyond the value of amusement as a criterion.

In contrast, film critics generally write for the magazines: *Film Quarterly, Cahiers du Cinema* (available in an English edition), *Film Culture, Sight and Sound, New Yorker,* and *Esquire.* Stanley Kauffmann in *New Republic* and Arthur Knight and Hollis Alpert in *Saturday Review* have written weekly pieces that combine previewing a film with deeper, more thoughtful, analysis. Recent well-known American film critics have been Andrew Sarris, Pauline Kael, Wilfrid Sheed, Jonas Mekas, Molly Haskell, and John Simon.

THE DOCUMENTARY FILM

In both England and America, the documentary film came of age in the 1930s through direct patronage by national governments, and matured, still under government auspices, during the troubled years of World War II. Perhaps this is not surprising, as a documentary's purpose is always partially social—setting forth public and private crises and victories, showing us where man has been and what, inevitably, man will become unless proper action is taken.

In England, the earliest documentaries are associated with the Empire Market Board Film Unit, headed by John Grierson. Grierson's first film, *Drifters* (1929), shot on location on the North Sea, portrays the daily existence of the herring fishermen. When the EMB Film Unit was shifted to the General Post Office in 1933, Grierson and the film unit continued the production of quality documentaries, including *Weather Forecast* (1934), *Song of Ceylon* (1934), *Coal Face* (1935), *Night Mail* (1936), and *North Sea* (1938). "By the time the war broke out," Arthur Knight writes, "the British documentary movement—headed by men like Paul Rotha, Stuart Legg, Basil Wright, Harry Watt, Alberto Cavalcanti, Arthur Elton and Edgar Anstey—had achieved a worldwide reputation and inspired scores of directors outside England to attempt documentary movements in their own countries."

In America, the Depression and the New Deal gave rise to a remarkable series of documentaries (see Chapter 15).

World War II gave impetus to increased documentary film production, ranging from training films for United States service personnel to informative films for a civilian population needing instruction in wartime procedures. As well, Hollywood directors like John Huston, William Wyler, and John Ford began making films for the military. *San Pietro* (1944), *Memphis Belle* (1944), and *Battle of Midway* (1944) are memorable documentaries filmed on and around World War II's battlegrounds.

In England, the documentary filmmakers, now working under the aegis of the Ministry of Information, also turned their attention to wartime subjects, producing such films as *London Can Take It* (1940), depicting London during a Nazi air raid; *Target for Tonight* (1941), documenting an air force bombing mission; and *Desert Victory* (1942), an account of the North African campaign. Early in the war, the English independent film studios were mobilized to produce training films as well as to continue in the production of feature films. As Arthur Knight has observed, "for the first time, the documentary and fiction film-makers of Britain joined forces. Some, like Alberto Cavalcanti and Harry Watt, moved from documentary to fiction; while fiction directors like John Boulting, Thorold Dickinson and Carol Reed became, at least for the time, documentalists."

Basic to many recent documentaries is a problematic cinema technique known as cinéma vérité, spontaneous cinema, or direct cinema. The term *cinéma vérité* applies to film that uses the camera to record reality in an unbiased and unmanipulated way. In presenting the essence of a situation, the director does not work from a preconceived shooting script, and, to all intents and purposes, does not direct—if by directing one means organizing and controlling what happens before the camera. By making use of the new lightweight cameras and recording equipment, the filmmaker goes into the field where he or she, and camera, act as witnesses and scribes. The intent is to provide either minimal or no interpretation and to retain the spontaneity and natural character-istics of the actual event.

In practice, documentary films exhibiting pure cinéma vérité are hard to find. Either consciously or unconsciously, most filmmakers impose an interpretation on their subject matter through in-camera editing, or editing after the film has been shot. Others "edit" reality before any filming occurs by carefully selecting the persons and objects to be photo-graphed and only then applying cinéma-vérité filming techniques. For example, *Chronique d'un Eté,* by Jean Rouch and Edgar Morin, shows evidence of rather stringent preshooting "editing," although the most effective parts of the film result from the characters behaving in ways that could not have been predicted beforehand.

In contrast, *Showman* and *The Beatles* provide good examples of pure cinéma vérité. Directed and produced by Albert and David Maysles, these films have been criticized for their superficiality. But, the Maysleses contend, their vow has been to avoid interfering with the subject during filming; any superficiality, therefore, is inherent in the subject and is inevitably part of the truth that the film depicts.

Robert Drew, Richard Leacock, Donald Pennebaker, and Gregory Shuker have produced many outstanding documentary films under the label The Drew Associates. *On the Pole* depicts the ambitions, anguish, and ultimate failure of an Indianapolis race-car driver named Eddie Sachs. *Primary* concerns the Hubert Humphrey–John F. Kennedy primary contest in Wisconsin. *Crisis* depicts the Robert Kennedy–Governor Wallace fight over the token integration of the Alabama schools. *The Chair* is about an effort to prevent a young black from going to the electric chair. *Jane* is a film portrait of Jane Fonda on the opening night of an unsuccessful play.

Other notable documentaries include Lionel Rogosin's *On the Bowery,* filmed on location in New York City, and Frederick Wiseman's controversial *Titicut Follies, High School,* and *Hospital.* Still others are Allan King's *Warrendale,* which concerns the treatment of emotionally disturbed children, and Frank Simon's *The Queen,* on a "Miss America" contest for transvestites.

In recent years, television has provided a ready market for documentaries. A fine example of a television documentary, and one that also makes use of cinéma vérité techniques, is "Royal Family," produced by a consortium of BBC and England's independent television companies and shown on American television. Richard Cawston served as producer-director, working with an eight-person crew throughout an almost full year of shooting forty-three hours of film. Cawston has attributed the success of this film to the royal family's freedom to talk without restraint, ad-libbing in front of the cameras, in the knowledge that Queen Elizabeth and Prince Philip had the right to veto any sections they found unacceptable in retrospect. "I decided it could be done only with some sense of humor and with a sort of cinéma-vérité technique," Cawston has said. "Therefore, nothing was really rehearsed. We would discuss beforehand what would happen, and then simply shoot it. It worked out very well."

Other television documentaries are considerably shorter and understandably more humble in subject matter and technique, ranging from film accounts of war maneuvers in Vietnam to Charles Kuralt's "On the Road" segments for CBS News. The television news magazines, like "Chronolog," and timely news specials provide excellent documentaries on such subjects as a U.S. Olympic sky-diving team and a Stone Age New Guinea tribe, photographed with precision and sensitivity by a team of Japanese cinematographers. Other outstanding documentaries have been ABC's Cousteau and *National Geographic* series and "Sadat: Action Biography"; Public Broadcasting Laboratory's "Birth and Death"; CBS's "Hunger in America" and "The Selling of the Pentagon"; and NBC's "Pensions: The Broken Promise."

Arthur Knight has conjectured that in the near future regional filmmakers may be celebrating their region through film as, traditionally, novelists, poets, and musicians have done. Certainly, the field for documentary production is wide open. Invariably, it seems, truth is stranger and more interesting than fiction. As a purveyor of facts and feelings, as a conveyor of an increasingly important photographic reality, and as a molder of public opinion, the documentary film is a powerful force in modern communications.

FILMS FOR INDUSTRY, GOVERNMENT, AND EDUCATION

This is a mushrooming industry in which an estimated 1200 firms are at work in the United States, producing pictures on a multiplicity of topics for showing to industrial and sales groups, schools and universities, government and community organizations, the armed forces, and professional and religious bodies. These firms might be compared to the hundreds of small trade journals in the magazine field. Few of them are major organizations, but in the mass they form an influential channel for communicating information and ideas.

Nontheatrical filmmaking is heavily financed by American industry, which has found in this type of motion picture a highly effective means for presenting its purposes, methods, and achievements. Approximately 15,000 nontheatrical films are produced each year. Most are on 16 mm film, the standard size for projection by small and portable machines. A few of the more elaborate are made on 35 mm, some even for widescreen projection. This total includes some 9400 business and industrial pictures, 1900 government films, 1700 educational films, 250 for medical and health use, 300 for community organizations, and 150 religious films. Nearly $1.5 billion is being spent annually to produce these films and for other audiovisual aids, such as filmstrips, slides, and equipment.

The price of making and distributing a good company film averages nearly $150,000, with some major productions exceeding $500,000. As many as 200 prints are made for some films to satisfy the demand. The average total audience for such a film is estimated to be 1.5 million. Many educational and instructional films are produced on far smaller budgets, some of them only a few thousand dollars, and are shown to more limited audiences.

Production of educational and informational films began with the development of the 16 mm portable projector in 1923. At present more than 750,000 projectors are in use in the United States, mostly in schools and businesses, but also in clubs, libraries, homes, and churches.

A large proportion of these nontheatrical films are available for use by organizations and private citizens free of charge. The cost is underwritten by business organizations as part of their institutional public relations budget; by federal, state, and local governments; by social or economic organizations that seek to present educational material in their particular fields; or by tax-supported institutions such as public libraries or adult education schools. There are 2600 film libraries in the United States distributing 16 mm films. *The H. W. Wilson Educational Film Guide* lists more than 20,000 films that can be borrowed.

OPPORTUNITIES

There are abundant opportunities for young men and women in both theatrical and nontheatrical film areas today. Many of those entering the field begin their studies at the more than 800 colleges and universities that offer work in film (see Chapter 20). Beginning salaries compare favorably with those of other mass communications industries and professions, and almost limitless financial returns may be achieved by highly creative and productive individuals.

A *Saturday Review* article affirms that "the opportunities for young filmmakers have never been greater, not just in theatrical motion pictures, but also in the burgeoning industrial, educational, and commercial film fields." The article continues, "Writers with an ear for the dialogue of the contemporary life problem and an eye for the contemporary setting are in demand." Even the "much maligned producer function" is being reappraised and its important role reaffirmed. Undeniably, although at one time getting into film work was a hit or miss affair, the college student today can find a well-paved academic route into one of the many careers available in the thriving and many-faceted film industry.

CHAPTER 15
PHOTOGRAPHIC COMMUNICATION

THE VISUAL DIMENSION

Photographic communication has emerged dramatically in recent decades as a key mode of mass communication—a visual dimension, capable of providing a wealth of description and detail not communicable through the written or spoken word.

The art of telling a story with photographs—both still and motion pictures—developed centuries later than the technique of telling it with words. Photographic equipment was relatively slow to become available, and the men who worked with pictures needed time to develop the editorial methods of photographic narration. The rapid development of equipment in recent years and of man's comprehension of how to use his sophisticated new tools, however, has made photojournalism a fundamental mode of mass communication.

Photojournalism for newspapers and magazines developed rapidly during the 1930s. Film, first used in the motion picture theater to provide entertainment, news, and documentaries for mass audiences, became in the 1950s and 1960s a dominant ingredient of televised news, public affairs, documentary, and advertising communication. Photojournalism thus has expanded in concept and function and today is part of the larger field known as photographic communication.

To have full knowledge of the communication process, the student needs to understand the functions performed by pictures, how photography developed, and the essential techniques used by professional photographers and editors. This chapter discusses those topics, as well as the opportunities and working conditions for visual communicators.

Less than 150 years elapsed from the moment when a man first produced a photographic image until a fascinated world watched astronauts Neil Armstrong and Edwin Aldrin transmit a live television picture from the surface of the moon. In that century and a half the growth of photography as a medium of communication has been spectacular, especially when we realize most of the progress has been in the last fifty years.

HOW PHOTOGRAPHY DEVELOPED

Pioneering Photography

Joseph Nicéphone Nièpce, a retired French lithographer, began searching for a method to capture the photographic image in 1813. Three years later he is believed to have succeeded in producing a negative image, but he could only partially fix the image after exposure—that is, desensitize it to light. In 1826 he made a photograph on a pewter plate showing a view from his workroom window. He called this process Heliographie (sun drawing).

Photography took a significant step forward with creation of the Daguerreotype by another Frenchman, Louis Jacques Mandé Daguerre, in 1839. In this process an invisible (latent) image was developed by using mercury vapor. The exposure time was reduced from 8 hours to 30 minutes, giving photography a practical application. The Daguerreotype process had three great limitations: (1) The image could be only the size of the plate in the camera; (2) the image was unique in itself and could be duplicated only by reshooting; and (3) the image was a *negative,* coated on a mirrored metallic surface, so a viewer could see it as a *positive* only if the mirror reflected a dark background.

Wet Plates

The third important approach to photography was the collodion wet plate process, developed in 1851 by Frederick Scott Archer, an English sculptor. The collodion process required the coating of a glass plate with a light-sensitive solution that had to be kept wet until exposed in the camera and processed in a darkroom. Very sharp paper prints could be made from a collodion negative. A photographer could use this process outdoors to record exposures of only 10 seconds to a minute, a spectacular improvement in photographic speed. He was required, however, to work from a portable darkroom on location.

It was with this wet plate process, so clumsy by modern standards, that Mathew Brady produced his magnificent photographs of the Civil War. A successful portrait photographer, Brady asked President Lincoln for permission to document the conflict. He sent out twenty teams of photographers, headed by Timothy O'Sullivan and Alexander Gardner, who followed the Union soldiers onto the battlefields and into their bivouacs. Brady's photographs have preserved for posterity a fascinating record of the war. For the first time, photography proved its value as a news medium.

Flexible Film

The next leap forward, opening the door for modern photography, came in 1889 when the Eastman Kodak Company, headed by George Eastman, introduced a transparent film on a flexible support. Creation of this film made the motion picture possible. It increased the picture-taking possibilities for still photographers, too; they could use smaller, less obtrusive cameras and no longer were burdened with heavy glass plates.

In 1912 the famous Speed Graphic press camera, which was to become the "workhorse" for news photographers for a half-century, was introduced. The small camera came into use in America in the 1920s. Ernst Leitz's Leica, a German camera using 35 mm film, was followed by another German make, the Rolleiflex, a larger $2\frac{1}{4}$ x $2\frac{1}{4}$ camera. Both remain popular in professional circles today.

The small camera freed the photographer from carrying bulky film or plate holders. It enabled him or her to operate less obtrusively, to take thirty-six pictures in rapid succession, and to use the fast lens to take pictures without flash in low-level lighting situations. The pictures thus were less formal, more candid, and honest. A German lawyer, Dr. Erich Salomon, who declared himself to be the first photojournalist, began using such a camera in 1928 as a photographer of European nobility. Two other Europeans who influenced the development of photojournalism were Stefan Lorant, who edited German and English illustrateds, and Alfred Eisenstaedt, a West Prussian, who moved from the Berlin office of the Associated Press to become one of *Life* magazine's first photographers.

Color photography became a commercial reality when the Eastman Kodak Company announced development of its Kodachrome color film in 1935. In the same year the first motion picture in Technicolor, a high-fidelity color process, was presented on the American screen.

Two more fundamental breakthroughs in photographic equipment followed World War II. In 1947 Edwin H. Land introduced the Polaroid system for producing a positive black and white print 60 seconds after exposure. Soon this time was reduced to 10 seconds. Then in 1963 a 50-second Polaroid color print process opened new avenues for amateurs and professionals alike. The second of these breakthroughs came in the mid 1950s: the recording of moving pictures on magnetic videotape. This was an electronic approach; all the other advances in the photographic process had depended on chemistry.

Newspaper Photographs

From a mass communication viewpoint, taking good photographs was not enough: a way had to be found to reproduce them in newspapers and magazines. Woodcuts had been used in the Civil War period, but they were slow to produce, expensive, and not exact. A direct photographic method was needed.

This was achieved by two men working separately, each of whom developed a halftone photoengraving technique. Frederic Eugene Ives published a halftone engraving in his laboratory at Cornell University in June 1879, and Stephen Horgan published a photograph "direct from nature" in the New York *Daily Graphic* in March 1880. Several years passed, however, before such photographs came into frequent use in newspapers; by the middle of the 1890s halftone engravings were appearing in supplemental inserts of the New York newspapers, and in 1897 the New York *Tribune* was the first to publish a halftone in the regular pages of a high-speed press run.

During the early years of the twentieth century, pictures in newspapers generally were used singly, to illustrate important stories. The newspaper picture page, making use of special layouts and unusual picture shapes, was developed during World War I. A major new force in American journalism, the picture tabloid, came into being shortly after World War I. In these newspapers with their small page size and flashy makeup, designed to appeal to street sale readers, the photograph was given the dominant position, often overshadowing the text of the news stories. The tabloid front page usually consisted of a headline and a dramatically blown-up news photo.

The New York *Daily News* began publication in 1919, followed by Hearst's *Daily Mirror* and the *Evening Graphic*. Intense picture competition among these three New York tabloids led at times to the publication of photographs that violated many people's sense of good taste. The *Evening Graphic* illustrated major stories with faked composograph photos, and the *Daily News* shocked readers by printing a full-page photograph of the electrocution of Ruth Snyder, a murderess. Of these three original New York tabloids, only the *Daily News* survives, still sharply edited but less flamboyant and less a "picture" paper than in its earlier days.

During the 1920s, when the picture newspapers were flourishing, experiments were carried out in transmission of a photographic image by wire and by radio. The first American photos sent by wire were transmitted from Cleveland to New York in 1924. A decade of development passed before the Associated Press established its Wirephoto network on January 1, 1935. Distribution of news photos by wire enabled newspapers across the country to publish pictures from other cities only a few hours after they were taken.

The Picture Magazines

The expanded interest in all forms of photographic communication in the 1930s led Time Inc. to found the weekly picture magazine *Life* in November 1936. *Life* was patterned after photographic publications developed in Germany and England. In 1937 the Cowles organization established *Look,* published every other week and more feature-oriented than *Life,* with less emphasis on news. *Look* ceased publication in 1971 and *Life* followed in 1972.

Both *Look* and *Life* emphasized editorial research and investigation preceding assignment of photographers to all but spot news stories. Photographers were well briefed as to the significance of a story before arriving on the scene to begin interpreting it with their cameras. In that sense photographers on the two magazines controlled a mind-guided camera. In its early years *Life* was even more stringent in controlling its photographers, suggesting to them before they left the office exactly how key pictures should be made. This practice diminished during World War II, which provided swiftly changing stories that did not fit an editor's preconceived plan.

From the mid 1930s into the 1950s a small group of well-known magazine photographers contributed to the development of the photographic essay and interpretive picture story. Dorothea Lange's sensitive images of America's depression conditions stand as examples of still photography at its finest. So also do the pictures of Margaret Bourke-White and photographs by Gordon Parks, whose creative abilities transcended the photographic medium to include writing, musical composition, and Hollywood film. Henri Cartier-Bresson, a French photojournalist, defined the "decisive moment" during this period, and Robert Capa showed how the still camera could record the reverberations of war. W. Eugene Smith and David Douglas Duncan were major contributors to *Life* during and after World War II. Smith's picture essays, including "Spanish Village," "Country Doctor," and "Nurse Midwife," stand as classics. David Duncan's word-and-picture reports of the Korean War have been matched only by his equally powerful Vietnam War magazine stories and picture books.

Motion Pictures

Only two years after Eastman's development of flexible film, Thomas A. Edison developed the Kinetoscope in 1891, thereby laying the foundation for the motion picture. The Kinetoscope was a motion picture projector designed to show still pictures in rapid succession to produce the visual illusion of motion on a screen in a darkened room.

The Lumiere brothers presented the first public performance of a

Margaret Bourke-White and Gordon Parks, whose creative photography has been among the nation's best. (Photo of Margaret Bourke-White courtesy of the estate of Margaret Bourke-White, © Time Inc.; photo of Gordon Parks by Alfred Eisenstaedt, Time-Life Picture Agency © Time Inc.)

motion picture for pay in the Grand Cafe of Paris in 1895. Edison made jerky, primitive motion pictures of President William McKinley's inauguration in 1896, Admiral Dewey at Manila in 1898, and McKinley's speech in Buffalo, New York, shortly before his assassination in 1901. William Randolph Hearst personally took motion pictures of action in Cuba during the Spanish-American War. These early efforts showed the motion picture's potential as a recorder of history. Exhibition of commercial motion picture films began with regularity about 1900.

Edison's pioneer efforts at recording news events on film led within a few years to creation of the newsreel, a staple short item on virtually every motion picture theater program for half a century until the faster news coverage of television drove the last newsreel out of business during the 1960s. The first regular newsreel series is credited to the Pathé *Journal* of 1907. Among the familiar newsreel names in American theaters were Pathé, Fox Movietone News, Metrotone, and International Newsreel.

The documentary film, a more elaborate method of recording the lives and activities of real people, had its start in 1922. Hired by a New York fur company to film the life of an Eskimo family, Robert Flaherty overcame great technological difficulties in the Arctic climate to produce *Nanook of the North.* From this film developed the documentary tradition that has given filmmaking some of its finest products.

During the Depression years Pare Lorentz produced *The Plow That Broke the Plains* for the Farm Security Administration in the same spirit of the FSA team of photo documentarians who, under the guidance of Roy E. Stryker, made more than 272,000 negatives and 150,000 prints of the United States and its dustbowls and migratory workers. Lorentz's 1937 film, *The River,* visualized the problems of erosion in the Mississippi River basin with more power than his previous documentary.

A third form of factual storytelling on film, halfway between the newsreel and documentary, was the *March of Time,* a weekly news magazine of the screen. Started by Time Inc. in 1935, it played for sixteen years. At its peak in the late 1930s and the early years of World War II it was seen by audiences of nearly 20 million a week in more than 9000 American theaters. Louis de Rochemont, the producer, used real events and actors, skillfully blended, to present an interpretative account of an event in relation to its background.

When television became a commercial force in the late 1940s, the tools and techniques developed by the motion picture industry were adopted for presenting news on television. A motion picture camera was relatively small and portable, and film shot at news events could be shown on the television screen. Until remote telecasting became technically practical, visual presentation of on-the-spot news had to be done with motion picture film and, later, with magnetic tape.

The television documentary became an established part of the networks' programing. Some outstanding examples have been CBS's "The Selling of the Pentagon" and its "Hunger in America," done in the tradition of Edward R. Murrow's earlier documentary, "Harvest of Shame"; NBC's documentary on chemical and biological warfare, a part of its "First Tuesday" series, "The Battle of Newburgh," shown on the NBC "White Paper" series; and a religious documentary, "A Time for Burning," aired over many educational stations. CBS's "Sixty Minutes" and ABC's "Reasoner Reports" reflect another documentary trend.

PRINCIPLES OF PHOTOGRAPHY

A photograph reproduced in a newspaper, magazine, or book is a two-dimensional representation of a subject that originally had four dimensions: length, width, depth, and existence and perhaps movement through time. Moreover, the printed image in almost every instance differs in size from its original model. Frequently it is a black and white representation of a subject with many colorful hues. The photographic communicator must master the technique of condensing these dimensions and conditions into a space having only length and width.

Photography is capable of high-fidelity reproduction of very fine details and textures. A skillfully made photograph can communicate the essence of tactile experience. It can be controlled to represent a subject in various perspectives, determined by the photographer as he or she selects a particular lens and the camera-subject relationship for the picture. Black and white photographs provide the photographer almost unlimited control in representing the original subject in shades of gray and the extremes, black and white. Thus the photographer's technical skill and mental attitude influence the picture that is taken. Two persons photographing the same subject may produce widely dissimilar pictures.

Since photography relies upon a lens to form a clear, sharp image and a shutter to control the length of time during which light strikes the sensitive film, two additional visual qualities are unique in photographic communication. As the lens aperture is opened or closed to allow varying amounts of light to strike the film, a change occurs in the depth of field, that is, the area in front of and behind the subject that appears in sharp focus. The photographer may render only the subject sharp, with details in foreground and background blurred to reduce their importance. Or, by controlling the aperture size of the lens, he or she may render an entire scene in sharp focus, from the nearest to the farthest object shown.

By selecting a shutter speed for a picture, the photographer begins control over the fourth dimension, time. He or she may use a long exposure, in which case a moving subject might blur in the finished photograph, or a very short exposure time to freeze a moving subject at a precise instant. Having determined a shutter speed for the effect desired, the photographer must decide which moment to capture out of the millions available. The French photojournalist Henri Cartier-Bresson refers to this act as determining the *decisive moment.*

Still Pictures

Photographic communication for the printed page may be in the form of a single picture, a series, a sequence, or a picture story. The series of pictures can be distinguished from the sequence by noting that the series is generally photographed from more than one viewpoint and has been made over a relatively long period of time. The sequence is a group of pictures made from the same viewpoint and generally covering a very short period of time, such as a group of pictures on the sports page on a Sunday morning newspaper showing stages of a sensational touchdown run. Most picture magazines today present picture *series* rather than picture *stories;* the latter are the most complex form of photographic communication in the print media, requiring logical visual continuity built upon a well-researched idea. Excellent examples of the picture story include W. Eugene Smith's "Spanish Village" and David Duncan's "This Is War," both published in *Life* during the 1950s. In book form, Edward Steichen's *The Family of Man* has been widely acclaimed as a photo essay.

In attempting to re-create the essence of an event, photographic communicators feel the need to couple their pictures with some sort of "sound track." They use the written word in the form of captions, headlines, and overlines. When one looks at a picture and reads its word accompaniment, one's eye serves two sense functions. While it studies the image, it functions as a normal eye; when it begins reading words, the eye functions as an ear, picking up the sound track. This reading and seeing occur through time, thus further developing the fourth dimension in a two-dimensional photograph.

Wilson Hicks, for many years executive editor of *Life,* contributed in the introductory chapter of *Photographic Communication* a definition of the photojournalistic form. In its simplest unit it is a blend of words plus one picture. Words add information the picture cannot give, and the picture contributes a dimension the words cannot. When the two have been blended, there emerges a greater meaning for the reader than could be received from either words or picture separately. Hicks suggests that this blend develops a communicative overtone.

Moving Pictures

Although the characteristics of the still photograph apply to motion picture film and television magnetic tape, both of which are sequences of still pictures, there are important distinctions about the moving picture as a medium. Films and videotape reproduce natural movement and sound, two elements extremely difficult to communicate in still photography. Moving picture communicators in addition have as their most important tool creative control over the fourth dimension, time. An audience viewing a message on film or tape is captive to the communicator in terms of pace, emphasis, and rhythm. A reader can spend as much or as little time as he or she chooses in studying a picture, and can do it whenever desired, returning later for another look. When one is a member of an audience in a motion picture theater or in front of a television screen, one does not have these options.

The producer of film and videotape is concerned with the continuity, the sequence of images. He or she knows how to use the "establishment" shot at the beginning of a particular scene and medium shots and closeups to continue the action, adding variety and emphasis. During the shooting and editing of film or tape, photographer and editor concern themselves with such visual techniques as screen direction, cutaways, cover material, reverse angles, and sound effectiveness. Film may be shot as silent footage, with a narrator adding description later in a studio, or it may be shot with natural lip-sync sound. Electronic videotape recording is used in place of film for some stories and advertisements on television. The first moon pictures sent back by Armstrong and Aldrin were an example of live presentation of moving pictures produced electronically without film or tape.

FUNCTIONS OF PHOTOGRAPHERS AND EDITORS

Photographs are used, just as are words, to inform, persuade, and entertain users of the mass media. Their effectiveness depends upon how well they are taken by the photographer and how well they are assembled for presentation to the audience by the editor. Each medium has special problems of picture presentation that require special knowledge and experience. Television is not radio with a picture of the announcer added; there is an important visual dimension. The still photograph is not "decoration," as it was in the newspaper and magazine early in this century. The development of candid photography with its quick, intimate glimpses of subjects off guard has given photojournalists exciting new possibilities by permitting them to avoid the stilted aspect so common in older pictures with slower cameras.

Daily newspaper photographers perform one of the fundamental tasks in photojournalism. On a typical day they receive three or four assignments, usually to happenings fairly close to the office. They likely will use a staff car, equipped with a two-way radio. The editor has written an assignment sheet describing the event and what is wanted, and perhaps has discussed the job in detail. On many newspapers photographers use their own equipment, for which the publication pays a monthly depreciation allotment; on others, they use office-owned cameras.

Once at the scene, the photographer makes from two to twenty pictures, gathering names and important caption material. Back at the office, the film will be processed, either personally or by a laboratory assistant, and finished prints delivered to the editor. On most assignments, only one of the pictures taken will be published; in fact, frequently none of the pictures will be printed because of space limitations or the development of later, bigger news stories.

A photographer on a general magazine staff works on more elaborate projects than does the daily newspaper staffer, often taking several weeks or even months to complete a single job. Assignments at times range far from home. The photographer is well briefed by researchers concerning the background of the story, and receives large research folios for "homework." On a major assignment he or she will shoot from 1000 to 5000 images, sending them home to the editors in "takes"; they keep the photographer posted on how the work has turned out. After all this effort, a dozen to a score of pictures likely will appear in print.

Life had a staff of fifteen photographers in the early 1970s, plus various contract and freelance contributors. These men and women as a group were shooting nearly 1,000 pictures a day—300,000 a year—for the magazine, which printed about 75 in each weekly issue. At *Look,* which had been published biweekly, about 150,000 photographs were

Student photographers at work in a large laboratory. (Courtesy of Henry W. Grady School of Journalism and Mass Communication, University of Georgia.)

shot each year by an eight-person staff. Some of those picture editors and photographers joined the staffs of the *National Geographic,* the *Smithsonian,* and other expanding visually attuned magazines.

The local television station news photographer works in a manner similar to that of his or her daily newspaper colleague. He or she has four to six assignments a day, usually travels in a radio-equipped staff car, and carries both silent and sound 16 mm camera equipment. In addition, there may be an audio tape recorder to pick up background sound. The photographer takes notes (spot sheets), including the names of those appearing in various scenes. Camera operators may work alone, with a reporter, or with a full crew to handle lighting and sound. After their return to the station, their film is processed by a laboratory specialist while the photographer perhaps writes an accompanying script. Much depends upon the size of the station.

With so much more film being shot than can be used either in print or on the air, the role of the editor is essential. The editors of film and still pictures have three functions: to procure the picture by assigning staff photographers, buying material from freelancers, and subscribing to syndicate services; to select the pictures to be used; and to present them in an effective manner.

Once the raw material has been obtained, the editor makes a selection from the entire "take" submitted. In the print media, he or she must crop and scale the pictures to emphasize their most interesting aspects and to work them into a layout. In television, the editor is concerned with juxtaposition effects from scene to scene and with time considerations. The presentation each editor puts together represents a blending of pictures and words, a designing of space and time.

PHOTOJOURNALISM AS A CAREER

Qualifications

Stimulating opportunities await young men and women who decide to enter the photographic side of mass communications. The work at times is exciting, and always interesting; each day brings new assignments that give the photographer room for creative expression and the use of professional techniques.

Anyone contemplating such a career should be healthy and possessed of physical stamina, because the work can be dangerous on assignments such as fires and riots; and the hours frequently are irregular. The photographer must carry equipment that is cumbersome and, particularly in television news, often quite heavy. Both physical and emotional exhaustion can affect a photographer involved in a long, difficult assignment.

Career photographic communicators also should have initiative, energy, and creative motivation. A degree of aggressiveness is necessary, but it should be tempered by thoughtfulness. Visual imagination is essential—the ability to see various interpretations of a subject in a given visual form. They should have an interest in design and the knack of examining pictures for each one's special qualities. They must be curious about the world about them and have an ability to mix with people. Being able roughly to sketch scenes and individuals is an important asset, but by no means a requirement.

Photographic communicators should have a good general education. About one-fourth of their studies should be spent in learning how to relate general knowledge to the discipline of photo communication. Those who plan to work in the news and information function of the mass media should include courses in basic reporting, editing, law and history of the press, and graphic design and typography.

In photography courses they must develop foundations in both the technical and visual dimensions of the medium. They should include courses in both still and motion photography, both black and white and color. Attention to the picture story, the documentary film, and advertising illustration is all-important. They should study the history of film and photography and also include courses in basic design.

Technical qualifications include an understanding of the photographic medium in terms of optics, lighting, color theory, and photographic processes, which include basic photo chemistry and physics. With the growing importance of electronics in nearly all areas of photographic communication, an understanding of electronic theory is desirable.

Earnings

A college graduate with photographic skills will start on a daily newspaper at from $7,000 to $9,500 a year. An experienced newspaper photographer, with five years or more on the job, may earn from $12,000 to $20,000 annually in large cities. The starting salary for a college graduate photographer on a local television station will vary from $6,500 to $9,000; after five years the range is $9,500 to $15,000. A staff photographer for a general or specialized magazine can expect to earn $9,000 to $15,000 in early career years. His or her salary can rise rapidly, faster than in newspaper or television work. Top professionals on the *National Geographic* earn as much as $50,000.

Some photographers prefer to freelance; that is, to work for themselves and sell their pictures to clients either directly or through picture agencies. The agencies take a commission of 25 to 35 percent of the selling price of the pictures. A freelancer also may work on contract, under which a magazine guarantees an agreed-upon earning in return for a commitment to be available to it on call. A freelancer usually begins as a staff photographer, then branches out after establishing a reputation and a group of clients. Freelance photographers can earn around $40,000 a year if very successful, although they start far lower in their early years. To be a successful freelancer, one must have good business sense and know how to market pictures as well as take them. The American Society of Magazine Photographers sets minimum rates for its members. The rate in effect in 1978 exceeded $200 per day plus expenses.

CHAPTER 16
PRESS ASSOCIATIONS

THE ROLE OF PRESS ASSOCIATIONS

For decades the chatter of press association teleprinters has been a symbol of news excitement. The dispatches typed out by their automatic keys on continuous rolls of paper represent the world of action, under datelines of Washington, London, Moscow, state capitals, and a thousand other cities.

Supplying the news dispatches that come in such abundance are the Associated Press and United Press International, the largest, most intricate, and fiercely competitive newsgathering agencies in the world. Without the service of a press association, a daily newspaper or broadcasting station would find distribution of a well-balanced news report to its audience virtually impossible.

In the electronic revolution sweeping the printed media, the traditional teletype has begun to disappear, just as the Morse telegraph key did. Some large newspapers do not have a teleprinter left in their newsrooms; dispatches are transmitted directly from a press association office computer into their computers, for editing on a video display terminal.

The press associations take over where the local and area news coverage of the city desk ends. Even the largest dailies and the broadcasting networks with extensive staffs of their own correspondents in Washington and abroad are heavily dependent upon the press associations for domestic and foreign dispatches.

Intense hour-to-hour rivalry between AP and UPI exists in their effort to deliver simply written dispatches that are comprehensive, accurate, objective, and perceptive—and to get them there first.

This competitive urge is one of the attractions of press association work, especially for younger reporters and editors; it adds a zest to newsgathering that has disappeared to some degree from the local news staffs in many cities where only one newspaper now exists. Commercially, this competition to be faster and better than your rival has great importance, because the AP and UPI are in constant battle to take away customers from each other. (The AP calls them members; the UPI refers to them as clients.)

Although the services they deliver to newspapers, television, and radio stations here and abroad are similar, the two press associations are or-

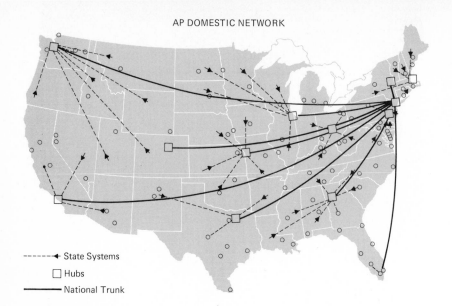

----◄ State Systems
☐ Hubs
─── National Trunk

FIGURE 16.1 The communications network of the Associated Press in the United States. "Hubs" are regional bureau offices. The AP also has an extensive worldwide communications network. (Courtesy of the Associated Press.)

ganized quite differently. The Associated Press, which is much older, is a cooperative newsgathering association. Each American newspaper that purchases its services becomes a member of the cooperative and has a voice in setting the association's newsgathering and financial policies; also, it is obligated to turn over its local news coverage to the cooperative. Television and radio stations taking AP service become associate members without voting rights; the total now exceeds that of newspaper members. The Associated Press was founded in 1848 by six New York publishers, primarily to cooperate in the gathering of news from ships arriving in eastern harbors from Europe. It has been in continuous existence ever since, having gone through several major reorganizations including one in 1900 that established it in its present form.

United Press International is a privately owned company, dealing on a contract basis with newspapers, television and radio stations, and other organizations that have need for a news report. Its individual clients influence the shape of the UPI news report through their suggestions and criticism, solicited by the UPI management, or through their ultimate power to cancel the service. The UPI has advisory boards of newspaper and broadcast clients to help management set goals and policies. The United Press was founded in 1907 by E. W. Scripps, the owner of a large group of newspapers, with the purpose of supplying news to papers that could not obtain Associated Press membership under the then-existing rules. In 1958 the United Press absorbed the International News Service, which had operated as a relatively weak third American competitor in the field since William Randolph Hearst founded it in 1909. The combined service became known as United Press International.

The Associated Press and United Press International are now comparable in strength, the UPI having improved its position by the merger with INS.

The Associated Press reported that in the late 1970s it was serving more than 10,000 newspapers and radio and television stations around the world; the United Press International reported that it had more than 6,000 clients for its news and picture services. Each organization operates in more than one hundred countries. Both press associations lease more than 400,000 miles of telephone wires in the United States for transmission of news and pictures, and both use satellites, cables, and radio teletype circuits to move their dispatches around the world.

Regardless of whether it is called a member or a client, the net result for each daily newspaper is much the same. It receives the UPI or AP news report for a specified number of hours each day, for which it pays a fee based upon its circulation and the amount of news received. Both news agencies offer supplemental sports and financial services, used by the larger newspapers.

Most small dailies, and even some very large ones, operate successfully with only one of the two major wire services. Of the 1750 American daily newspapers, approximately 45 percent subscribe only to AP, 30 percent only to UPI, and 25 percent to both services. More than 425 dailies purchase news from both to have a wider choice of news stories to publish. When both services provide stories on the same news events, as they do scores of times daily, the telegraph editor of the two-service newspaper selects the dispatch that arrives first, if an urgent news break is involved, or the one that seems to him more complete, concise, and interesting. Sometimes the two dispatches are combined to provide a more well-rounded and complete story.

The rival agencies keep close watch on selected lists of these two-service papers to determine the "play" their respective stories receive. Bad "play" on a big story—or worse, being badly beaten by the rival agency on a news break—brings sharp backstage criticism from the New York home office to the head of the offending bureau.

HOW PRESS ASSOCIATIONS FUNCTION

The news reports of each press association traditionally have been carried to newspapers and broadcasting stations by leased circuits and delivered on teleprinters in newsrooms. During the electronic upheaval of the mid- and late 1970s, delivery of the report by wire direct into the newspaper's computer for VDT editing grew increasingly popular with large newspapers using advanced techniques. The soaring expense of leasing wires caused the two press associations to explore an even more dramatic form of transmission, by satellite. The proposal was to transmit the news report not by the standard leased ground wire, but by beaming it to a communications satellite in orbit 22,000 miles above the equator and having it relayed back to earth; each press association newspaper and broadcast client would receive the satellite signals via a local "dish" capable of bringing in multiple channels. The news report would be delivered into the recipient's computer or into teletype and photo machines, as he or she chose. Transmission by satellite at 1200 words a minute would be an astounding contrast to the unreliable 30-word-a-minute Morse dot-and-dash methods the press associations used in their early days.

Each press association divides its flow of news into P.M. and A.M. reports, or cycles, the former for afternoon newspapers and the latter for morning papers. These reports always begin with a "budget," or checklist, of the most important stories that are to be transmitted. The budget is a summary of the basic stories then available, or known to be forthcoming during the next few hours, plus sports and feature highlights. Usually it contains ten or twelve items. The news editor is thus able to plan makeup to ensure space for stories that the paper most likely will want to run. Since the large majority of American newspapers are published in the afternoon, and most news occurs during daytime hours, the P.M. reports are generally handled with a greater sense of urgency.

Basic stories on major news situations are transmitted early in each cycle. If later developments occur on a story, a new "lead" is moved on the wire. This reports the latest news on the situation and ends with a transitional paragraph that blends into the earlier dispatch at a specified place. On big, fast-breaking stories a press association may carry half a dozen leads in a cycle; these are edited so compactly that the dispatch which ultimately appears in a client newspaper reads with smooth continuity, even though it may contain segments of several leads.

Such methods are necessary because press association clients are constantly going to press and must print what is available on a given situation at press time. To use a phrase popular with United Press International, somewhere there is a deadline every minute. This is a major difference between press association and ordinary newspaper writing:

the press association correspondent must keep feeding latest developments in a "spot" story onto the news wires immediately, even when their meaning and ramifications are not fully disclosed; the newspaper staff correspondent (called a "special" by the wire services) usually has more time before deadline to digest and consolidate the information. Press association writers and editors usually work under time pressure. When we consider this, the amount of background and interpretation an experienced press association writer can weave into a fast-breaking story is remarkable.

Press associations have main trunk distribution circuits running across the country, serving the major metropolitan newspapers. Regional and state circuits from regional centers serve the smaller papers in different areas of the country. The editors who control the flow of news onto these secondary wires must see that the newspapers on each receive a balanced menu of regional news along with the most important national and foreign dispatches. Thus an Associated Press member in Arizona will receive some stories of interest only to readers in the Southwest that will not be delivered to another member in Florida. These members will receive identical dispatches on the day's major news from Washington and London, however. Proper channeling of the daily news report, so that each newspaper gets the largest possible number of stories pertinent to its needs, is a basic problem for press association editors. Many stories are shortened when relayed on secondary circuits because smaller newspapers do not have the space to publish them in full. Dispatches from the press association bureaus abroad are sent to the New York home offices for processing and filing on the domestic circuits.

The press associations use video display terminals, on which reporters write their dispatches. Their stories go into computer storage from which they are called by editors on control desks. Once edited, the stories are ready for transmission to newspaper and broadcasting clients. They may be delivered as teleprinter roll "hard copy," as punched teletypesetter tape for newspapers still using hot metal typesetting machinery, as "hard copy" on special white paper that can be inserted into an OCR electronic scanner, or direct as electronic signals into the newspaper's computer. Although newspapers with the direct computer intake system no longer require teletype machines, they have a special supplementary high-speed printer that provides a copy for reference when desired.

Since the teletype circuit operates at sixty-six words a minute, press

Close-up view of a press association dispatch called up for editing on a newspaper copy desk video display terminal. (Courtesy of the South Bend *Tribune*.)

associations always have faced the problem of having large stacks of copy on hand awaiting transmission. Newspapers receive stories under this traditional method in the sequence determined by the editors who control the news wires. Newly developed computer-to-computer transmission techniques are changing this. A brief abstract of each story is sent to the newspapers. With all the accumulated day's news stored in the newspaper computer within a short time, instead of having to await its arrival piece by piece, the newspaper's telegraph editor can select and edit the stories desired for publication, then release them from the newspaper's computer to be put into type. Spot-breaking stories are transmitted on a priority basis from computer to computer as they develop.

A still further modification called "demand" service is offered by UPI. This provides the telegraph editor of the individual newspaper with abstracts of all stories available in the UPI news report but does not transmit the stories automatically to the newspaper. Instead, the telegraph editor orders transmission from the press association computer of only the stories desired. The editor of another newspaper might order quite a different set of stories. The purpose of "demand" service is to cut down the huge wasted effort of transmitting stories that a paper does not use and must throw away.

During this transitional period, when some newspapers are far advanced into computerized operations while others hesitate to abandon traditional methods, press association managements must serve their customers in a variety of ways. The pace at which newspapers change over to the new transmission methods depends largely upon their financial ability to do so and the foresight of their management. By the early 1980s, the gathering momentum of the electronic techniques will be felt in a large majority of American newspapers, with technical advances beyond those described here.

SPECIAL WRITING TECHNIQUES

It is evident that a news story which goes through all these vicissitudes of editing from reporter to client editor's desk requires special writing techniques. It may be published 500 words long in one newspaper and only 100 words in another. Thus the writer must keep his fundamental information near the top of the story so the dispatch can be trimmed easily without having key facts omitted.

A press association reporter must write concisely, in simple sentences. Because the dispatches will be printed in newspapers of differing political persuasions, the writer must be carefully objective, especially in handling complicated, controversial stories. The primary goal of press association writing is clear and swift communication of events and ideas. The staff writer's basic stock in trade is straight news, well written. More distinctive forms of self-expression increasingly find their way onto the wires; usually, however, those who wish to concentrate on this type of writing choose other, less restrictive outlets.

Television and radio's instant news coverage of events in progress has had a heavy impact on the press associations. Like newspapers, broadcast news staffs have changed their operating methods, increasing the stress on interpretive and analytical material. Until approximately the mid 1950s, press association reports primarily were happening-oriented, concentrating on reporting events as they took place. Today, they are more situation-oriented. Recognizing that the newspapers they serve no longer can be first with big news stories, the associations supplement spot news with background and interpretive dispatches that help the reader understand the "why" of the situation.

Although the press associations permit their established writers more

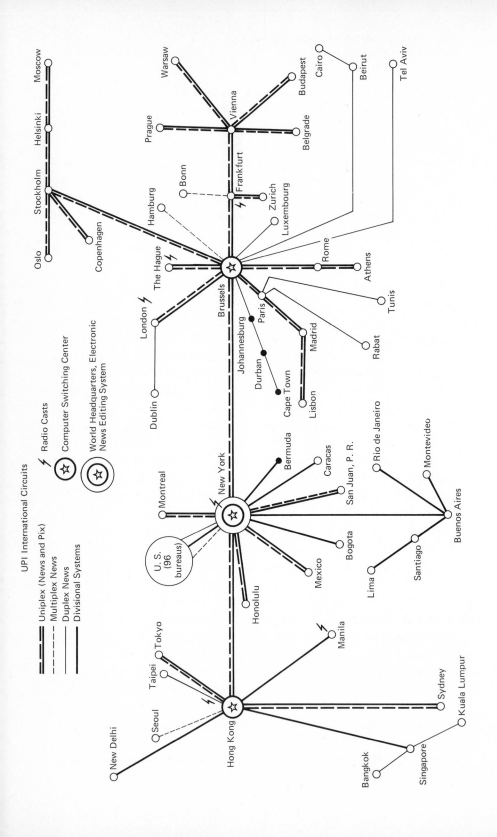

UPI International Circuits

—— Uniplex (News and Pix)
--- Multiplex News
—— Duplex News
▬▬ Divisional Systems

⚡ Radio Casts

✪ Computer Switching Center

◎ World Headquarters, Electronic
   News Editing System

freedom in interpreting news situations than in the past, they are on guard against political or social slanting of dispatches. The more complicated the world becomes, the more difficult it is for press associations to find a proper balance between quick-breaking facts and interpretation that gives them perspective without distortion. This calls for highly skilled reporting and editing.

OTHER PRESS ASSOCIATION ACTIVITIES

Both the United Press International and Associated Press were founded to provide news for American newspapers. That remains their basic function, but they have branched out into additional services. Each supplies specially written news reports to thousands of radio and television stations in the United States, and news to newspapers and broadcasting stations in many foreign countries. A constant flow of news originating in the United States is being sent abroad while foreign news is arriving in New York by a complex network of circuits. In Europe, the American associations distribute their dispatches on leased circuits for translation into the local language in each country. Translation into Spanish for Latin American countries is largely done in the New York offices. Bulletins on important news breaks can be flashed by teletype within a minute or two on a Rome-London-New York-San Francisco-Tokyo transmission network, spreading the word around the world almost instantly. Pictures are transmitted throughout the world by radio facilities.

The foreign bureaus of the American press associations usually are headed by an American, but they also employ local nationals in substantial numbers as reporters, editors, and translators. The number of foreign correspondent jobs available to Americans in the press associations is thus smaller than many people may believe. In normal times approximately 500 American citizens serve overseas as media correspondents, the majority of them for the press associations. It is apparent that the commonly held desire of young writers to become foreign corre-

FIGURE 16.2 The worldwide communications network of United Press International. Leased cables, satellites, and radio circuits speed the flow of news. The UPI also has an extensive communications network in the United States. (Courtesy of United Press International.)

spondents is not easily fulfilled. During the peak years of the Vietnam War the overseas contingent was much enlarged. Often sharp differences existed between the correspondents' reports from Saigon and the usually optimistic official U.S. government version of the conflict. When American troops were withdrawn from Southeast Asia, so were most reporters.

At many points around the world the American organizations are in sharp competition, in both newsgathering and sales, with such foreign news agencies as Reuters of Great Britain and Agence France-Presse. The impact of these foreign agencies upon the American press is negligible, however, since only a very few metropolitan papers purchase any of their material.

The American press associations have become important transmission belts for presenting a picture of life in America to foreigners. The hunger in many countries for news about the United States reflects this country's major role in world affairs. The Associated Press and United Press International carry a heavy responsibility in their selection and writing of news for the overseas audience, so that a well-balanced picture is presented. This does not imply censorship, the hiding of unpleasant news, or peddling of propaganda, but a judicious budget of stories to provide a multifaceted view of American life. For a great many citizens of foreign countries, press association dispatches provide the chief source of information about life, political policies, and attitudes in the United States.

The only foreign press association with important news outlets in the United States is Reuters, the British agency. The Reuters news report, which is edited principally in London, is purchased by some metropolitan American newspapers and TV-radio network news departments as a supplementary service.

Special news service for television and radio stations is a major part of the agencies' operations. This is transmitted on different teletype circuits from the newspaper service and is rewritten from the stories in the basic report to please the ear rather than the eye. The style is more conversational, with simpler sentence structure and less detail. Distribution of this specially processed radio report was inaugurated by the United Press in 1935. The Associated Press followed reluctantly five years later.

Another important service provided to newspapers by the press associations is news picture coverage. Both AP and UPI operate coast-to-coast circuits for transmission of news photographs, a growing number of them in color. Newspapers connected to these circuits receive photographs instantaneously as they are transmitted. The news agencies supply pictures to foreign clients by satellite, radio photo, leased circuits, and mail.

Some newspapers purchasing the nationwide direct service receive the news photos in their offices over facsimile machines, which translate the electrical impulses of the transmission circuit into black and white photographs by means of a scanning device; these pictures are ready for immediate printing in the newspapers. During the 1970s, the Associated Press introduced a new system of photo transmission by wire called Laserphoto, which uses a laser beam to provide improved clarity in the dry glossy prints it delivers to the member papers. Both AP and UPI have staffs of photographers who are assigned to stories much as are reporters. In addition, the Associated Press distributes many pictures taken by photographers on the staffs of member papers. UPI also supplements its staff picture coverage with photos from newspaper sources.

Both press associations deliver an audio news service for radio station voice pickups on news events. UPI operates a daily motion picture newsfilm service to TV stations, an Ocean Press radio news report to passenger vessels at sea, and a voice-over-photo news TV service by satellite. Among its supplementary offerings the AP includes a color slide service for television stations, a mailed tape service, and a book division that produces a news annual and other special volumes.

On still another front, the Associated Press and United Press International, the latter through its subsidiary United Feature Syndicate, provide comic strips, women's features, political columns, and a host of other syndicated material for newspaper publication.

Thus the two organizations have journeyed far afield from their original purpose of providing dispatches for newspapers. However, the daily newspaper report continues to be the core of each agency's operations. The UPI and AP now serve not one but three of our mass communications media—newspapers, television, and radio, plus special services to magazines.

CRITICAL VIEWS OF AGENCIES

Students of the American press sometimes are critical of the heavy dependence of newspapers and broadcasting stations on the press associations; this criticism is aimed more at the role of the wire services than at their daily performance. There is an undercurrent of uneasiness among these critics because more than 1700 daily newspapers and nearly 9000 broadcast stations look to these two organizations for the great bulk of their nonlocal news. Anyone who listens to a succession of radio newscasts and hears the identical words from the radio news wires spoken to him repeatedly on different wavelengths realizes the dependence of radio stations in particular on the press associations. In fact, an overwhelming percentage of the American people are largely dependent on the two organizations, through their various newspaper and TV-radio ramifications, as well as their use by the weekly news magazines, for knowledge of what is happening in the world. In the eyes of the critics this constitutes a danger involving conformity of reporting and thought, and some question the qualifications of wire service editors to select the news that is transmitted.

The argument is more philosophic than practical. The economics of newspaper publishing makes it impossible for even the largest, richest newspapers to have staff reporters stationed around the world in sufficient numbers to give them exclusive reports, for the costs would be prohibitive. Therefore some form of cooperative newsgathering is necessary. So long as the United Press International and Associated Press remain free of government control or subsidy, operate in a highly competitive manner, and hold to their principles of objective news coverage, the perils of undue conformity are relatively small. The efficient and far-reaching news lines of the press associations contribute greatly to the mammoth amount of information about the world available to readers and listeners throughout the United States.

The editors of client and member newspapers, and wire service executives themselves, subject the press association news report to constant scrutiny for accuracy and completeness. When instances of insufficient or inaccurate coverage come to light, steps are taken quickly to remedy the weakness. The competitive factor is a very wholesome one. The Associated Press Managing Editors Association has committees making continuous studies of AP operations.

The press associations are scolded at times by critics because they use the reporting services of part-time local "string" correspondents in some parts of the world. When a major story breaks in a remote area, they must use the sometimes inadequate services of these part-timers until an American-trained correspondent can reach the scene. Governments of developing countries complain that the Western news services give a distorted colonialist view of their countries. At New Delhi in 1976 some of them formed a government-financed Non-Aligned News Pool in competition. While admitting basis for their complaint, the Western press saw this as an attempt to distribute government-manipulated and censored news.

Another criticism of the press associations is shared by the newspapers themselves—an alleged preoccupation with "crisis" reporting. That means trying to find conflict and excitement in every situation, to the point of distorting the news. In particular, this charge has been made about the handling of political and legislative news. It is stated that too much emphasis is placed on the routine partisan postures of the two major parties. This allegation results from the striving of each association to find sharp "angles" that induce telegraph editors to print its stories instead of its competitor's. Recently, however, both wire services have been broadening their coverage by offering more thoughtful, interpretive articles in such fields as religion, race, education, labor, and social problems. They are much less open to charges of "crisis" overemphasis than they were a decade ago. The news services are also criticized for not carrying enough foreign news, to which they reply that their newspapers will print only a limited amount of such news, and there is no use in taking wire transmission time to give them what they won't use.

Actually, the conformity in presentation of national and foreign news by newspapers is less than might be expected. Checks of representative groups of newspapers receiving the same wire service show a surprisingly wide variation in the stories chosen from the telegraphed news report by editors for publication in their newspapers. Stories selected for prominent front page play by some editors may be dismissed by others with brief mention on inside pages, or omitted entirely. This is not surprising when we realize that the press association wire delivers far more dispatches than most newspapers can use, and the pressures of local news vary from city to city. So do the news judgments of the individual editors.

Another way editors have found to broaden their national and foreign news coverage is purchase of a supplementary news service, such as those offered by the New York *Times* and the Los Angeles *Times–*Washington *Post* Service. These services supply to their clients by wire a daily news report that includes dispatches on major Washington and foreign events, plus background dispatches under many datelines. They leave the hourly spot coverage to the press associations, but seek to round out the picture with news material that is exclusive in each client's territory. Because of the cost, supplementary services are used primarily by the larger newspapers.

JOB OPPORTUNITIES

The press associations are among the finest training grounds in the entire field of mass communications for young men and women interested in a career of working with news. The work is challenging. It puts a premium on speed, conciseness, and judgment. These organizations have a tradition of hiring young writers of limited professional experience and training them. Since the turnover in press association personnel is relatively high, there are quite a few job openings each year. A large increase in the number of women on press association staffs has occurred in recent years. The same is true of members of racial minorities.

A beginner in press association work usually is given routine stories to rewrite from the local newspapers, items to check by phone, and similar simple duties. The writer must learn to look outward from the local community, to weigh each story for its interest to readers in other cities. Quite soon, the relative newcomer may be named night manager of a small bureau, an opportunity to exercise a limited amount of administrative responsibility. Because of the nature of press association work, staff members do more editing and less original reporting than newspaper staffs do.

Those who stay with the press associations for a number of years, as many do, usually become managers of small or middle-sized bureaus or are transferred into such large offices as Chicago, Washington, or the New York general headquarters. Members of the foreign staffs normally are given experience in New York or Washington before being sent abroad.

Salaries for press association work are approximately in line with those on large daily newspapers. Although quite a few men and a few women spend virtually their entire careers in the press associations, there is a fairly heavy turnover in personnel. Some wire service staff members grow tired of the time pressures and the writing restrictions. They believe that although advancement is relatively fast when they are starting, it slows down as they mature.

They may find better salary opportunities in special reporting jobs and editorships on newspapers or in public relations, radio, television, and other related fields of mass communications. Many of the country's best-known reporters, writers, television commentators, and editors worked for the press associations in their younger years; almost unanimously they are grateful for the experience, especially for the writing discipline it taught them.

NEWSPAPER FEATURE SYNDICATES

The other major source of editorial material used by daily newspapers, and one that tends to bring uniformity to the American press, is the feature syndicate. Syndicates sell to the newspapers a multitude of material for the entertainment and education of their readers, edited and ready for publication upon delivery. Comic strips and some other features are provided in proof form for newspaper reproduction; text features are available in proof or duplicated form, prepunched TTS tape, on "scanner-ready" paper for newspapers using electronic typesetting machinery, or by transmission directly into the purchaser's computer system.

An editor can load the newspaper with as much syndicated material as conscience and budget will allow. The larger the feature "package" in a paper, the less space is available to be filled with locally created news and press association dispatches. A publication too full of such "canned" features gets a reputation of being more an entertainment medium than a newspaper and of being deficient in editorial enterprise. Readership polls show, however, that a very strong desire exists among readers for certain syndicated features.

So the newspaper editor tries to strike a suitable balance. There is no firm rule of thumb about this; one good newspaper of substantial circulation and a reasonably large editorial "hole" (the space left in a newspaper after the advertisements have been inserted) will publish 16 comic strips daily while a comparable one runs only 10 or 12. The same is true of political columns and other material offered by the syndicates.

Examination of a typical well-edited newspaper with 50,000 daily circulation shows this material purchased ready-made from national feature syndicates: 12 comic strips, 12 cartoon panels, 5 political columns, medical column, personal advice column, crossword puzzle, astrological forecast, political cartoon, 2 entertainment columns, and juvenile information feature.

Some features, especially comic strips, have run in newspapers so many years that they have become household words, a commonplace in contemporary American life. Millions of readers every day look to see how Dick Tracy is getting along in his pursuit of a clever criminal, how Mary Worth's soap opera plots are unfolding, and how Dagwood, the ordinary family man, is dealing with his domestic problems. The political opinions of columnists Jack Anderson and Carl Rowan and the humorous satirical comment of Art Buchwald cause discussion among business people at lunch. Such free-swinging advice columns as "Dear Abby" are the predinner fare of many homemakers. An increase in subtlety and sophistication has been noted with the rise of such strips as "Peanuts" and "The Wizard of Id." Efforts to inject political and social relevance into the comic world, of which the strip "Doonesbury" is a striking example, have had moderate success. Reflecting the changing social scene, comic strip artists have been using black characters in prominent roles since the late 1960s.

Approximately a dozen major syndicates provide the bulk of the features appearing in American newspapers, although there are more than a hundred smaller companies, some of which operate in specialized fields like boating and book serializations. The major syndicates have from 25 to more than 100 different features in the lists they offer for sale to editors. An editor who has trouble saying "no" to the sales talk of the syndicate representative soon finds the paper overloaded with material for which the total weekly fee can run uncomfortably high. But an editor who can't say "no" is a contradiction in terms. On comics especially, many editors make a habit of dropping one feature whenever they buy a new one. Papers make occasional readership surveys to determine which comics and daily features are most popular. So attached do readers become to individual comic strips that the dropping of one sometimes provokes a torrent of complaints; consequently, fewer changes are made than many editors desire.

Features are sold to newspapers for prices scaled to the paper's circulation. Although some are sold for specific contract periods, many are on a t.f. basis—the abbreviation for the phrase "till forbid"—meaning that the feature runs until the editor sends in a cancellation, usually on 30- to 90-day notice.

Competition among the syndicates to sell their features is intense. There are more than 250 daily comic strips on the market, many of which are also issued in color for Sunday comic sections; about 40 health columns, 75 religious features, and a dozen competing columns on stamp collecting. Although many well-established "name" features go on year after year, a new group of comic strips, panels, and text columns is brought onto the market annually. Features that lose popular appeal are dropped by the syndicates.

As a rule an editor organizing a comic page tries to offer readers a mixture of adventure continuity, serial stories similar to TV soap opera drama with strong feminine appeal, children's interest, a strip slanted to teenagers, and gag-a-day strips without continuity except in the characters themselves. Until a few years ago, most comic strips ran five columns wide; now almost all are in four columns. Closely connected with the comic strip is the cartoon panel, usually two columns wide, in which some familiar characters, such as Dennis the Menace, are involved in daily humorous misadventure; there is no continuity of action in these panels, which resemble those published in magazines. Several exceptionally popular comic strip and cartoon characters have been transformed into "live" versions on television, with uneven success. The creators of popular strips like "Peanuts" earn large additional income through merchandising tie-ins featuring their cartoon characters.

The feature syndicates do not offer very great potential for the young man or woman seeking a job. Their editorial and sales staffs are small and mostly drawn from professional journalists with several years of editorial or business experience. Most of the artists and writers whose material is distributed by these organizations do their work outside the syndicate offices and send or bring it in for editing and approval. Usually they work on a percentage arrangement with the syndicate, receiving a portion of the fees paid by the newspapers. Syndicate editing requires knowledge of the public taste, as well as the space problems, buying habits, and idiosyncracies of the various newspaper editors who are the customers for the syndicate products.

CHAPTER 17
ADVERTISING

ADVERTISING AND THE FUTURE

Advertising plays a unique and central role in the American economic system. Although the energy crisis, the shortage of certain critical materials, pollution, and economic recessions have caused difficulties, production is no longer our primary concern, as is still the case in most countries. Instead, distribution bears the chief responsibility for maintaining a high level of employment and general prosperity. And the distribution of goods and services depends largely on the effective use of advertising in the media.

As Frederick R. Gamble, former president of the American Association of Advertising Agencies, has pointed out:

Advertising is the counterpart in distribution of the machine in production. By the use of machines, our production of goods and services has been multiplied. By the use of mass media, advertising multiplies the selling effort. Advertising is the great accelerating force in distribution. Reaching many people rapidly at low cost, advertising speeds up sales, turns prospects into customers in large numbers and at high speed. Hence, in a mass-production economy, advertising has the greatest opportunity and the greatest responsibility for finding customers.

The people engaged in advertising are a creative and resourceful lot, but even they have not been able to find the proper words to describe adequately the tremendous rise of advertising since World War II. In 1947 American business spent slightly over $4 billion to cry its wares. From 1965 to 1975 advertising growth failed to keep pace with the economy, but the pattern was reversed in 1976, when an unusual 14 percent growth rate was registered. By 1978 advertising expenditures exceeded $37 billion annually, and the Department of Commerce predicted that advertising spending would increase at an 8 percent annual rate, reaching $54.7 billion by 1982.

Like it or not, Americans live in an advertising environment. A Harvard study, for example, indicates that the average adult is exposed potentially to 500 advertisements daily in television, radio, newspapers, and magazines. Throw in billboards, direct mail, such specialty items as book matches and ballpoint pens, and the packages in which most products are displayed so attractively, and you have many additional advertising exposures each day. Without advertising most Americans would not be able to afford the cost of broadcast programs, newspapers, and magazines; even book matches, now distributed so freely, would bear a cost.

In the United States advertising is serving a population now exceeding 215 million and expected to reach almost 240 million by 1990. The production of goods and services inevitably must expand accordingly, and advertising will expand right along with them. Advertisers will concentrate mainly on two segments of the market—the age group thirty to forty-five, expected to rise from 36.5 million to about 60 million, and the age group sixty-five and over, which should increase from 22.1 million to about 30 million. This is almost the reverse of the pattern for the fifteen years ending in 1975, when increases were recorded mainly in the school-age and young adult population and in persons forty-five years of age and older.

A historic surge of research and development by American industry, education, and government has produced more efficient manufacturing as well as countless new products. Research expenditures of well over $15 billion each year have revolutionized much of American business. For example, in only a decade it increased the production of plastics by 300 percent, electronics 240 percent, and aluminum products 200 percent. The manufacturing and marketing of semiconductors alone is well over a half-billion-dollar a year business. Approximately 10,000 new products account for 10 percent of all sales each year, and the volume of new products is increasing, although at a slower rate during periods of economic recession. Advertising, along with its marketing aids of sales promotion, product design, packaging, point-of-purchase displays, product publicity, and public relations, has its work cut out for it.

J. Davis Danforth, formerly executive vice president of one of the largest advertising agencies, Batten, Barton, Durstine & Osborn, Inc., took a look at the future in a speech before an advertising group, and declared:

If our national productivity increases, as most economists predict, advertising will have to grow to move the mountain of goods which will be produced. New color television sets, fuel injection automobiles, hundreds of new appliances that are in laboratory stages now, millions of new homes with advanced radiant heating and cooling equipment, and the astonishing new furnishings that will go into them . . . And we'll have to help sell them all!

We will be selling windows that close themselves when it rains, and food that will be practically nonperishable, irradiated by electronic rays to keep it fresh almost indefinitely. Perhaps you will shop by TV by just sitting at home and dialing a number, color TV will hang in a picture frame on your wall, phones will come equipped with viewing screens so you will be able to see as well as hear (is that good?). Already we can dial long distance almost anywhere in the country without ever contacting an operator. We will have doubledeck streets in the high traffic centers, daily newspapers may be printed in color, and perhaps you will have a unit in your house so that your morning newspaper will be printed right in your own home while you are sleeping. With the new science of geriatrics, everybody is going to live longer—maybe even advertising men! . . .

Advertising men and women certainly will want to live longer, for they will be caught up in the key role of helping to bring about a dazzling pattern of living in the future. Hundreds will find their opportunities overseas, for American business has truly gone international. Every one of the 100 leading corporations in the United States is involved with international trade, and most of them have their own manufacturing facilities overseas. Well over 100 American advertising agencies are represented abroad, and the top ten agencies alone place more than $3.3 billion in international advertising each year.

As more and more countries become industrialized and personal incomes increase, American business and advertising people will explore new frontiers of worldwide expansion and opportunity. These pioneers of the future will be paid well, in both money and satisfaction, for their ability to help move the products of a new age into the hands of people everywhere. Small wonder that advertising as a career is appealing to an increasing number of the most mentally alert and imaginative of today's youth.

THE LURE OF ADVERTISING

Few careers provide the day-by-day satisfactions inherent in advertising. Each sales problem that must be solved and each advertisement that must be conceived, produced, and presented to the public challenge the creativity and the skill of the men and women so engaged. At times as many as a half-dozen campaigns are created for a single product so that each may be tested in the marketplace.

The industry richly rewards people with imagination, and those with the ability to think for themselves. It brings a sense of fulfillment to those who have cultivated the "whole person"—who have obtained a liberal education through delving into philosophy, foreign languages, literature, art, music, astronomy, and other such fields. It enables them to call upon their own inner resources, to test new ideas and new approaches, and to seek results through subtle means as well as directly. Like fiction writers, although dealing with facts, they have the opportunity to *create* the mental images they want to evoke in the minds of the public. Those whose talents lie in research and other aspects of producing and selling advertising are equally well rewarded.

There's an intensely satisfying thrill in seeing one's ideas assume form and substance in an advertisement or an advertising campaign that actually produces the intended response. There's an accompanying thrill in viewing the creativity of others. "It's probably terrible to say this, but I buy the *New Yorker* to read the ads," exclaimed a young advertising career woman. The advertisements, she explained, excite her esthetic sense and produce the same stimulation that a young voice student experiences on hearing a famous operatic singer.

HOW ADVERTISING DEVELOPED

Until the advent of mass selling in the nineteenth century, advertising played only a minor role in the conduct of business. In early Greek and Roman days signboards were placed above the doors of business establishments, and town criers proclaimed that merchants had certain wares for sale. These were merely means to attract customers to a shop, however; in contrast with modern advertising and sales techniques, the display of merchandise and personal selling were depended on to make the sale.

After the invention of movable type accelerated printing in the mid-fifteenth century, handbills, posters, and then newspapers were used in increasing quantities to advertise products. Advertisements appeared in early American newspapers, but the volume did not grow to sizable proportions until trade began to flourish in the metropolitan centers in the early days of the republic. Almost all selling was local until about 1840, when the development of railroad transportation enabled industry to send its products to consumers who lived far from the manufacturing plants. National advertising resulted as businessmen used both magazines and newspapers to broaden their markets. The first advertising agency in the United States was organized by Volney B. Palmer in 1840 or 1841. His agency, and those that followed his, did not prepare copy but served primarily as publisher's representatives. Some thirty agencies were selling space for more than 4000 American publications by 1860. Since there were no public lists of these publications and no way of substantiating circulation claims, the agents could manipulate the buying and selling of space to substantial personal advantage.

In 1869, however, George P. Rowell began publishing *Rowell's American Newspaper Directory,* a rather complete list of newspapers, together with careful estimates of circulation. The same year F. Wayland Ayer founded N. W. Ayer & Son, Inc. (with his father) to buy space in the interest of his clients rather than to sell it for newspapers, and his agency began its continuing directory of all periodicals in 1880. Soon other agencies were started along professional lines of providing planning and space-buying services for their clients. There was an upsurge in the use of pictorial art in advertisements, and the nation began to be conscious of the first widely quoted slogans such as Ivory Soap's "99 $\frac{44}{100}$ Per Cent Pure" and "It Floats," Eastman Kodak's "You Press the Button—We Do the Rest," and "Good Morning, Have You Used Pears' Soap?"

As newspaper and magazine circulations increased and new technological advances were made, advertising at the turn of the century developed new slogans, better copywriters and artists, and better analysis of products, media, and markets. A crusade was begun in 1911 against the gross exaggerations and misleading claims of some advertisers, notably those selling patent medicines. The various advertising organizations that were formed helped elevate the ethics of the business. To promote truth in advertising, many states adopted a model statute proposed by *Printers' Ink,* a magazine formerly published for advertising people, at the behest of the Association of Advertising Clubs. The first Better Business Bureau was formed in 1913, and the next year saw the establishment of the Audit Bureau of Circulations, a nonprofit organization making unbiased periodical audits and statements concerning a publication's circulation.

The advent of radio and a steady improvement in the techniques of advertising, such as copy-testing, the study of psychological appeals, and plans for integrated campaigns, characterized the 1920s. Advertising fought to hold its own during the depression years of the 1930s against both the near-paralysis of business and the organized objections of consumers to what they considered to be improper practices in advertising. In 1938 the Wheeler-Lea Act was passed to protect the consumer against false advertising by business firms, mainly in selling foods, drugs, and cosmetics. During this decade, however, advertisers increasingly used research methods, such as readership studies and audience measurement.

During World War II the War Advertising Council was established by advertising agencies, media, and advertisers as a voluntary contribution to the total war effort. So successful was the council in promoting the sale of war bonds, donation of blood, rationing, and the like, that it has been continued as the Advertising Council, Inc., headquartered in New York. This private, nonprofit organization conducts about twenty-five major public service campaigns each year pertaining to health and safety, education, the environment, the disadvantaged, consumerism, the economy, and community and international subjects.

Many of the council's campaigns have become part of America's consciousness and language. For example, Smokey the Bear (forest fire prevention), an Indian shedding a tear over pollution; "America. It only works as well as we do" (productivity); "A mind is a terrible thing to waste" (United Negro College Fund); "The good neighbor is you" (American Red Cross); "Don't forget. Hire the vet" (National Alliance of Businessmen); and "High blood pressure. Beat it and live" (high-blood-pressure education). Total media contributions to council campaigns have amounted to more than $8.5 billion.

The booming economy after World War II produced rapid growth in all areas of advertising. Staffs were enlarged, branch offices of advertising agencies proliferated, and small agencies formed networks to provide reciprocal services for their clients across the country. The development of television as an advertising medium accelerated the trend to larger agencies, however, because it increased the complexities of advertising. Television arrived at a most opportune time, for advertisers were introducing hundreds of new products and consumers were eager to learn their merits. The older media, also growing, soon adjusted to television, although radio and the national magazines felt the new competition most keenly. Advertisers turned increasingly to research to provide facts about their products and to discover the motivations of consumer markets.

Advertising in the late 1970s was confronted with the staggering task of helping to move into the hands of consumers an unprecedented volume of manufactured goods and then, midway in the decade, also with the problems of economic recession. More money was entrusted to advertising personnel, and their responsibilities mounted. Management demanded more efficient methods of measuring the effectiveness of advertising as distinguished from other marketing functions. Many large agencies "went public"—that is, converted their proprietorship into shares that were traded and priced on the stock market. In order to generate greater profits for principals and stockholders, some agencies began diversifying into side businesses, such as retail stores and product manufacturing.

The computer, long used for such housekeeping chores as accounting, billing, and reports, came into more sophisticated use to provide the breakouts and analyses necessary for sound manufacturing and advertising decisions. As information multiplied, the computer helped management, advertising, and marketing people understand the new world of product proliferation, market segmentation, automated distribution, population shifts, and the profit squeeze. National computer networks were established by some large agencies using high-speed data transmission telephone lines and communications facilities. The computer was used to analyze consumer surveys, to assist in media buying, to calculate television program cost efficiencies in relation to client objectives, and in numerous other ways.

At the same time, the attention paid to creativity, cleverness, and wit in the preparation of print and broadcast messages and campaigns led to a widely discussed "cult of creativity" in the industry. Although many television commercials are ill received by the public, others often are so full of wit and humor that many viewers consider them more entertaining than the programs. Prime examples are the creations of satirist Stan Freberg for Jeno's Pizza and Chun King products, the ad campaign and marketing overhaul for Braniff Airways, and the advertising prepared for such companies as Avis, Volkswagen, and Benson & Hedges. Many new agencies were established as the most creative advertising personnel went into business for themselves.

Some advertising people decried the extensive use of wit and humor, contending that it might be entertaining but that it does not always sell goods and services. Because of the business slowdown during the recession, many commercials of a humorous, awareness, and image-building variety gave way to "hard-sell" advertisements. "Less emphasis on showmanship, more on sellmanship," is the way one observer put it. Creative research, entailing repeated testing and weeks, even months of hard work, became even more important. Humor, however, remained a basic ingredient for many spots. For example, a Speidel watchband commercial showed the faces of a man and a woman on watches rotating on and off the screen as they talked. To cap it off, the man's face finally asks the woman's face what she's doing tonight. "Oh, I'm flexible," she replies, and her watchband flexes once again. Three weeks of filming and four months of "rotoscoping" were required to produce the 30-

second commercial, but product, demonstration, and interest all were present, and the commercial brought immediate sales.

In comparison with the "product era" of the 1950s and the "image era" of the 1960s, positioning emerged as a primary characteristic of the present decade. In a media-oriented society, many companies have found it necessary to "position" a product in the public's mind—a position taking into consideration not only its own strength and weaknesses, but those of its competitors as well. Examples are Seven-Up's "Un-Cola" campaign, *Sports Illustrated's* "Third Newsweekly" program, a beer company's "First class is Michelob" assertion that it is the first American-made premium beer, and the positioning of Beck's beer against Lowenbrau with the advertising line, "You've tasted the German beer that's the most popular in America. Now taste the German beer that's the most popular in Germany."

Comparative advertising emerged as another weapon in the battle for sales. In 1965 advertising leader Fairfax Cone had summed up the industry's general sentiment on the practice when he said, "It's bad manners and I can't believe the public will stand for it." In the 1970s, however, both the public and the majority of advertising practitioners seemed to favor the technique. Some commercials named competitive products, others merely alluded to them. For example, a campaign for Scotti automobile mufflers explicitly scoffed at "the Midas touch," pointing out that Midas, Inc.'s famous lifetime replacement muffler guarantee did not include other parts of the exhaust system installed by the company, whereas under Scotti's guarantee customers could get off "Scot free." A Dictaphone commercial proclaimed, "Bad news for IBM." Seneca apple juice commercials showed a set of triplets, each with Hi-C, Hawaiian Punch, and Seneca apple juice; all three children "love" those products, the commercial stated, but only Seneca contained 100 percent fruit juice. Without naming its competitor, the Scope campaign referred to a competing "medicine breath" mouthwash, whereupon Listerine retaliated by proclaiming that its product lasted "two times longer than the leading sweet-tasting mouthwash." Comparative advertising also was widely practiced in print advertising.

Industry code review boards watched carefully over the technique, condoning comparisons considered significant to product performance, but banning disparagement, unqualified language, and dangling comparisons. Legitimate comparison was viewed as saying "ours is better than his" and disparagement as saying "his is worse than ours."

Other recent trends include the rise of advocacy advertising, in which corporations run paid ads that take sides on important public issues; a major increase in government advertising; a movement toward world-wide conglomerates, consortiums, and working alliances by which agencies cooperate or interact without actual partnership or crossownership; and the merging or near-merging of the advertising and public relations departments of companies and agencies.

The criticisms leveled at the advertising industry, and the chief problems confronting it, are discussed in Chapter 7. The threat of government regulation loomed as the largest of these problems as the powerful consumer movement with its multiple pressures on industry spread rapidly. How to recruit, and hold, able young men and women so as to refresh and replenish the industry's more than $15 billion pool of advertising talent was another major problem. "Talent napping" was a continuing practice, and the agencies' annual turnover rate stood at 35 percent. Mounting areas of friction between clients and agencies, caused by poor communications, account conflicts, comparative advertising, the feeling by some clients that agencies overcharge or are overpaid, failure to agree on how to measure the effectiveness of ads, and other reasons contributed to the annual shifting of about 20 percent of all advertising accounts in the nation from one agency to another. The problems in this mercurial, exciting business were many; but few deserted it, and the level of earnings remained high.

THE SIZE OF THE ADVERTISING FIELD

In the United States

More than 400,000 persons are employed in all phases of advertising in this country. This estimate by industry spokespeople includes those who create or sell advertising for an advertiser, medium, or service, but not the thousands behind the scenes such as printers, sign painters, and clerical help. Manufacturing and service concerns employ the largest number of advertising workers. Next in order are the mass media, including radio, television, magazines, outdoor, direct mail, and transportation advertising departments. Following them are retail establishments, advertising agencies, wholesalers, and miscellaneous specialty companies.

In addition, it has been estimated that approximately 1 million persons fill jobs related to advertising. They include paper salespeople, representatives of media, advertising printing, and typography companies, and other such persons. Almost 75,000 men and women are employed in the approximately 6,600 advertising agencies in the United States. Of the approximately 20,000 newcomers attracted into the advertising business each year, about 1,500 are hired by the advertising agencies directly from college, although this number diminishes considerably during periods of economic recession.

International Advertising

United States advertisers, agencies, and advertising personnel have been engaged in international advertising for decades. Today our participation is steadily and dramatically increasing. Standards of living in Europe, the Far East, Latin America, and other heretofore untapped marketing areas are constantly improving. Literacy rates have been rising, and the growth of both print and broadcast media in many countries has provided a larger audience for advertising. American wares are in great demand. We are exporting billions of dollars worth of products each year. These join the flow of goods produced by overseas plants in which Americans have invested well over $50 billion.

As a consequence, giant corporations such as IBM World Trade, Exxon, Coca-Cola Export, General Motors, and Monsanto, long in the international field, are being joined by countless other companies seeking their share of the world market. IBM World Trade alone has more than 330 sales locations, 235 data processing centers, and approximately 140,000 employees in 127 countries outside the United States. Almost all are nationals of the countries in which they work. The company's gross income abroad exceeds $9 billion.

In 1977 the top ten U.S. agencies engaged in advertising in other countries grossed $647 million in income through their non-U.S. operations. Of this total, McCann-Erickson and the J. Walter Thompson Company grossed almost a third. The Thompson company pioneered in global agency operations, opening its first overseas office in London in 1889. Today it has more than 5600 employees at work in 60 offices in 25 countries. McCann-Erickson staffs its more than 70 full-service offices largely with nationals of the 47 countries in which they are located. The firm is a part of Interpublic, Inc. The other agency leaders in gross income earned in other countries in 1977 are SSC&B, Young & Rubicam, Ogilvy & Mather International, Ted Bates & Co., Compton Advertising, BBDO International, D'Arcy-MacManus & Masius, and the Leo Burnett Company.

The smaller domestic agencies operate overseas in four ways: through subsidiaries, of which they own part or all of the stock; through exclusive affiliations; through account affiliations with overseas agencies that may also work with other American agencies; and through export media, such as *Reader's Digest International* and *Vision.* The fourth method often is used along with any of the other three.

The total number of advertising employees serving overseas with American companies and agencies has never been estimated. Despite automation, or partly perhaps because of it, the number is certain to increase. L. T. Steele, executive vice president of Benton & Bowles, Inc., has summed up the opportunities in this fashion:

Young people coming into advertising . . . will discover, in the international scope of the business, a whole world of opportunities. Advertising men and women of our generation are rightfully proud of their contributions to the American economy. The new, young breed will extend these contributions to many other economies in other countries. If we, in our time, have found excitement, stimulation, and rich rewards in our careers in advertising, think how much greater their achievements can be!
It is they who will truly be co-architects of the world of tomorrow.

WHAT ADVERTISING PEOPLE DO

Advertising may be defined as the dissemination of sales messages through purchased space, time, or other media to identify, inform, or persuade. What people do to accomplish this objective can be described by examining briefly the roles they play in advertising agencies, in advertising departments of the mass media, in retail store and company advertising departments, and in the planning of a national advertising campaign.

Advertising Agencies
An agency first studies its client's product or service to learn the advantages and disadvantages of the product itself in relation to its competition. It then analyzes the present and potential market for which the product or service is intended. Taken into consideration next are the distribution and sales plans of the client, which are studied with a view to determining the best selection of media. A definite plan is then formulated and presented to the client.

Once the plan is approved the agency staff writes, designs, and illustrates the proposed advertisements or prepares the broadcast commercials; contracts for space or time with the media; produces the advertisements and sends them to the media with instructions; checks and verifies the use of the ads; pays for the services rendered and bills the client; and cooperates in such merchandising efforts as point-of-purchase displays.

Who are the persons who perform these services? The answer varies, since advertising agencies range in size from small operations to those employing a thousand persons or more. The executive heads of an agency usually are people who have proved they can produce sales for their clients through print, broadcasting, and other media and who are capable of procuring new business for the agency. These executives may be organized into a plans board, giving general direction to such departments as research, planning, media, copy, art and layout, television production, print production, traffic, merchandising, checking, and accounting.

The key persons in servicing an account—that is, in providing liaison between the agency and the client—are the account executives. These men and women must have a general knowledge of all phases of advertising, merchandising, and general business practices, as well as the ability to be creative in solving a client's special advertising problems and in planning campaigns. Account executives call on the agency's various departments for assistance and correlate their efforts in behalf of clients.

Copy and art chiefs are responsible for the actual creation of advertisements. Copywriters are salespersons, inventors, interpreters, and perhaps artists, but always competent writers. Art directors are salespersons, inventors, interpreters, perhaps writers and sometimes producers, but also visually sensitive persons who usually can draw. They see to it that all the visual elements come together at every phase of the work from rough layouts to finished ads. They supervise every aspect from the graphic approach to selection of type. For television, they begin by making a storyboard, the series of pictures representing the video portion of the commercial. Often they help choose the film techniques, music and other sounds, and models.

The broadcasting department selects, recommends, and contracts for the programs best suited to the product to be advertised. The agency also creates the television and radio commercials and supervises their actual production.

From the moment an ad is designed and written to the time it actually appears in magazines and newspapers or on billboards, it is in the hands of the print production people. They are up to date on typography, printing, photoengraving, electrotyping, and allied crafts and pro-

ADVERTISING AGENCY ORGANIZATION CHART

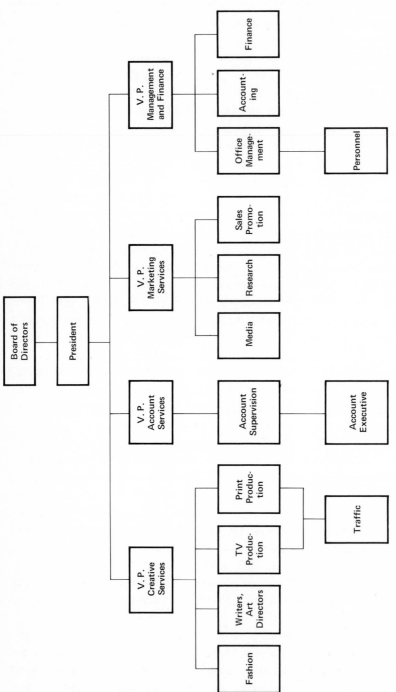

FIGURE 17.1

cesses. They know what is practical for reproduction and help to guide the creative departments in planning their work. They buy graphic arts services and materials and see assignments through to completion.

Because so many agency functions, including copy, art, production, and media, are involved in the same assignment—that of producing a single ad or commercial or an entire campaign—it is vital to keep everyone working smoothly and on schedule. Planning the flow and timing of all the work is the function of traffic control. Whether the project is large or small, traffic sees that all do their parts on time in order to meet deadlines and publishers' closing dates.

The marketing research department gathers the facts that make it possible to solve sales problems. Research findings provide vital intelligence for the agency. Facts—for instance, about what type of people use a product and why—may help provide creative people with the central idea for an advertising approach. Or media people may plan an entire advertising campaign based on research about the way people read certain magazines or which television stations they watch. Most agencies depend upon their clients for the bulk of their marketing information.

Media people select and buy print space for ads and air time for commercials. They get the facts and figures from the research department. They must know the moods of magazines, the psychological environments of TV shows, and the editorial tone of any given newspaper. From daily and weekly newspapers, national magazines, business magazines, radio and television stations, outdoor posters, and direct mail lists they choose the most effective combinations for each advertisement and product. And they must be able to stay within a budget.

Agencies also have people who handle sales promotion, merchandising, public relations, fashion, home economics, and personnel. Then too, like other firms, agencies need comptrollers, secretaries, general office workers, bookkeepers, and billing clerks. (Figure 17.1 shows a typical organization chart.)

The Advertising Checking Bureau determines if the advertisements have been used by the media as planned. The agency's commission then is computed. This is generally 15 percent of the medium's published rate; if the advertising space or time cost $100, the agency collects that amount from the client and pays the medium $85. Most agencies today operate under the commission system because the bulk of their compensation comes from commissions allowed by media. This averages about

75 percent of income. The remaining 25 percent compensation to these agencies is from clients. It consists of fees plus out-of-pocket expenditures for special services and collateral work performed at the client's request, and service charges, or commissions as they are more commonly called, added to the cost of materials and services purchased in the preparation of advertising. The suppliers of materials and services used in preparing advertising, typography, plates, filmed commercials, artwork, printing, etc., do not allow a commission to the agencies as do the media. When these charges are billed to the advertiser, commission generally is added. Until recent years commission was usually 15 percent on the net bill, but it is becoming more standard to make the commission 17.65 percent in order to receive 15 percent on the gross bill. After all expenses have been met, the agencies generally wind up with 2 to 3 percent net profit on their gross income each year. There is a movement now for agencies to charge entirely by the fee system.

Advertising Departments of Mass Media

All the media employ space or time sales personnel and almost all engage national sales representatives to obtain advertising for them. Let us consider several actual newspaper and radio operations.

One newspaper publishes both morning and evening newspapers with a combined circulation of 38,000. The combined retail advertising staff consists of six sales representatives and a retail manager; one of the salespeople is a woman. Advertisements handled by the department comprise 70 percent of the newspaper's total advertising volume, the remainder being in classified and national.

Each salesperson handles between 75 and 100 accounts, ranging from department stores to small shops. Unlike the practice on large newspapers, they are not assigned to specific territories. After calling on their accounts, they prepare semicomprehensive layouts using artwork from one of several advertising layout service books. The layouts are then sent to the offset composing room. Proofs are delivered to any retailer placing an ad that contains 15 or more inches of space.

These salespeople work from 8:30 A.M. to 6 P.M. five days a week. Each is required to produce at least one "speculative" layout each week. They are paid a base salary plus commission, and annual incomes average $10,000. Commissions are paid when the amount of space sold at the same time the previous year is exceeded, and in connection with the fifteen or so special editions ("back-to-school") printed each year, color ads, and departmental sales contests.

In contrast, thirty-two salespersons are employed by a nearby morning, evening, and Sunday newspaper selling more than 350,000 copies primarily in a fifteen-county metropolitan area. Each must serve accounts only in a specified area. If the ad is too elaborate for the salesperson to prepare, the newspaper's art department lends assistance. After the typed copy and artwork are arranged on the dummy ad, it is printed on a proof sheet exactly as it is to appear in the newspaper. The salesperson checks the ad and may send it to the customer for signed approval before it is printed. These salespersons work in air-conditioned, carpeted offices with easy access to a covered parking lot. They earn commissions above their base salary if they produce more sales than their monthly quotas.

A nearby 1000-watt medium-market AM station employs four salespersons. Among them is the commercial manager, a woman, who doubles as station manager but spends most of her time calling on accounts. One salesman also announces occasional play-by-play sports broadcasts. The station owner handles all national accounts as well as a dozen local ones. The sales staff earns $9,000 to $10,000 annually in commissions. The commercial manager receives a salary plus 15 percent of the collections on her own accounts and a graduated percentage of the sales volume of the entire staff.

A copywriter prepares the commercials and the station announcers tape them. The spots are played over the telephone for client approval before being aired. The traffic manager then schedules them on cartridge tapes (called "carts"). Many of the commercials also are aired on the station's 5200-watt FM station.

Space limitations will not permit other examples. All advertising personnel provide fresh, up-to-date information about the markets that their newspaper, magazine, or station covers and about the "pulling power" of the medium itself. These facts are provided regularly by their own research and promotion departments or by national trade associations or bureaus.

Most magazines deal directly with national advertisers or indirectly through national representatives. As is true with the other media, copywriters, artists, and production, promotion, and merchandising personnel supplement the sales force. And there is a similar ladder of promotion to executive positions.

Retail Store Advertising

Retail firms employ more than 80,000 persons in their advertising departments. These range from one-person staffs to those employing dozens of persons. In a large store the advertising manager works closely with sales promotion and marketing specialists. In one large Chicago department store, the staff consists of a copy chief, production manager, and proofreader; an art director and assistant art director, together with six layout artists, five "finish" artists, and two apprentices; and five copywriters, mostly women with a high degree of creativeness who specialize in women's and children's apparel, men's apparel and accessories, and home furnishings. In addition, two copywriters are assigned to the basement store and the suburban store. Other journalistic personnel may be found in the public relations and publicity office and in the radio-television division preparing special product demonstrations. Mary Wells Lawrence, today's highest paid advertising executive, started at the retail copy department level.

Those charged with planning a store's advertising must be familiar with all aspects of the market, consumer behavior and attitudes, and such factors as product images and characteristics. The steps normally taken in planning a campaign include these: (1) setting a sales goal or budget, based to a large extent on sales the preceding year; (2) deciding how much advertising is needed; (3) determining which products or services to promote and when; and (4) preparing a day-to-day schedule. Store displays and other merchandising efforts are coordinated. The volume of sales produced during each advertising period is carefully monitored to determine the success of the advertising and to help in future planning.

Industrial and Trade Advertising

The public is well aware of consumer goods advertising: We see and hear advertisements almost every moment of the waking day, and often advertising jingles course through our brains even as we sleep. Not so with industrial and trade advertisements, for they are not addressed to the general public. *Industrial* advertising is employed by producers of industrial goods, such as steel, machinery, lubricants, packaging, and office equipment, in order to sell these products to other industries. *Trade* advertising is employed by the producers and distributors of branded and nonbranded consumer goods in order to reach the retailers and wholesalers of consumer goods. They, in turn, sell these goods to their own customers.

The industrial or trade advertising department may employ only one person, the advertising manager, or as many as 400 or more persons. The typical department, however, employs about seven. These are likely to include the advertising manager, secretarial help, a writer, perhaps an artist, and one or two persons engaged in marketing research, media evaluation, or production work.

The department handles inquiries and prepares catalogs and technical data sheets, direct mail, exhibits, and sales promotion materials such as slide films, movies, and props for sales meetings. It likely will engage in market research, but most departments obtain market data without charge through business paper research services.

Almost all industrial and trade advertising departments employ outside agencies to handle trade advertisements. More than half the advertising placed in business publications comes from general agencies. Others identify themselves as industrial advertising agencies, although most of them also handle consumer goods advertising. They specialize in industrial, technical, scientific, commercial, and merchandising products and services. A few agencies confine themselves to such fields as financial or pharmaceutical advertising.

The industrial agency is most likely to emphasize the services of account executives who work directly with the client, write copy, and make media-buying analyses and decisions largely on their own. There is a minimum of creative direction by an overall planning board. Between 20 and 50 percent, or more, of industrial agency income is derived from fees rather than media commissions. This is caused by the fact that commissions are limited, generally amounting to only $150, often even $25 or $50, per insertion. And an agency may be called upon to prepare between 50 and 100 different advertisements each year per $100,000 in annual space expenditures. With costs for research, layout, merchandising, and public relations running high and commissions low, the charging of supplemental fees for these services is a necessity.

National Campaigns

Selecting appropriate media for a particular advertising campaign demands great business acumen and reliance on research studies. If an advertiser decides to use magazines as his vehicle, for example, he must next decide which class or group, such as women's magazines, to choose, and then must select the specific publication, such as *McCall's*. The size of the advertisement and the frequency of publication also must be determined. Similar choices must be made for all the media to be employed.

In introducing its 1975 Granada automobile, the Ford Motor Company combined thorough market research with an advertising, sales promotion, and public relations campaign that, through sheer size, achieved the nationwide "impact and awareness" that were its stated goals. Ten-second "teaser" spots were run in major television markets about three weeks before the new model was announced. These were followed by a heavy schedule of preannouncement commercials aired primarily during professional football games. During announcement week, commercials on television specials and major football telecasts reached 170 million households an average of three times each.

Three-page black and white preannouncement advertisements were placed in *Time, Sports Illustrated, U.S. News & World Report,* and *Newsweek.* Readers of those four magazines and *Reader's Digest* saw spectacular five-color, four-page advertisements during announcement week and immediately thereafter. Sixty-five million copies of a preprint insert were placed in Sunday, daily, and weekly newspapers, reaching virtually every home in the country. Although the insert supported Ford's entire line, the Granada was featured on the cover and in the first two pages.

Company spokespersons said this was the largest concentration of media ever to launch a new car. During the preannouncement period alone, it was estimated that 99 percent of U.S. households were reached an average of 6.6 times each. The average family was exposed to Granada advertising 16 times during the entire announcement period and for a month thereafter.

Promotional support was equally strong. Development of the car from early marketing research studies to the design center drawingboards to the finished prototypes was detailed in sixty early special briefings for newsmen and women from major dailies and the wire services. A conference for magazine writers and photographers resulted in several cover stories; *Road Test* magazine announced that the Granada was its "car of the year" and *Motor Trend* magazine pronounced the model its "value" car of the year.

A national preview conference in Detroit attended by more than 100 news personnel was followed a month later by individual test drives by 200 or more persons, resulting in countless feature articles. Broadcast media representatives attended the national conference and conducted interviews with company officials. A 60-second film clip was distributed to 210 TV stations and local talk shows were solicited on which company people discussed the car. Ford Division's thirty-four sales districts set up speakers' bureaus through which company executives spoke to local civic groups and offered free loans of the Granada for a week.

After a number of major publications misspelled "Granada," a series of humorous news releases was distributed involving the mayors of Grenada, Mississippi, and Granada, Minnesota, battling over for which city the car had been named.

The results? Granada immediately became the best-selling new American car in a decade. In only nine months, despite the recession, Ford dealers sold more than 176,000 cars, reportedly more than all the other new models offered by other companies combined.

Few advertising and promotional budgets can be this extensive. The procedure, however, is the same in each: the judicious expenditure of an allotted sum in a carefully coordinated campaign involving research, marketing, advertising, and public relations personnel, and using every medium necessary to accomplish the specified sales objective.

QUALIFICATIONS

Men and women with a wide variety of interests and talents qualify for careers in advertising. As the American Association of Advertising Agencies puts it:

Whether your career interests lie in marketing or management, design or decimals, psychology or public service, fashion or finance, computers or copywriting, people or products, ideas or imagery, the medium or the message, personnel or photography, communications or commerce, sales or show business, math or music, graphics or global markets, packaging or printing, research or retail promotion, television . . . or you name it . . . the multifaceted world of advertising offers opportunities to get involved in all these areas—and more.

The advertising world is made up of people who have creative, analytical, selling, or management abilities. Successful advertising people are said to be constructive, adaptable, and eternally curious. They must be constructively optimistic because they are called on to originate ideas and to initiate action—to visualize in full operation something that has not yet been started. They must be adaptable because of the infinitely varied problems and the different types of persons they meet almost daily. And they must have an unceasing interest in people and things and the operation of business in general and the industry in particular. They must keep abreast of developments in advertising and remain keen and interested students in many fields throughout their careers.

Imagination, foresight in sensing trends, the ability to reason analytically, and a sense of form are characteristics of advertising men and women that are frequently cited. Also emphasized is a broad general education in the liberal arts, obtained either in conjunction with the offerings of schools of communication or commerce or entirely in the humanities, social sciences, or sciences. Generally, professional preparation in advertising opens doors most quickly.

Young men and women with talent and ability rise rapidly in advertising, particularly in the agency field. More than one-fifth of the 450 agencies that belong to the American Association of Advertising Agencies (4As) are run by executives who were under forty when they stepped up to the chief executive's chair. About 50 percent of all agency jobs are held by women. At the professional level, the percentage approximates 25 per cent, and in New York City about 33 percent.

Women play important roles in practically every phase of advertising. Many women graduates go to work immediately as copywriters for department stores and other companies and for the agencies. A few sell space and time for the media or enter the classified advertising departments of newspapers, A number of national advertising campaigns have been masterminded by women functioning as account executives. The advertising directors of some of the largest department stores are women, and women also have achieved success as media buyers for agencies. More and more women are being made vice presidents of agencies, and several very successful women now head firms of their own.

Approximately 7 percent of the professionals in the 4As' member agencies belong to minority groups, while minorities account for about 20 percent of nonprofessional jobs.

Rewards, both financial and psychological, come quickly for those who are imaginative and quick-thinking, can work under pressure, and have a bent for solving problems. About half the people in a typical agency, for example, are professionals or executives. The sharing of ownership and profits with such key employees is practiced more often in agencies than in most businesses.

SALARIES

The overall trend in advertising agency salaries is up, surveys have disclosed. These advances include across-the-board increases, partly to take care of cost-of-living hikes. The main reason for the raises, however, lies in the fact that most agencies today are handling far more business than they did before and immediately after World War II.

Agencies in metropolitan areas (New York, Chicago, Los Angeles, Detroit, and Boston were those surveyed) pay from 10 to 15 percent higher salaries than those in smaller cities. In both metropolitan and nonmetropolitan areas, respectively, salaries now vary little from one section of the country to the other. In both large and small cities, however, one fact stands out: the heavier the gross billings by an agency, the greater the salary scale. There are agencies that gross less than $250,000 a year, whereas those in the giant category take in $300 million to $800 million or more a year.

A survey taken by Rubel & Humphrey and published in *Advertising Age* shows the average salaries paid in 1975 by all-size agencies combined. These figures do not include bonus or stock option plans, which are a part of most compensation programs.

AVERAGE AGENCY SALARIES, 1975
(in thousands of dollars)

Work Function	High	Low	Average
Administrative			
Chief executive officer	$61.6	$31.6	$45.3
Chief financial officer	38.1	18.4	26.9
Chief accounting officer	18.3	9.6	13.5
Contact, Public Relations			
Account supervisor	43.0	19.0	28.4
Account executive	28.4	10.3	18.5
Copy/contact account executive	22.9	10.6	16.4
Public relations director	28.4	14.0	20.1
Public relations account executive	20.8	10.1	15.1
Creative			
Creative director	39.1	20.4	28.5
Executive art director	33.3	17.8	24.4
Art director	22.3	12.0	17.1
Layout artist, senior	17.5	8.8	12.9
Layout artist, junior	12.9	6.8	9.3
Copy chief	31.8	15.8	22.3
Copywriter, senior	23.1	11.9	16.6
Copywriter, junior	13.6	7.9	10.5
Broadcast			
Commercial production manager/producer	24.6	12.9	19.0
Associate producer	15.7	9.1	12.3
Administrative/business manager	15.3	8.3	11.8
Media and Research			
Media director	23.5	13.6	16.8
Associate media director	16.0	8.6	12.1
Buyer—space/time	12.4	6.9	9.4
Research director	32.1	16.4	24.0
Research analyst	18.3	9.1	13.5
Print Production and Traffic			
Production manager	18.9	10.8	14.4
Production assistant	12.8	7.2	9.6
Traffic manager	12.1	7.2	9.4

Source: Courtesy of Rubel & Humphrey, Inc., and *Advertising Age.*

As their skills and experience increase, advertising specialists generally find that they possess knowledge for which there is great demand. In moving from one agency to another, often taking accounts with them, they naturally move into higher pay brackets. A somewhat similar promotion situation is true in media and company advertising departments. The top advertising executives in the office of newspapers, magazines, and other media and in client companies generally earn about two-thirds of what their counterparts with the agencies receive. Other factors, however, such as security and fringe benefits, often more than make up for the lower salaries.

In the general magazine field, advertising directors earn from $12,000 to $50,000, depending largely on circulation. Business paper advertising managers earn from $11,000 to $35,000. Advertising managers for newspapers are paid about the same. And commercial managers for radio and television stations earn from $9,000 to $30,000.

Beginning salaries in both print and broadcast media and in company advertising departments for recipients of bachelor's degrees average $8,000, whereas those possessing master's degrees are paid average starting salaries in excess of $9,000. Once they have proved their worth, qualified advertising people generally move rapidly upward.

CHAPTER 18
PUBLIC RELATIONS

A NEW FIELD

Public relations is one of the newest and fastest growing fields in communications. It is estimated that as many as 100,000 persons are employed in various kinds of public relations jobs, some at high levels of management. More are being attracted every year from the mass media of communications and from among the graduates of journalism schools. As our society becomes more complex—and the need for effective communications between our numerous institutions and the individuals they serve becomes more essential—the field of public relations practice is likely to continue its steady growth.

The term *public relations* means many different things to different people. It has been used, and abused, to cover a wide range of activities from legitimate attempts at persuasive communication to the bribery efforts of unscrupulous lobbyists. In its best and narrowest sense, public relations is the planned and organized effort of a company or institution to establish mutually beneficial relationships with its various *publics*. Publics, in turn, may be defined as the various groups of people who are affected by—or who can affect—the operations of a particular firm or institution. Each public is bound together by a common interest vis-à-vis the organization.

Thus, for a manufacturing corporation, such publics would include employees, stockholders, citizens of the community in which it is located, dealers who handle its products, and the ultimate purchasers or users of its products. Similarly, for a nonprofit hospital, these publics may include its professional staff, its employees, its patients and their families, the citizens in the community in which it is located, and its financial supporters.

Although many persons tend to consider "public relations" and "publicity" as synonymous terms, it should be obvious that more than effective communication is required to initiate and execute a sound public relations program. Effective public relations programing begins with the establishment of fair and equitable policies by management. The essence of these policies must be explained to those who work for the organization or who represent it, and to the interested publics, in varying forms of communication. In short, communication must explain the policies and actions of management, but the policies and actions must support the words. Finally, the responses of these publics to what the organization says and does must be reflected back to management so that appropriate adjustments may be made in policies and operations.

Public relations has been defined by *PR News,* a weekly newsletter in the field, as "the management function which evaluates public attitudes, identifies the policies and procedures of an individual or an organization with the public interest, and plans and executes a program of action to earn public understanding and acceptance." In recent years, managements have tended to look to their public relations executives for a continuing analysis of social, economic, and political trends that may have an impact on the operations of the business or institution so that future problems may be avoided or alleviated. In this capacity, the public relations people may be required to evaluate developments in such areas as consumer activism, the environmental protection movement, and government responses to minority problems. In these areas, public relations practice—at its best—affords genuine opportunities for meaningful service to society. As this function develops more fully, the value of public relations people to management and the social significance of the public relations function will offer greater opportunities to those who wish to follow a public relations career.

The student who desires a successful career in corporate public relations (the largest area of public relations practice) should be committed to the capitalist system. But, beyond this, the proper exercise of the public relations function in corporate management offers opportunities for improving the profit system and making it work more effectively to serve society. Thus, careers in corporate public relations may provide compensations beyond the relatively good salaries and fringe benefits for idealistic young people.

HISTORY AND DEVELOPMENT

The roots of public relations go far back into history. Caesar's *Commentaries,* the four Gospels of the New Testament, and *The Federalist* are examples of persuasive communications long before the public relations concept was crystalized. In times nearer our own, we have had the nineteenth-century press agents who achieved a less than respectable reputation for persuading—or duping—the masses. But if contemporary practice is the offspring of nineteenth-century press agentry, the child is quite unlike its parent.

The modern public relations concept was born shortly after the turn of the century when Ivy Ledbetter Lee, a newspaperman who had covered business news, conceived the idea of setting up a Business News

Bureau to disseminate information to the press on behalf of business corporations. It was Lee's belief that much of the public's antipathy toward business at that time—an antipathy stirred up and exploited by the muckrakers—resulted from the fact that most businesses operated in complete secrecy and most businesspeople would not discuss their policies or operations with the public. Lee offered to provide a service that would enable businesspeople to address the public. His idea proved attractive. Among Lee's early clients were the Pennsylvania Railroad (then one of America's greatest corporations, known as the "standard railroad of the world"), anthracite coal mine operators who were involved in labor strife, and later John D. Rockefeller, Jr.

A second dimension was added to the public relations concept during World War I, when the Committee on Public Information was established by the federal government under George Creel. The committee conducted a massive and successful publicity effort to mobilize the American public behind the war effort. The values of such massive communications efforts were impressed upon those who worked with Creel, and some of them became pioneers in the establishment of public relations agencies designed to conduct similar campaigns for private clients. They included Edward L. Bernays, who subsequently became the author of a classic but badly named book on public relations, *The Engineering of Consent,* and Carl Byoir, who established what has become one of the largest and most successful public relations agencies in the world, Carl Byoir and Associates.

Bernays generally is credited with adding another aspect to the public relations concept: the counseling function. He theorized aptly enough that if the public relations practitioner has the responsibility for explaining management's policies and actions to the public, then the public relations specialist also should have a voice in advising management on the formulation of its policies and the development of programs affecting the public. Although some managements still have not recognized this aspect of public relations practice, in many of America's largest corporations today the public relations executive is a vice-president who has strong influence on the development of management policy.

Still another dimension was added to the public relations concept in the 1930s with the development of modern public opinion and marketing survey techniques by George Gallup, Elmo Roper, Claude Robinson, and others. This development provided a tool by which public relations counselors and executives could evaluate public attitudes quantitatively.

Public relations people help to arrange press conferences and meetings like this one, in which insurance executives are briefed on developments affecting them in the federal government. (Courtesy of Insurance Information Institute, New York.)

Thus, instead of simply relying upon their own estimates of public opinion, they could achieve some degree of objective measurement. Public opinion measuring techniques still are far from perfect and their results subject to error, but they have become more reliable as the result of refinements over the years. Public attitude surveys have become a standard tool of public relations practitioners.

Another refinement in public relations practice in recent years, as has been mentioned earlier, is the idea that the public relations executive should be the monitor of social, economic, and political trends that may affect the business or institution he or she represents. Thus, contemporary public relations, when practiced at the optimal level, involves three general responsibilities:

1 *Continuing analysis of the social, economic, political, and human environment in which the business or institution operates to provide a basis for advising management.*
2 *Counseling management on the development of policies and operations to develop sound relationships with the various pertinent publics.*
3 *Communicating essential information concerning managerial policies and practices, products, and services to the concerned publics.*

In short, the public relations function, effectively implemented, helps correlate the private interests of management with the overriding public interest to facilitate the growth and development of the particular institution. No public relations program can expect to succeed if the private interests of the business or institution run counter to the public interest. Only where the private and the public interests are effectively correlated can an organization expect to have a healthy environment in which to operate. As an expert communicator, both to management and to its publics, the public relations executive helps to bring about this correlation.

PUBLIC RELATIONS AND THE MASS MEDIA

Public relations at its best has a unique relationship with the mass media of communication. The communicative function of public relations practice has become an inextricable part of the mass communications network in the United States. It would not be too extreme to state that, without the contributions of tens of thousands of public relations communicators, our media would not be nearly as accurate or as well-rounded in content as they are.

Consider, for example, that no newspaper—not even the New York *Times* or the *Wall Street Journal*—nor any magazine, wire service, or broadcasting station or network can afford to support a staff large enough to have experts in every field of human endeavor. Even the largest media rely upon the public relations persons representing companies and institutions to provide the expertise, background, explanations, and translations from the language of the experts to the language of the lay person that enable journalists to write understandably about complex and arcane subjects. The smaller papers and the smaller news staffs of the broadcast media are even more dependent on public relations people for this kind of help. In one sense, then, public relations practitioners provide a necessary link between the media and many specialized areas of activity in our society, a link that the media generally could not afford to provide for themselves.

Inasmuch as public relations people also are responsible for presenting their companies and institutions in the best possible posture, the question may arise as to whether this situation leads to abuse of the channels of public communication. The answer is that, although admittedly it is possible for public relations people occasionally to take advantage of the media, over the long range it is imperative that public relations communicators establish their integrity with the media people. They cannot afford to dupe them, at the risk of ending their usefulness.

Most journalists recognize this fact, and over a period of time come to know which public relations people can be trusted. Thus, mutually honest and beneficial relationships are developed.

Although public relations people are dependent to a considerable extent on the mass media in their communications activities, public relations communications are not limited to the mass media. Public relations staffs and counselors develop many specialized (or controlled) forms of communication, such as printed booklets or periodicals; exhibits; and motion pictures, slide films, and other audiovisual presentations aimed at specific publics. In this area also, public relations communicators should be influenced not only by an innate sense of honesty but also by the knowledge that their long-range effectiveness must be built on a reputation for integrity.

TYPES OF PUBLIC RELATIONS EMPLOYMENT

Although many firms and some other types of institutions established their public relations departments many years ago (notably the American Telephone and Telegraph Company, which early recognized the importance of good public relations for a regulated monopoly), the major expansion in public relations has occurred since World War II. The initial thrust of this expansion occurred in business and industry, but it was followed by an expansion of organized public relations programs in many other kinds of institutions (known as institutional public relations): public school systems and universities, hospitals, non-profit health and welfare organizations, government agencies, business and professional associations, and even the military. Although federal law prohibits the employment of public relations people by U.S. government agencies, essentially the same function is carried out by information officers. The army, navy, and air force all have designated public information officers who have been especially trained in military public relations policy at service schools or who have been sent for the same purpose to universities with good public relations programs, such as those whose public relations sequences have been accredited by the American Council on Education for Journalism.

The largest subgroup of practitioners is engaged in public relations on behalf of business corporations. In 1975, Jack O'Dwyer, publisher of *O'Dwyer's Newsletter* in New York City, made a survey of the 1000 largest industrial companies, as ranked by *Fortune* magazine, along with about 50 of the largest corporations in each of six other areas including commercial banking, life insurance, diversified finance, retailing, transportation, and utilities. The results, published in *O'Dwyer's Directory of*

Corporate Communications, disclosed that 919 of 1293 companies employed approximately 6300 public relations communications professionals in departments bearing such titles as public relations, corporate communications, communications, advertising and public relations, public affairs, corporate relations, public information, and external relations.

More than one-third (457) of the companies retained external public relations counseling firms. Of the companies that retained outside public relations counsel, 125 had no internal departments; the other 332 relied on both internal and external public relations people.

The 1977 edition of this same directory was expanded to cover 2001 of the largest companies in the United States, but it does not provide as much detail. Of the 2001 companies, only 1310 had full-time staff people employed in a public relations or communications capacity. Another 138 firms employed external public relations counsel. The remaining 553 had no professional help at all.

Additionally, many thousands of public relations practitioners are employed in the 4000 national trade and professional associations, as well as in some of the 40,000 state, regional, and local associations of the same type. Although many associations have small public relations departments with relatively few people, some have extensive staffs with budgets of several million dollars.

Most public relations people are full-time employees of the institutions they represent. But, also since the end of World War II, there has been a mushroom-like growth of public relations counseling firms. Like an advertising agency, a public relations counseling firm may serve a number of clients on a fee-plus-expenses basis. Such counseling firms range in size from those with only one practitioner and a secretary to a complex organization such as Hill and Knowlton or Carl Byoir and Associates, with 300 to 600 employees and a variety of departments.

The public relations counseling firm often is in a position to offer a more objective point of view about a company's or an institution's problems than the internal public relations department. The counseling firm also is in a position to provide extra manpower to supplement the internal staff in periods of intensified activity or to provide experts in certain fields that may not be represented on the internal staff. Scott M. Cutlip and Allen H. Center, in the 1978 edition of the textbook, *Effective Public Relations,* estimated that there are more than 1700 PR counseling firms in the United States. But the 1977 edition of O'Dwyer's directory lists only 719, presumably the largest or better known.

In large counseling organizations, separate departments may specialize in newspaper publicity, placing clients on television talk shows, developing and placing magazine articles, producing audiovisual presentations, developing special programs aimed at educators and educational institutions, and so on. A similar pattern prevails in respect to in-house public relations staffs. Some smaller business firms and institutions may have only a one-man, one-woman public relations department. Others, like General Motors and the U.S. Steel Corporation, may have scores or hundreds of people in numerous subdepartments specializing in different areas of public relations or in differing communications techniques.

When one analyzes the overall situation it becomes clear that, broadly speaking, there are two types of public relations people: *generalists* and *specialists*. The generalists, a definite minority, are usually at the executive or managerial level. They are responsible for analyzing problem situations, developing programs to resolve these situations, participating in management-level discussions of policy, and supervising the implementation of programs. The specialists, a much larger number, are the experts in various techniques of communication and in the specialized areas of public relations practice. These men and women work under the direction of the generalists. The specialists write news releases, speeches, and booklets; answer inquiries from the press; arrange press conferences and special events; develop audiovisual presentations and educational materials; and so on. Most public relations careers start at the specialist level—for example, in publicity writing or magazine editing. After the individual gains experience and shows promise of generalist potential, he or she moves to a higher level.

Overall, the growth of public relations jobs since World War II has been spectacular. Although in the early 1970s the rate of growth diminished with the economy, prospects for well-trained and competent public relations people seem promising. As more and more companies and institutions compete for public understanding and support, as more and more managements recognize the values of—and the utter necessity for—effective public relations efforts, the demand for competent practitioners should continue. As a matter of fact, today there are more top-level public relations opportunities than there are experienced and competent men and women to fill them.

PUBLIC RELATIONS ASSIGNMENTS

Consider a male university journalism or communications graduate who goes to work for a public utility, such as the telephone company, after preparing himself for publishing, broadcasting, public relations, or advertising work. He joins the staff of one of the AT&T operating companies, perhaps as a member of the three-person employee magazine staff. His next assignment is in the company news bureau, preparing stories for the hometown newspapers in cities where the company operates—stories about personnel changes and promotions in the local telephone office, about retirements of old-time employees, about additional services or improvements in long-distance dialing, and so on. He is working at the "tool" level, using his journalistic skills. He is not immediately making policy, although he attends staff meetings in the public relations department at which policy is discussed. He is being indoctrinated in company policy and procedures, and he is beginning to understand the total nature of the company operation.

Next the graduate may be sent to the community relations section, where he is more of an "idea" man. He consults with the local office manager in a town in which customer attitude survey studies have shown dissatisfaction with service or misunderstanding of billing procedures and rates. They decide they need better employee communication and arrange group meetings; they check to see if local managers are making effective use of company films that can be shown to civic groups; they plan an institutional advertising series in the local newspaper that will explain the company's costs and needs for revenue if the town is to have the best possible telephone service; and they plan other measures by which the firm can show responsiveness to community attitudes.

Next the young communicator returns to employee relations work, perhaps as editor of a magazine or as an information specialist who develops manuals and programs for the use of supervisory management. He attends employee meetings as a consultant, and suggests ways in which employees can be made more interested in the company's financial problems. He may help run orientation sessions for higher supervisory personnel in which the public relations objectives of the company are explained. Why should a local manager spend time working with the local newspaper editor? How should he go about becoming a news source? Why should the manager belong to the Rotary or Kiwanis Club and spend time "doing good"? The employee relations specialist tries to relate the total public relations program to the personal interests of employees.

There are other assignments. If he has had advertising experience, the public relations man may be placed in charge of institutional advertising. If he has had training in sampling procedures and statistical methods, he may take charge of a customer attitude survey and its interpretation. He may head the audiovisual section and handle films, slides, and pic-

A "highway booby trap" survey is conducted as part of a public service project sponsored by the Insurance Information Institute. Public relations people are involved in many projects of this nature. (Courtesy of Insurance Information Institute, New York.)

tures. He may return to the news bureau as director in charge of the major company stories. He may edit the company's annual report for a time and do shareholder relations work. He may become a policy thinker, preparing speeches for the company president, writing a manual explaining the public relations policies of the company, or working with various executives on long-range planning. He may in time become assistant director of the department. And finally he may become vice-president in charge of public relations, a member of the company's management group. Or, he may move on to the central public relations staff of the parent company, American Telephone and Telegraph. More likely he will remain in a median-level assignment, rounding out a comfortable and satisfying career as a telephone company employee who serves the community and other employees in a specialized staff role demanding technical journalistic skills and policymaking ability.

Another example might be a young woman journalism graduate who is not convinced she wishes to do newspaper work, but who has acquired some understanding of journalistic routines through her classes and a vacation stint on a newspaper. She is more interested in magazine writing and layout and begins as assistant editor of a company employee magazine. A year later she becomes editor. Later she marries and decides to relinquish full-time employment but still work professionally. She finds that the local hospital needs someone to edit its informal staff bulletin, handle the printing of occasional brochures and reports, and represent the hospital with the local media when newsworthy events take place. She is able to advise the hospital administrator on both printing matters and news policy and develops interesting stories of value both to the hospital and to readers.

A third example might be a five-year veteran of metropolitan newspaper work who is offered a position with a major automotive company. She starts in information work, moves on to employee relations, and becomes assistant director for a major branch plant. Three years later she is shifted to Detroit, where she becomes an assistant manager in the company's public relations department. She decides she would prefer to enter a public relations counseling firm, and becomes an account executive for one specializing in automotive clients. At forty she is a vice-president of the firm and receives as much pay as a major executive of the largest metropolitan dailies. In a counseling firm she is freer to carry out her own plans and ideas than in a company staff role. But she also needs to be more daring, for she has less personal security.

These are only three examples of an infinite variety of career possibilities in public relations. It is hardly necessary to point out that the highest salaries are earned by the generalists who reach the executive level and who are capable of analyzing problems, planning programs, and administering large staffs and budgets.

QUALIFICATIONS

There was a time when most public relations people were hired away from the communications media. Many of the top-level executives in public relations today began their careers as journalists. Their progress and development as public relations people was the result of on-the-job training, usually on a trial-and-error basis. That they succeeded is a tribute to their intelligence, their adaptability, and their willingness to keep on learning throughout their careers. (Some news-oriented persons, however, found they could not make this transition and returned to news work.) But this senior generation is fading away. Although many employers still look to the media for public relations recruits, more and more employers are looking to young college graduates to fill beginning jobs in public relations departments.

Education for public relations practice dates from 1923, when Edward L. Bernays taught the first course in public relations at New York University. Since 1945, there has been a substantial proliferation of public relations courses and programs at both the undergraduate and the graduate levels. Dr. Ray Eldon Hiebert, dean of the College of Journalism at the University of Maryland, made a study of public relations education under a 1970 grant from the Foundation for Public Relations Research and Education. He found that, in all, 303 institutions provided some education in public relations. By 1975, according to another foundation-sponsored survey by Dr. Albert Walker of Northern Illinois University, this figure had grown to 320. Of the 144 institutions that responded to Dr. Walker's survey, almost one-half offered an undergraduate sequence or a major program in public relations, and about 18 percent offered graduate sequences or major fields of concentration in public relations. As of 1978, sixteen undergraduate programs in public relations were accredited by the American Council on Education for Journalism, the official accrediting agency.

Along with the graduates of public relations programs, many other graduates of journalism and communications schools, as well as from liberal arts programs, are being employed in beginning public relations jobs—provided they have the quintessential ability to write and speak well. One of the few things that experienced public relations practitioners agree upon is that the primary qualification for anyone wishing to succeed in the field is the ability to articulate: to write well and clearly and with facility, and to express oneself well orally. No one can hope to succeed in public relations without the ability to use words effectively. Words are the basic tool of the public relations practitioner. To be successful, he or she must have an intimate understanding of language.

Additionally, there is need for the ability to empathize with other people, to anticipate and understand their point of view. In the managerial structure, the public relations executive bears the responsibility for estimating how a particular policy or action on the part of management will be greeted by the public or publics affected. More than intuitive ability is necessary here. Whatever inherent abilities public relations practitioners may have in this area of human understanding should be supplemented by background education in the social sciences, particularly sociology and psychology, so that their estimates of public reactions will be more than mere guesses. Of course, in many situations, when the magnitude of the problem justifies such research, public relations practitioners will supplement their own interpretation of the situation, however well-equipped they may be to make an assessment, with formal surveys of public opinion and attitudes.

SALARIES

In 1977 a survey by the *PR Reporter,* a weekly newsletter, showed that the typical public relations practitioner who had reached the executive level was in his mid-forties, had about fourteen years of experience in the public relations field, and earned $27,800 annually. This median salary figure is misleading, however, inasmuch as salaries for these practitioners ranged from $11,350 to $90,000. This part of the survey dealt with public relations vice-presidents or department directors, or the equivalent, in consumer product companies, conglomerates and other industrials, utilities, banks and insurance companies, trade and professional associations, and hospitals.

For the presidents or owners and principals of public relations counseling firms, the survey found the average age to be fifty, the years of experience in public relations twenty-two, and the median salary $39,000, with a salary range of $24,000 to $100,000. Counseling firms tend to pay better than do other employers of public relations practitioners. One must take into account, however, that counseling firms offer less stability in employment and that frequently the fringe benefits for people in the counseling business are less extensive than in other fields.

Obviously, the new college graduate is not going into a beginning public relations job at these salary levels. In 1977, he or she was more likely to be offered between $9,400 and $14,000 depending upon the locale and the type of job. Salaries are likely to be higher in large cities such as New York, Washington, Chicago, and Los Angeles, and lower in smaller cities. A job with a profit-making corporation, an industry association, or a counseling firm is likely to pay more than a job with a nonprofit educational institution, a government agency, a hospital, or a charitable institution. Nevertheless, the kind of rounded experience that one gains in some of these lower-paying jobs can be valuable later.

PROFESSIONALISM IN PUBLIC RELATIONS

Among public relations practitioners there are considerable differences of opinion as to whether public relations is simply a craft or a developing profession. Certainly, at its present level, public relations does not qualify as a profession in the same sense that medicine and the law are considered to be professions. Public relations does not have prescribed standards of educational preparation, a mandatory internship, or barriers to admission to the field.

On the other hand, many persons in the field believe the practice can become a profession and are working toward that end. Much of this effort has been conducted through the Public Relations Society of America, which has more than 8000 members. To become an accredited member of the society, a man or woman must have at least five years experience in public relations practice or teaching, must have two sponsors who will testify as to integrity and ability, and must pass written and oral examinations. The PRSA accreditation program, instituted in 1965, has been a major step toward professionalizing the field. To be an associate member of PRSA, one need have only one year's experience in the field. For students who have just earned their college degrees and who have been members of the Public Relations Student Society of America, there is a preassociate form of membership in PRSA. The student organization, sponsored by PRSA, has chapters in more than seventy colleges and universities.

Additionally, both PRSA and the public relations division of the Association for Education in Journalism have worked to improve and standardize the curricula for programs of public relations studies at the bachelor's and master's levels. The society has developed a code of professional standards for the practice of public relations. Although parts of the code are phrased in general terms, such as requiring public relations practitioners to adhere to generally accepted standards of accuracy, truth, and good taste, other clauses and interpretive supplements deal with specifics. For example, a PRSA member cannot represent conflicting or competing interests without the express consent of both parties, nor can he or she reveal the confidences of present or former clients or employers.

The Foundation for Public Relations Research and Education, established in 1956 with the support of the society but now independent, seeks to advance professionalism through grants for research studies, publications, and sponsorship of a quarterly, the *Public Relations Review*. Under a grant from the foundation, Morton J. Simon, a lawyer who specializes in the law as it affects public relations and advertising, has published a book entitled *Public Relations Law*. It correlates for the reference of the public relations practitioner all aspects of the general laws, as well as regulations of the Securities and Exchange Commission and other government agencies, that affect the conduct of public relations practice. It is an example of the growing body of specialized knowledge pertaining to public relations practice.

Thus, although public relations still suffers some stigma as a result of the occasional misuse of the term, it has come a long way from the time when the public relations practitioner was scorned by his colleagues in journalism as a "publicity hound" or a "flack." Nevertheless, public relations still has a long way to go before it achieves the distinction of becoming a genuine profession. Today, at the very least, it is an essential link in the nation's mass communications network.

While public relations practice originated in the United States, it has spread to many other countries of the free world. The art, or profession, is well developed in the Western European countries, and it is growing rapidly in Latin America, Africa, the Near East, and the Far East.

The International Public Relations Association, an individual membership society for public relations professionals with international interests, was organized in 1955. IPRA now has more than 400 members in about 50 nations. Every third year it sponsors a World Congress of Public Relations, which attracts more than a thousand persons.

This worldwide interest in the developing public relations profession is an encouraging sign for the future. The burgeoning of public relations, especially in countries where people can speak freely, is an encouraging indication of a bright future for all who excel in the practice.

CHAPTER 19

MASS COMMUNICATIONS RESEARCH

THE NEED FOR RESEARCH

The enormous growth of the various forms of mass communication in the twentieth century has resulted in an increasing need for better knowledge of the processes and effects of mass communication. The complex mass media system has produced a need for research not only among practicing communicators, but also among policymakers, consumers, and various social groups. Many of the problems and criticisms discussed in Part II, for example, have led to research questions. Consequently, a core of specially trained research men and women has risen to search for and supply this knowledge.

Much of the mass communication research conducted today attempts to answer the questions of broadcasters, advertising specialists, and other communicators. The magazine or newspaper editor, for example, needs to know such things as these: How many persons read my publication? (Typically, each copy has several readers so the total audience may be something quite different from the total circulation.) What kinds of persons read my publication? (The New York *Times,* for example, is aimed at a different audience from that of the *Daily News;* the audience of *True Story* is almost completely different from that of *Boys' Life.*) How am I doing as an editor? Am I printing the kinds of things my audience wants to read about? Are my stories easy to read or hard to read? How can I improve the content of my publication? How can I improve the presentation of this content in terms of layout and typography?

Time was when an editor could know many of these things pretty well by personal contact with the people in the community or area. By informal means, through experience, the editor developed a rough idea of the composition of the audience and how well the publication was liked. This unsystematic, informal "intuitive" method no longer is adequate for the modern communicator for several reasons:

1. *The increasing number of communications media.* In the present-day community, the average person has access to many media—local and out-of-town newspapers, a number of television and radio stations, and hundreds of magazines, books, and films.

2. *Increasing competition among the media for the attention of the public.* Since no individual has enough time to read or listen to all the

media, or even to pay attention to all the output of just one medium, this means a small fraction of the available output will be selected, and the rest ignored. This leads to intense competition among the different media to capture as much of the public's time and attention as possible—obviously, the newspaper or magazine or station that succeeds in satisfying the needs of the public, whose messages are interesting and easy to absorb, will get a good share of public attention. Those that do not succeed in doing this will eventually fall by the wayside.

3. *The increasing number of people in the audience.* An editor or broadcaster has from several thousand to several million readers, viewers, or listeners, and the tendency is constantly toward larger audiences. No communicator can possibly have personal contact with everyone in the audience and knowledge of all their varying needs, likes, dislikes, and opinions.

4. *The changing tastes of the public.* People are becoming better educated and more sophisticated; they travel more, know more about the rest of the world, and are constantly developing broader interests through exposure to more communications from outside their immediate environment. Any communicator's audience is in a constant state of turnover and interest change. Decisions cannot be based on what was known to be true ten years or five years or even one year ago. It is a fickle public in the sense that it is constantly changing in taste and mood.

These are all good reasons why the effective communicator—whether advertising copywriter, editor, or broadcaster—can no longer rely on hunches and intuition alone to capture and hold the attention of the public. As Harry Henry says in *Motivation Research:* "There are examples, of course, of 'hunch-merchants' who hit on successful ideas with enormous success, and finish up as classic case histories. But no case histories are written up of the 99 equally self-confident but not so lucky venturers whose only spell of glory is in a brief trip to the bankruptcy courts."

In the face of all these changing requirements, then, just how do modern mass communicators get the precise information they need to make their media successful? They turn to communications research, a specialty that has grown up in the past two decades, to help answer some of the questions they do not have the time or training to answer for themselves. The communications researcher is just one member of the team of writers, editors, artists, advertising persons, and others working together to help a medium do its job, which is to transmit information, opinion, and entertainment to a mass public. Or again, the researcher may be a scholar in a university setting whose main objective is that of adding to our general knowledge of the communication process.

Modern communicators also face criticism and questions about their role in society. For example, do TV commercials in children's programs mislead or take advantage of young viewers? Is there any relationship between television programing and violent behavior? Do news media distort the news? Such questions often lead to research that is as important as that describing the changing tastes of the public. Thus, although the media need research telling them how to compete with one another and how to serve their audiences, they also need answers to broader questions about their role in modern society. Much research of this type is being conducted in schools of journalism and mass communications.

WHAT IS COMMUNICATIONS RESEARCH?

A broad definition of research is simply "careful investigation" or a diligent inquiry into any subject. This broad term would include almost any kind of study—the literary scholar who reads through all of Shakespeare's works, the biographer who finds out all he can about a famous man, or the historian who compiles a history of American newspapers.

Mass communications research, however, has taken on a somewhat more specialized meaning. First of all, it is usually (though not always) considered *behavioral* research—the study of human beings (rather than inanimate or nonhuman objects). It is a branch of the behavioral sciences such as psychology, sociology, and anthropology.

Thus we see it is also *interdisciplinary* research. That is, it borrows the tools and knowledge of various other fields of study that will help in the understanding of mass communications problems. It does not confine itself to any particular point of view or theory or subject matter. It may borrow from linguistics, general semantics, philosophy, economics, or any other discipline that might help communications effectiveness.

It is *scientific* research, since it uses scientific methodology in solving communications problems. As in any science, its aim is to explain, predict, and control. In achieving this end, its methods must be objective (as opposed to subjective) and systematic (as opposed to unsystematic). Although most mass communications research is done on specific problems, the goal—as in any scientific field—is to formulate general principles and theories that can bring about more effective communication. Being scientific, it is, of course, *quantitative* research. Random sampling methods, the laws of probability, and mathematical statistical techniques all help to make more precise and meaningful the findings from any particular investigation.

It is generally *primary* research rather than secondary. That is, the mass communications researcher customarily gathers new and original information rather than relying on printed source material. This is not always the case, however, since one may, for example, have to consult year-by-year statistical figures gathered in the past by other researchers in order to spot a trend over a period of time.

And, of course, the subject matter of communications research is communication. More specifically, it is concerned with mass communications, the communications behavior of large numbers of people, particularly those who make up the audiences for the different media. But other groups can be studied, too, of course—newspaper reporters, news sources, magazine editors, or public relations specialists, for example. In order to understand the behavior of groups, however, it is usually necessary first to understand individual behavior.

To summarize the definition of mass communications research: It is generally the scientific study of the mass communications behavior of human beings, usually in current situations requiring the gathering of primary quantitative information. It also includes the study of the communicators, their media, and the content of their message.

This is not the only definition that might be legitimately applied. It leaves out other kinds of research done in the field of journalism and mass communications (historical, literary, biographical, legal, economic, international aspects), which are discussed in Chapter 20 on journalism teaching; editorial research of the "fact-checking" variety; and the creative synthesizing of ideas and research findings. It also includes some topics that might be claimed by other disciplines. It is, however, a reasonably comprehensive definition of the specialized type of mass communications research that has grown up in recent decades.

AREAS OF COMMUNICATION RESEARCH

The volume of communication research has grown in recent years as an increasing number of scholars have been attracted to the subject. Two trends have accompanied that growth. The breadth of communication research has grown as scholars with varying interests have delved into different areas—those of political communication, consumer interests, and media economics, for example. And the depth of communication research has increased as scholars taking different avenues have tended to specialize within one area or another. Consequently, communication research could be divided in a number of ways. One approach is to categorize research within the four aspects of the communication process described in Chapter 1: the communicator, the message, the channel, and the audience. Extensive research has been done in each area.

Communicator Research

One way to improve communication is to find out what kinds of people are best suited for the job and what factors affect communicator performance. We need to know the essential characteristics of good reporters, editors, and advertising people, among others, so that the proper training may be offered to future professionals. Even the most professional communicator, however, may be unaware of some of the factors affecting performance. In one study it was found that stories resulting from assignments by editors were more accurate than those originated by the reporter or stemming from coverage of general meetings. Another study disclosed that news personnel with "supportive images" (more establishment-oriented than others) reported so-called good news more accurately than bad news, whereas those with critical images of society did a more accurate job on bad news. Communicators increasingly are using sophisticated tools such as the computer to analyze complex problems. How will journalists adjust to the new demands placed upon them? How will reporters perform with the new technologies? These are questions for communicator research studies.

Message Research

The effects of different forms of the same message may be compared through variations in style, length, degree of difficulty, and the like, with attention paid to comprehensibility, interest, and attention value. We often vary our personal conversations as to complexity and word usage in terms of some determination of the sophistication of the intended receiver. With scientific content analysis we can easily determine the relative degree of difficulty of any message, and we can make inferences about the intent of the communicator as well.

Channel Research

The channel through which a message is transmitted is closely related to the effectiveness of the message. This is due in part to the differing characteristics of the various media, which perform somewhat differently the functions of informing, interpreting, entertaining, and selling. By their character, content, style, and geographic coverage, media, to a great extent, are able to select their desired audiences. Advertisers are especially interested in determining which media can best deliver their messages and in knowing something about the people who comprise the potential audience of a medium. And in face-to-face communication, we often use facial expressions—a smile, for example—to much greater advantage than a flow of pleasant words.

Audience Research

The bulk of communication research ultimately is concerned with mass media audiences. Communicators need to know the behavior, interests, tastes, attitudes, and opinions of the people whom they seek to reach. Advertisers must know the number and description of people in a medium's audience so they may reach the right kind of person for their products. For example, a baby food manufacturer may want to learn which of two magazines with equal circulations has the larger number of young married women. Publishers and editors require audience information so they may select editorial content that fits their readers' needs. The reading interests of young newspaper readers are quite different from those of older folk. More recently, researchers have gone beyond simply describing the audiences of mass media. In some studies, researchers are seeking to determine the motivations for media use; in others, the goal is to determine the gratifications people derive from using the media. Still other scholars are focusing on children of different ages, trying to learn how children understand what they see and hear on television. Specialists in political communication are examining how people use the media to follow candidates and their campaigns. One strain of research focuses on the relationship between the media's inventories of campaign issues and the personal lists of readers and viewers.

The overall goal is to find out how mass communications affects audiences, just as we individuals need to know how our words affect other individuals with whom we communicate. The object of mass communications is to affect human behavior and attitudes. The object of communications research is to find out how and to what degree human behavior and attitudes are affected by mass communications.

COMMUNICATIONS RESEARCH METHODS

Communications research uses the same basic methods as other branches of the behavioral sciences. And, depending on the needs of the researcher, any of the following methods may be applied to practically any problem.

In *survey research* the scientific sample is studied to gather demographic information or sociological facts as well as psychological information—opinions and attitudes. As opposed to the status survey, which produces an inventory of facts, survey research gathers both factual information and the opinions of subjects. Thus, the researcher is able to talk about the relationships among variables—for example, the relationship between educational level and media usage, or between sex and opinion concerning a particular political candidate.

A similar method, but one in which independent and dependent variables are related and hypotheses tested, is the *field study*. Whereas in a third method, the *field experiment,* the independent variable is introduced by the researcher in an environment in which considerable control of extraneous variables is possible, the field study is ex post facto. In both the field study and field experiment an attempt is made to establish causal relationships between independent and dependent variables. The most closely controlled method of study of causal relationships is the *laboratory experiment,* in which all except the independent variable to be studied are eliminated.

The survey is frequently used to determine relationships between demographics and mass communications behavior, as in determining the relationships of sex and age to television program viewing. An example of a field study is a case in which it is hypothesized that the grade performance of school children has a stronger and more consistent relationship to the extent of usage and comprehension of mass communications than do other variables in the school and home environment. In a field experiment, one might designate two groups or communities that are similar in relevant characteristics and introduce variables, such as two forms of advertising of the same new product, to determine which form of advertising is more conducive to the purchase of the new product. Both the field study and the field experiment are difficult to control because variables other than those studied may affect the measured or dependent variable without the researcher's being able to know what really happened.

The laboratory experiment provides the best opportunity for control of variables since the researcher can be practically certain that the causal variable introduced actually brings about the measured effect. For example, using two equivalent or matched groups, the researcher might present a message in oral form to one group and in written form to the other. If a standard test then demonstrates that comprehension was consistently higher for the oral message group than for the written message group, one could be reasonably certain that the oral message was more easily understood by people like those in the two groups.

EXAMPLES OF COMMUNICATIONS RESEARCH

Research is used by every kind of communicator—newspaper and magazine editors and writers, television and radio personnel, advertising and public relations experts, government information specialists, book publishers, and film producers. Some research has immediate utility in that it can be applied by changing the content or layout. In a sense this can be called *feedback* research, since it is one way in which members of the audience may inform the editor or broadcaster what they like or dislike. In readership studies subscribers tell what they prefer to read, in graphics research readers disclose what types of displays they find most attractive, in advertising research readers tell which ads are most effective, in public opinion research the public relates how it feels about a medium, and in content analysis the communicator learns how much print space or broadcast time is being devoted to various kinds of stories. Other research, such as that dealing with the processes and effects of mass communication, also provides important information for communicators. While it may have less immediate application, it is of great concern to policymakers, critics, social groups, and other consumers.

Readership Studies
Sometimes called "reader traffic" studies, these tell the editor how many and what kinds of people have read each item in a publication. For example, story A had 40 percent readership whereas story B had 10 percent, picture A had 37 percent readership whereas picture B had 12 percent. Such information, gathered by trained personnel in personal interviews with representative samples of readers, provides a check on editorial judgment. It is useful to the editor in following trends of audience interest, in evaluating effects of typographical makeup and display of stories on readership, in deciding which of several syndicated features should be retained or dropped, and so on. Effectiveness of various types of advertising also can be studied.

Similar research is conducted on television and radio programs. The various rating services can determine how many sets were tuned in to each of a number of programs, how many people were listening to each set, and what kinds of people they were. One TV-radio research service gets its information from an electronic device permanently attached to the television or radio sets of a sample of households. Another rating service makes personal telephone calls to homes while programs are on the air. Another method is to have listeners keep diaries.

Graphics Research

Typography, layout, and makeup fall within the area generally called graphics by the print media. By experimentation with different methods of presentation, the researcher can tell the editor the most effective means of presentation of a given item. A book publisher or magazine or newspaper editor may choose to test, say, audience preference for one kind of typeface as compared with another; the use of one large illustration instead of several smaller pictures; or the effectiveness of a news item published in an area two columns wide and 5 inches deep, as contrasted with the same item set in one column 10 inches deep. Much research has been done on the legibility of typefaces and esthetic preferences for them.

Advertising people, too, are strongly interested in graphics research. Which ad gets across the most information—an ad with a big picture and a little text, or a little picture and a lot of text? Such research may be done by split runs in the publication, so that the alternatives are presented to two different samples of readers whose reactions then can be compared after a readership survey, or by experimentation with a relatively small group of persons before publication.

Graphics research has its parallel in the broadcasting media. Research can tell whether 3 minutes of commercial time are most effective at the beginning of a program, at the end, or spread through it. Or it can tell whether, on a radio newscast, a summary of headlines at the start of the program will increase interest in the news items that follow.

Advertising Research

The various media and almost all advertising agencies conduct advertising research to help them in their job of persuading people to buy. *Market* research has been carried on since the start of the century and was the forerunner of other public opinion research. It includes consumer surveys on potential markets for new products, dealer studies, customer attitude surveys, and studies of effectiveness of brand names and package designs. Media use by advertisers is determined in part by market research results, and various media seek to point out their usefulness by undertaking market research studies for particular advertisers' products. *Copy* research includes analysis of advertisement readership studies, pretesting of advertisements, evaluation of printed advertisement campaign effectiveness, and graphics. In broadcasting, commercials and programs may be tried out on small samples of listeners by means of response recording devices. The same is true of films.

Public Opinion Research

All communicators are interested in knowing the state of public opinion about themselves or their medium. Publishers want to know how the public feels about their newspapers, magazines, or books. Broadcasters and film producers are equally sensitive to public approval. Public relations and advertising specialists want to know if they have succeeded in creating a favorable image for their companies or products in the public mind. Surveys of attitudes held by specific customer groups, and by the public generally, give them some answers.

Communicators are interested in public opinion from an additional viewpoint—that is, public attitudes toward social and economic issues, government officials and their policies, and important events. The familiar national polls conducted by George Gallup, Elmo Roper, and others offer a check on prevailing opinion. And since public opinion is news in itself, the polls are sold to many newspapers; in addition, some newspapers conduct their own polls and report the outcomes as news stories. Large companies subscribe to opinion survey services as a part of their public relations programs. Government also uses public opinion research—the United States Information Agency has a survey research division whose sole function is to measure public opinion toward the United States in other countries and the effects of our various foreign information programs, including the Voice of America. Politicians are increasingly using public opinion surveys to gauge campaign progress and important issues.

Content Analysis

Much can be learned about a publication merely by studying its contents. (This falls somewhat outside the definition of behavioral research.) Content analysis provides a clue to an editor's or writer's intentions and to the kind of audience a publication or broadcast attracts. Combined with readership studies, it gives clues to what people want to read about. This form of research can be especially valuable when more precise kinds of research are inappropriate or unavailable. For example, a content analysis of German wartime broadcasts gave the Allies useful clues to the enemy's war strategy. An analysis of Soviet cold war propaganda helped the U.S. Information Agency in the formulation of its own propaganda, since it revealed the themes that were currently being stressed and enabled us to combat them.

Processes and Effects Research

What are the effects of mass communication? For many years this question directed the work of scholars interested in mass media processes. The model of communication outlined in Chapter 1 provided the elements, with arrows indicating that the major flow is from communicator to message to audience. More recently researchers have noted that the model is too simple: TV viewers and newspaper readers are not just passive agents reacting to what they see and read. As a consequence, research projects have sought to determine what people seek in the media, what happens when they use them, and what they get out of them. The more complex perspectives recognize that people have varying interests, biases, and needs which they "take with them" to the media. At the same time, other researchers have chosen to work with families, groups, and communities rather than with individuals. The following are a few examples of current trends in mass communication research.

1. *Community media systems.* One strain of research has focused on the role of the mass media in communities. Editors, broadcasters, and other communicators act as "gatekeepers," deciding what information community residents will receive about various issues. Are there differences in the types of information conveyed by communicators in small as contrasted with large communities? One study suggests that editors in smaller, more homogeneous communities tend to avoid controversial issues and concentrate on more positive, socially supportive information. Editors in larger communities, which have organized interest groups and more mechanisms for handling disputes, distribute more conflict information and are more likely to stress opinion leadership.

2. *Information diffusion.* People are provided with an abundance of information by the mass media, and technologies in the not too distant future will accelerate this "information explosion." In coping with this barrage, people must be selective. They learn things from the mass media, but not necessarily the same things nor the same amount. For example, those who use more of the print media—newspapers, magazines, and books—tend to be more knowledgeable than those who rely mainly on radio and television for their information.

3. *Media socialization.* Adults do not suddenly appear with full-blown reading, viewing, and listening habits. They acquire these habits, among others, through many years and under the influence of many

factors. One approach to understanding the development of communication behavior is called socialization research. Scholars try to specify the social origins and processes by which people learn and maintain such things as reading and viewing habits. In a sense they are turning around the question of effects and asking what leads to use of the mass media. Researchers taking this perspective have found varying TV viewing patterns among children from different family environments. In families in which a child is encouraged to explore new ideas and to express them openly, children spend far less time with TV and pay more attention to news and public affairs programs when they do watch. By contrast, in families placing greater emphasis on obedience and social harmony, children spend the most time with TV of any group and their interest is concentrated on entertainment rather than on news and public affairs programs.

4. *Agenda-setting Function.* For years researchers have been interested in the relationship between media use and attitude change. More recently, studies have focused on information and the new cognitions acquired from the media. An example of this trend is the notion of an agenda-setting function of the press. The view is that the media often may not be successful in telling people what to think, but they have considerable success in telling people what to think about. Studies here, for example, look at the relationship between the agenda of political campaign issues set by the media and the personal agendas of the audience.

5. *Children and television.* Parents, broadcasters, government regulators, and others have been concerned with violence shown on television. This has led to a large number of studies trying to determine whether there is any relationship between watching TV violence and real acts of violence. Do children use the violent characters shown on TV as models for their own behavior? How do children understand the violence they view on the TV screen? These are among the questions researchers are asking. Obviously small children have more limited capacities than adults for understanding the world around them. For example, do children under the age of seven have difficulty relating the different parts of a plot sequence? This has implications for their TV viewing, since they may be unable to connect the punishment accorded a TV murderer with the criminal act or the motive.

6. *Motives, uses, and gratifications.* As noted earlier, researchers are delving into the motives people have for using the mass media, and are

trying to identify the uses and gratifications associated with newspaper reading, TV viewing, and the like. In one study, readers relied on the newspaper for help in deciding how to vote in a nonpartisan election. In another study, people who had switched to a four-day work week started watching TV programs that had direct application to activities planned for expanded weekends. Other researchers are examining the different things people seek in the media—specific information, a chance to relax, favorite programs, and so on.

The preceding examples demonstrate the range of communication research today. Each area has implications for communicators. For example, editors may want to rethink their coverage of political candidates if their readers' "issue agendas" are not closely linked with a newspaper's campaign coverage. Media consumers also need to understand how communication works, and much of the research discussed helps to provide that information.

One of the most satisfying aspects of communications research is in doing original, imaginative thinking and investigation. Creative researchers try to think of different ways to do a particular communications job and then test the alternatives to see which is the most effective. They critically analyze the long-standing traditions and accepted practices of the media and then test these tricks of the trade to see if they are really the most effective ways to communicate. They devise new and original research techniques and methods to solve particular problems. They keep abreast of developments in related disciplines such as psychology and sociology, applying the findings and theories from those fields to communications problems. Creative communications researchers also make valuable contributions to theory and practice in those related disciplines. They both borrow from and contribute to other areas of knowledge.

A glance through a few issues of such journals as the *Journalism Quarterly,* the *Journal of Communication,* and *Public Opinion Quarterly* will reveal in more detail some of the directions that mass communications research now takes. Although some of the questions or problems explored do not differ greatly from those explored thirty years ago, the emphasis now is on the use of more scientific methods of studying those questions. Earlier expressions of subjective opinion by communications experts are being subjected to scientific scrutiny and the "folklore" of the media are being tested.

OPPORTUNITIES IN RESEARCH

Research is being conducted in every kind of communications and business enterprise today. All the media are engaged in research to some degree: newspapers, magazines, radio, television, publishing houses, film producers. So are the supporting agencies: press associations, advertising agencies, public relations films, specialized commercial research firms. So are manufacturers of consumer and industrial products, retail and wholesale business firms, the federal government, and colleges and universities.

Surveys have shown that four out of every five United States companies have a department (one person or more) engaged in market research, which almost always includes some form of communications or opinion research in its activities. Even among the smaller firms—those with sales under $5 million annually—three out of every five have a research department. Advertising agencies are the most avid users of research; more than 90 percent of all United States agencies have a research department. And the large publishing and broadcasting organizations employ researchers.

Naturally, the larger the firm, the more likely it is to have a research department. However, both it and the smaller firm frequently turn to commercial research firms, whose sole business it is to conduct research for outside clients. Most medium and large cities in the country today have at least one commercial research firm, and the number of such firms is increasing yearly. Many of these firms serve clients on a national basis, and a few conduct research in foreign countries. Some of the largest are the Opinion Research Corporation of Princeton, New Jersey; International Research Associates and Alfred Politz Research of New York City; A. C. Nielsen Company in Chicago; and Field Research on the west coast.

Advertising agencies tend to have larger research staffs than other kinds of businesses; the largest agencies employ an average of fifty persons in their research departments. Large publishing and broadcasting firms average four research employees, but a few have departments more the size of those in the agencies.

How is the pay for the worker in communications research? Because of the extensive amount of advanced training and specialized knowledge required, researchers are well paid compared with other mass communications personnel. The holder of a master's degree who has specialized in research may expect a starting salary of $10,000 to $15,000 a year. The more advanced student in communications research—who has completed most or all of his or her doctoral training—can initially command $15,000 to $18,000 a year. These figures vary, of course, with location and size of firm. With experience, communications research specialists rise in salary to $25,000 or higher. Research analysts exceed the $10,000 level. Women are frequently employed in analyst positions and increasingly in higher ones.

Opportunities for advancement in mass communications research are good because of the expansion taking place in the field. Not only can research be a rewarding and satisfying vocation in itself, but it also serves as a steppingstone to other kinds of work, both in the creative and business aspects of communications. One example is Dr. Frank Stanton, who started in research and became head of the Columbia Broadcasting System. Two others are A. Edward Miller, who became publisher of *McCall's,* and Marion Harper, Jr., who became head of McCann-Erickson advertising agency.

Another excellent opportunity for researchers exists in schools of journalism and mass communications. More and more universities are adding communications researchers to their staffs, both to do research and to teach and train students in the skills involved. In addition, such schools often contract to do research for the media or for civic and government agencies. A doctoral degree is generally considered a requirement for such a faculty position.

TRAINING FOR RESEARCH POSITIONS

Until just after World War II, most scientifically trained researchers on mass communications problems came from psychology and sociology. The importance of research as a specialty has since led some of the nation's leading schools of journalism and mass communications to set up graduate programs in quantitative scientific research methods.

In some of these schools, mass communications research is offered as just one of several communications fields graduate students may elect in their courses of study; in others, the entire graduate program is devoted to courses in behavioral research theory and methodology, with a minimum of emphasis on the "communications" aspect. In almost all, however, the research specialization requires a sampling of appropriate courses drawn from several different disciplines and heavy emphasis on statistics and scientific method courses.

A typical graduate program calls for a major in mass communications or journalism with a minor in psychology, sociology, or statistics. Various other departments—anthropology, philosophy, economics, political science, speech communication, marketing, to name a few—may also figure in the program to a lesser extent, depending on the individual interests of the student. Some individuals prefer to major in social psychology or sociology and minor in communications or journalism.

It is generally considered desirable—though not necessary—for graduate students in communications research to have professional experience in one or more of the mass media. The first wave of communications research Ph.D.s—those receiving degrees in the 1950s—almost without exception had practical journalism experience as newspaper reporters and editors, radio news personnel, and so on. The value of a practical journalism background lies in the greater awareness of crucial communications problems, a better knowledge of the questionable assumptions of the trade, and a generally more critical perspective based on an understanding of journalistic processes and folkways.

It should be emphasized, however, that prior journalistic experience is not a requirement, but merely helpful for the person interested in mass communications research. He or she can acquire knowledge of the media and of journalistic techniques in journalism courses and in post-degree professional work. It should be noted, too, that the only distinction between the graduate program of a mass communications researcher and that of the less specialized behavioral scientist is the former's preoccupation with mass communications as the subject matter of the research; in practice, the student may engage in almost any kind of social research.

CHAPTER 20
MASS COMMUNICATIONS EDUCATION

THE ROLE OF EDUCATION

Informing and enlightening the public is a difficult task. Few can succeed as practitioners in mass communications without mastering the principles and practices of broad areas of knowledge that comprise the basic ingredients of a college education. Society has become so complex, its specialties so numerous, and its varying relationships so involved that only a person with a sure intelligence and a comprehension of many facets of human activity can understand the meaning of events. And without understanding, any attempt at reporting or interpreting is not only superficial but actually dangerous to the security of a democratic nation.

It is true that the exceptional individual can acquire a broad education without entering the portals of an institution of higher learning. A number of men and women with limited academic backgrounds are exerting genuine leadership in the mass media offices of the country today. But for most of us the only certain path to acquiring knowledge about our world lies in formal courses of instruction in the social sciences, the natural sciences, and the humanities. Here we discover the precise methodology of the researcher and the scientist and the skills of the writer or artist; we have guided access to the accumulated wisdom of the ages; we learn what men and women have considered to be the good, the true, and the beautiful; and we study the behavior of human beings, both as individuals and in their relationships with others.

Acquiring such a basic education has special importance to future communicators. For one thing, they are exposed to areas of thought and criticism that give them opportunities to become cultured persons of discrimination and taste in their own right. From these experiences they should be able to acquire a sound working knowledge of society and a sensitivity to its many problems that will enable them to exercise the type of forthright citizenship so essential in our democracy. If their exposure to the processes of education has been productive, they will be enabled, in the words of Newman, "to see things as they are, to go right to the point, to disentangle a skein of thought, to detect what is sophistical, and to discard what is irrelevant."

Education, however, assumes an even greater importance to future communicators: almost every bit of knowledge and every insight that they acquire in college, from a study of the love life of the oyster to

Thorstein Veblen's views on "conspicuous consumption," eventually seem to become grist for the mill as they report and interpret the kaleidoscopic nature of life in the most practical of working assignments.

CHANNELS OF EDUCATION
FOR MASS COMMUNICATIONS

Men and women desiring to equip themselves for careers in mass communications may follow several avenues in reaching their goal. The most common method is to enroll in a school or department of journalism or communications offering a four-year program leading to a degree in journalism. Approximately 300 colleges and universities in the United States provide such courses of study. Some of these institutions have provided separate administrative units (colleges, schools, divisions) for their journalism or communications instruction. The majority have located the school or department of journalism or communications within the liberal arts college. In either case, students typically take no more than 25 to 30 percent of their course work in journalism or communications; the remainder is spread through the social sciences, humanities, and natural sciences, as well as physical education or military fields, in accordance with the university's requirements for both breadth and depth of study in the various areas of learning. In effect, students elect a major specialization in professional studies that give them instruction in basic communication skills and in social science-oriented courses that relate journalism and communications to society. They do this just as other students elect a major concentration in geology, physics, political science, or English—and they are no more "specialized" in one subject than are these others.

Many practitioners in mass communications are college graduates who have pursued noncommunications majors in liberal arts institutions. Some employers among the mass media seek out such students, in the belief that their background in general liberal arts study best equips them for full development within their organizations. It seems more reasonable, however, that the men and women who acquired both professional and general liberal arts education while enrolled in schools and departments of journalism, television-radio, speech, or communications would be better prepared for professional work and would be employed more readily. This fact has been corroborated by numerous surveys.

Journalism educators know about this increasing reliance by newspapers upon their graduates through the operations of their placement offices. The placement service is one of the most important functions of a journalism school as far as the prospective graduate is concerned. Employers rely on the schools to recommend applicants for both beginning and advanced positions and make calls directly to the journalism offices rather than to the college's general placement service. A large journalism or communications school will receive several hundred requests each year from newspapers, press associations, television and radio stations, magazines, advertising agencies, major industrial companies seeking advertising and public relations personnel, and others wishing to employ graduates with communications skills.

Many students are introduced to the mass communications field through study at the more than 500 four-year institutions in the United States that offer some journalism courses but not a full major. High schools and junior colleges provide the beginning courses for thousands of other students. Some work on campus newspaper, yearbook, and television or radio staffs, or find part-time employment with local newspapers and broadcast stations while still in school. Many eventually find jobs in communications and related fields.

Students desiring careers in advertising and communications management frequently find the courses of study they want under the professional and liberal arts listings of schools and departments of journalism, speech, radio-television, and communications. Much of the background they need is offered through schools of business. In many universities a cooperative arrangement exists so that, regardless of the type of degree sought, such students obtain their specialized courses in both business and communications areas. The business major must become familiar with the peculiar problems and structure of the branch of the communications industry he proposes to enter; the communications major must learn principles of sound business practice.

With the tremendous expansion of industry since World War II, public relations has risen to prominence as a career sought by thousands. Most schools and departments of journalism offer one or two orientation courses in combination with preparation in basic journalistic training; they and those schools with more fully developed curriculums suggest programs emphasizing electives in economics, psychology, sociology, and other social sciences, and in business areas. Few schools of business offer separate courses in public relations, although they incorporate course units emphasizing the theory and overall knowledge of public relations essential to successful management. Journalism school courses seek to offer the student both this background and the instruction necessary for becoming an actual practitioner in public relations.

In the broadcast area, students desiring careers in performance and production generally concentrate on courses in speech and radio-television. Those desiring to become radio and television newscasters and writers combine journalism, speech, and radio-television courses. Those headed for sales, promotion, public relations, and management positions may choose to major in business with allied instruction in journalism and radio-television. Those entering educational broadcasting frequently obtain teaching certificates while also acquiring a background in radio-television and speech. Television production students likely will take as much work in theater and dramatic literature as possible. The possible variations in these emphases are almost endless, depending on the students' objectives. Common to all these career paths, however, is a strong background in the liberal arts. The interlocking nature of broadcast instruction is a factor in the recent development of schools or colleges of communications, linking speech, radio-television, film, advertising, public relations, and journalism.

Courses in the film are offered by more than 800 radio and television, speech communication, journalism, theater arts, and education schools and departments. They range from a single film appreciation course in some institutions to multiple courses in production, history, and esthetics leading to a film major in others. Among institutions emphasizing study in the film are Southern California, University of California at Berkeley, Boston, Indiana, Columbia, New York, Northwestern, Michigan State, Kansas, Texas, and San Francisco State University.

Combination programs have been developed at many universities to enable the student interested in a career as a communications specialist in such areas as agriculture, home economics, medicine, or science to obtain basic proficiency through courses made available in two or more departments, schools, or colleges.

Students often supplement classroom and laboratory instruction with part-time jobs on campus and with nearby commercial media and by accepting internships, normally ten-week to three-month summer stints, with media, government agencies, business firms, and institutions. Upon permanent employment they often are placed in training programs.

In an effort to identify talent at institutions with no journalism programs, the Newspaper Fund, Inc., of Dow Jones and Company since 1960 has awarded more than $500,000 in intern scholarships to 1140 students. Approximately 520 students, mainly enrolled in journalism schools and departments, have received grants totaling more than $300,000 to participate in the Fund's newspaper editing program.

Journalism, a comparative fledgling among university disciplines, gained its foothold on college campuses early in this century. Formal education for journalism was inevitable in the face of the steadily increasing complexities of the twentieth century, which demanded better-trained personnel on American newspaper staffs. None other than General Robert E. Lee first proposed a special college education for printer-editors. That was in 1869, when the general was president of Washington College, now Washington and Lee University, in Virginia. Little came of his proposal. Other early attention was given to printing instruction, such as that beginning at Kansas State College in 1873.

In 1904 the first four-year curriculum for journalism students was organized at the University of Illinois, and journalism instruction began the same year at the University of Wisconsin. Four years later the first separate school of journalism was founded at the University of Missouri by an experienced journalist, Dean Walter Williams. In 1912 the Columbia University School of Journalism, endowed with $2 million from Joseph Pulitzer, opened its doors. By that year more than thirty colleges and universities were offering courses in journalism.

The first courses were largely vocational in nature as pioneer teachers in the field endeavored to prepare college students for careers on newspapers, then the primary medium of mass communication. During the 1920s, however, emphasis on technique lessened and curriculums began to reflect an increasing interest in the social, ethical, and cultural aspects of journalism. Dr. Willard G. Bleyer, director of the University of Wisconsin School of Journalism until his death in 1935, is credited with leading the movement away from a preoccupation with techniques. Also influential was exposure to methods of teaching the social sciences that journalism instructors were receiving in graduate programs. Courses in the history and the ethics of journalism became popular, and they were followed by studies of the newspaper as a social institution, of the interpretation of current affairs, and of public opinion.

These courses, together with those dealing with foreign news channels and legal aspects of the press, heightened respect for journalism as a discipline among other college teachers. At the same time, products of journalism departments were earning a grudging acceptance from curmudgeons of the editorial offices who, as Horace Greeley put it, learned their journalism through eating ink and sleeping on the exchanges. Teachers began to offer courses to prepare students for careers in newspaper management, advertising, photography, and other such specialized fields. And while recognizing the importance of the humanities and the natural sciences in the total educational program of their students, teachers came to achieve the closest working relationships with the social sciences.

As both the breadth and depth of subject matter in journalism increased, master's degrees were offered. In 1935 the Pulitzer School at Columbia restricted its year's course to holders of a bachelor's degree, and the Medill School of Northwestern University established a five-year plan for professional training in 1938. Graduate study for journalism majors developed at a rapid pace after World War II, as the schools themselves and some of the media units began to urge advanced study in both journalism and the social sciences. Many of those who obtained master's degrees entered journalism teaching, but increasing numbers spent five years of study in preparation for professional careers.

At the doctoral level, most graduate schools that recognized journalism instruction followed the lead of the University of Wisconsin in providing a minor or a double minor in journalism for candidates who generally majored in such fields as history or political science. The University of Missouri, however, awarded the first degree of Doctor of Philosophy in journalism in 1934, and by the 1940s other programs were under way. Some were based on strong supporting emphasis in the social sciences; others related the study of mass communications to psychology and sociology as a behavioral science. In the 1970s the Ph.D. degree in mass communications was offered at eighteen universities. Some Ph.D. recipients entered the communications industry or other research areas, but most became faculty members.

The growth of the philosophy that journalism and communications schools should develop research scholars capable of critical analysis of the media and their social environment coincided with television's rise and the increased importance of departments of speech communication and radio-television in providing preparation for broadcast careers. New, integrated instructional units emerged, a few merely for administrative convenience, but most devoted to the serious study of communication as the common denominator linking several academic areas of study. For example, Michigan State University brought its speech communication, journalism, advertising, and broadcast instruction together into a College of Communication Arts, with a research unit at its center. The University of Texas similarly combined its speech communication, radio-television-film, journalism, and advertising programs into a School of Communication. Today, "Communication" or "Communications" is a part of the name of instructional units at many institutions.

Because of their diversity of interests, mass communication educators find teaching and research inspiration and assistance through membership in a number of regional, national, and international organizations. They include the Association for Education in Journalism, Speech Communication Association, International Communication Association, Broadcast Education Association, American Academy of Advertising, Popular Culture Association, and a number of others.

The Association for Education in Journalism, founded in 1912, is the so-called umbrella organization for many scholars in such fields of study as mass communication and society, theory and methodology, law, media history, international communication, photojournalism, graphics, newspaper, magazine, advertising, public relations, and radio-television. AEJ publishes *Journalism Quarterly, Journalism Educator, Journalism Monographs,* and *Journalism Abstracts.* It has two administrator organizations as coordinate members. They are the American Association of Schools and Departments of Journalism (AASDJ), composed of schools with sequences accredited by the American Council on Education for Journalism (ACEJ), and the American Society of Journalism School Administrators (ASJSA), to which both administrators of schools with ACEJ-accredited sequences and those that have not sought or have not obtained such accreditation belong.

All three groups—AEJ, AASDJ, and ASJSA—have representatives on the American Council on Education for Journalism, together with representatives of nineteen industry and professional organizations: the American Society of Newspaper Editors, American Newspaper Publishers Association, Southern Newspaper Publishers Association, National Newspaper Association, and Inland Daily Press Association (the five groups which helped establish the council in 1939); and the National Association of Broadcasters, Magazine Publishers Association, Public Relations Society of America, International Newspaper Advertising Executives, International Association of Business Communicators, National Conference of Editorial Writers, National Press Photographers Association, Radio Television News Directors Association, Associated Press Managing Editors Association, Western Newspaper Foundation, Associated Press Broadcasters Association, Broadcast Education Association, Women in Communications, Inc., and the Society of Professional Journalists, Sigma Delta Chi.

Through its accrediting committee the council evaluates sequences of instruction in American universities, visiting schools on invitation approximately every six years. Currently accredited are programs in news-editorial, advertising, broadcast news, radio-television general (telecommunications), public relations, magazine, photojournalism, publishing, and technical, agricultural, and home economics journalism.

The Speech Communication Association, founded in 1914, consists of teachers and administrators at all educational levels, speech scientists and clinicians, media specialists, theater artists and craftsmen, communication consultants, students, and industry representatives. Primary publications are *The Quarterly Journal of Speech, Communication Monographs,* and *The Speech Teacher,* as well as a newsletter, annual directory, bibliographic annual, and convention abstracts. Its divisions are forensics, instructional development, interpersonal and small group interaction, interpretation, mass communication, public address, rhetorical and communication theory, speech sciences, and theater. Administrators of speech communication departments are organized as the Association for Communication Administrators.

The International Communication Association, formed twenty-five years ago, brings together academicians, other professionals, and students whose interest is focused on human communication. Publications are *The Journal of Communication, Human Communication Research,* and a newsletter. Its divisions are information systems and interpersonal, mass, organizational, intercultural, political, instructional, and health communication.

A recently organized Council of Communication Societies brings together leaders of the ICA, SCA, American Business Communication Association, American Forensic Association, American Medical Writers Association, American Translators Association, Industrial Communication Council, Society for Technical Communication, and Society of Federal Linguists. The council publishes a news digest and a communication calendar.

A COMMUNICATIONS EDUCATION NEVER ENDS

It's a truism, of course, to point out that a college diploma, or its equivalent in individual attainment, is only the beginning of a lifetime of education. For no other group does this fact hold greater validity than for those who embark on careers in mass communications. Every aspect of human experience and emotion can become their concern; the world changes and so must their ability to understand and interpret those changes.

Men and women who want to develop their fullest potential in the field of mass communications cannot neglect their reading, both fiction and nonfiction, and the selective viewing of films, televised documentaries, and the like. Just as a physician peruses periodicals to keep abreast of advances of knowledge in medicine, so must the communicator read journals in his own and allied fields. These include such research journals as *Journalism Quarterly, Public Opinion Quarterly,* and the *Journal of Communication;* trade journals such as *Editor & Publisher, Broadcasting,* and *Advertising Age;* and general interest professional journals such as *Nieman Reports, Quill,* and *Columbia Journalism Review.*

Maintaining active membership in organizations that seek to improve their crafts also is the mark of the professional communicator. Highly stimulating to many are the conferences and literature of the groups previously listed as supporting journalism accreditation, state and local associations, wire services, Women in Communications, and the Society of Professional Journalists, Sigma Delta Chi.

Many media people return to college for regular courses as well as for such continuing education activities as institutes, workshops, and forums. Dow Jones and Company's Newspaper Fund, Inc., has sent more than 6500 high school and junior college journalism teachers back to college for special summer training. Several hundred newspaper men and women have been selected by the Nieman Foundation for a year's study at Harvard University. The American Press Institute provides seminars regularly at Reston, Virginia. The Southern Newspaper Publishers Association sponsors both public affairs and newspaper skills seminars. These are only examples of numerous such activities available to mass media personnel.

MASS MEDIA TEACHING
IN THE SECONDARY SCHOOL

There are more potential openings for teachers of journalism in the secondary schools of the United States than in any other field for which journalism training provides preparation. The best estimates are that approximately 45,000 senior and junior high school publications—newspapers, magazines, and yearbooks—are issued regularly. More than 1 million students work on these publications, which cost collectively around $50 million a year. About 175,000 students are enrolled each year in journalism courses offered at approximately 5,000 high schools. Many others learn the principles of radio and television production in classes and activity clubs.

A phenomenon of the last decade has been the establishment of thousands of high school courses designed to acquaint students with the operations of the mass media and to consider the effects of mass communications on their lives. These courses, offered through language arts, speech, journalism, and other departments, have been one of the principal causes of the steady growth in mass communications enrollments in colleges and universities.

Secondary school journalism can be traced to the founding of the first known high school paper, the *Literary Journal,* in 1829 at the Boston Latin Grammar School. It was not until 1912, however, that the first known class in high school journalism was started in Salina, Kansas. Secondary school journalism matured during the 1930s and 1940s as school boards, superintendents, and principals noted its educational value.

Those who have taught high school journalism over the years speak with genuine enthusiasm about the satisfactions they have found in handling journalism classes and advising school publications. For one thing, they enjoy having many of their school's most brilliant students on their publications staffs; frequently the highest ranking group of students in the English placement tests is assigned to the teacher producing the school paper. These imaginative and creative youngsters are stimulated by actually writing for print. Many of them go on to other fields of study at the universities, but some become the prize students of journalism or communications schools and eventually take their places in professional work. The school paper and the annual are major activities at the high school level; this gives their advisers additional prestige as teachers. They also are brought into close contact with school administrators, and quite a number of able journalism teachers have moved into administrative work.

Several organizations issue publications and guidebooks for teachers and students and conduct critical services providing professional evaluation and ratings of school media. They include the Columbia Scholastic Press Association, at Columbia University; National Scholastic Press Association, at the University of Minnesota; National School Yearbook/Newspaper Association, at Texas Tech University; and Catholic School Press Association, at Marquette University. They publish, respectively, *School Press Review, Scholastic Editor, Photolith,* and *Catholic School Editor.* Quill and Scroll, the honorary society of high school journalists, with headquarters at the State University of Iowa, publishes a magazine bearing the society's name.

There are also regional associations, such as the Southern Interscholastic Press Association, with headquarters at the University of South Carolina, and the Mid-America Association for Secondary Journalism, at the University of Missouri, as well as state associations. The teachers themselves are organized as the Journalism Education Association, affiliated with NSPA, which publishes *Communication: Journalism Education Today.*

A recent study published in the latter periodical disclosed that about 30 percent of the states have no specific journalism certification requirements, about 30 percent grant journalism certification for completing fewer than fifteen semester hours of college journalism course work, and about 40 percent require the equivalent of a minor in journalism. Only two states require a major in journalism.

Some prospective teachers major in journalism and minor in an area such as English or the social sciences, meanwhile acquiring sufficient hours in education courses to qualify for certificates. Others major in education and take first and second minors in journalism and some other field. Still others major in English or language arts and take as many journalism courses as they can work into a four-year program. All realize that they likely will be teaching only one or two courses in journalism, with the balance of their instructional assignments in another subject. During the recent declining market for teachers, those with the greatest preparation in journalism were more likely to be employed.

TEACHING JOURNALISM
IN THE COMMUNITY COLLEGE

Hundreds of opportunities for teaching journalism are available in community colleges throughout the United States, which are growing steadily in enrollment and importance as the population increases.

Fifty-nine percent of the 936 community colleges that responded to a recent survey conducted by Dr. Frank Deaver of the University of Alabama offer some courses in journalism. Most often these courses include introduction to mass communications, beginning newswriting and reporting, news editing, and photography. Two-thirds of the courses serve as laboratories for student publications—newspaper, magazine, or yearbook. In most of these two-year colleges the journalism program is designed to encourage these student publications and to give basic preparation for students planning to major in journalism or communications at four-year colleges and universities. A number of community college educators state that their primary purpose is to acquaint students with the mass media and to teach them to become discerning "consumers" of news and opinion so they will be better able to discharge their responsibilities as citizens. In some community colleges enough advanced instruction is available to prepare graduates to take jobs with the media.

Two-year college educators are organized as the Community College Journalism Association, an affiliate of the Association for Education in Journalism. The Newspaper Fund worked with the educators to develop their organization through annual seminars at the University of Texas. In California, more than sixty two-year and city colleges belong to the Journalism Association of Community Colleges. The typical degree of the two-year college educators is the M.A., earned by 75 percent. Many serve as advisers to student publications or as college publicity directors. A substantial number are women.

THE FOUR-YEAR COLLEGE AND UNIVERSITY LEVEL

Journalism and communications faculty members at the university or college level are engaged in three major activities: teaching, research, and service. They have one or more specialties in the journalistic techniques, acquired through their own professional experience with the mass media: Reporting, news editing, magazine writing, radio and television news, typography and graphic arts processes, advertising, public relations, news photography, film, critical writing, broadcast programing and production, and editorial writing are among these technique fields. Teachers usually start at this techniques level, but they are well advised to be equipped for teaching and research in one or more of the scholarly fields of interest. They should be interested, too, in performing services for the mass media with which the school or department is in close contact and in spending long hours offering advice and counsel to students who turn to them for guidance and stimulation.

Those who aspire to the top ranks of university or college teaching in journalism and mass communications usually seek master's degrees in the field. They then undertake study toward the Ph.D. degree in a college or university that offers either a major or a minor in the subject and that has a journalism and communications faculty of graduate school caliber. Some prefer to minor in journalism or communications and to do their major doctoral work in political science, history, psychology, sociology, economics, speech, American studies, or another related field; others enter universities that award Ph.D. degrees in journalism or in communications. In either case, there is a blending of study and research in journalism or communications with study and research in the social sciences, behavioral sciences, or the humanities.

Not all college journalism or communications faculty members need undertake doctoral work; some with sound professional experience and specialized abilities in such fields as graphic arts, news photography, weekly journalism, or radio and television writing, production, and programing find their services amply rewarded at the M.A. level. There have been shortages of qualified teachers in the advertising and broadcast media fields, particularly.

Opportunities for scholarly teaching, research, and publication in the mass communications field are almost unlimited. Many aspects of the history of communications remain to be explored, despite the fact that this area traditionally has been a favorite one for journalism professors. The literary aspects of journalism constitute another little-plowed field. Important studies of the relationships between the press and society, and of the conflicts between press and government, await future scholars. Only a start has been made on penetrating studies of the economics of the mass media. Advertising offers wide opportunities for advanced study and research projects of both basic and applied character. As explained in Chapter 19, the fields of mass communications theory and research, of public opinion and propaganda, and of other studies allied to the behavioral sciences have barely been opened by scholars. Particularly, there is a need for interpretive analysis of scientific findings and quantitative data by those who can relate what the researchers have found to the everyday problems of the mass media. The processes of international communications and the study of foreign journalism have become more important in recent years also, with few faculty members qualified to do advanced teaching and research in the field.

Offering assistance to the publications adviser at the junior college and college level are the Associated Collegiate Press, companion organization of the National Scholastic Press Association, the National Council of College Publications Advisers, and the National School Yearbook/Newspaper Association. The ACP, NSYA, and NNS issue guidebooks and other publications for college publications staffs and maintain critical services for newspapers, annuals, and magazines.

Salaries for communications teachers in colleges and universities run somewhat above the averages for other disciplines, because of the competitive bidding from the mass media for the services of those who are preparing for teaching careers. University and college salaries have improved substantially in recent years, and those who reach professorial status can look forward to nine-month salaries running from $15,000 to $30,000 or more a year. There also are opportunities for additional income from summer teaching, summer "refresher" work in the media, consultantships to advertising agencies and other groups, research projects, and book publication and other writing.

BIBLIOGRAPHY

BIBLIOGRAPHY

This is a selected, annotated bibliography of books dealing with mass communications and journalism. It is organized to correspond with the four principal sections and twenty chapters of this book.

It is the authors' aim to introduce readers to some of the basic books that, if they have the time and interest to explore them, will take them beyond the necessarily limited syntheses of an introductory survey of mass communications. A student reader who has the interest and opportunity to elect further studies in the field will meet many of these books again in advanced courses; if she or he goes no further, this bibliography will provide a personal reading list for more detailed examination of various facets of the field. It is in no sense an all-inclusive bibliography; for that purpose the reader is referred to Warren C. Price's *The Literature of Journalism: An Annotated Bibliography* (Minneapolis: University of Minnesota Press, 1959), and a ten-year supplement to it compiled by Price and Calder M. Pickett, *An Annotated Journalism Bibliography* (1970). Another excellent aid is Eleanor Blum's *Basic Books in the Mass Media* (Urbana: University of Illinois Press, 1972). *Mass Media Booknotes,* edited since 1969 by Christopher H. Sterling and published monthly (mimeograph) by the Department of Radio-Television-Film, Temple University, offers extensive reports on books in all areas. See also the research journals listed below. A general source book is the annual Directory issue of *Journalism Educator,* published by the Association for Education in Journalism for the American Society of Journalism School Administrators.

This bibliography also lists the principal journals and trade publications with which students of mass communications should be familiar, and in a few instances makes references to articles in them. In cases where books have gone through revised editions, the date given is for the most recent revision. In subsequent listings of a book, place and date of publication are not repeated.

PERIODICALS, ANNUAL PUBLICATIONS, AND DIRECTORIES

General Research Journals
Journalism Quarterly: published by the Association for Education in Journalism, devoted to research articles in journalism and mass com-

munications. Contains extensive book reviews, bibliographies of articles in American and foreign journals, news of journalism education.

Public Opinion Quarterly: Emphasizes political and psychological phases of communication. Book reviews and summaries of public opinion polls. Published by the American Association for Public Opinion Research.

Gazette: International journal, published in Amsterdam, devoted to research in mass communications. Book reviews and bibliographies.

Journal of Communication: Research quarterly focusing on methodology; material in speech and interpersonal communication areas; book reviews. Published by International Communication Association.

Communication Research: International quarterly focusing on research methodology. Published by Sage Publications.

AV Communication Review: Reports on research activities and findings in the communication area. Previously published quarterly by the Department of Audiovisual Instruction of the NEA; now published by the Association for Educational Communications and Technology.

Quarterly Journal of Speech: Research articles, book reviews. Published by the Speech Communication Association.

Journal of Popular Culture: Quarterly with wide interests in field; articles, book reviews. Published by Bowling Green State University in cooperation with the Popular Culture Association.

Journalism History: Research quarterly; articles, notes, book reviews for mass communications history. Published by the California State University Northridge Foundation with the support of the American Association of Schools and Departments of Journalism.

Mass Comm Review: Quarterly publication of the Mass Communications and Society Division of AEJ; articles.

Journal of Typographic Research: Research quarterly of the graphic arts area, published by the Cleveland Museum of Modern Art.

Journalism Monographs: Published serially by the Association for Education in Journalism, beginning in 1966, for research findings falling between article and book lengths; approximately quarterly.

General Professional Journals

Professional journals with general interest articles on press problems: *Nieman Reports* (Nieman Foundation); *Columbia Journalism Review* (Columbia University Graduate School of Journalism); *Quill* (Society of Professional Journalists, Sigma Delta Chi); *Matrix* (Women in Communications, Inc.); *Journalism Educator* (AEJ for American Society of Journalism School Administrators); *Communication: Journalism Educa-*

tion Today (Journalism Education Association); *IPI Report* (International Press Institute).

Newspapers

Professional journals: *ASNE Bulletin* (American Society of Newspaper Editors); *Masthead* (National Conference of Editorial Writers); *News Photographer* (National Press Photographers Association); formerly *National Press Photographer.*

Trade journals: *Editor & Publisher,* whose focus is on the daily newspaper and general industry problems, but which reports on advertising, marketing, and public relations areas; *Publishers' Auxiliary* (National Newspaper Association), primarily covering weeklies and small dailies; *Guild Reporter* (American Newspaper Guild); *Circulation Management; Inland Printer,* for the printing industry.

Annual publications: *APME Red Book,* containing the record of the annual meeting and the reports of the continuing studies committee of the Associated Press Managing Editors Association; *Problems of Journalism,* covering the annual meeting of the American Society of Newspaper Editors; *News Research for Better Newspapers,* a compilation of materials published by the ANPA News Research Center.

Directories: *Editor & Publisher International Year Book,* source for statistics and information about dailies; N. W. Ayer and Son, *Directory of Newspapers and Periodicals,* covering all newspapers and magazines.

Television, Radio, and Film

Research journals: *Journal of Broadcasting* (Broadcast Education Association); *Television Quarterly* (National Academy of Television Arts and Sciences); *Public Telecommunications Review* (National Association of Educational Broadcasters); *American Film* (American Film Institute). Articles, book reviews, notes.

Professional journals: *RTNDA Communicator* (Radio Television News Directors Association); *Film Critic* (American Federation of Film Societies); *Film Quarterly Communication Arts* (photography, television); *TV Communications* (cable television).

Trade journals: *Broadcasting,* the voice of that industry; *Television/ Radio Age; Variety,* voice of the entertainment world; *Billboard.*

Directories: *Broadcasting Yearbook,* source for statistics and information about radio and television; *Television Factbook; Broadcasting Cable Sourcebook.*

Magazines and Book Publishing

Professional and trade journals: *Folio,* for the magazine area; *Publishers' Weekly,* for the book publishing industry, whose focus is primarily on general trade and children's books; *The Retail Bookseller; Bookbinding and Book Production; Author and Journalist, Writer,* and *Writer's Digest,* for freelance magazine writers.

Directories: *Literary Market Place,* for book publishing; N. W. Ayer and Son, *Directory of Newspapers and Periodicals,* for magazine statistics and information; *Writer's Market* and *Writer's Year Book,* guides for magazine article writers; Gebbie Press, *House Magazine Directory.*

Advertising and Public Relations

Research journals: *Journal of Marketing* (American Marketing Association), articles and book reviews: *Journal of Marketing Research* (Advertising Research Foundation); *Journal of Advertising* (American Academy of Advertising); *Public Relations Review* (Foundation for Public Relations Research and Education), annual bibliography.

Professional journals: *Public Relations Journal* (Public Relations Society of America); *PR News* (newsletter).

Trade journals: *Advertising Age,* the major organ of the advertising industry; *Advertising Agency; Advertising Requirements; Sponsor,* for buyers of broadcast advertising; *Industrial Marketing; Sales Management; Direct Marketing.*

Directories: Standard Rate and Data Service, *Consumer Markets; Editor & Publisher Market Guide; Broadcasting Marketbook.*

General

The Aspen Handbook on the Media, 1977–79 Edition, edited by William L. Rivers, Wallace Thompson and Michael J. Nyhan (New York: Praeger, 1977), and *The Mass Media: Aspen Guide to Communication Industry Trends,* edited by Christopher H. Sterling and Timothy R. Haight (1978), are valuable reference-research guides.

PART I: THE ROLE OF MASS COMMUNICATIONS

William L. Rivers and Wilbur Schramm's *Responsibility in Mass Communication* (New York: Harper & Row; 1969) is the best treatment of communication ethics. It discusses the role of the mass communicator in developing the political, social, and economic fabrics of a democratic society, and the development of modern mass communications. In a similar vein are John C. Merrill, *The Imperative of Freedom* (New York:

Hastings House, 1974); Lee Brown, *The Reluctant Reformation* (New York: David McKay, 1974); and William L. Rivers, Theodore Peterson, and Jay Jensen, *The Mass Media and Modern Society* (San Francisco: Rinehart, 1971). Examining advertising's role in the economy and its social contribution are John S. Wright and John Mertes, *Advertising's Role in Society* (St. Paul: West, 1976); Jules Backman, *Advertising and Competition* (New York: New York University Press, 1967); and Kim B. Rotzoll, James E. Haefner and Charles H. Sandage, *Advertising in Contemporary Society* (Columbus, Ohio: Grid, 1976).

An excellent introduction to the study of the communication process and to research in mass communication is found in Wilbur Schramm's *Men, Messages, and Media: A Look at Human Communication* (New York: Harper & Row, 1973), a readable survey of communication theory, mass communication audiences, effects, and social controls. John C. Merrill and Ralph L. Lowenstein contributed their prize-winning *Media, Messages, and Men: New Perspectives in Communication* (New York: McKay, 1971), analyzing the changing role of the mass media, the communicators and their audiences, and media concepts and ethics. Charles R. Wright updated his 1959 pacesetter, *Mass Communication: A Sociological Perspective* (New York: Random House, 1975). All three are in paperback editions.

Communication effects are analyzed in W. Phillips Davison, James Boylan and Frederick T. C. Yu, *Mass Media Systems and Effects* (New York: Praeger, 1976); *The Process and Effects of Mass Communication,* edited by Wilbur Schramm and Donald F. Roberts (Urbana: University of Illinois Press, 1971); and Joseph T. Klapper, *The Effects of Mass Communication* (New York: Free Press, 1960).

Several books of readings deal with the role of mass communications in society. Listed in order according to the increasing complexity of their materials, they are *Interpretations of Journalism,* edited by Frank Luther Mott and Ralph D. Casey (New York: Crofts, 1937), a historical collection of utterances about the press over 300 years; *Enduring Issues in Mass Communication,* edited by Everette Dennis, Arnold Ismach and Donald Gillmor (St. Paul: West Publishing, 1978), a study of media impact, roles and reforms; *Communications in Modern Society,* edited by Wilbur Schramm (Urbana: University of Illinois Press, 1948), fifteen essays on communications problems and research trends; *Mass Communications,* edited by Wilbur Schramm (Urbana: University of

Illinois Press, 1960), selected readings on mass communications "through the windows of the social sciences"; *Reader in Public Opinion and Communication,* edited by Bernard Berelson and Morris Janowitz (New York: Free Press, 1966), dealing with public opinion theory, media content, audiences, and effects; *People, Society, and Mass Communication,* edited by Lewis A. Dexter and David M. White (New York: Free Press, 1964), dealing with communication research with a sociological emphasis; and *Dimensions of Communication,* edited by Lee Richardson (New York: Appleton-Century-Crofts, 1969), focusing on problems of communication and persuasion at both personal and media levels.

The complex and specialized area of communications theory may be approached through a readable survey of contemporary theory by Melvin L. DeFleur and Sandra Ball-Rokeach, *Theories of Mass Communication* (New York: McKay, 1975), a revision of DeFleur's 1970 edition with the same title. Reed H. Blake and Edwin O. Haroldsen provide brief explanations of basic concepts of communication in *A Taxonomy of Concepts in Communication* (New York: Hastings House, 1975). C. David Mortensen edited *Basic Readings in Communication Theory* (New York: Harper & Row, 1973). Provocative discussions are found in Marshall McLuhan's *Understanding Media: The Extensions of Man* (New York: McGraw-Hill, 1964), his earlier *The Gutenberg Galaxy: The Making of Typographic Man* (Toronto: University of Toronto Press, 1962), and his 1967 attention-getter, *The Medium Is the Massage* (Bantam Books).

A thousand-page reference volume for the serious scholar of communication theory is *Handbook of Communication* (Chicago: Rand McNally, 1973), edited by Ithiel de Sola Pool and Wilbur Schramm. Among collections of scholarly articles on mass communications research are three annual reviews published by Sage Publications of Beverly Hills, California: *Current Perspectives in Mass Communication Research,* edited by F. Gerald Kline and Phillip J. Tichenor (1972); *New Models for Mass Communication Research,* edited by Peter Clarke (1973); and *The Uses of Mass Communications: Current Perspectives on Gratification Research,* edited by Jay G. Blumler and Elihu Katz (1974). W. Phillips Davison and Frederick T. C. Yu edited *Mass Communication Research: Major Issues and Future Directions* (New York: Praeger, 1974). An earlier collection of essays on subjects ranging from cognitive dissonance to voting behavior was offered by Wilbur Schramm in *The Science of Human Communication* (New York: Basic Books, 1963). Among other books in the theory area are William Stephenson, *The Play Theory of Mass Communication* (Chicago: University of Chicago Press, 1967); Alfred G. Smith, *Communication and Culture: Readings* (New York: Holt, Rinehart and Winston, 1966); and Charles E. Osgood, George Suci, and Percy Tannenbaum, *The Measurement of Meaning* (Urbana: University of Illinois Press, 1957).

The effects of the mass media on the social fabric are discussed in various articles in *Mass Culture: The Popular Arts in America,* edited by Bernard Rosenberg and David M. White (New York: Free Press, 1957). There are sections on the mass literature, motion pictures, radio, and television. An updated version by the same authors is *Mass Culture Revisited* (Princeton, N.J.: Van Nostrand Reinhold, 1971).

Among the leading books on public opinion are Bernard C. Hennessy, *Public Opinion* (Scituate, Mass.: Duxbury Press, 1975), a text in third edition; Alan D. Monroe, *Public Opinion in America* (New York: Harper & Row, 1975), emphasizing the political process; V. O. Key Jr., *Public Opinion and American Democracy* (New York: Knopf, 1961); Erwin P. Bettinghaus, *Persuasive Communication* (New York: Holt, Rinehart and Winston, 1973); Robert E. Lane and David O. Sears, *Public Opinion* (Englewood Cliffs, N.J.: Prentice-Hall, 1967), focusing on voting; and Curtis D. MacDougall, *Understanding Public Opinion: A Guide for Newspapermen and Newspaper Readers* (Dubuque, Iowa: Brown, 1966).

The impact of public opinion and the mass media upon politics is analyzed by Walter Lippmann in his classic *Public Opinion* (New York: Harcourt, Brace, 1922); by Douglass Cater in *The Fourth Branch of Government* (Boston: Houghton Mifflin, 1959), a study of the key role of the Washington press corps; by Bernard C. Cohen in *The Press and Foreign Policy* (Princeton, N.J.: Princeton University Press, 1963), a study of Washington diplomatic reporting; by James Reston in another study of press influence on foreign policy, *The Artillery of the Press* (New York: Harper & Row, 1967); by Elmer Cornwell Jr. in *Presidential Leadership of Public Opinion* (Bloomington: Indiana University Press, 1965); and by William L. Rivers in his *The Opinionmakers* (Boston: Beacon, 1965), a study of leading Washington journalists, and his *The Adversaries* (Boston: Beacon, 1970), a study of press manipulation by public officials. A research-oriented contribution to the subject was made in the 1975 Sage Publications review of communication research edited by Steven H. Chaffee, *Political Communication: Issues and Strategies for Research*. Others are Bernard Rubin, *Media, Politics, and De-*

mocracy (New York: Oxford, 1977); Donald L. Shaw and Maxwell E. McCombs, editors, *The Emergence of American Political Issues* (St. Paul: West, 1977), studies of the agenda-setting function; Sidney Kraus and Dennis Davis, *The Effects of Mass Communication on Political Behavior* (State College: Penn State Press, 1976); L. John Martin, editor, *Role of the Mass Media in American Politics,* a special issue of the *Annals* of the American Academy of Political and Social Science (September, 1976); and Thomas E. Patterson and Robert D. McClure, *The Unseeing Eye* (New York: Putnam, 1976), television's election role.

International communication research and theory are reported upon in Lucian W. Pye, *Communications and Political Development* (Princeton, N.J.: Princeton University Press, 1963); Wilbur Schramm, *Mass Media and National Development* (Stanford, Calif.: Stanford University Press, 1964); Wilson P. Dizard, *Television: A World View* (Syracuse, N.Y.: Syracuse University Press, 1966); Daniel Lerner and Wilbur Schramm, *Communication and Change in the Developing Countries* (Honolulu: East-West Center, 1967); Wilbur Schramm and Daniel Lerner, *Communication and Change: The Last Ten Years—and the Next* (Honolulu: University of Hawaii Press, 1976); Alan Wells, *Mass Communication: A World View* (Palo Alto, Calif.: National Press, 1974); and Heinz-Dietrich Fischer and John C. Merrill, editors, *International and Intercultural Communication* (New York: Hastings House, 1976), with articles by scholars of many countries.

PART II: THE HISTORICAL PERSPECTIVE

The most widely ranging of the journalism histories is Edwin and Michael Emery, *The Press and America: An Interpretative History of the Mass Media* (Englewood Cliffs, N.J.: Prentice-Hall, 1978). It correlates the narrative of journalism history with social, political, and economic trends and is especially comprehensive in its treatment of twentieth-century journalism—newspapers, magazines, radio and television, press associations, and the relationship of the mass media to government and society.

Frank Luther Mott's *American Journalism: A History, 1690–1960* (New York: Macmillan, 1962) is designed for both classroom and reference shelf, contains much rich detail in its comprehensive treatment of newspapers, but puts little emphasis on other media. Alfred McClung Lee's *The Daily Newspaper in America* (New York: Macmillan, 1937) offers a sociological approach and much valuable data in its topical treatment of such subjects as newsprint, printing presses, labor, ownership and management, news, advertising, and circulation. Willard G. Bleyer's *Main Currents in the History of American Journalism* (Boston: Houghton Mifflin, 1927) remains an excellent account of American journalism until the early twentieth century, with emphasis on leading editors.

Kenneth Stewart and John Tebbel, in *Makers of Modern Journalism* (New York: Prentice-Hall, 1952), sketch early American journalism history and concentrate on twentieth-century journalistic personalities. Tebbel, in his *Compact History of the American Newspaper* (New York: Hawthorn, 1969) and his *The Media in America* (New York: Crowell, 1975), does the reverse, sketching twentieth-century journalism in only the broadest terms. Sidney Kobre adds details in his sociologically based *Development of American Journalism* (Dubuque, Iowa: Brown, 1969). Robert A. Rutland wrote a brief popularized account in *The Newsmongers* (New York: Dial, 1973), as did George N. Gordon in *The Communications Revolution* (New York: Hastings House, 1977).

The roles of women in American journalism history are explored by Marion Marzolf in *Up From the Footnote: A History of Women Journalists* (New York: Hastings House, 1977), a good synthesis.

Reproductions of full front pages of newspapers on an extensive, planned scale are found in Edwin Emery's *The Story of America as Reported by Its Newspapers 1690–1965* (New York: Simon and Schuster, 1965) and in *America's Front Page News 1690–1970,* edited by Michael C. Emery, R. Smith Schuneman, and Edwin Emery (New York: Doubleday, 1970).

Articles about twentieth-century journalists first published in the *Saturday Evening Post* are found in *Post Biographies of Famous Journalists,* edited by John E. Drewry (Athens: University of Georgia Press, 1942), and its sequel, *More Post Biographies* (1947). A collection of the best magazine articles about leading American newspaper editors and publishers of all periods is found in *Highlights in the History of the American Press, edited* by Edwin H. Ford and Edwin Emery (Minneapolis: University of Minnesota Press, 1954).

The best historical accounts of specific areas of mass communications are found in the following:

Radio and television: Erik Barnouw's three-volume history of U.S. broadcasting, *A Tower in Babel, The Golden Web,* and *The Image Empire* (New York: Oxford, 1966, 1968, 1970); Sydney W. Head,

Broadcasting in America (Boston: Houghton Mifflin, 1978); Gleason L. Archer's classics, *History of Radio to 1926* (New York: American Historical Society, 1938) and *Big Business and Radio* (1939); and Llewellyn White's *The American Radio* (Chicago: University of Chicago Press, 1947). For technical history, see Orrin Dunlap, *Communications in Space* (New York: Harper & Row, 1970).

Magazines: Frank Luther Mott's monumental *A History of American Magazines,* in five volumes (Vol. 1, New York: Appleton, 1930; Vols. 2–5, Cambridge, Mass.: Harvard University Press, 1938–68); James Playsted Wood, *Magazines in the United States* (New York: Ronald, 1956); Theodore Peterson, *Magazines in the Twentieth Century* (Urbana: University of Illinois Press, 1964); John Tebbel, *The American Magazine: A Compact History* (New York: Hawthorn, 1969).

Book publishing: Hellmut Lehmann-Haupt and others, *The Book in America: History of the Making and Selling of Books in the United States* (New York: Bowker, 1951); Frank A. Mumby, *Publishing and Bookselling: A History from the Earliest Times to the Present* (London: Jonathan Cape, 1956).

Films: Paul Rotha and Richard Griffith, *The Film Till Now* (London: Spring Books, 1967), world cinema survey; Richard Griffith and Arthur Mayer, *The Movies* (New York: Simon and Schuster, 1970), American film history.

Photography: Beaumont Newhall, *The History of Photography from 1839 to the Present Day* (New York: Museum of Modern Art, 1964); Helmut and Alison Gernsheim, *The History of Photography* (London: Oxford, 1970) and *A Concise History of Photography* (1965).

Press associations: Victor Rosewater, *History of Cooperative News-Gathering in the United States* (New York: Appleton, 1930); Robert W. Desmond, *The Information Process: World News Reporting to the 20th Century* (Iowa City: University of Iowa Press, 1978).

Advertising: Frank Presbrey, *The History and Development of Advertising* (New York: Doubleday, Doran, 1930), the standard account; James Playsted Wood, *The Story of Advertising* (New York: Ronald, 1958), more readable.

Graphics: Isaiah Thomas, *The History of Printing in America* (Albany, N.Y.: Joel Munsell, 1810 and 1874) is the earliest journalism history account; Daniel B. Updyke's two-volume *Printing Types: Their History, Forms and Use* (Cambridge, Mass.: Harvard University Press, 1937) is the standard work; S. H. Steinberg, *Five Hundred Years of Printing* (Baltimore: Penguin, 1974), is a briefer survey.

Additional references, by chapter topic, follow.

Chapter 3: Theories and Realities of Press Freedom

Companion books trace the story of American press freedom: Leonard W. Levy, *Freedom of the Press from Zenger to Jefferson,* and Harold L. Nelson, *Freedom of the Press from Hamilton to the Warren Court* (Indianapolis: Bobbs-Merrill, 1966). They are unexcelled surveys.

Lucy M. Salmon's *The Newspaper and Authority* (New York: Oxford, 1923) is an extensive historical survey of restrictions placed on newspapers. Important periods of the history of press freedom struggles are covered in Fred S. Siebert, *Freedom of the Press in England, 1472–1776* (Urbana: University of Illinois Press, 1952); Leonard W. Levy, *Legacy of Suppression: Freedom of Speech and Press in Early American History* (Cambridge, Mass.: Harvard University Press, 1960); Clyde A. Duniway, *The Development of Freedom of the Press in Massachusetts* (New York: Longmans, Green, 1906); John C. Miller, *Crisis in Freedom: The Alien and Sedition Acts* (Boston: Little, Brown, 1951); Frank Luther Mott, *Jefferson and the Press* (Baton Rouge: Louisiana State University Press, 1943); and Zechariah Chafee, Jr., *Free Speech in the United States* (Cambridge, Mass.: Harvard University Press, 1941), a study emphasizing the effects of modern wartime conditions. James E. Pollard, *The Presidents and the Press* (New York: Macmillan, 1947), covers presidential press relations from Washington to Truman, and is supplemented by his *The Presidents and the Press: Truman to Johnson* (Washington: Public Affairs Press, 1964).

Excellent discussions by newspaper editors of current problems in protecting freedom of information and access to news are found in James Russell Wiggins, *Freedom or Secrecy* (New York: Oxford, 1964), and Herbert Brucker, *Freedom of Information* (New York: Macmillan, 1949). More detailed studies are Harold L. Cross, *The People's Right to Know* (New York: Columbia University Press, 1953), and Zechariah Chafee, Jr.'s two-volume *Government and Mass Communications* (Chicago: University of Chicago Press, 1947).

Supreme Court trends are traced in William A. Hachten's *The Supreme Court on Freedom of the Press* (Ames: Iowa State University Press, 1968) and later in Kenneth S. Devol's *Mass Media and the Supreme Court* (New York: Hastings House, 1976). J. Edward Gerald's *The Press and the Constitution* (Minneapolis: University of Minnesota Press, 1948) analyzes constitutional law cases involving press freedom from 1931 to 1947. David L. Grey reports on court coverage in *The Supreme Court and the News Media* (Evanston, Ill.: Northwestern University Press, 1968). Donald M. Gillmor analyzes a major conflict in *Free Press and Fair Trial* (Washington: Public Affairs Press, 1966).

Two extensive case books on press law are Donald M. Gillmor and Jerome A. Barron, *Mass Communication Law: Cases and Comment* (St. Paul: West, 1978), and Marc A. Franklin, *Cases and Materials on Mass Media Law* (Mineola, N.Y.: Foundation Press, 1977). Two major general accounts are Harold L. Nelson and Dwight L. Teeter, Jr., *Law of Mass Communications* (Mineola, N.Y.: Foundation Press, 1978), and William E. Francois, *Mass Media Law and Regulation* (Columbus, Ohio: Grid, 1975). Briefer accounts are Don R. Pember, *Mass Media Law* (Dubuque, Iowa: Brown, 1977), and Paul P. Ashley, *Say It Safely* (Seattle: University of Washington Press, 1976).

Philosophical problems of press freedom are analyzed by the Commission on Freedom of the Press in *A Free and Responsible Press,* by William E. Hocking in *Freedom of the Press: A Framework of Principle* (Chicago: University of Chicago Press, 1947), and by Fred S. Siebert, Theodore Peterson, and Wilbur Schramm in *Four Theories of the Press* (Urbana: University of Illinois Press, 1956). Among discussions of press freedom by journalists are Walter Lippmann, *Liberty and the News* (New York: Harcourt, Brace, 1920); Elmer Davis, *But We Were Born Free* (New York: Bobbs-Merrill, 1954); and Alan Barth, *The Loyalty of Free Men* (New York: Viking, 1951).

The film area is covered by Ira H. Carmen, *Movies, Censorship and the Law* (Ann Arbor: University of Michigan Press, 1966), and by Richard S. Randall, *Censorship of the Movies* (Madison: University of Wisconsin Press, 1968); books by Richard McKeon, Robert K. Merton, and Walter Gellhorn, *The Freedom to Read: Perspective and Program* (New York: Bowker, 1957); and radio and television by Sydney W. Head, *Broadcasting in America,* and Walter B. Emery, *Broadcasting and Government* (East Lansing: Michigan State University Press, 1971). Movie and television censorship is decried in Murray Schumach's *The Face on the Cutting Room Floor* (New York: Morrow, 1964).

Chapter 4: Growth of the Print Media

The best historical discussion of the news function is Frank Luther Mott's *The News in America* (Cambridge, Mass.: Harvard University Press, 1952), a survey of the concepts, forms, and problems of news. No one interested in newspapers should miss reading it.

The best books on the opinion function and editorial page writing are John L. Hulteng, *Opinion Function* (New York: Harper & Row, 1973);

A. Gayle Waldrop's *Editor and Editorial Writer* (Dubuque, Iowa: Brown, 1967), and Curtis D. MacDougall's *Principles of Editorial Writing* (Dubuque, Iowa: Brown, 1973). Jim A. Hart traces the history of the editorial, 1500–1800, in *Views on the News* (Carbondale: Southern Illinois University Press, 1971), and Allan Nevins continues in the introductions for sections in his collection of editorials, *American Press Opinion: Washington to Coolidge* (New York: Heath, 1928).

Arthur M. Schlesinger, *Prelude to Independence: The Newspaper War on Britain, 1764–1776* (New York: Knopf, 1958), analyzes one period of major press influence. Nevins, *American Press Opinion,* has an excellent section on the partisan journalism of the 1790s. C. C. Regier, *The Era of the Muckrakers* (Chapel Hill: University of North Carolina Press, 1932), examines magazines during the Progressive era; Louis Filler, *Crusaders for American Liberalism* (New York: Harcourt, Brace, 1939), also covers newspaper people. So does Jonathan Daniels in *They Will Be Heard: America's Crusading Newspaper Editors* (New York: McGraw-Hill, 1965), a 200-year survey. Writings of the muckrakers are edited by Arthur and Lila Weinberg in *The Muckrakers* (New York: Simon and Schuster, 1961).

The best anthologies are *Voices of the Past,* edited by Calder M. Pickett (Columbus, Ohio: Grid, 1977); *A Treasury of Great Reporting,* edited by Louis L. Snyder and Richard B. Morris (New York: Simon and Schuster, 1962); Bryce W. Rucker's *Twentieth Century Reporting at Its Best* (Ames: Iowa State University Press, 1964), and John Hohenberg's *The Pulitzer Prize Story* (New York: Columbia University Press, 1959).

Top-flight biographies of key figures in the development of the news function include Carl Van Doren, *Benjamin Franklin* (New York: Viking, 1938); Oliver Carlson, *The Man Who Made News: James Gordon Bennett* (New York: Duell, Sloan and Pearce, 1942); Francis Brown, *Raymond of the Times* (New York: Norton, 1951); Fayette Copeland, *Kendall of the Picayune* (Norman: University of Oklahoma Press, 1943); Candace Stone, *Dana and the Sun* (New York: Dodd, Mead, 1938); Raymond B. Nixon, *Henry W. Grady: Spokesman of the New South* (New York: Knopf, 1943); Don C. Seitz, *Joseph Pulitzer* (New York: Simon and Schuster, 1924); W. A. Swanberg, *Pulitzer* (New York: Scribner's, 1967); Julian Rammelkamp, *Pulitzer's Post-Dispatch 1878–1883* (Princeton, N.J.: Princeton University Press,

1966); George Juergens, *Joseph Pulitzer and the New York World 1883–1887* (Princeton, N.J.: Princeton University Press, 1966); Oliver Knight, *I Protest: Selected Disquisitions of E. W. Scripps* (Madison: University of Wisconsin Press, 1966), both a biography and collection of Scripps' writings; W. A. Swanberg, *Citizen Hearst* (New York: Scribner's, 1961); John Tebbel, *The Life and Good Times of William Randolph Hearst* (New York: Dutton, 1952), Gerald W. Johnson, *An Honorable Titan: A Biographical Study of Adolph S. Ochs* (New York: Harper, 1946); Merlo J. Pusey, *Eugene Meyer* (New York: Knopf, 1974); James H. Markham, *Bovard of the Post-Dispatch* (Baton Rouge: Louisiana State University Press, 1954); Homer W. King, *Pulitzer's Prize Editor: A Biography of John A. Cockerill* (Durham, N.C.: Duke University Press, 1965); Mary E. Tomkins, *Ida M. Tarbell* (New York: Twayne, 1974); and Marion K. Sanders, *Dorothy Thompson* (Boston: Houghton Mifflin, 1973).

Leading biographies of opinion makers include John C. Miller, *Sam Adams: Pioneer in Propaganda* (Boston: Little, Brown, 1936); Mary A. Best, *Thomas Paine* (New York: Harcourt, Brace, 1927); Glyndon G. Van Deusen, *Horace Greeley: Nineteenth Century Crusader* (Philadelphia: University of Pennsylvania Press, 1953); George S. Merriam, *The Life and Times of Samuel Bowles* (New York: Century, 1885); Joseph F. Wall, *Henry Watterson* (New York: Oxford, 1956); and Joseph L. Morrison, *Josephus Daniels Says* (Chapel Hill: University of North Carolina Press, 1963). William Cullen Bryant and Edwin Lawrence Godkin are most easily read about in Allan Nevins, *The Evening Post: A Century of Journalism* (New York: Boni and Liveright, 1922). The McCormick and Patterson families and their Chicago *Tribune* and New York *Daily News* are analyzed by John Tebbel in *An American Dynasty* (New York: Doubleday, 1947).

The best autobiographies are Benjamin Franklin, *Autobiography* (New York: Putnam, 1909); *The Autobiography of William Allen White* (New York: Macmillan, 1946); *The Autobiography of Lincoln Steffens* (New York: Harcourt, Brace, 1931); Horace Greeley, *Recollections of a Busy Life* (New York: Ford, 1868); Frement Older, *My Own Story* (New York: Macmillan, 1926), the memoirs of a crusading San Francisco editor; Josephus Daniels, *Tar Heel Editor* (Chapel Hill: University of North Carolina Press, 1939), volume one of a five-volume series; and E. W. Howe, *Plain People* (New York: Dodd, Mead, 1929), the story of a Kansas editor and his readers, also told in Calder M. Pickett, *Ed Howe: Country Town Philosopher* (Lawrence: University Press of Kansas, 1969).

Excellent reminiscences of journalists include Melville E. Stone, *Fifty*

Years a Journalist (New York: Doubleday, Page, 1921); Will Irwin, *The Making of a Reporter* (New York: Putnam, 1942); Webb Miller, *I Found No Peace* (New York: Simon and Schuster, 1936); and Vincent Sheean, *Personal History* (Boston: Houghton Mifflin, 1969 reissue). The best of a great writer's news work is found in William White's *By Line: Ernest Hemingway* (New York: Scribner's, 1967), and in the biography by Carlos Baker, *Ernest Hemingway* (New York: Scribner's, 1969). Lee G. Miller, *The Story of Ernie Pyle* (New York: Viking, 1950), is very readable. Ishbel Ross, *Ladies of the Press* (New York: Harper, 1936), and John Jakes, *Great Women Reporters* (New York: Putnam, 1969), tell the story of dozens of women journalists. Helen Thomas in *Dateline: White House* (New York: Macmillan, 1975) tells the story of one.

Among important histories of individual newspapers are William E. Ames, *A History of the National Intelligencer* (Chapel Hill: University of North Carolina Press, 1972); Frank M. O'Brien's *The Story of the Sun* (New York: Appleton, 1928), covering the New York *Sun* from 1833 to 1928; Gerald W. Johnson and others, *The Sun-papers of Baltimore, 1837–1937* (New York: Knopf, 1937); Meyer Berger, *The Story of the New York Times* (New York: Simon and Schuster, 1951); Chalmers M. Roberts, *The Washington Post—The First Hundred Years* (Boston: Houghton Mifflin, 1977), heavy on recent years; Erwin D. Canham, *Commitment to Freedom: The Story of the Christian Science Monitor* (Boston: Houghton Mifflin, 1958); Will C. Conrad, Kathleen F. Wilson, and Dale Wilson, *The Milwaukee Journal: The First Eighty Years* (Madison: University of Wisconsin Press, 1964); and Jim A. Hart, *A History of the St. Louis Globe-Democrat* (Columbia: University of Missouri Press, 1961).

Two basic historical studies of the black press are Frederick G. Detweiler, *The Negro Press in the United States* (Chicago: University of Chicago Press, 1922), and Vishnu V. Oak, *The Negro Press* (Yellow Springs, Ohio: Antioch Press, 1948). A comprehensive survey is *The Black Press, U.S.A.* by Roland E. Wolseley (Ames: Iowa State University Press, 1971). *Perspective of the Black Press, 1974* (Kennebunkport, Maine: Mercer House, 1974) is an extensive anthology edited by Henry G. La Brie III.

Among the books on the New Journalism and protest press are a good survey by Everette E. Dennis and William L. Rivers, *Other Voices:*

The New Journalism in America (San Francisco: Canfield, 1974); an anthology edited by Tom Wolfe, *The New Journalism* (New York: Harper & Row, 1973); *The Reporter as Artist* (New York: Hastings House, 1974), edited by Ronald Weber; and Robert J. Glessing, *The Underground Press in America* (Bloomington: Indiana University Press, 1971.

Magazine editors and publishers are the subjects of books by Oswald Garrison Villard, *Fighting Years* (New York: Harcourt, Brace, 1939), the memoirs of the editor of the *Nation;* Peter Lyon, *Success Story: The Life and Times of S. S. McClure* (New York: Scribner's, 1963); S. S. McClure, *My Autobiography* (New York; Stokes, 1914); John Tebbel, *George Horace Lorimer and the Saturday Evening Post* (New York: Doubleday, 1949); George Britt, *Forty Years—Forty Millions: The Career of Frank A. Munsey* (New York: Farrar and Rinehart, 1935); James Thurber, *The Years with Ross* (Boston: Little, Brown, 1957), the story of editor Harold Ross and the *New Yorker;* Brendan Gill, *Here at the New Yorker* (New York: Random House, 1975); Norman Cousins, *Present Tense* (New York: McGraw-Hill, 1967), by the *Saturday Review editor;* W. A. Swanberg, *Luce and His Empire* (New York: Scribner's, 1972); and Robert T. Elson, *Time Inc.* (New York: Atheneum, 1968) and *The World of Time Inc.* (New York: Atheneum, 1973), a two-volume history covering 1923–1941 and 1941–1960.

Two individual histories of press associations are Oliver Gramling, *AP: The Story of News* (New York: Farrar and Rinehart, 1940), and Joe Alex Morris, *Deadline Every Minute: The Story of the United Press* (New York: Doubleday, 1957).

Chapter 5: The Growth of Radio, Television, and Film

An eight-year editing project by Lawrence H. Lichty and Malachi C. Topping resulted in more than 700 pages of *American Broadcasting: A Sourcebook on the History of Radio and Television* (New York: Hastings House, 1975). The best historical accounts are found in Erik Barnouw's *A Tower in Babel* and *The Golden Web,* Sydney W. Head's *Broadcasting in America,* Llewellyn White's *The American Radio* and in Christopher H. Sterling and John M. Kittross, *Stay Tuned: A Concise History of American Broadcasting* (Belmont, Calif.: Wadsworth, 1978).

Biographies include Alexander Kendrick, *Prime Time: The Life of Edward R. Murrow* (Boston: Little, Brown, 1969); Roger Burlingame, *Don't Let Them Scare You: The Life and Times of Elmer Davis* (Philadelphia: Lippincott, 1961); Carl Dreher, *Sarnoff: An American Success* (New York: Quadrangle, 1977); and Irving E. Fang, *Those Radio Commentators!* (Ames: Iowa State University Press, 1977).

Autobiographies are Lowell Thomas, *Good Evening Everybody* (New York: Morrow, 1976); Dan Rather, *The Camera Never Blinks* (New York: Morrow, 1977); *Father of Radio: The Autobiography of Lee De Forest* (Chicago: Wilcox & Follett, 1950); and H. V. Kaltenborn, *Fifty Fabulous Years, 1900–1950: A Personal Review* (New York: Putnam's, 1950). Two collections of writings are *In Search of Light: The Broadcasts of Edward R. Murrow 1938–1961* (New York: Knopf, 1967) and *Looking Ahead: The Papers of David Sarnoff* (New York: McGraw-Hill, 1968).

Relationships with government are analyzed in Walter B. Emery, *Broadcasting and Government* (East Lansing: Michigan State University Press, 1971), the best source; John E. Coons, ed., *Freedom and Responsibility in Broadcasting* (Evanston, Ill.: Northwestern University Press, 1963); Harvey J. Levin, *Broadcast Regulation and Joint Ownership of Media* (New York: New York University Press, 1960); and by Head and White. For sources, see Frank J. Kahn, *Documents of American Broadcasting* (New York: Appleton-Century-Crofts, 1972).

Motion pictures: Rotha and Griffith, *The Film Till Now,* and Griffith and Mayer, *The Movies,* are leading historical surveys. Alan Casty offered an account of world filmmaking in *Development of the Film: An Interpretive History* (New York: Harcourt Brace Jovanovich, 1973). Two other top accounts are Gerald Mast, *A Short History of the Movies* (New York: Bobbs-Merrill, 1971), and Arthur Knight, *The Liveliest Art* (New York: Macmillan, 1957).

The history of documentary films is told by Paul Rotha, Sinclair Road, and Richard Griffith in *Documentary Film* (London: Faber and Faber, 1966), and by A. William Bluem in *Documentary in American Television* (New York: Hastings House, 1965). Newsreels are covered in Raymond Fielding's *The American Newsreel, 1911–1967* (Norman: University of Oklahoma Press, 1972).

PART III: CRITICISMS AND CHALLENGES

An excellent basis for any discussion of the duties and the performance record of the mass media is the summary report of the Commission on Freedom of the Press, *A Free and Responsible Press* (Chicago: University of Chicago Press, 1947). The commission printed four studies already cited, Chafee's *Government and Mass Communications,* Hocking's, *Freedom of the Press,* White's *The American Radio,* and Ruth Inglis' *Freedom of the Movies,* as well as *Peoples Speaking to Peoples,* by Llewellyn White and Robert D. Leigh (Chicago: University of Chicago Press, 1946), an analysis of international news channels.

Criticisms of the mass media are summarized in John Hulteng's *The Messenger's Motives* (Englewood Cliffs, N.J.: Prentice-Hall, 1976), by analyzing 150 cases involving ethical problems. Criticism of press managers is the theme of Ben H. Bagdikian in *The Effete Conspiracy and Other Crimes by the Press* (New York: Harper & Row, 1972). Hillier Krieghbaum examines this topic in *Pressures on the Press* (New York: (Crowell, 1972). Probing the media scene are Everette E. Dennis, *The Media Society, Evidence About Mass Communication in America* (Dubuque, Iowa: Brown, 1978); David Shaw, *Journalism Today* (New York: Harper's College Press, 1977); and John Hohenberg, *The News Media* (New York: Holt, Rinehart and Winston, 1978). Bryce W. Rucker presents a comprehensive survey of media dilemmas while updating Morris Ernst's 1946 study by the same title, *The First Freedom* (Carbondale: Southern Illinois University Press, 1968).

Two books edited by Warren K. Agee provide extensive criticisms of the media: *The Press and the Public Interest* (Washington: Public Affairs Press, 1968) contains the annual William Allen White Lectures delivered by eighteen of America's leading reporters, editors, and publishers; in *Mass Media in a Free Society* (Lawrence: Regents' Press of Kansas, 1969) six media spokesmen discuss challenges and problems confronting newspapers, television, motion pictures, and magazines. Other criticisms of press performance are found in *The Press in Perspective,* edited by Ralph D. Casey (Baton Rouge: Louisiana State University Press, 1963), a series of seventeen lectures by leading journalists at University of Minnesota over sixteen years.

Ben H. Bagdikian's *The Information Machines* (New York: Harper & Row, 1971) projects the impact of technological change on the media and offers a wealth of research data based on findings of RAND Corporation research teams.

A comprehensive collection of articles focusing on major media issues and criticisms, revised biannually, is found in Michael C. Emery and Ted Curtis Smythe, *Readings in Mass Communication: Concepts and Issues in the Mass Media* (Dubuque, Iowa: Brown, 1977). Other books of readings include Alan Wells, *Mass Media and Society* (Palo Alto, Calif.: Mayfield, 1975); Francis and Ludmila Voelker, *Mass Media: Forces in Our Society* (New York: Harcourt Brace Jovanovich, 1975); Alan Casty, *Mass Media and Mass Man* (New York: Holt, Rinehart and Winston, 1973); John D. Stevens and William E. Porter, *The Rest of the Elephant* (Englewood Cliffs, N.J.: Prentice-Hall, 1973); and Leonard Sellers and William L. Rivers, *Mass Media Issues* (Englewood Cliffs, N.J.: Prentice Hall, 1977).

Among general surveys are Steven H. Chaffee and Michael J. Petrick, *Using the Mass Media: Communication Problems in American Society* (New York: McGraw-Hill, 1975), built around major problem areas; Frederick C. Whitney, *Mass Media and Mass Communications in Society* (Dubuque, Iowa: Brown, 1975); Don Pember, *Mass Media in America* (Palo Alto, Calif.: Science Research Associates, 1977); Ray Hiebert, Donald F. Ungurait, and Thomas W. Bohn, *Mass Media* (New York: McKay, 1974), research-oriented; David G. Clark and William B. Blankenburg, *You and Media* (San Francisco: Canfield, 1973), treating readers as media consumers; Peter M. Sandman, David M. Rubin, and David B. Sachsman, *Media: An Introductory Analysis of American Mass Communications* (Englewood Cliffs, N.J.: Prentice-Hall, 1976); and Robert D. Murphy, *Mass Communication and Human Interaction* (Boston: Houghton Mifflin, 1977).

Print media: Two studies of the status of the daily press are found in Ernest C. Hynds, *American Newspapers in the 1970s* (New York: Hastings House, 1975), and John L. Hulteng and Roy Paul Nelson, *The Fourth Estate* (New York: Harper & Row, 1971). A. Kent Mac-Dougall collected *Wall Street Journal* articles in *The Press: A Critical Look from the Inside* (New York: Dow Jones, 1972). Selections from the *Nieman Reports* make a comprehensive survey of news problems and trends in Louis Lyons, *Reporting the News* (Cambridge, Mass.: Harvard University Press, 1965). Hillier Krieghbaum treats one problem in *Science and the Mass Media* (New York: New York University Press, 1967). Curtis D. MacDougall, *The Press and Its Problems* (Dubuque, Iowa: Brown, 1964), is a revision of his *Newsroom Problems and Policies*. Lucy M. Salmon's *The Newspaper and the Historian* (New York: Oxford, 1923) is a classic historical study.

Among professionals' criticisms, Herbert Brucker's *Freedom of Information* is an enlightened defense and analysis of the newspaper press. By contrast, Carl E. Lindstrom uses for the title of his book *The Fading American Newspaper* (Garden City, N.Y.: Doubleday, 1960). Stanley Walker explains the problems facing editors in *City Editor* (New York: Stokes, 1934); he held that post on the New York *Herald Tribune*. A. J. Liebling brought together his satirical articles on press short-comings, written for the *New Yorker,* in *The Press* (New York: Ballantine, 1964) and in *The Wayward Pressman* (New York: Doubleday, 1948), devoted heavily to New York papers. Silas Bent, *Ballyhoo* (New York: Liveright, 1927) is strongly critical of the newspaper press of its day, as are Upton Sinclair's *The Brass Check* (Pasadena, Calif.: Published by the author, 1920), and George Seldes' *Freedom of the Press* (Indianapolis: Bobbs-Merrill, 1935). Oswald Garrison Villard, *The Disappearing Daily* (New York: Knopf, 1944), and Morris L. Ernst, *The First Freedom* (New York: Macmillan, 1946), exhibit a critical concern over newspaper ownership concentration trends but are not statistically accurate.

Broadcasting and film: A comprehensive collection of readings is Ted C. Smythe and George A. Mastroianni, *Issues in Broadcasting: Radio, Television, and Cable* (Palo Alto, Calif.: Mayfield, 1975). Two other substantial readers are David Manning White and Richard Averson, *Sight, Sound, and Society: Motion Pictures and Television in America* (Boston: Beacon, 1968), and Harry J. Skornia and Jack W. Kitson, *Problems and Controversies in Television and Radio* (Palo Alto, Calif.: Pacific Books, 1968). William Wood's readings in *Electronic Journalism* (New York: Columbia University Press, 1967) offer a defense of television news. Rosenberg and White, in *Mass Culture* and *Mass Culture Revisited,* cover broadcasting and film. Barry Cole edited 77 *TV Guide* articles for *Television* (New York: Free Press, 1970).

Leo Bogart objectively analyzes scores of research studies, seeking to determine the social impact of television, in *The Age of Television* (New York: Frederick Ungar, 1972). Two brief studies are *Broadcasting and Cable Television: Policies for Diversity* (New York: Committee for Economic Development, 1975), and Jack Lyle, *The People Look at Public Television: 1974* (Washington: Corporation for Public Broadcasting, 1975), updating a 1963 book by Schramm, Lyle, and Pool.

Among effective criticisms of broadcasting are Ron Powers, *The Newscasters* (New York: St. Martin's, 1977); Edwin Diamond, *The Tin Kazoo: Television, Politics, and the News* (Cambridge, Mass.: MIT Press, 1975), and Edward Jay Epstein, *News from Nowhere: Television and the News* (New York: Random House, 1973), an evaluation of 1968–1969 network news. Critical appraisals by the Alfred I. duPont–Columbia University Awards committee were begun with *Survey of Broadcast Journalism 1968–1969,* edited by Marvin Barrett (New York: Grosset & Dunlap, 1969). Harry J. Skornia contributed *Television and the News: A Critical Appraisal* (Palo Alto, Calif.: Pacific Books, 1968) and *Television and Society* (New York: McGraw-Hill, 1965), with an "agenda for improvement." Robert E. and Harrison B. Summers wrote *Broadcasting and the Public* (Belmont, Calif.: Wadsworth, 1972).

Coming from the Aspen Institute Program on Communications and Society are *The Future of Public Broadcasting,* edited by Douglass Cater (New York: Praeger, 1976); *Television as a Social Force* and *Television as a Cultural Force,* edited by Douglass Cater and Richard Adler (Praeger, 1975, 1976); *Cable and Continuing Education,* edited by Richard Adler and Walter S. Baer (Praeger, 1973); Richard M. Polsky, *Getting to Sesame Street: Origins of the Children's Television Workshop* (Praeger, 1974); and *The Electronic Box Office: Humanities and Arts on the Cable,* edited by Richard Adler and Walter S. Baer (Praeger, 1974).

Additional references, by chapter topic, follow.

Chapter 6: Crisis of Credibility

A thousand-page study of the Watergate years of 1972–1974 objectively presented with detailed documentary support and constant cross-references integrating various facets of the episode, forms the basis for analysis of that gigantic crisis of media and presidential credibility. The volume is *Watergate: Chronology of a Crisis* (Washington: Congressional Quarterly, 1975), edited by Mercer Cross and Elder Witt with a staff of thirty from that research organization and contributors.

Among the most useful books about Watergate are Carl Bernstein and Bob Woodward, *All the President's Men* (New York: Simon and Schuster, 1974); Jimmy Breslin, *How the Good Guys Finally Won* (New York: Viking, 1975); William E. Porter, *Assault on the Media* (Ann Arbor: University of Michigan Press, 1976); and the fifth Dupont–Columbia University survey of broadcast journalism, *Moments of Truth?* (New York: Crowell, 1975). Backgrounds for the government and political leaders involved in a decade of credibility crisis are provided in Dan Rather and Gary Paul Gates, *The Palace Guard* (New York: Harper & Row, 1974), and David Halberstam, *The Best and the Brightest* (New York: Random House, 1972).

Television news crises are covered admirably in William Small, *To Kill a Messenger* (New York: Hastings House, 1970), covering the 1960s with its crises of war, violence, rioting, and political polarization. Small was then CBS Washington bureau chief. One of television's problems was the subject of Newton Minow, John Bartlow Martin, and Lee M. Mitchell in *Presidential Television* (New York: Basic Books, 1973).

A first-hand criticism of network policy affecting CBS News appears in Fred W. Friendly, *Due to Circumstances Beyond Our Control . . .* (New York: Random House, 1967). The 1969 speeches of Vice-President Spiro T. Agnew attacking the fairness of television commentators and other media news are collected in Spiro T. Agnew, *Frankly Speaking* (Washington, Public Affairs Press, 1970). Even stronger attacks were made by Edith Efron in *The News Twisters* and *How CBS Tried to Kill a Book* (Los Angeles: Nash, 1971, 1972).

One of the best reports on the 1972 campaign press corps was Timothy Crouse, *The Boys on the Bus* (New York: Random House, 1973). Another aspect of political reporting is surveyed in fifty selections edited by Robert Blanchard for *Congress and the News Media* (New York: Hastings House, 1974). Two interesting studies of press performance during political campaigns are Nathan B. Blumberg's *One Party Press?* (Lincoln: University of Nebraska Press, 1954), a report on how thirty-five metropolitan dailies covered 1952 presidential campaign news, and Arthur E. Rowse's *Slanted News: A Case Study of the Nixon and Stevenson Fund Stories* (Boston: Beacon, 1957).

For details on studies of violence in riots, see Robert K. Baker and Sandra J. Ball, *Violence and the Media* (Washington: Government Printing Office, 1969), a staff report to the National Commission on the Causes and Prevention of Violence giving a historical treatment and a review of research. Two major citations in commission reports are *Report of the National Advisory Commission on Civil Disorders* (Kerner Report), 1968), chapter 15, "The News Media and the Disorders," and *Rights in Conflict,* the Walker Report to the National Commission on the Causes and Prevention of Violence, 1968, pages 287–327, "The Police and the Press."

The *Aspen Notebook on Government and the Media,* edited by William L. Rivers and Michael J. Nyhan (New York: Praeger, 1973), offers a spirited debate of government-media relations and regulatory issues.

Chapter 7: The Media and Social Issues

Violence and sensationalism: There are two collections of articles on the issues. One, with reasoned but conservative views, is edited by Victor B. Cline, *Where Do You Draw the Line? An Exploration into Media Violence, Pornography, and Censorship* (Provo, Utah: Brigham Young University Press, 1974). The other is the research-based *Violence and the Mass Media* (New York: Harper & Row, 1968), edited by Otto N. Larsen. Of historical importance are Helen M. Hughes, *News and the*

443

Human Interest Story (Chicago: University of Chicago Press, 1940), a sociological study; and Simon M. Bessie, *Jazz Journalism: The Story of the Tabloid Newspapers* (New York: Dutton, 1938).

Research findings have been reported by George Gerbner, et al., annually, as in *Violence Profile No. 8: Trends in Network Television Drama and Viewer Conceptions of Social Reality, 1967–1976* (Philadelphia: Annenberg School of Communication, University of Pennsylvania, 1977).

Marshall McLuhan's major books have been *The Gutenberg Galaxy* (1962) and *Understanding Media* (1964) although his *The Medium Is the Massage* (1967) created the most public attention.

Advertising: Jules Backman, *Advertising and Competition,* and Charles H. Sandage and Vernon Fryburger, *The Role of Advertising,* show its importance to the economy. Otis Pease, *The Responsibilities of American Advertising* (New Haven, Conn.: Yale University Press, 1958), emphasizes national advertising. Neil H. Borden, *The Economic Effects of Advertising* (Chicago: Irwin, 1942), is a lengthy study of the role advertising plays in the national economy; a portion is reprinted in Wilbur Schramm, *Mass Communications.* E. S. Turner, *The Shocking History of Advertising* (New York: Dutton, 1953), is constructively critical; so is Martin Mayer, *Madison Avenue, U.S.A.* (New York: Harper, 1958), primarily a study of advertising agencies. Vance Packard assigned almost unlimited powers to advertising men in *The Hidden Persuaders* (New York: McKay, 1957). Both the Mayer and Packard books are available in paperback editions.

Media organizations: There are two histories of media organizations, Edwin Emery's *History of the American Newspaper Publishers Association* (Minneapolis: University of Minnesota Press, 1950), and Alice Fox Pitts' *Read All About It—Fifty Years of the ASNE* (Reston, Va.: American Society of Newspaper Editors, 1974).

Chapter 8: Economic Problems of the Media
Ownership of media: Bryce Rucker, *The First Freedom* (Carbondale: Southern Illinois University Press, 1968), has a wealth of statistics and analysis. A major study is Jon G. Udell, *The Economics of the American Newspaper* (New York: Hastings House, 1978), sponsored by the American Newspaper Publishers Association. Trends in concentration

of newspaper ownership are reported in chapter 24 of Emery, *The Press and America*, and by Raymond B. Nixon in *Gazette* (*1968, No. 3*) and in the winter 1961 *Journalism Quarterly*.

Audience: *The Continuing Study of Newspaper Reading*, sponsored by the American Newspaper Publishers Association and the Advertising Research Foundation from 1939 to 1952 and covering readership studies of 142 newspapers, offers evidence of readership trends. The results were analyzed by Charles E. Swanson in "What They Read in 130 Daily Newspapers," fall 1955 *Journalism Quarterly*. Gary A. Steiner, *The People Look at Television* (New York: Knopf, 1963), is a voluminous study of viewing habits and attitudes of the American people by sex, education, income, religion, and so on.

PART IV: THE MASS COMMUNICATIONS INDUSTRIES AND PROFESSIONS

The listings in this section are confined to books dealing with the operations of the mass communications industries and professions, and books describing professional techniques and qualifications. For histories of the various media, see the bibliography for Part II; for books dealing with the role of the mass media in society and with media performance, see the bibliographies for Part I and Part III. Research journals, professional journals, trade publications, and directories for the various fields of mass communications are listed at the opening of the bibliography.

Chapter 9: Newspapers

Textbooks on reporting and newswriting: Curtis D. MacDougall, *Interpretative Reporting* (New York: Macmillan, 1977), a 45-year veteran; Mitchell and Blair Charnley, *Reporting* (New York: Holt, Rinehart and Winston, 1978); Melvin Mencher, *Reporting and Writing the News* (Dubuque, Iowa; Brown, 1977); Michael Ryan and James W. Tankard, Jr., *Basic News Reporting* (Palo Alto, Calif.: Mayfield, 1977); William Metz, *Newswriting* (Englewood Cliffs, N.J.: Prentice-Hall, 1977); Fred Fedler, *Reporting for the Mass Media* (New York: Harcourt Brace Jovanovich, 1973); Ralph S. Izard, Hugh Culbertson, and Donald A. Lambert, *Fundamentals of News Reporting* (Dubuque, Iowa: Kendall/Hunt, 1977); David L. Grey, *The Writing Process* (Belmont, Calif.: Wadsworth, 1972), using the behavioral approach; Julian Harriss, Kelly Leiter, and Stanley Johnson, *The Complete Reporter* (New York: Macmillan, 1977); and Judith L. Burken, *Introduction to Reporting* (Dubuque, Iowa: Brown, 1976), aimed at community college classes particularly. A valuable adjunct to the reporting texts is E. L. Callihan, *Grammar for Journalists* (New York: Ronald, 1978).

Two books combine coverage of reporting, writing, and editing for print and broadcast media with mass media introductory material: Verne E. Edwards, Jr., *Journalism in a Free Society* (Dubuque, Iowa: Brown, 1970), and William L. Rivers, *The Mass Media: Reporting, Writing, Editing* (New York: Harper & Row, 1975).

Special fields of reporting: Paul Williams, *Investigative Reporting* (Englewood Cliffs, N.J.: Prentice-Hall, 1978); Philip Meyer, *Precision Journalism* (Bloomington: Indiana University Press, 1973), a reporter's introduction to social science methods; George S. Hage, Everette E. Dennis, Arnold H. Ismach, and Stephen Hartgen, *New Strategies for Public Affairs Reporting: Investigation, Interpretation, Research* (Englewood Cliffs, N.J.: Prentice-Hall, 1976); Chilton R. Bush, *Newswriting and Reporting of Public Affairs* (Philadelphia: Chilton, 1971); Louis I. Gelfand and Harry E. Heath, Jr., *Modern Sports Writing* (Ames: Iowa State University Press, 1968); Claron Burnett, Richard Powers and John Ross, *Agricultural News Writing* (Dubuque, Iowa: Kendall/Hunt, 1973); Todd Hunt, *Reviewing for the Mass Media* (Philadelphia: Chilton, 1972).

News editing and copyreading: Bruce Westley, *News Editing* (Boston: Houghton Mifflin, 1978); Alfred A. Crowell, *Creative News Editing* (Dubuque, Iowa: Brown, 1975); Gene Gilmore and Robert Root, *Modern Newspaper Editing* (Berkeley, Calif.: Glendessary, 1970); Floyd K. Baskette and Jack Z. Sissors, *The Art of Editing* (New York: Macmillan, 1977); Robert E. Garst and Theodore M. Bernstein, *Headlines and Deadlines* (New York: Columbia University Press, 1961).

Community journalism: John Cameron Sim, *The Grass Roots Press: America's Community Newspapers* (Ames: Iowa State University Press, 1969); Morris Janowitz, *The Community Press in an Urban Setting* (New York: Free Press, 1967); Bruce M. Kennedy, *Community Journalism: How to Run a Country Weekly* (Ames: Iowa State University Press, 1974).

Graphics and production: Edmund C. Arnold, *Modern Newspaper Design* (New York: Harper & Row, 1969), and *Ink on Paper 2* (New York: Harper & Row, 1972); Arthur T. Turnbull and Russell N. Baird, *The Graphics of Communication: Typography, Layout and Design* (New York: Holt, Rinehart and Winston, 1975); Ruori McLean, *Magazine*

Design (London: Oxford University Press, 1969); Roy Paul Nelson, *Publication Design* (Dubuque, Iowa: Brown, 1972); Allen Hurlburt, *Publication Design* (New York: Van Nostrand Reinhold, 1976).

Advertising and management: Frank W. Rucker and Herbert Lee Williams, *Newspaper Organization and Management* (Ames: Iowa State University Press, 1974); Leslie W. McClure and Paul C. Fulton, *Advertising in the Printed Media* (New York: Macmillan, 1964).

Chapter 10: Magazines

An overview of the magazine field is provided by Roland E. Wolseley's *Understanding Magazines* (Ames: Iowa State University Press, 1969), which treats editorial and business operations of consumer, business, and specialized publications. Wolseley's *The Changing Magazine* (New York: Hastings House, 1973) traces trends in readership and management. *Magazine Profiles* (Evanston, Ill.: Medill School of Journalism, 1974) presents studies by twelve graduate students of nearly fifty current magazines. John Tebbel's *The American Magazine: A Compact History* (New York: Hawthorn, 1969), emphasizes a current industry-wide survey. Robert Root, *Modern Magazine Editing* (Dubuque, Iowa: Brown, 1966), gives a general introduction; Russell N. Baird and Arthur T. Turnbull, *Industrial and Business Journalism* (Philadelphia: Chilton, 1961), covers the business press area in detail. James L. C. Ford, *Magazines for Millions* (Carbondale, Ill.: Southern Illinois University Press, 1970), tells the story of specialized publications in such fields as business, religion, labor, homemaking.

Views of specialized magazine work can be obtained from Rowena Ferguson, *Editing the Small Magazine* (New York: Columbia University Press, 1958, paperback 1963); DeWitt C. Reddick and Alfred A. Crowell, *Industrial Editing: Creative Communication Through Company Publications* (New York: Bender, 1962); William C. Halley, *Employee Publications* (Philadelphia: Chilton, 1959); Julien Elfenbein, *Business Journalism* (New York: Harper & Row, 1960).

Textbooks on magazine editing and feature writing include J. W. Click and Russell N. Baird, *Magazine Editing and Production* (Dubuque, Iowa: Brown, 1974); Roy Paul Nelson, *Articles and Features* (Boston: Houghton Mifflin, 1978); George L. Bird, *Modern Article Writing* (Dubuque, Iowa: Brown, 1967); Stewart Harral, *The Feature Writer's Handbook* (Norman: University of Oklahoma Press, 1966); Helen M. Patterson, *Writing and Selling Feature Articles* (Englewood Cliffs, N.J.: Prentice-Hall, 1956). Richard Gehman, *How to Write and Sell Magazine Articles* (New York: Harper & Row, 1959), is by a freelancer.

Chapter 11: Book Publishing

Charles G. Madison's *Book Publishing in America* (New York: McGraw-Hill, 1967) is the definitive survey of the book publishing industry by a former editor and publisher. There are many useful insights into the art of publishing and the history of the major companies. A well-rounded picture of the trade or general side of the book publishing industry is given by a score of specialists in *What Happens in Book Publishing,* edited by Chandler B. Grannis (New York: Columbia University Press, 1967).

Sir Stanley Unwin, *The Truth About Publishing* (New York: Bowker, 1960), is highly readable. John P. Dessauer, *Book Publishing: What It Is, What It Does* (New York: Bowker, 1974), gives an overview. William Jovanovich, *Now, Barabbas* (New York: Harper & Row, 1964) presents thoughtful essays on his field by a publishing executive.

Roger Smith, ed., *The American Reading Public: A Symposium* (New York: Bowker, 1964), is a particularly succinct and useful collection of authoritative essays by a number of publishing executives.

The first two volumes of a projected three-volume work by John Tebbel, *A History of Book Publishing in the United States* (New York: Bowker, 1972, 1975), cover the years 1630–1865 and 1865–1919.

Chapter 12: Radio and Recordings

Introductory books for radio include Robert L. Hilliard, *Radio Broadcasting: An Introduction to the Sound Medium* (New York: Hastings House, 1974), and Giraud Chester, Garnet R. Garrison, and Edgar Willis, *Television and Radio* (New York: Appleton-Century-Crofts, 1971). Sydney W. Head's *Broadcasting in America* (Boston: Houghton Mifflin, 1978) is one historical survey. For recordings, a popular history is C. A. Schicke, *Revolution in Sound: A Biography of the Recording Industry* (Boston: Little, Brown, 1974). Another is R. Serge Denisoff, *Solid Gold: The Popular Record Industry* (New York: Transaction Books, 1975).

In radio management and production, two key books are Edd Routt, *The Business of Radio Broadcasting* (Blue Ridge Summit, Pa.: TAB Books, 1972), one of a series issued by that publisher, and Robert Oringel's *Audio Control Handbook* (New York: Hastings House, 1972), a guide to radio sound.

Books dealing with radio news include John and Denise Bittner, *Radio Journalism* (Englewood Cliffs, N.J.: Prentice-Hall, 1977), including documentaries; F. Gifford, *Tape: A Radio News Handbook* (New York: Hastings House, 1977); G. Paul Smeyak, *Broadcast News Writing* (Columbus, Ohio: Grid, 1977); and 1940s texts.

See the listings for Chapter 13 for books dealing with both radio and television.

Chapter 13: Television

Introductory books for television include Robert L. Hilliard, ed., *Understanding Television: An Introduction to Broadcasting* (New York: Hastings House, 1974); Giraud Chester, Garnet R. Garrison, and Edgar Willis, *Television and Radio* (New York: Appleton-Century-Crofts, 1971); Horace Newcomb, *TV: The Most Popular Art* (Garden City, N.Y.: Doubleday Anchor, 1974), an analysis of popular TV programing; and A. William Bluem and Roger Manvell, *Television: The Creative Experience* (New York: Hastings House, 1967), a collection of 37 articles by leading American and British television professionals that originally appeared in *Television Quarterly* and the *Journal* of the British Society of Film and Television Arts.

Books that deal with television news are Irving E. Fang, *Television News* (New York: Hastings House, 1978); John M. Patterson, *Writing News for Broadcasting* (New York: Columbia University Press, 1971); Robert C. Siller, *Guide to Professional Radio and TV Newscasting* (Blue Ridge Summit, Pa.: TAB Books, 1972); Vernon Stone and Bruce Hinson, *Television Newsfilm Techniques* (New York: Hastings House, 1974); Jim Atkins, Jr., and Leo Willette, *Filming TV News and Documentaries* (New York: Amphoto, 1965); and Edd Routt, *Dimensions of Broadcast Editorializing* (Blue Ridge Summit, Pa.: TAB Books, 1974).

Books treating various types of writing are Edgar E. Willis, *Writing Television and Radio Programs* (New York: Holt, Rinehart and Winston, 1967); Robert L. Hilliard, *Writing for Television and Radio* (New York: Hastings House, 1976); and Norton S. Parker, *Audiovisual Script Writing* (New Brunswick, N.J.: Rutgers University Press, 1968).

Management and production: Ward L. Quaal and James A. Brown, *Broadcast Management* (New York: Hastings House, 1976), a standard account for radio and TV station management; Gerald Millerson, *The Technique of Television Production* and *Effective TV Production* (New York: Hastings House, 1972, 1976); Michael Murray, *The Videotape Book: A Basic Guide* (New York: Taplinger, 1975); Arthur Englander and Paul Petzold, *Filming for Television* (New York: Hastings House, 1976); Richard L. Williams, *Television Production: A Vocational*

Approach (Salt Lake City: Vision, 1976); Howard W. Coleman, editor, *Color Television* (New York: Hastings House, 1968). Two books on graphics are Walter Herdeg, *Film and TV Graphics* (New York: Hastings House, 1967), and Roy Laughton, *TV Graphics* (New York: Reinhold, 1966). A reference work for the technologies of film and television is *The Focal Encyclopedia of Film and Television: Techniques* (New York: Hastings House, 1969).

The advertising area is described in Elizabeth J. Heighton and Don R. Cunningham, *Advertising in the Broadcast Media* (Belmont, Calif.: Wadsworth, 1976); Eugene F. Seehafer and Jack W. Laemmar, *Successful Television and Radio Advertising* (New York: McGraw-Hill, 1959), and Charles A. Wainright, *Television Commercials* (New York: Hastings House, 1970).

Chapter 14: The Film

Gerald Mast's *A Short History of the Movies* (New York: Bobbs-Merrill, 1976), offers detailed, highly readable descriptions and analyses, primarily of American and European films. To the major film histories, Rotha and Griffith's *The Film Till Now* and Griffith and Mayer's *The Movies,* may be added Arthur Knight, *The Liveliest Art* (New York: Macmillan, 1957, also Mentor paperback), particularly good for the years 1895–1930; D. J. Wenden, *The Birth of the Movies* (New York: Dutton, 1975), covering 1895–1927; Alan Casty's *Development of the Film: An Interpretive History* (New York: Harcourt Brace Jovanovich, 1973); and James Monaco, *How to Read a Film* (New York: Oxford, 1977). The best social history is Garth Jowett, *Film: The Democratic Art* (Boston: Little, Brown, 1976), updating Lewis Jacobs' *The Rise of the American Film* (1939). Another is Robert Sklar, *Movie-Made America* (New York: Random House, 1975).

The standard work on the history, principles, and technique of the documentary motion picture is Paul Rotha, Sinclair Road, and Richard Griffith, *The Documentary Film* (London: Faber and Faber, 1966). Others are Lewis Jacobs, *The Documentary Tradition: From Nanook to Woodstock* (New York: Hopkinson and Blake, 1971); Alan Rosenthal, *The New Documentary in Action: A Casebook in Film Making* (Berkeley: University of California Press, 1971); Richard M. Barsam, *Nonfiction Film: A Critical History* (New York: Dutton, 1973); Richard D. MacCann, *The People's Films* (New York: Hastings House,

1973), a history of U.S. government documentaries; and Erik Barnouw, *Documentary: A History of the Non-Fiction Film* (London: Oxford University Press, 1974), a well-integrated analysis.

John L. Fell's *Film: An Introduction* (New York: Praeger, 1975) is designed for survey courses as is Roy P. Madsen's *The Impact of Film* (New York: Macmillan, 1973). Suitable for text use is Thomas W. Bohn and Richard L. Stromgren, *Light and Shadows: A History of Motion Pictures* (Port Washington, N.Y.: Alfred Publishing, 1975).

Lewis Jacobs, *The Emergence of Film Art* (New York: Hopkinson and Blake, 1969), offers carefully selected essays to illustrate the evolution of the motion picture as an art from 1900 to the present. Roger Manvell, in *New Cinema in Europe* (New York: Dutton, 1966), gives brief descriptions of movements, filmmakers and films in postwar feature filmmaking in Europe. Gregory Battcock's *The New American Cinema* (New York: Dutton, 1967) is a stimulating collection of essays covering theory and practice of contemporary experimental filmmakers.

Film direction is examined by Eric Sherman in *Directing the Film* (Boston: Little, Brown, 1976), and by Louis Giannetti in *Understanding Movies* (Englewood Cliffs, N.J.: Prentice-Hall, 1972). Personalities from the silent film era are interviewed in Kevin Brownlow, *The Parade's Gone By* (New York: Knopf, 1968). Also of note is Andrew Sarris, *The American Cinema: Directors and Directions 1929–1968* (New York: Dutton, 1968).

Chapter 15: Photographic Communication
History and development: Beaumont Newhall, *The History of Photography from 1839 to the Present Day* (New York: Museum of Modern Art, 1964); Helmut and Alison Gernsheim, *History of Photography* (London: Oxford University Press, 1970); Peter Pollack, *Picture History of Photography* (New York: Abrams, 1969); Nathan Lyons, *Photographers on Photography* (Englewood Cliffs, N.J.: Prentice-Hall, 1966); R. Smith Schuneman, *Photographic Communication: Principles, Problems and Challenges of Photojournalism* (New York: Hastings House, 1972); A. William Bluem, *Documentary in American Television* (New York: Hastings House, 1965); Paul Rotha, Sinclair Road, and Richard Griffith, *Documentary Film* (London: Faber and Faber, 1966).

Techniques: Phil Davis, *Photography* (Dubuque, Iowa: Brown, 1975); Robert B. Rhode and Floyd H. McCall, *Introduction to Photography* (New York: Macmillan, 1976); David H. Curl, *Photo-Communication* (New York: Macmillan, 1978); Philip C. Geraci, *Photojournalism* (Dubuque, Iowa: Kendall/Hunt, 1976); Clifton C. Edom, *Photojournalism* (Dubuque, Iowa: Brown, 1976); Arnold Roth-stein, *Photojournalism: Pictures for Magazines and Newspapers* (New York: Amphoto, 1965); Wilson Hicks, *Words and Pictures* (New York: Harper, 1952); Roy Pinney, *Advertising Photography* (New York: Hastings House, 1962).

Biographical: James Horan, *Mathew Brady: Historian with a Camera* (New York: Crown, 1955), and *Timothy O'Sullivan: America's Forgotten Photographer* (New York: Crown, 1966); Judith Gutman, *Lewis W. Hine and the American Social Conscience* (New York: Walker, 1967); Richard Griffith, *The World of Robert Flaherty* (New York: Duell, Sloan and Pearce, 1953); Margaret Bourke-White, *Portrait of Myself* (New York: Simon and Schuster, 1963); David Douglas Duncan, *Yankee Nomad* (New York: Holt, Rinehart and Winston, 1966); Carl Mydans, *More Than Meets the Eye* (New York: Harper & Row, 1959); Gordon Parks, *A Choice of Weapons* (New York: Harper & Row, 1966); Edward Steichen, *A Life in Photography* (Garden City, N.Y.: Doubleday, 1963); Cornell Capa, *Robert Capa* (New York: Grossman, 1974).

Picture books: Alfred Eisenstaedt, *Witness to Our Times* (New York: Viking, 1966); David Douglas Duncan, *War Without Heroes* (New York: Harper & Row, 1970); John Szarkowski, *The Photographer's Eye* (New York: Museum of Modern Art, 1966); Leonard Freed, *Black in White America* (New York: Grossman, n.d.); Cornell Capa, ed., *The Concerned Photographer* (New York: Grossman, 1969), 200 photos of protest by six leading photographers; Charles Harbutt and Lee Jones, *America in Crisis* (New York: Holt, Rinehart and Winston, 1969); Associated Press, *The Instant It Happened* (New York: Associated Press, 1974), great news photos from the Civil War to Watergate.

Chapter 16: Press Associations

There is no one book describing the press associations. Frank Luther Mott paints a picture of the Associated Press operation in a chapter of *The News in America.* Emery traces their history in *The Press and America* and Ault tells youthful readers how big stories are covered in *News Around the Clock* (New York: Dodd, Mead, 1960).

Oliver Gramling, *AP: The Story of News,* and Joe Alex Morris, *Deadline Every Minute: The Story of the United Press,* capture a good deal of the reportorial excitement of the press associations. Hugh Baillie, *High Tension* (New York: Harper & Row, 1959), is the readable autobiography of a former president of UP. *Kent Cooper and the Associated Press* (New York: Random House, 1959) is the second personal account by the most famous general manager of AP; the first, *Barriers Down* (New York: Farrar and Rinehart, 1942), is Cooper's story of his effort to break up international news monopolies. Melville E. Stone, *Fifty Years a Journalist,* is the autobiography of the first AP general manager.

A UNESCO publication, *News Agencies: Their Structure and Operation* (New York: Columbia University Press, 1953), gives summary accounts of AP, UP, and INS and analyzes other world news agencies. John C. Merrill, Carter R. Bryan, and Marvin Alisky, *The Foreign Press* (Baton Rouge: Louisiana State University Press, 1970), includes world news agencies in its overall picture. UNESCO's *World Communications: A 200-Country Survey of Press, Radio, Television, Films* (New York: UNESCO, 1975) is a reference work for international communications. John Hohenberg covers foreign correspondents generally in *Foreign Correspondence—The Great Reporters and Their Times* (New York: Columbia University Press, 1964).

Other books describing the international media the press associations serve include John C. Merrill, *The Elite Press* (New York: Pitman, 1969), a study of a selected worldwide group of papers; Kenneth E. Olson, *The History Makers* (Baton Rouge: Louisiana State University Press, 1966); a survey of European press history; Graham Storey, *Reuters* (New York: Crown, 1951), and Theodore E. Kruglak, *The Two Faces of Tass* (Minneapolis: University of Minnesota Press, 1962), two press association histories; James W. Markham, *Voices of the Red Giants* (Ames: Iowa State University Press, 1970), a study of the Soviet and Chinese mass media systems; Burton Paulu, *Radio and Television Broadcasting on the European Continent* (Minneapolis: University of Minnesota Press, 1967), and *Radio and Television Broadcasting in Eastern Europe* (Minnesota Press, 1974); and Walter B. Emery, *National and International Systems of Broadcasting* (East Lansing: Michigan State University Press, 1969).

The annual July *Syndicate Directory* issued by *Editor & Publisher* updates Elmo Scott Watson, *A History of Newspaper Syndicates, 1865–1935* (Chicago: Publishers' Auxiliary, 1936).

Chapter 17: Advertising

Among the general text and reference books on advertising are Charles H. Sandage and Vernon Fryburger, *Advertising Theory and Practice* (Homewood, Ill.: Irwin, 1971); S. Watson Dunn and Arnold Barban, *Advertising: Its Role in Modern Marketing* (New York: Holt, Rinehart and Winston, 1974); Edgar Crane, *Marketing Communications* (New

York; Wiley, 1972); John S. Wright, Daniel S. Warner, and Willis L. Winter, Jr., *Advertising* (New York: McGraw-Hill, 1977); Philip Ward Burton and J. Robert Miller, *Advertising Fundamentals* (Columbus, Ohio: Grid, 1976); Stanley Ulanoff, *Advertising in America* (New York: Hastings House, 1977), persuasion; Otto Kleppner and Stephen Greyser, *Advertising Procedure* (Englewood Cliffs, N.J.: Prentice-Hall, 1973); Dorothy Cohen, *Advertising* (New York: Wiley, 1972); Barbara Davis Coe, *Advertising Practice* (Englewood Cliffs, N.J.: Prentice-Hall, 1972).

Four collections of readings are Wright and Warner, *Speaking of Advertising* (New York: McGraw-Hill, 1963); Sandage and Fryburger, *The Role of Advertising;* Arnold M. Barban and C. H. Sandage, *Readings in Advertising and Promotion Strategy* (Homewood, Ill.: Irwin, 1968); and James E. Littlefield, *Readings in Advertising* (St. Paul: West, 1975).

Media is the topic of Arnold M. Barban, Donald W. Jugenheimer and Lee F. Young in *Advertising Media Sourcebook and Workbook* (Columbus, Ohio: Grid, 1975) and of Jack Z. Sissors and E. Reynold Petray in *Advertising Media Planning* (Chicago: Crain, 1976).

Copywriting techniques are described by David L. Malickson and John W. Nason in *Advertising—How to Write the Kind That Works* (New York: Scribner's, 1977) and by Philip Ward Burton in *Advertising Copywriting* (Columbus, Ohio: Grid, 1974). They are also described by Aesop Glim (George Laflin Miller) in *Copy—The Core of Advertising* (New York: Dover, 1963) and *How Advertising Is Written—and Why* (1961); Hanley Norins, *The Compleat Copywriter* (New York: McGraw-Hill, 1966); Clyde Bedell, *How to Write Advertising That Sells* (New York: McGraw-Hill, 1952).

Graphics and design: Arthur T. Turnbull and Russell N. Baird, *The Graphics of Communication: Typography, Layout, Design* (New York: Holt, Rinehart and Winston, 1975); Roy Paul Nelson, *The Design of Advertising* (Dubuque, Iowa: Brown, 1977); Edmund C. Arnold, *Ink on Paper 2* (New York: Harper & Row, 1972); Stephen Baker, *Advertising Layout and Art Direction* (New York: McGraw-Hill, 1959); Peter Croy, *Graphic Design and Reproduction Techniques* (New York: Hastings House, 1968); Carl Dair, *Design with Type* (Toronto: University of Toronto Press, 1967).

Advertising agencies: Roger Barton, *Advertising Agency Operations and Management* (New York: McGraw-Hill, 1955) is a practical guide. Martin Mayer, *Madison Avenue, U.S.A.,* provides a good picture of advertising agencies, Ralph M. Hower, *The History of an Advertising Agency: N. W. Ayer & Son at Work, 1869–1939* (Cambridge, Mass.: Harvard University Press, 1939) is a documented history of one. David Ogilvy tells a fascinating story about life in an agency in *Confessions of an Advertising Man* (New York: Atheneum, 1963; Dell paperback, 1964). The story of the pioneering Albert Lasker is told by John Gunther in *Taken at the Flood* (New York: Harper & Row, 1960).

Chapter 18: Public Relations

The best book to read in exploring the public relations field is Scott M. Cutlip and Allen H. Center, *Effective Public Relations* (Englewood Cliffs, N.J.: Prentice-Hall, 1978).

Other general books include those by Doug Newsom and Alan Scott, *This Is PR: The Realities of Public Relations* (Belmont, Calif.: Wadsworth, 1976); Bertrand R. Canfield and Frazier Moore, *Public Relations: Principles, Cases, and Problems* (Homewood, Ill.: Irwin, 1973); John Marston, *The Nature of Public Relations* (New York: McGraw-Hill, 1963); Charles S. Steinberg, *The Creation of Consent, Public Relations in Practice* (New York: Hastings House, 1975); Roy L. Blumenthal, *The Practice of Public Relations* (New York: Macmillan, 1972); Allen H. Center, *Public Relations Practices, Case Studies* (Englewood Cliffs, N.J.: Prentice-Hall, 1975). Otto Lerbinger and Albert J. Sullivan edited *Information, Influence & Communication: A Reader in Public Relations* (New York: Basic Books, 1965), focusing on research and theory.

Groups of public relations professionals contributed chapters for *Public Relations Handbook,* edited by Philip Lesly (Englewood Cliffs, N.J.: Prentice-Hall, 1971), and *Handbook of Public Relations,* edited by Howard Stephenson (New York: McGraw-Hill, 1971). A leading counselor, John W. Hill, tells his story in *The Making of a Public Relations Man* (New York: McKay, 1963). New York's practitioners are described by Irwin Ross in *The Image Merchants* (Garden City, N.Y.: Doubleday, 1959). Edward L. Bernays, in *Public Relations* (Norman: University of Oklahoma Press, 1952), presents a case history type of discussion by a longtime practitioner. His memoirs are in *Biography of an Idea* (New York: Simon and Schuster, 1965). Ray E. Hiebert contributed the biography of another pioneer in his *Courtier to the Crowd: The Life Story of Ivy Lee* (Ames: Iowa State University Press, 1966). Alan R. Raucher traced early PR history in *Public Relations and Business 1900–1929* (Baltimore: The Johns Hopkins Press, 1968).

Publicity practices are described in David L. Lendt, ed., *The Pub-*

licity Process (Ames: Iowa State University Press, 1975); Clarence A. Schoenfeld, *Publicity Media and Methods* (New York: Macmillan, 1963); and Howard Stephenson and Wesley F. Pratzner, *Publicity for Prestige and Profit* (New York: McGraw-Hill, 1953).

Among books on specialized subjects are Ray E. Hiebert and Carlton Spitzer, eds., *The Voice of Government* (New York: Wiley, 1968), with two dozen Washington information men discussing their work; James L. McCamy, *Government Publicity* (Chicago: University of Chicago Press, 1939); Benjamin Fine, *Educational Publicity* (New York: Harper, 1951); Harold P. Levy, *Public Relations for Social Agencies* (New York: Harper & Row, 1956); Louis B. Lundborg, *Public Relations in the Local Community* (New York: Harper, 1950); and Sidney Kobre, *Successful Public Relations for Colleges and Universities* (New York: Hastings House, 1974).

Bibliographies are Scott M. Cutlip, *A Public Relations Bibliography* (Madison: University of Wisconsin Press, 1965), and its extension, Robert L. Bishop, *Public Relations: A Comprehensive Bibliography* (Ann Arbor: University of Michigan Press, 1974).

Chapter 19: Mass Communications Research

The reader interested in this field can gain an impression of its scope and methods by examining *Introduction to Mass Communications Research,* edited by Ralph O. Nafziger and David M. White (Baton Rouge: Louisiana State University Press, 1963). It has eight chapters by leading research specialists in journalism and mass communications.

A book that describes more varied types of journalism research is *An Introduction to Journalism Research,* edited by Ralph O. Nafziger and Marcus M. Wilkerson (Baton Rouge: Louisiana State University Press, 1949). Wilbur Schramm surveyed "Twenty Years of Journalism Research" in the spring 1957 *Public Opinion Quarterly,* while Allan Nevins discussed "American Journalism and Its Historical Treatment" in the fall 1959 *Journalism Quarterly.*

Four books that introduce the reader to research methods are David M. White and Seymour Levine, *Elementary Statistics for Journalists* (New York: Macmillan, 1954); Charles H. Backstrom and Gerald D. Hursh, *Survey Research* (Evanston, Ill.: Northwestern University Press, 1963); at a more sophisticated level, Richard W. Budd, Robert K. Thorp, and Lewis Donohew, *Content Analysts of Communication* (New

York: Macmillan, 1967); and Julian Simon, *Basic Research Methods in Social Science* (New York: Random House, 1969).

Advertising research methods are outlined in Daniel Starch, *Measuring Advertising Readership and Results* (New York: McGraw-Hill, 1966), in Charles Ramond, *Advertising Research* (New York: Association of National Advertisers, 1976), summarizing knowledge, and in Darrell Blaine Lucas and Steuart Henderson Britt, *Measuring Advertising Effectiveness* (New York: McGraw-Hill, 1963). A discussion of research opportunities in the newspaper area is found in Jack B. Haskins and Barry M. Feinberg, *Newspaper Publishers Look at Research* (Syracuse, N.Y.: Newhouse Communications Center, 1968).

Many of the references listed for Part I of this bibliography also are pertinent to this chapter, especially those dealing with effects, the communication process, and public opinion.

Chapter 20: Mass Communications Education

The growth of journalism education is reviewed in Albert A. Sutton, *Education for Journalism in the United States from Its Beginning to 1940* (Evanston, Ill.: Northwestern University Press, 1945). *The Training of Journalists* (Paris: UNESCO, 1958) is a worldwide survey on the training of personnel for the mass media, updated by *Mass Communication: Teaching and Studies at Universities,* edited by May Katzen (Paris: UNESCO, 1975).

William R. Lindley's monograph, *Journalism and Higher Education* (Stillwater, Okla.: Journalistic Services, 1976), traces the development of four major American journalism schools.

Books about career opportunities include Herbert Brucker, *Journalist: Eyewitness to History* (New York: Macmillan, 1962); Edward W. Barrett, ed., *Journalists in Action* (New York: Channel Press, 1963), stories of sixty-three Columbia University journalism graduates; Leonard E. Ryan and Bernard Ryan, Jr., *So You Want to Go into Journalism* (New York: Harper & Row, 1963); M. L. Stein, *Your Career in Journalism* (New York: Messner, 1965); George Johnson, *Your Career in Advertising* (New York: Messner, 1966; Gregory Jackson, *Getting Into Broadcast Journalism* (New York: Hawthorn, 1974); John Tebbel, *Opportunities in Publishing Careers* (Louisville: Vocational Guidance Manuals, 1975), book publishing; Elmo I. Ellis, *Opportunities in Broadcasting* (Skokie, Ill.: National Textbook Co., 1978); and Roland E. Wolseley, *Careers in Religious Communications* (Scottdale, Pa.: Herald Press, 1977).

Available in paperback are Arville Schaleben's *Your Future in Jour-*

nalism, Edward L. Bernays' *Your Future in Public Relations,* and *Your Future in Advertising* (New York: Popular Library).

Career information is available from the office of the Executive Secretary, Association for Education in Journalism, 118 Reavis Hall, Northern Illinois University, DeKalb, Ill. 60115. *Education for a Journalism Career* is available from the American Council on Education for Journalism, School of Journalism, University of Missouri, Columbia 65201.

Other pamphlets available are *Your Future in Daily Newspapers* (American Newspaper Publishers Association), *Broadcasting the News, Careers in Television,* and *Careers in Radio* (National Association of Broadcasters), *Magazines in the U.S.A.* (Magazine Publishers Association), *Careers in the Business Press* (American Business Press, Inc.), *Occupational Guide to Public Relations* (Public Relations Society of America), and *Careers Unlimited* (Women in Communications).

Quill & Scroll, University of Iowa, publishes annually *Careers in Journalism,* in magazine form. The Newspaper Fund, Inc., issues a *Journalism Scholarship Guide* annually.

Catalogs describing the curricular offerings of individual schools and departments of journalism are available upon request to the school or department concerned or to the registrar of the institution.

INDEX

INDEX